Concepts and Principles
of Physical Education:
What Every Student Needs to Know

Bonnie S. Mohnsen, Editor

Published by the

**National Association for Sport and Physical Education
(NASPE)**
an association of the
American Alliance for Health, Physical Education,
Recreation and Dance

1900 Association Drive
Reston, VA 20191-1599
(703) 476-3410
naspe@aahperd.org

Address orders to:
AAHPERD Publications, P.O. Box 385, Oxon Hill, MD 20750-0385,
call 1-800-321-0789, or order on line at www.aahperd.org/naspe.
Order Stock No 304-10261.

Printed in the United States of America.

ISBN 0-88314-744-0

Preface

NASPE is pleased to provide a revised edition of this very successful publication that supports and complements the National Standards for Physical Education (1995). The first edition represented a re-conceptualization of a much earlier project known as Basic Stuff, which in two editions of nine volumes each provided the scientific foundations for physical activity and performance at a level relevant and understandable to students at each educational level.

This edition helps physical education contribute to the ongoing educational reform agenda that has been the focus of educational leaders and public concern for the last ten years. The content makes clear connections between cognitive information about physical activity and actual physical activity performance. Physically educated individuals know about physical activity as well as have developed abilities to engage safely and skillfully in a variety of movements. The authors of the various chapters in this new edition support application of physiology, biomechanics, sociology, motor learning, psychology, history, philosophy and aesthetics concepts and information to human movement. This information helps to make physical education a rich experience that is well integrated with the overall educational program.

I would like to acknowledge Bonnie Mohnsen and each of the chapter authors for their expertise and willingness to translate the latest research related to performing and understanding physical activity for delivery to students in relevant and meaningful ways. This information facilitates support of other content areas and helps physical education take its rightful place in the total educational programs in elementary, as well as middle and high schools. Physical activity is not only a leisure time luxury — it is an essential component of a healthy lifestyle for individuals of all ages. The contents of this book will provide teachers and students with the context for physical activity education by providing multiple perspectives and approaches to the study of physical activity.

Judith C. Young, Ph.D.
Executive Director

Acknowledgements

I would like to extend my thanks to the individual authors who worked on this project. Chosen for their expertise in the respective subdisciplines of physical education, these individuals have committed numerous hours and tremendous energy to produce this significant body of work.

Judith Alter – Aesthetics and Exercise Physiology
Judith Rink – Motor Learning
Gail Evans and Susan Hall – Biomechanics
Gayle Hutchinson and Rita Mercier – Social/Psychology
Jan Patterson – Historical Perspectives
Kathleen Williams and Greg Payne – Motor Development

In addition, I wish to extend my appreciation to the individuals who reviewed this second edition of *Concepts and Principles of Physical Educaiton; What Every Student Needs to Know.* They provided input regarding the selection of concepts and principles along with insightful recommendations on the writing of the book.

Tony Amorose   Kathleen Knutzen
Jerry Ballew   Jerry Landwer
Ruel Barker   Angela Lumpkin
Jennifer Beller   Richard Magill
Kris Berg   Karen Meaney
Lanie Dornier   Tom Nesser
Mary Duquin   Deborah J. Rhea
Cathy Ennis   Synthia Sydnor
Larry Hensley   Gene White

I am also grateful to Kathy Stark and Pia McCarthy, from the NASPE office, for seeing this project through from start to finish! Their dedication and commitment to this project is to be commended.

Bonnie Mohnsen
Editor

Contents

Preface iii

Setting the Stage 1
Bonnie S. Mohnsen

Motor Learning 31
Judith E. Rink

Motor Development 65
Kathleen Williams and Greg Payne

Biomechanics 107
Susan J. Hall and Gail G. Evans

Exercise Physiology 143
Judith B. Alter

Historical Perspectives 205
Jan Patterson

Social Psychology 245
Rita Mercier and Gayle Hutchinson

Aesthetic Experience 309
Judith B. Alter

Putting It All Together 353
Bonnie S. Mohnsen

Appendix 387

Index 411

Resources 423

Chapter **1**

Setting the Stage

Bonnie S. Mohnsen

The year is 2030. Our students, now adults in their 30s, are working, pursuing careers, and/or raising families. As business executives, automobile designers, digital engineers, health professionals, service professionals, and teachers all are living their lives and using the knowledge, skills, and attitudes they gained during their K-12 education. As a result of the concept-based physical education program in which they participated during their K-12 years, they are able to address the significant issues/questions facing them on a daily basis:

> *What is the best type of exercise program for me so I can have lifelong good health? At what age should I enroll my children in youth sports programs? What is wrong with my golf swing and what can I do to improve it? What is the best way to resolve the conflicts I am having with my recreational softball team? What should I look for in the performances when I am watching Olympic figure skating? As a school board member, how should I vote on the elimination of eleventh and twelfth grade physical education programs?*

One of the most significant questions that all educators will face during the coming decade is "what knowledge and experience do high school graduates need in order to live *high quality* lives in the 21st century?" The answer to this question will continue to evolve as we experience change in the world around us. However, the National Association for Sport and Physical Education (NASPE) initially addressed this topic in 1986 when it appointed an Outcomes Committee to answer the question, "What should students know and be able to do?" related to physical education. The committee's answer (Franck, 1992) provided the definition of a physically educated person as someone who:

- Has learned skills necessary to perform a variety of physical activities.
- Is physically fit.
- Participates regularly in physical activity.
- Knows the implications and the benefits of involvement in physical activity.
- Values physical activity and its contribution to a healthful lifestyle.

The committee further expanded the definition to 20 outcome statements and defined sample benchmarks for selected grade levels. In order to align the physical education curriculum documents with those being developed in other subject areas at the time, NASPE's Standards and Assessment Committee (NASPE, 1995a) altered the course and identified seven content standards for physical education:

1. Demonstrates competency in many movement forms and proficiency in a few movement forms.
2. Applies movement concepts/principles to the learning and development of motor skills.
3. Exhibits a physically active lifestyle.
4. Achieves and maintains a health-enhancing level of physical fitness.
5. Demonstrates responsible personal and social behavior in physical activity settings.
6. Demonstrates understanding and respect for differences among people in physical activity settings.
7. Understands that physical activity provides opportunities for enjoyment, challenge, self-expression, and social interaction.

The committee further defined each of these standards for kindergarten, second grade, fourth grade, sixth grade, eighth grade, tenth grade, and twelfth grade (see Figure 1 for the definitions and areas of emphasis for Standard 5). These standards represent a philosophy of physical education that goes beyond fitness or sport education into a comprehensive view of the subject area known as physical education. Both the Outcomes and the National Standards brought us closer to answering the

Figure 1

Definition and Emphasis Related to National Standard 5

Demonstrates responsible personal and social behavior in physical activity settings.

Twelfth Grade

Twelfth grade students demonstrate the ability to initiate responsible behavior, function independently, and positively influence the behavior of others in physical activity settings. They demonstrate leadership by holding themselves and others responsible for following safe practices, rules, procedures, and etiquette in all physical activity settings. They act as a neutralizer in avoiding conflict or as a mediator in settling conflicts.

The emphasis for the twelfth grade student will be to:
- Initiate independent and responsible personal behavior in physical activity settings.
- Accept the responsibility for taking a leadership role and willingly follow as appropriate in order to accomplish group goals.
- Anticipate potentially dangerous consequences and outcomes of participation in physical activity.

Eighth Grade

Students are beginning to seek greater independence from adults. They make appropriate decisions to resolve conflicts arising from the powerful influence of peers and to follow pertinent practices, rules, and procedures necessary for successful performance. They practice appropriate problem-solving techniques to resolve conflicts when necessary in competitive activities. Students reflect on the benefits of the role of rules, procedures, safe practices, ethical behavior, and positive social interaction in physical activity settings.

The emphasis for the eighth grade student will be to:
- Recognize the influence of peer pressure.
- Solve problems by analyzing causes and potential solutions.
- Analyze potential consequences when confronted with a behavior choice.
- Work cooperatively with a group to achieve group goals in competitive as well as cooperative settings.

Fourth Grade

Students identify the purposes for and follow, with few reminders, activity-specific safe practices, rules, procedures, and etiquette. They continue to develop cooperation skills to enable completion of a common goal while working with a partner or in small groups. They can work independently and productively for short periods of time.

The emphasis for the fourth grade student will be to:
- Follow, with few reminders, activity-specific rules, procedures, and etiquette.
- Utilize safety principles in activity situations.

Continued on next page

Figure 1 *(continued)*

- Work cooperatively and productively with a partner or small group.
- Work independently and on task for short periods of time.

Kindergarten
Students begin to learn and utilize acceptable behaviors for physical activity settings. The focus is directed toward understanding safe practices as well as classroom rules and procedures. Students begin to understand the concept of cooperation through opportunities to share space and equipment with others in a group.

The emphasis for kindergarten students will be to:
- Apply, with teacher reinforcement, classroom rules, procedures, and safe practices.
- Share space and equipment with others.

From NASPE's *Moving into the Future: National Standards for Physical Education: A Guide to Content and Assessment,* 1995.

question, "What do students need to know and be able to do?" However, neither defined the specific content that must be taught so students can become physically educated. In 1998, the first edition of *Concepts of Physical Education: What Every Student Needs to Know* (Mohnsen, 1998) was published. Building on the earlier work of the Basic Stuff Project (Kneer, 1981), the book described the concepts that should be taught in grades K through 12 based on the National Standards (Standard 2 in particular). This second edition of *Concepts and Principles of Physical Education: What Every Student Needs to Know* refines the answer and brings the concepts/principles up-to-date in light of the significant changes in our society. In the following sections, we will examine the trends related to business, health, leisure, education, and physical education along with their impact on the selection of the concepts/principles identified in Chapters 2 through 8.

Business Trends

In the late 1800s, with the advent of new technologies, America moved from an agricultural society to an industrial society (Davidow & Malone, 1992). During the late 1900s, another transition occurred as the nation moved from an industrial society to an information society. Today we have unlimited access to vast amounts of information. And, with the Internet and other digital media, we are on the verge of another transition, this time to a communication society in which everyone is linked together. People will have immediate access to anyone, anywhere, and at any time.

Business leaders have a keen interest in how we are preparing students for a changing work force. In 1991, the Secretary of Labor's Commission on Achieving Necessary Skills (SCANS) identified five competencies that business leaders want from high school graduates. In 2000, the Commission updated the list to address the continuing changes in society:

Effective workers can productively use:

Resources:	They know how to allocate time, money, materials, space, and staff.
Interpersonal skills:	They can work on teams, teach others, serve customers, lead, negotiate, and work well with people from culturally diverse backgrounds.
Information:	They can acquire and evaluate data, organize and maintain files, interpret and communicate, and use computers to process information.
Systems:	They understand social, organization, and technological systems; they can monitor and correct performance; and they can design or improve systems.
Technology:	They can select equipment and tools, apply technology to specific tasks, and maintain and troubleshoot equipment.

Competent workers in the high-performance workplace need:

Basic skills:	Reading, writing, arithmetic and mathematics, speaking and listening.
Thinking skills:	The ability to learn, reason, think creatively, make decisions, and solve problems.
Personal Qualities:	Individual responsibility, self-esteem and self-management, sociability, and integrity.

These competencies help to answer the question, "What knowledge and experience will young adults need to live high-quality lives in the 21st century?" A physical education curriculum (based on the National Standards) contributes to all of these areas. In particular are the interpersonal (aligns with Standards 5 and 6) and information (aligns with Standards 2 and 4) skills identified for effective workers and the personal qualities (aligns with Standards 5 and 6) and thinking skills (aligns with Standards 2 and 4) identified for competent workers in high-performing workplaces.

Interpersonal skills and personal qualities are significant attributes in view of our increasingly multicultural society. In such a society, beliefs differ dramatically and there are conflicting norms of behavior. Thirty-six percent of all job listings explicitly mention *teamwork* as a requirement for the job (Thornburg, 2002). When schools fail to teach interpersonal skills, businesses must send their upper level managers to team-building seminars so they can learn to work more efficiently and effectively together. These seminars may include Outward Bound experiences, challenge courses (e.g., high ropes courses), or other types of physical challenge that require participants to work together to succeed. These are the same types of experiences that many physical educators provide for their students! Physical educators must provide the instruction necessary for students to learn to work on teams, teach others, lead, and work well with people from diverse backgrounds. Burrus (1993), a noted futurist, recognized the role of physical education in the development of social skills when he stated, "Many subjects that teach interpersonal skills, such as sports [sic] and music, are subjects that are being cut back at the present time, but shouldn't be" (p. 242).

Information today is doubling every year. By the year 2020, information experts predict that knowledge will double every 70 days! Information and thinking skills continue to retain their importance, since the ability to access, filter, and assess information along with the desire for lifelong learning are the keys to success in the 21st century. Students in physical education can learn how to access, filter, and assess the information they need to plan valid and effective exercise, wellness, and activity programs. Students are constantly bombarded with claims of "new" and "quick" solutions to weight loss and health issues. They must be able to differentiate between claims and effective programs.

Health Trends

Life expectancy averages worldwide have increased during the last century. In the United States today, the life expectancy is 77 years (United States Census Bureau, 2000), and the number of centenarians is increasing weekly. Many children born today can expect to live well into the 22nd century. On June 26, 2000, nearly five years ahead of schedule, a working draft of the human genome was completed. This draft depicts the layout of 100,000 human genes along with the sequence of the nearly three billion DNA base pairs. This document and the refinements to follow will have a dramatic impact on molecular medicine and the quality of health care. Futurists predict that the health care of tomorrow may be found in health kiosks located at local malls, where one-stop check-ups, diagnosis, and up-to-date advice will replace doctor visits.

On July 11, 1996, the United States Department of Health and Human Services produced a report titled *Physical Activity and Health: A Report of the Surgeon General*. The report concluded that regular physical activity directly relates to improved health benefits and that there is a direct link between physical activity and physical fitness. The report recommended moderate amounts of physical activity be performed on most days of the week. Following this simple guideline can reduce the risk of death from coronary heart disease, hypertension, colon and ovarian cancer, and non-insulin-dependent diabetes along with the symptoms of anxiety and depression.

This good news, however, should be tempered by several alarming statistics. Heart disease still kills 950,0000 people annually (American Heart Association, 2001). While cardiovascular disease primarily affects the elderly, 5 percent of all heart attacks occur in individuals younger than 40 years of age and 34 percent occur in individuals younger than 75. Cardiovascular disease also is a significant contributor to physical disability, dramatically affecting the lives of many survivors. The economic cost of cardiovascular disease in 2001 was estimated at $298.2 billion (American Heart Association, 2001).

The Centers for Disease Control (CDC, 2001) concludes that only 64.6 percent of youngsters participate in activities that make them sweat and breathe hard for 20 minutes or more three days per week (see Figure 2), and only 25.5 percent participate in moderate activities for 30 minutes or more five days per week. An estimated 40 percent of adults do not get any exercise. This is conclusive evidence that inactivity among children is a precursor to sedentary lifestyles among adults. A total of 10.5 percent of today's youngsters are overweight, and an additional 13.6 percent are at risk of becoming overweight. In the adult population, this figure escalates to an estimated 66 percent of overweight Americans. Obesity-related diseases cost the American public more than $1 billion every year, while inactivity and poor diet lead to at least 300,000 deaths each year (Koplan, 2000).

Concerns regarding obesity and the lack of physical activity among U.S. adults have reached a critical mass. Significant documents from the U.S. Department of Health and Human Services and the CDC (see reference section), along with the *Healthy People 2010 Physical Activity and Fitness Objectives* (see Figure 3) have aroused White House attention. On June 20,

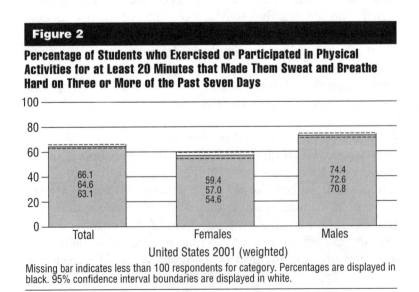

Figure 2

Percentage of Students who Exercised or Participated in Physical Activities for at Least 20 Minutes that Made Them Sweat and Breathe Hard on Three or More of the Past Seven Days

United States 2001 (weighted)

Missing bar indicates less than 100 respondents for category. Percentages are displayed in black. 95% confidence interval boundaries are displayed in white.

2002, President George W. Bush announced the *Healthier Us* initiative, which is based on four principles of healthy living:

- Be physically active every day.
- Eat a nutritious diet.
- Get preventive screenings.
- Make healthy choices.

This initiative focuses attention on the importance of daily physical activity. Of equal importance is the focus on the risks associated with inactivity.

Figure 3

Healthy People 2010: Physical Activity and Fitness Objectives
- Increase the proportion of adolescents who engage in moderate physical activity for at least 30 minutes on five or more of the previous seven days.
- Increase the proportion of adolescents who engage in vigorous physical activity that promotes cardiorespiratory fitness three or more days per week for 20 or more minutes per occasion.
- Increase the proportion of children and adolescents who view television two or fewer hours per day.
- Increase the proportion of trips made by walking.
- Increase the proportion of trips made by bicycling.
- Increase the proportion of the nation's public and private schools that require daily physical education for all students.
- Increase the proportion of adolescents who participate in daily physical education.
- Increase the proportion of adolescents who spend at least 50 percent of school physical education class time being physically active.
- Increase the proportion of the nation's public and private schools that provide access to their physical activity spaces and facilities for all persons outside of normal school hours (that is, before and after the school day, on weekends, and during summer and other vacations).
- Increase the proportion of middle, junior high, and senior high schools that provide comprehensive school health education to prevent health problems in the following areas: unintentional injury, violence, suicide, tobacco use and addiction, alcohol or other drug use, unintended pregnancy, HIV/AIDS and STD infection, unhealthy dietary patterns, inadequate physical activity, and environmental health.

Source: U.S. Department of Health and Human Services, *Healthy People 2010: Understanding and Improving Health*, 2000.

Leisure Pursuit Trends

Trends in recreation are correlated with personal "habits, lifestyles, resource opportunities, and economic and social contexts" (Kelly, 1987, p. iii). Thus, with the change from agricultural society, to industrial society, to information society came changes in the ways individuals used their leisure time. The increased use of technology has taken much of the physical labor (a natural source of physical activity) out of our work and out of our daily lives as well. This has created a greater need for moderate to vigorous exercise pursuits.

It is interesting to note that, in the 1960s, futurists predicted a shorter work week and more leisure time. However, the reality is that it now takes two incomes for most families to maintain a middle class lifestyle, and that's an 80-hour work week per family (Popcorn, 1992). In addition, people today spend a large amount of time traveling to work, watching television, and playing computer games (Kelly, 1987). It is more important than ever that physical educators provide information on time management, stress reduction, and maximizing leisure time through moderate to vigorous activity.

Education Trends

Throughout the last several decades, the education community has strived to keep pace with the rapidly occurring changes in society. However, many educational leaders will argue that schools have, in fact, remained in the industrial age. For example, secondary students are still, in most schools, moved from class to class throughout the day, much like a new product is moved from station to station along an assembly line.

Standards: Statements that identify the essential knowledge and skills that should be taught and learned in school.

Today, as we enter the communication age, futurists are predicting what schools of the future may look like. Thornburg (1992, p. 118), a noted educational futurist, says that rather than have assigned classrooms, schools might become huge resource centers where students, teachers, and others can co-mingle, conduct research, discuss projects, and interact freely. The structure of classes and assignments may be provided via "telecomputing." This is a very different picture from what schools look like today. For starters, everyone at school would be there because they wanted to be. School sites would bustle with excitement and activity.

In Thornburg's view, schools will be more like museums, where students can exchange ideas and socialize with other students around the world. With this idea in mind, it is interesting to note what individuals from outside the education realm are saying about the future of education. Anglin (1991, p. 265), a computer designer, says that in addition to providing access to facilities that are not affordable on an individual basis—such as chemistry labs and gymnasiums—schools may become institutions whose most cherished aim is to deliver those services now considered to be of secondary importance: sports, art, choir, socialization, and individual attention.

Assessment: Process of quantifying, describing, gathering data, or giving feedback about performance.

Several trends relating to the effective education of students for the 21st century emerge from the current literature on educational reform. They include:

- All students have equal access to instruction and information.
- Teachers assume the role of facilitators of learning rather than disseminators of information.
- The approach to learning is interdisciplinary, to ensure the integration of important principles across the curriculum.
- The curriculum promotes lifelong learning.
- The curriculum emphasizes "how to learn" as opposed to "what to learn."
- The curriculum emphasizes critical thinking skills, creative thinking skills, decision making skills, and problem finding and solving skills.
- Instruction is meaningful for the learner.
- Students take responsibility for their own learning.
- Instruction emphasizes active learning where students learn by doing.
- Learning is enhanced by the use of new technologies.
- Assessment measures student learning in performance-based settings, as it relates to predetermined standards of knowledge.

Standards-based assessment: Criterion-referenced assessment in which the criteria are taken directly from standards.

These trends are accompanied by the understanding that we don't know what exact knowledge will be needed in the future. For example, will foreign languages continue to be taught in our schools when hand held devices will provide instantaneous translations? The only thing we know for certain is that lifelong learning will be our insurance policy against obsolete information (Thornburg, 2002). This understanding certainly focuses our attention on developing the capacity and desire for learning in our students—including the learning of motor skills and fitness.

Physical Education Trends

As indicated in Chapter 6 (historical perspectives), physical education has been viewed with varying degrees of esteem throughout the history of humankind. Within the last decade, the importance of physical education in promoting good physical and mental health has again risen. The current thrust began with the publication of the Surgeon General's report on physical activity and health in 1996. It recommended, "every effort should be made to encourage schools to require daily physical education in each grade and to promote physical activities that can be enjoyed throughout life" (p. 6). This recommendation is based on research that shows favorable attitudes toward physical education and physical activity are related positively to adolescent participation in such activity (Ferguson et al., 1989; Zakarian et al., 1994; Tappe et al., 1990).

The Surgeon General's report was followed by three other documents that continue to view physical education in a positive and necessary vein:

■ *Guidelines for School and Community Programs to Promote Lifelong Physical Activity Among Young People* (CDC, 1997). These guidelines summarize the benefits of physical activity, the consequences of physical inactivity, and data on participation in physical activity by young people. They identify key principles for effective policies and programs and they list guidelines and recommendations. In terms of physical education, the guidelines recommend, "implement sequential physical education curricula and instruction in grades K-12 that: 1) emphasize enjoyable participation in lifetime physical activities such as walking and dancing, not just competitive sports; 2) help students develop the knowledge, attitudes, and skills they need to adopt and maintain a physically active lifestyle; 3) follow the National Standards for Physical Education; and 4) keep students active for most of class time."

- *Promoting Better Health for Young People Through Physical Activity and Sports: A Report to the President* (CDC, 2000a). This report from the Secretary of Health and Human Services and the Secretary of Education, released by the White House on November 29, 2000, states "physical education is at the core of a comprehensive approach to promoting physical activity through schools. All children, from prekindergarten through grade 12, should participate in quality physical education classes every school day."

- *Fit, Healthy, and Ready to Learn: A School Health Policy Guide* (National Association of State Boards of Education [NASBE], 2000). This document is designed to help state and local decision makers establish effective policies to help students adopt lifelong healthy habits and achieve their academic potential. In terms of physical education, it advocates "a sequential physical education curriculum taught daily in every grade, prekindergarten through twelfth, that involves moderate to vigorous physical activity; that teaches knowledge, motor skills, and positive attitudes; that promotes activities and sports that all students enjoy and can pursue throughout their lives; that is taught by well-prepared and well-supported staff; and that is coordinated with the comprehensive school health education curriculum ."

Additionally, NASPE, the CDC, the National Board for Professional Teaching Standards (NBPTS), and numerous physical educators across the United States have worked hard during the last decade developing public service announcements and position statements, promoting physical education with state and federal legislatures, and defining high-quality 21st century physical education programs. Numerous documents (see Figure 4) are available to help physical educators assess and improve their programs. From a comprehensive perspective, consider:

- *School Health Index for Physical Activity and Healthy Eating: A Self-Assessment and Planning Guide.* This docu-

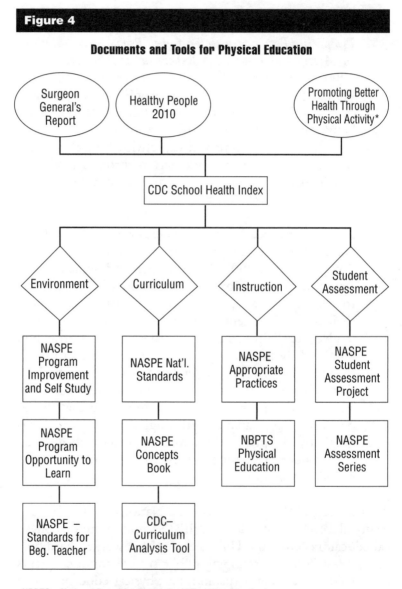

Figure 4

Documents and Tools for Physical Education

NBPTS – National Board for Professional Teaching Standards
NASPE – National Association for Sport and Physical Education
School Health Index – School Health Index for Physical Activity and Healthy Eating:
A Self-Assessment Planning Guide

ment available from the CDC is available in an *Elementary School* (2000b) and a *Middle/High School* (2000c) version. Both documents enable schools to identify strengths and weaknesses of their physical activity and nutrition policies and programs; develop an action plan for improving student health; and involve teachers, parents, students, and the community in improving school services. Eight modules assist educators and other stakeholders in assessing the school policies and environment; health education program; physical education program; nutrition services; school health services; school counseling, psychological and social services; health promotion for staff; and family and community involvement. Within the physical education module, there are 20 assessment points that cover the learning environment, curriculum, instruction, and assessment.

Standards-based: A descriptor that suggests that a clear and direct relationship exists among any combination of activities, materials, instructional processes, and assessments and that all relate to each other and to identified standards.

In addition to the *School Health Index for Physical Activity and Healthy Eating* overview document, there are other documents specific to environment, curriculum, instruction, and assessment that can assist physical educators in assessing and improving their programs. The curriculum documents look at *what* is taught; the instruction documents look at *how* content is delivered; the assessment documents look at *how well* students learn the information and skills; and the environment documents look at the *setting* in which instruction is delivered.

The curriculum documents include:

- *Moving into the Future: National Physical Education Standards* (NASPE, 1995a). This document defines the National Physical Education Standards and sets the framework for curriculum development.

- *Concepts of Physical Education: What Every Student Needs to Know* (Mohnsen, 1998). The first edition of this book further defined the content for inclusion in a physical education curriculum.

- *Physical Education Curriculum Analysis Tool* (PECAT) from the Centers for Disease Control (CDC, -in press). The PECAT is designed to be a simple, user-friendly tool to assist states, school districts, and schools in assessing how well their curricula meet National Standards, guidelines, and best practices for teaching physical education and in making revisions to their curricula based on the assessment.

The instructional publications include numerous textbooks on teaching methods, books on *how to* teach specific activities, and documents on effective instructional delivery:

- *Appropriate Practices for Elementary School Physical Education* (NASPE, 2000a), *Appropriate Practices for Middle School Physical Education* (NASPE, 2001), and *Appropriate Practices for High School Physical Education* (NASPE, 1998a). These documents address the key aspects of instructional strategy and practice that are essential to the delivery of quality physical education to students.

- *NBPTS Physical Education Standards* (NBPTS, 1999). This document includes a listing of 13 standards that define accomplished teaching. Demonstrating accomplishment of these standards leads to National Board certification. National Board certification is a demonstration of a teacher's practice as measured against high and rigorous standards.

The assessment publications also include numerous textbooks on assessment, books on *how to* assess specific areas of physical education (e.g., fitness), and booklets on effective assessment:

- *Assessment Series* (NASPE) – includes numerous booklets that include current and innovative assessment ideas, tactics, and strategies along with how to use them in K-12 physical education classes. Each booklet in the series focuses on a different assessment topic (e.g., authentic assessment, portfolio assessment, assessing student responsibility).

- *Assessment Project* (NASPE) – In 1999, NASPE appointed a task force of university and public school professionals to consider how to advance physical education throughout the United States. The charge was to create a set of performance indicators, assessment tasks, protocols, and scoring rubrics that are based on and complement the National Standards for Physical Education. The work of this committee is currently in progress.

Learning opportunities: Recommended practices to support all students in attaining the standards. These are presented for access, instruction, assessment, connections, and best practices in the fields of knowledge; represent areas that can be influenced by the teacher; and are supported by current research and best practices.

The area of learning environment is addressed as a component of quality physical education in numerous textbooks (e.g., *Teaching Middle School Physical Education [Mohnsen, 2003]*). However, NASPE has developed several documents that focus exclusively on establishing the opportunity to learn:

- *National Standards for Beginning Physical Education Teachers* (NASPE, 1995b). This document describes what new teachers should know and be able to do prior to entering the teaching profession.

- *Physical Education Program Improvement and Self-Study Guide* (NASPE). This document is available in a middle school (1998c) and a high school (1998b) version. Both documents assist physical educators in developing and implementing programs. They provide the essential ingredients in the learning environment that will produce quality middle school and high school physical education programs and services. Both documents are being updated and will return as *Opportunities to Learn Standards*.

- *Opportunities to Learn Standards for Elementary Physical Education* (NASPE, 2000a). This document addresses program elements that are essential for providing full opportunity for *all* students to learn in physical education. It includes a self-evaluation checklist for use in planning, evaluation, program development, and advocacy efforts by anyone interested in the availability of quality physical education programs.

All of these documents, taken together, have raised the bar for physical education in our schools. They provide a vision for what physical education *can be*—placing the responsibility for the delivery of quality physical education (as defined in these documents) squarely on the shoulders of the physical educators. These documents, along with press releases from schools that are providing outstanding physical education programs, have brought attention to the importance of quality physical education programs and put pressure on districts and schools to produce *like* programs.

Concepts and Principles of Physical Education

Built on the earlier work from the *Basic Stuff* series and aligned with the National Physical Education Standards, this second edition of *Concepts and Principles of Physical Education* asked leaders in the respective subdisciplines to review the current information and to summarize the most significant material in a form that allows K-12 teachers to share it with their students. The standards are deliberately presented as broad-based demonstrations of learning. The concepts/principles define the content that will allow students to accomplish the grade-level benchmarks and prepare for lives in the 21st century. Chapters 2 through 8 of this book represent the seven subdisciplines (motor learning, biomechanics, exercise physiology, social psychology, historical perspectives, motor development, and aesthetics) of physical education. Each chapter is organized as follows:

- Introduction to the subdiscipline. This section establishes a working definition of the subdiscipline and sets the stage for learning important concepts/principles.
- Importance of the subdiscipline. This section answers the question *why study this area of physical education?*
- Link to the National Standards. This section addresses the relationship between the subdiscipline and the National Physical Education Standards.
- Significant subdiscipline concepts/principles. This section identifies and explains the important concepts/principles that a physically educated adult needs to know.
- Lesson ideas. This section provides ideas for the teaching and learning of the concepts/principles.
- Assessment ideas. This section provides ideas for evaluating students' understanding of the concepts/principles.
- Resources for more information. This section provides references for additional information regarding concepts/ principles related to the subdiscipline.

Chapter 9 pulls together the information presented in Chapters 2 through 8 in an integrated fashion. It answers the question, "What next?" In addition, it shows how to integrate the information from various subdisciplines and standards into learning experiences. And, it shows various ways in which the subdisciplines can be integrated into other subject areas to create an interdisciplinary approach.

Before we can apply the grade level concepts/principles, instructional ideas, and student assessment ideas discussed in Chapters 2 through 8, we must identify a common language and knowledge base. The final sections in this chapter explain the concept/principle selection process, instructional considerations, and assessment tools that are used throughout the book.

Concept/Principle Selection Process

Alignment: Directness of the link among standards, local curriculum, instructional materials, instructional methods, and assessments.

The concepts/principles included in the following chapters align with and expand on the kindergarten, second grade, fourth grade, sixth grade, eighth grade, tenth grade, and twelfth grade benchmarks identified in the National Standards. However, instead of simply listing the standards, this book provides the critical concepts/principles that must be addressed or learned by the students if they are to demonstrate their learning related to each of the standards. The majority of the concepts/principles are related to Standard 2; however, you also will find concepts/principles related to the other six National Physical Education Standards.

Some of you will follow the concepts/principles presented in this book verbatim, while others will create and follow your own paths for different reasons. But reasons you must have; it is important that you be able to explain your decisions. Certainly, your selection of concepts/principles will be based on values held by you and other teachers in your district. Certainly, there must be an alignment between the concepts/principles you select and your specific physical education standards. However, be sure that you also can link the concepts/principles to the specific needs of your students. Remember: selecting fewer more significant concepts/principles that can be addressed in depth is a better choice than selecting many "less significant" concepts/principles that at best can be glossed over. An in-depth approach aligns more closely with trends in business and education in general.

Instructional Considerations

There are many ways to include cognitive concepts/principles in the teaching of physical education. First and foremost, teachers must model the application of these concepts/principles as they provide instructional experiences for students. Second, they must plan and provide specific learning activities that teach the concepts/principles. Careful planning, based on the information contained in the concept/principle and the various learning styles of the students in the class, will ensure that learning occurs.

One model to consider when developing activities for all students is Gardner's theory of multiple intelligences. According to Gardner (2000), there are currently eight identified areas of intelligence: linguistic intelligence, logical-mathematical intelligence, spatial intelligence, bodily-kinesthetic intelligence, musical intelligence, interpersonal intelligence, intrapersonal intelligence, and naturalist intelligence. Every individual has varying degrees of ability in each of these areas. When developing learning experiences, it is important for the teacher to consider each of the eight areas in order to provide learning opportunities that relate to the various capabilities (see Figure 5). Students can rotate through various learning stations or they may be allowed to select the one learning opportunity they feel is best suited to their strengths.

A second model to consider is interdisciplinary instruction. When considering this model remember that physical educators must first be true to their own subject area. They must ensure that they are facilitating student learning as it relates to the physical education grade level standards and concepts/principles. However in many cases, integration with other subject areas can facilitate this process. There are several educational models available for integrating information with other subject areas. The model described next is based on the work of Fogarty (1991), and is used here as a framework for integrating information between physical education and other sub-

---

Figure 5

Gardner's Multiple Intelligences
Linguistic: Capacity to use words effectively
Logical-Mathematical: Capacity to use numbers and reason effectively
Spatial: Capacity to perceive the visual-spatial world accurately
Bodily-Kinesthetic: Capacity to use bodies effectively
Musical: Capacity to perceive musical forms accurately
Interpersonal: Capacity to understand others effectively
Intrapersonal: Capacity to understand themselves effectively
Naturalist: Capacity to discriminate among living things

---

ject areas. Specific examples for using this model are presented in Chapter 9.

The **sequenced model** encourages teachers to rearrange the order of their topics so that similar units in different subject areas coincide with one another. In the case of two related disciplines, teachers sequence content so that common subject matter is taught at the same time. In this way, learning in one subject area enhances the learning in another with very little interaction between the instructors. An example of this model is a health educator teaching a nutrition unit while the physical educator teaches a body composition or health-related fitness unit.

In the **shared model**, teachers work together to look for common areas of curriculum. The focus is on shared concepts/ principles, skills, and attitudes. This model extends the sequenced model, since it requires the teachers to plan overlaps in course content to provide support for information from both subject areas and not simply to repeat information. An example of this model is a movement education unit in which the language arts educator introduces a story and students illustrate the characters and their emotions through movement during physical education.

The **webbed model** is a thematic approach to integrating subject matter. Planning for instruction begins with a theme, and information related to that theme is integrated into different subjects. Themes that can cross various subject areas include transportation, patterns, space, and oceanography. In this model, the theme becomes central to the learning and the teachers provide information that supports the theme. Themes might include wellness, transitions, change, and space travel. In the space travel theme, physical education students explore the need for exercise in a weightless environment.

In the **threaded model**, the teacher selects concepts/principles (e.g., social skills, multiple intelligences, technology) that are then threaded into the existing curriculum. This model does not require additional units; it simply requires that important concepts/principles be revisited throughout the curriculum. Typical interdisciplinary concepts/principles include writing across the curriculum and technology across the curriculum. The significance of this model is that the more reinforcement that occurs, the more likely students are to retain and use the concepts/principles. An example might be the science educator addressing Newton's Laws during the first month of school and the physical educator addressing the application of Newton's Laws to various physical activities throughout the rest of the school year.

The **integrated model** is an expansion of the shared model. It represents a crossdisciplinary approach involving four or more subject areas. This model involves setting curricular priorities in each area and then finding the overlapping skills, attitudes, and concepts/principles in the other areas. Again, the emphasis is on subject areas supporting one another, not the repetition of information in each subject area. An example is a health-related fitness unit in which the health educator focuses on personal health, the physical educator on conditioning and training, the science educator on the digestive system, and the math educator on word problems involving the input and output of calories.

In the **immersed model**, teachers select a concept/principle and then design a project that requires students to select and study an area related to the concept/principle. In this model, the learner integrates the concept/principle with little outside intervention. This approach targets student interest areas. It also requires more time than most instructional approaches. Examples of interest areas include baseball, dinosaurs, robotics, and astronomy. In the robotics unit, students might explore ways to make a robot appear more human in its movement.

Assessment Tools

Assessment measures progress as students work toward achieving the identified benchmarks and standards. In addition, assessment reveals the effectiveness of the instructional program and provides insight into how physical educators can make learning more successful and meaningful. In order for these outcomes to occur, the assessment must be aligned to the standards and tools selected based on their ability to measure progress related to a particular standard. It also is important to let students know how they will be assessed and how they will be provided with feedback throughout the learning process.

Assessment in K-12 education tends to fall into one of three major categories: traditional, alternative, and authentic. In the traditional approach, assessment is based on standardized motor skill tests for accuracy and distance; written tests on rules, history, and strategy; and physical fitness tests. Alternative assessment tools, as identified in the National Standards, include self-assessment, video analysis, open-ended questions, and focused journal writing. Authentic assessment takes this one step farther by requiring students to use alternative assessment tools to apply their learning to real-world situations.

Authentic assessment: Process of gathering evidence and documentation of a student's learning and growth in ways that resemble real life as closely as possible.

In each chapter of this book, the authors include ideas on how students can demonstrate their learning in relation to the standard or concept/principle learned. These assessment ideas are based on the application of a number of different assessment tools and concepts/principles, including checking for understanding, observation, reports, projects, role playing and simulations, student logs and focused journals, 30-second wonders, and written tests. (NASPE is developing more comprehensive assessment strategies through its assessment project.)

Checking for Understanding

With this quick technique, the teacher simply asks a question and then calls on several students to answer the question. It is important to query a heterogeneous group of students (low achievers, high achievers, boys, girls) in sufficient numbers to get an accurate reading of the students' cognitive understanding.

Observations

Observations are performed by the teacher, peers, or the students themselves. An observation requires a judgment to be made about a particular motor skill. When assessing performance based on observation, teachers use either a checklist or rubric (see the section on rubrics), or a simple counting system (e.g., number of serves in the court, number of free throws made). In some situations, students assess themselves, have a peer validate their assessment, and then have the teacher complete the assessment cycle by making the formal observation.

Reports

Rubric: A set of scoring guidelines for assessing student work. Good rubrics consist of a fixed measurement scale (e.g., four-point), a set of clear criteria, performance descriptions for each criterion at each point on the scale, and sample responses (anchors) that illustrate various levels of performance.

Reports are a commonly used assessment technique. They may encompass several subject areas, providing an interdisciplinary assessment (e.g., the language arts teacher assesses the writing, and the physical education teacher assesses the content).

Projects (Individual and Group)

Student projects take the report technique one step farther by asking students to create products other than written reports. These products might take the form of videos, multimedia presentations, or oral presentations. Many students find projects intrinsically motivating, since they often can use skills that are associated with their primary intelligence. However, projects also can be very time consuming for students to do and for teachers to evaluate.

Role Playing and Simulations

Role playing and simulations provide students with the opportunity to respond as if they were in a real-life situation. They require students to use higher-level thinking and problem solving skills.

Student Logs and Journals

Student logs and journals are used to document perceptions, feelings, attitudes, and evidence of progress. Journal reflections are typically made at the end of each class, when students describe what they did, what they learned, what risks they took, and what they would change about their performance. In logs, on the other hand, students record levels of performance (number of curl-ups, times for the mile run, etc.) or specific behaviors collected at regular intervals throughout a period of time.

Thirty-Second Wonders

The 30-second wonder is another quick assessment tool that can demonstrate whether students understand the concepts/ principles the teacher has presented. The teacher simply asks a question and has each student write an answer on a piece of paper. Teachers can assess the answers to determine the lesson for the following day.

Written Tests

Written tests are typically used to assess cognitive understanding. They can include multiple choice, true/false, matching, fill-in-the blank, short answer, and essay questions. However, the recent shift has been to emphasize essay or open-ended questions. This is often referred to as going "beyond the bubble," indicating a shift from filling in a Scantron™ sheet to using cognitive and strategic problem-solving skills.

Criteria: The dimensions or characteristics of standards used to judge student work.

Rubrics

Rubrics are scoring criteria that are used to assess student work. They provide a description of various qualitative levels of performance on a specific task or product. The rubric presents criteria by which the quality of the final product is assessed. The rating can take the form of any number of scales, but a range of one through six (with six being ideal), or one through four (with four being ideal), is the most common. Initially, the teacher develops the rubric, but as confidence grows the development of rubrics becomes a joint effort involving teacher and students.

Portfolios

A portfolio is a permanent collection of a student's best work. It demonstrates progress toward identified standards. It is similar to an artist's portfolio, and can contain a variety of assessment tools. Most portfolios include a reflective essay in which the student comments on the portfolio. At the end of the year, the portfolio provides the teacher and the student with concrete information that can be used to discuss progress and to set goals for the next year.

Portfolio: Purposeful, integrated collection of student work showing effort, progress, or achievement in one or more areas.

Concluding Comments

This book is the most recent attempt to provide physical educators with up-to-date content that will assist students in becoming physically educated. As we move into the next seven chapters, it is imperative that readers challenge their existing assumptions about education in general and physical education in particular, and dare to create high-quality learning experiences that are relevant for the 21st century.

References

American Heart Association. (1991). *Heart and stroke facts*. Needham, MA: Author.

_____. (2001). *Heart and stroke facts: 2001 statistical supplement*. Dallas: Author.

Anglin, G. J. (Ed.). (1991). *Instructional technology: Past, present and future*. Englewood, CO: Libraries Unlimited.

Burgeson, C. R., Wechsler, H., Brener, N. D., Young, J. C., & Spain, C. G. (2001). Physical education and activity: Results from the school health policies and programs study 2000. *Journal of School Health, 71*(7), 293-300.

Burrus, D. (1993). *Techno trends*. New York: Harper Business.

Carr, J. F., & Harris, D. E. (2001). *Succeeding with standards: Linking curriculum, assessment, and action planning*. Alexandria, VA: Association for Supervision and Curriculum Development.

Carr, N. J. (Ed.). (1987). *Basic stuff series II*. Reston, VA: AAHPERD.

Centers for Disease Control and Prevention. (1997). Guidelines for school and community programs to promote lifelong physical activity among young people. *MMWR, 46*, 1-36 (No. RR-6).

_____. (1999). Youth risk behavior surveillance—United States. *MMWR. 49*(No. SS-5).

_____. (2000a). *Promoting better health for young people through physical activity and sports: A report to the president from the secretary*. Atlanta, GA: Author.

_____. (2000b). *School health index for physical activity and healthy eating: A self-assessment and planning guide–middle school/high school*. Atlanta, GA: Author.

_____. (2000c). *School health index for physical activity and healthy eating: A self-assessment and planning guide–elementary school*. Atlanta, GA: Author.

_____. (2001). Youth risk behavior surveillance—United States. Web site: http://apps.nccd.cdc.gov/YRBSS/index.asp.

_____. (in press). *Physical education curriculum analysis tool*. Atlanta, GA: Author.

Corbin, C. B., & Pangrazi, R. P. (1998). *Physical activity for children: A statement of guidelines.* Reston, VA: NASPE.

Davidow, W. H., & Malone, M. S. (1992). *The virtual corporation.* New York: Harper Business.

Doolittle, S., & Fay, T. (2002). *Authentic assessment of physical activity for high school students.* Reston, VA: NASPE.

Ferguson, K. J., Yesalis, C. E., Pomreh, P. R., & Kirkpatrick, M. B. (1989). Attitudes, knowledge, and beliefs as predictors of exercise intent and behavior in school children. *Journal of School Health, 59*(1) ,112-115.

Fogarty, R. (1991). *The mindful school: How to integrate the curricula.* Palatine, IL: IRI/Skylight.

Franck, M. (1992). *Outcomes of quality physical education programs.* Reston, VA: NASPE.

Gardner, H. (2000). *Intelligence reframed: Multiple intelligences for the 21st century.* New York: Basic Books.

Holt/Hale, S. A. (1999a). *Assessing and improving fitness in elementary physical education.* Reston, VA: NASPE.

_____. (1999b). *Assessing motor skills in elementary physical education.* Reston, VA: NASPE.

Kelly, J. R. (1987). *Recreational trends toward the year 2000.* Champaign, IL: Management Learning Laboratories.

Kneer, M. (Ed.). (1981). *Basic stuff series I.* Reston, VA: AAHPERD.

Koplan, J. (2000). *Obesity continues climb in 1999 among American adults.* Atlanta, GA: National Center for Chronic Disease Prevention and Health Promotion. Web site: http://www.cdc.gov/nccdphp/dnpa.

Lambert, L. T. (1999). *Standards-based assessment of student learning: A comprehensive approach.* Reston, VA: NASPE.

Lund, J. L. (2000). *Creating rubrics for physical education.* Reston, VA: NASPE.

Melograno, V. J. (1999). *Preservice professional portfolio system.* Reston, VA: NASPE.

Mitchell, S. A., & Oslin, J.L. (1999). *Assessment in games teaching.* Reston, VA: NASPE.

Mohnsen, B. (1999). *The new leadership paradigm for physical education: What we need to lead.* Reston, VA: NASPE.

_____. (2003). *Teaching middle school physical education.* Champaign, IL: Human Kinetics.

Mohnsen, B. (Ed.). (1998). *Concepts of physical education: What every student needs to know.* Reston, VA: NASPE.

National Association for Sport and Physical Education. (1995a). *Moving into the future: National physical education standards. A guide to content and assessment.* Reston, VA: Author.

_____. (1995b). *National standards for beginning physical education teachers.* Reston, VA: Author.

_____. (1998a). *Appropriate practices for high school physical education.* Reston, VA: Author.

28

_____. (1998b). *Physical education program improvement and self-study guide for high school.* Reston, VA: Author.

_____. (1998c). *Physical education program improvement and self-study guide for middle school.* Reston, VA: Author.

_____. (1999). *Sport and physical education advocacy kit (SPEAK) II.* Reston, VA: Author.

_____. 2000a. *Oppotunities to learn standards for elementary physical education.* Reston, VA: Author.

_____. 2000b. *Appropriate practices for elementary school physical education.* Reston, VA: Author.

_____. 2000c. *Appropriate practices in movement programs for young children, ages 3-5.* Reston, VA: Author.

_____. (2001). *Appropriate practices for middle school physical education.* Reston, VA: Author.

National Association of State Boards of Education. (2000). *Fit, healthy and ready to learn: A school health policy guide.* Alexandria, VA: Author.

National Board for Professional Teaching Standards. (1999). *Physical education standards (ages 3-18+).* Southfield, MI: Author.

O'Sullivan, M., & Henninger, M. (2000). *Assessing student responsibility and teamwork.* Reston, VA: NASPE.

Popcorn, F. (1992). *The Popcorn report.* New York: Harper Collins.

Popcorn, F., & Marigold, L. (1996). *Clicking: 16 trends to future fit your life, your work, and your business.* New York: HarperCollins.

Secretary's Commission on Achieving Necessary Skills. (1991). *What work requires of schools: A SCANS report for America 2000.* Washington DC: U.S. Department of Labor.

_____. (2000). *What work requires of schools.* Washington, DC: U.S. Department of Labor.

Staff. (September 13, 1988). Youth problems are frightening. *Deseret News.*

Staff. (July-August, 2002). The technology timeline. *The Futurist,* pp. 33-36.

Tappe, M. K., Duda, J. L., & Menges-Ehrnwald, P. (1990). Personal investment predictors of adolescent motivation orientation toward exercise. *Canadian Journal of Sport Sciences, 15,* 185-192.

Thornburg, D. D. (1992). *Edutrends 2010: Restructuring, technology and the future of education.* San Francisco, CA: Starson.

_____. (2002). *The new basics: Education and the future of work in the telematic age.* Alexandria, VA: Association for Supervision and Curriculum Development.

United States Census Bureau. (2000). *World Population.* Washington, DC: Author.

United States Department of Health and Human Services, Public Health Service. (1990). *Healthy people 2000: National health promotion and disease prevention objectives.* Washington, DC: Author.

_____. (1996). *Physical activity and health: A report of the Surgeon General.* Atlanta, GA: Author.

_____. (2000). *Healthy people 2010: Understanding and improving health.* Washington, DC: Author.

_____. (2001). *The Surgeon General's call to action to prevent and decrease overweight and obesity* (2001). Rockville, MD: Office of the Surgeon General.

Zakarian, J. M., Hovell, M. F., Hofstetter, C. R., Sallis, J. F., & Keating, K. J. (1994). Correlates of vigorous exercise in a predominantly low SES and minority high school population. *Preventive Medicine, 23,* 314-321.

Chapter **2**

Motor Learning

Judith E. Rink

*S*hould I practice my golf stroke in parts or as one complete movement? What do I look for when selecting a tennis instructor? Should I concentrate my weekly practice time in one day or spread it over several practice sessions? How should I alter my tennis practice sessions now that I have developed competency in the basic skills?

The answers to all of these questions are rooted in the field of study known as motor learning. In this chapter, we will look at motor learning concepts as they relate to the learning and refinement of motor skills. These concepts are an important part of the cognitive foundation for a physically educated person, and understanding them can enhance the experience of acquiring or maintaining a physically active lifestyle.

What Is Motor Learning?

Motor learning is the study of change in the ability of a person to perform a skill. The degree of learning is inferred from improvement in performance over time as a result of practice or experience. Like all learning, motor learning is inferred from behavior and represents a relatively permanent change in behavior. However, it is possible to observe performance without observing learning. Changes in behavior are attributed to experience or practice and not to changes in the organism (such as increased strength).

Why Is Motor Learning Important?

Teachers must be committed to the process of learning *how to learn*. They must be knowledgeable in the basic concepts of learning if they are to help students understand how to learn and why particular practices are important to learning. Helping students develop learning skills and giving students the knowledge they need to learn independently will help them be better learners today and will help them later in life when they choose to acquire new skills. Adults who have a strong background in basic and fundamental movement patterns and who know how to learn new skills will be better prepared for an active life. Thus, at a minimum, students should understand the basic concepts that equip them to become independent learners of motor skills.

Linking Motor Learning to the National Standards

Motor learning concepts/principles can stand by themselves as content for physical education. Motor learning concepts are specifically targeted in Standard 2 (Applies movement concepts and principles to the learning and development of motor skills). However, they can be successfully integrated with all of the other standards as well. This is particularly true of aspects of the following National Standards:

- National Standard 1: Demonstrates competency in many movement forms and proficiency in a few movement forms.
- National Standard 4: Achieves and maintains a health-enhancing level of physical fitness.
- National Standard 6: Demonstrates understanding and respect for differences among people in physical activity settings.
- National Standard 7: Understands that physical activity provides opportunities for enjoyment, challenge, self-expression, and social interaction.

The intent of the National Standards is not that physical education will become a classroom course in motor learning and motor control. Rather, the concepts/principles should be selected carefully, be developmentally appropriate for the age of the learner, and be integrated with physical activity. This is particularly true with motor learning concepts. It is repetition through the program that will provide the reinforcement the student needs to learn the concepts and to be able to transfer them to new learning experiences.

Selected Motor Learning Themes

It is important for physical education teachers to understand and be able to apply the information contained in the textbooks on motor learning. While physically educated individuals do not need the same depth of understanding, it is important for students to grasp certain concepts if they are to be independent learners of motor skills. These concepts are organized around five major themes:

1. How do people get better at motor skills?
2. What is good performance?
3. What stages do individuals pass through to become proficient at motor skills?
4. What kind of practice facilitates learning?
5. Will learning one motor skill help a person learn another motor skill?

Each of these themes is briefly developed in the following section. Critical student concepts that fall under each theme are developed in a K-12 format.

How Do People Get Better at Motor Skills?

Improvement in motor skills is usually the result of changes in growth and/or learning. As students grow bigger and stronger, many of their skills—particularly those requiring force production (jumping, throwing, etc.)—will improve. However, the ability to improve the process characteristics (form) of a motor skill is not dependent on age or strength. Learning might be described as a change in behavior that is the result of practice and experience using motor skills. Learning is inferred from performance, and it can only be measured indirectly.

For example, we infer that students have learned when they do well on an assessment of the product or product characteristics of a movement. And, we infer that they have not learned when

Continuous skills: Skills that are repeated one after another (e.g., basketball dribble) and do not have a clearly defined beginning and end.

they do poorly. Because we are measuring performance, learning may or may not have occurred. We can measure learning by looking at performance after time has elapsed between practice and testing. Short-term improvement in motor performance can be achieved without actual learning if the movement responses are not committed to long-term memory. This means that teachers might be able to elicit a good performance from a student who has not learned the skill and, therefore, will not be able to repeat it. When students have learned, performance becomes more consistent.

Discrete skills: Skills that are unconnected to other skills (e.g., volleyball forearm pass) and have a clear beginning and end.

Again, when we observe performance after a period of time has elapsed between practice and testing, we are more likely to accurately determine the degree of learning that has occurred. Once motor skills are committed to long-term memory, they will be retained for long periods of time. It should be noted here that continuous skills (riding a bike) are remembered for longer periods of time than discrete skills (the tennis serve).

When we say that an individual has learned a motor skill, we are actually talking about several different kinds of change that take place as performance improves. The most obvious is the physical change that occurs with practice. The movement becomes more mechanically efficient and coordinated; the goal of the movement is accomplished to a greater extent; and the use of different muscle groups to accomplish the movement becomes more efficient. Cognitive change also is likely as skill develops. More skilled performers attend to different parts of the performance. They can focus on how to use a skill, and they have greater ability to correct their own performance.

Concepts/Principles

Kindergarten: *Practice and experience makes you better at motor skills.* Many students in physical education think that people are born "good" or "not good" at motor skills. Helping students attribute success in motor skills to their own effort and experience is a critical concept for students. It should begin early and continue throughout a good program.

Second Grade: *Knowing how to perform a skill will help you learn that skill.* The role of cognitive knowledge in learning a motor skill is often underestimated. Students need to know that "knowing how" can help them be better performers. Teachers are likely to find that students are more likely to attend to efforts to communicate "how to do it" if they know why this information is important.

Fourth Grade: *You get better at many motor skills as you get bigger and stronger.* Strength and size are factors that affect many motor skills. Given the same level of motor competence in a skill, bigger students often are more effective at skills requiring force production simply because they are bigger and stronger. For young children who are growing rapidly, knowing that body size does make a difference is likely to help them accept what they can do and accept the differences between what they can do and what older and bigger students can do.

Fourth Grade: *If you can identify the cues for a skill you are more likely to perform it correctly.* This concept is a more advanced notion of the idea of "knowing how." Being able to identify the specific cues for a skill will facilitate using knowledge and practice.

Sixth Grade: *Different skills require different physical abilities that can be developed through training programs.* This concept presents a great opportunity for teachers to integrate knowledge of the fitness components and their development with the role of the components in motor skill development. Students not only should be able to identify the fitness components that play a major role in a skill or sport, but they also should be able to develop them in the context of the sport or activity.

Eighth Grade: *Motor skills that are learned well enough to be included in long-term memory are kept for a long period of time.* This concept is an advanced version of the importance of practice. Students must understand that it takes a lot of practice for a skill to be really learned and that if it is really learned it is not likely to "disappear" at the next practice.

Tenth Grade: *Short-term improvement in motor skills can be achieved without learning if the practice isn't long enough.* Sometimes when students are successful in the short term it is difficult to get them to continue to practice. Understanding why practice must be extensive should help motivate students to practice.

Twelfth Grade: *As you move into adulthood you will want to learn different motor skills.* Although students leave us as young adults, our responsibility as physical educators is to educate for a lifetime of physical activity. This concept stresses the importance of helping students project their needs for learning and continued physical activity into the future.

What Is Good Performance?

There are two aspects to good performance. The first is the ability to correctly select what to do; the second is the ability to execute that selection appropriately. For example, I may correctly select a drop shot in badminton, but I may not be able to execute that shot correctly. Or, I may be able to do a drop shot but may not select the appropriate time to use it. Knowledge

Example 1

Threading Motor Learning Concepts into the Curriculum
Elementary School Example: Second Grade

Concept/Principle: Two or more skills (serial) are combined correctly when they flow smoothly from one skill to another without any breaks (e.g., running into a jump).

The content area the teacher is working with is combining locomotor actions. As part of the planned experiences for this part of the curriculum, students will combine locomotor movements on small equipment (hurdles, low boxes, and hoops) into a sequence. The teacher has decided to thread the concept that combined skills are called serial skills and are performed well when the transitions between the movements are smooth. The teacher focuses instruction on how to make the transitions smooth and assess the degree to which students have knowledge of good transitions and can execute good transitions.

The teacher has decided to thread the concept of serial skills and smooth transitions into work with fielding and throwing a ball. Students are reminded that fielding and throwing are serial skills, and that it is important to make the transitions between these movements smooth. Students explore how they can make the transitions smooth.

Each time the teacher teaches serial skills, he or she reintroduces the idea of what a serial skill is and what constitutes good performance. The potential for students to transfer the concept of serial skills into new experiences increases with the amount of reinforcement threaded throughout the curriculum.

plays a critical role in skill execution. I may execute a motor skill according to the knowledge I have about how to do that skill, but my knowledge may be incorrect.

When a performance is not good, it is important to know whether the problem is related to the skill that was selected or to how it was executed. Different kinds of skills put different demands on each aspect of a performance. Skills that are performed in complex environments put more emphasis on what to do (response selection) than skills that are not performed in complex environments. Closed skills that must be performed with consistent form (e.g., gymnastics, diving) put more emphasis on correct execution.

Closed skills: Motor skills that are performed in an environment that is stable and predictable (e.g., archery).

There are several ways in which types of motor skills are differentiated, and these will affect what is learned and how it is learned. The most critical differentiation of motor skills is related to the continuum of closed and open skills. Closed skills are performed in stable and predictable environments. Gymnastics, diving, and the foul shot in basketball are all examples of closed skills. The environment in which the skill is performed is largely stable and predictable. Although no skill is ever performed in exactly the same conditions (e.g., wind and mental

---

Example 2

Threading Motor Learning Concepts into the Curriculum
Secondary School Example: Sixth Grade

Concept/Principle: Game tactics are a decision of what to do in a competitive situation. Some tactics are correct but are executed poorly.

The activity the teacher is working with is badminton. As part of the planned experiences for this unit, the teacher will work with net game offensive and defensive strategies. The teacher has decided to thread the concept that there are two parts to performance in a strategy: the decision and the execution of the decision.

Part way through the unit, the teacher videotapes the play of students and asks them to analyze their play. As part of this analysis, students determine whether their errors resulted from their choice of what to do (their intent) or the manner in which they executed what they did. Students then make a list of those problems on which they need to work. They divide their list into problems with choosing a strategy and problems executing a strategy.

The teacher threads this concept through all of the sports that are included in the curriculum, increasing the potential that students will be able to use the concept to learn new sports independently.

Example 3

Webbing a Concept into the Curriculum
Secondary School Example: Eighth Grade

Concept/Principle: Good performance of closed skills should result in prac-tice and performance that is done in the same way each time. Some closed skills are done in different environments and require adaptation.

The teacher has chosen to assign a few days at the end of the school year to the development of this concept. He or she has identified all of the closed skills that students have learned during their basketball, volleyball, badmin-ton, archery, and bowling units, and has set up stations around the gym where each of these skills can be practiced.

After identifying and developing the concept with several examples, the teacher asks the students to rotate through each of the stations. At each station, students must identify the important cues for the skill. Students then have the opportunity to practice the skill 10 times with a peer observer. The peer observer identifies aspects of performance that are not consistent from trial to trial—including preparation and what the student does follow-ing performance—and gives feedback. After students have had an opportu-nity to perform and to be an observer, they may move on to the next station.

state of the performer), the environment for closed skills is more stable and the object or person is not moving.

Open skills are characterized by variable and unpredictable en-vironments. In most open skills, either the object or the per-former is moving. The tennis forehand, the field goal shot in basketball, and the soccer pass all are examples of open skills. There also are some skills that are essentially closed skills but are performed in variable environments, such as in golf and

Open skills: Motor skills that are performed in a changing environment.

bowling. For these skills, the performance must be adjusted to suit different situations.

Motor skills also are characterized as discrete skills, serial skills, and continuous skills. Discrete skills are single skills performed in isolation from other motor skills. Examples of discrete skills are the soccer penalty kick, the tennis backhand, the golf stroke, and the standing long jump. These skills are usually not per-formed with, or are not followed by, other skills. Serial skills consist of two or more different skills performed with each other. Examples include fielding a ball and throwing it, trap-ping a soccer ball and passing it, dribbling a basketball and shooting it, and performing a gymnastics dance routine. Most team sports require that players combine two or more complex skills in a serial fashion. Continuous skills include two or more repetitions of the same skill, such as dribbling in basketball or soccer ball.

Good performance of serial and continuous skills requires that the performer link movements together in a smooth fashion. Preparation for the next movement actually occurs during the previous movement. Consider, for example, going from a handstand into a forward roll, or fielding and throwing a ball. If I am going to move into a forward roll from a handstand, I will have to make adjustments to both the handstand and the forward roll. How I field a ball and how I come up from fielding a ball is determined in large part by the kind of throw I need to make. Players actually prepare for the throw while they are fielding. In serial skills such as the dribble, one movement leads into the next.

It is important to determine how the links between skills should be made and to practice movements in sequence. Sports such as soccer—where many skills are performed in a serial fashion—require players to practice many different combinations of skills (i.e., receive an aerial ball, dribble and pass, receive a ground ball, dribble and shoot).

Good performance for open skills requires performers to adapt their performance to the open environment. For example, basketball players must make a decision about what to do based on their opponents' and their teammates' positions and abilities. They also must adjust their movements to meet the demands of different situations. More skilled individuals are able to choose appropriate motor responses and execute those choices in complex and changing environments.

Defining good performance is a critical theme in our work with students in physical education. It is difficult to strive to be good at something if you do not know what "good" is. Several concepts have been selected as critical concepts to be learned in a K-12 program for this theme.

Concepts/Principles

Kindergarten: *You are good at a motor skill when you perform the skill with the correct cues.* One of the difficulties teachers face in teaching motor skills is that they are trying to teach "process" while students are focused on product. Helping students to understand at an early age that good performance is linked to how well they perform in terms of the movement process is important. Linking this concept to the importance of cues in learning (previous theme) is important.

Second Grade: *Two or more skills (serial) are combined correctly when they flow smoothly from one skill to another without any breaks (e.g., running into a jump).* By the second grade, students should be linking skills together. Performing skills in a serial fashion requires a focus on preparing for the second skill while performing the first. Teachers who help students focus on transitions and the importance of transitions will give students a valuable tool with which to learn additional skills.

Second Grade: *Continuous skills (same skill performed over and over again) need to be modified when more than one skill is performed in a row.* This concept is similar to the previous one, but it is important for students to distinguish when skills are being performed in a continuous fashion and when they are being performed in a serial manner. Again, the focus is on helping students understand that they will need to make adjustments and understand the specific adjustments they must make.

Fourth Grade: *Good performance of open skills requires a performer to adapt performance to an environment (e.g., modifying a forward roll to meet the size of a mat or to coordinate a performance with a partner).* As students begin to use skills in more complex environments, they must not only know how to change what they do, they must understand that they must adapt and adjust what they do as environments change.

Sixth Grade: *Game tactics are a decision of what to do in a competitive situation. Some tactics are correct but are executed poorly.* As students begin to participate in game situations they need to understand the difference between the correct decision of what to do and the correct execution of what to do. These are two distinct aspects of game play; they should be discriminated for the student. This can happen more effectively if students are rewarded for the right idea, even if they are not yet able to execute it. Likewise, drawing attention to what a skill is used for will help develop good decisions.

Sixth Grade: *The selection of a game tactic is dependent on what your teammates and opponents do in a game.* Players do not operate in a vacuum. Early emphasis should be placed on understanding the need for developing an awareness of what opponents and teammates are doing and the implications of the interactive environment for changes that must be made in performance.

Sixth Grade: *The goal should be for movement sequences, routines, and combinations of skills to flow smoothly from one to another. Preparation for a subsequent movement occurs in the previous movement.* Like the concept of serial and continuous skills, as students begin to develop sequences for performance they must be helped to understand the concept of "flow" in relation to combined movements. They also must learn how "flow" is achieved.

Eighth Grade: *Good performance of closed skills should result in practice and performance that is done in the same way each time. Some closed skills are done in different environments and require adaptation.* Not only should students begin to identify when a skill is closed and when it is open, they also should know how to practice for these different types of skills.

Tenth Grade: *Open skills are performed in unpredictable and unstable environment and should be practiced in variable conditions.* Practice conditions for open skills are more difficult to identify and require skills in game analysis. Older students should be capable of this level of analysis.

Twelfth Grade: *Learning is assessed after a break between practice and testing (retention).* This concept is an advanced version of the previous concept. It emphasizes the importance of students knowing when they have learned a skill.

What Stages Do Individuals Pass Through To Become Proficient at Motor Skills?

An individual must pass through three stages to become proficient at a motor skill (Fitts & Posner, 1967):

- Stage 1. This is the **cognitive stage**. At this point, the individual is trying to figure out how to do the skill and is generating beginning attempts. The emphasis here is on "what to do." Performance is very inconsistent, and attention demands are very high. For example, a beginning volleyball player who is trying to do a forearm pass is likely to have difficulty getting set in the right position to hit the ball. The player is likely to send the ball in many different directions until he or she learns how to place his or her arms to control the direction. This player is not able to deal with what may be happening with teammates or opponents, and may be completely unaware of their movements. A performer at this level is likely to commit different errors with each attempt.

- Stage 2. This is the **associative stage** of learning. The emphasis here is on trying to perfect the movement response. Learning continues to involve cognitive processes of performance. Consistency improves. Performers begin to attend to other environmental aspects of performance. A good example of this stage of development is the basketball player who can make some defensive adjustments in the dribble to accommodate the movements of an offensive player, but who cannot quite take his or her eyes off the ball. Performers at this level become overloaded easily and the skill breaks down. At this level, most adjustments to the environment are made very much at a conscious level of awareness.

- Stage 3. This is the **automatic stage**. At this point, movement responses flow. There is little cognitive involvement, and the level of performance is consistently high. Performers at this stage can function in highly complex environments such as games. They can focus on what to do without having to think about how to do it. The soccer player moving into scoring position can focus on where teammates and opponents are located on the field and can anticipate their movements without having to worry about dribbling, passing, or shooting skills.

It is important for learners to know how learning progresses from being a beginner to being a competent performer of a skill. The following concepts have been identified as critical for addressing stages of development in the K-12 program.

Example 4

The Immersion (Project) Approach to Teaching Motor Learning Concepts
Secondary School Example

Concepts/Principles
In the first stage of learning a motor skill, you should seek to get a clear idea of how to do the skill. You also should be able to describe what you should be doing.

In the second stage of learning a motor skill, you should work toward consistent performance in more complex environments.

In the third stage of learning a motor skill, your movement responses should be automatic. Difficult motor skills will never reach 100 percent reliability.

The teacher wants students to be able to identify the stages through which they pass as they become proficient in a motor skill. Students may do this by teaching a skill to a peer, younger sibling, or younger friend. They also may do this project with themselves as the learner. Students are encouraged to choose a skill that does not require a great deal of time in which to develop proficiency.

Students must identify the stages of learning and provide videotape and descriptions of the learner at the different stages. The final project report should include:

1. An introduction describing the stages of learning through which individuals pass as they are learning a motor skill.
2. Videotape of the learner at the stages of learning described in the first part of the report.
3. Descriptions of the learner at different stages of learning.

The project should result in at least a three-page report describing the conditioning for the activity. The teacher should collect the reports, share the best ones with the class, and spend a class session comparing and contrasting the conditioning for different activities and sports. Students who are interested in a particular sport or activity should be provided with access to the reports for those activities or sports.

Concepts/Principles.

Kindergarten: *When you first begin to learn a motor skill you will not be good at it.* The major message of this concept for learners is that it is okay to be a beginner. Students need to know that beginners, no matter the age, are not good at motor skills. They should be encouraged to try new skills even though they are not good at them. This needs to be a continuous message throughout our programs.

Kindergarten: *Self-assessment of how good you are at learning a motor skill should be considered in terms of your improvement.* Using improvement as a measure of personal success in physical education will facilitate student motivation. Students are in control of their effort, and effort and practice should lead to improvement. Since not all students start at the same point, giving students a guide to measure personal success that is achievable is more likely to result in lifelong participants in physical activity.

Second Grade: *You can do a motor skill more consistently when you get good at it.* This concept identifies consistency as a criterion for getting better at motor skills. Students can be helped to understand the lack of consistency in the beginning stages and the gradual increase in consistency as they become more skilled.

Fourth Grade: *You can begin to concentrate on other parts of performance after you develop some consistency in the skill itself (e.g., dribble by yourself before you have a defender).* This concept differentiates Stage 1 from Stage 2 in learning a motor skill. It may help teachers motivate students to practice at Stage 1 if they know how Stage 1 affects game play.

Sixth Grade: *In the last stage of learning a motor skill the skill becomes automatic.* Consistency of performance, smooth flow of movement, and the ability of the performer to concentrate on very complex environments are the rewards of reaching the automatic stage of learning a motor skill. Students should be able to identify when they and others have reached this stage. They should know that they are working toward this stage.

Sixth Grade: *Good practice will help you move more quickly from one stage to another.* Good practice should be identified as what helps you to move from one stage to another. Concepts that identify good practice (the next theme) should be integrated with this concept.

Eighth Grade: *In the first stage of learning a motor skill you should seek to get a clear idea of how to do the skill. You should be able to describe what you should be doing.* This is a more advanced version of identifying Stage 1. Students should learn that they must understand how to do a skill when they are beginning to learn it. If they don't understand how to do a skill, they should get the information they need at this stage. This can be facilitated through the use of written/web/visual material.

Eighth Grade: *In the second stage of learning a motor skill you should work toward consistent performance in more complex environments.* This concept is a more advanced version of recognizing Stage 2. Learners in Stage 2 should be focused on developing consistency in their performance. Students should be able to identify the factors that make a movement response complex and should order that complexity so it is added gradually to Stage 2 learning.

Tenth Grade: *In the third stage of learning a motor skill your movement responses should be automatic. However, you will never reach 100 percent reliability.* This is a more advanced version of identifying Stage 3. Learners at this stage should be helped to move their focus away from how to perform. They should know that it is not possible to reach absolute consistency in motor skills. Even professional and Olympic performers "miss".

Twelfth Grade: *Good practice plans allow game players to spend the majority of practice working to get better at combining and adapting skills.* Students who understand the stages of learning a motor skill are ready to connect those stages with concepts related to facilitating practice. This is particularly important for skills that are performed in complex environments like games.

What Kind of Practice Facilitates Learning?

Practice is the most critical variable in learning a motor skill. The literature tells us that the quality of practice (the degree to which the movement response resembles the "appropriate" movement response) is related to learning. Practice alone does not produce learning; the practice must be of high quality. If you consistently practice something in an incorrect manner,

---

Example 5

The Immersion (Project) Approach to Teaching Motor Learning Concepts
Secondary School Example

Concepts/Principles
In the first stage of learning a motor skill you should seek to get a clear idea of how to do the skill. You also should be able to describe what you should be doing.

In the second stage of learning a motor skill you should work toward consistent performance in more complex environments.

In the third stage of learning a motor skill your movement responses should be automatic. Difficult motor skills will never reach 100 percent reliability.

Distributed practice is better than massed practice.

Most skills should be practiced as a whole so that you maintain the rhythm of the skill. If you practice parts, they should not be practiced for too long a period before they are put back in the whole.

Skills should be practiced in conditions that are game-like and performance-like as much a possible.

Open skills are performed in unpredictable and unstable environments and should be practiced in variable conditions.

Good performance of closed skills should result in practice and performance that is done in the same way each time. Some closed skills are done in different environments and require adaptation.

The teacher wants students to be able to set up their own practice schedule for a skill of their choice. The students must:

1. Identify the skill for which they will develop a practice schedule, and list the implications for practice.
2. Identify the stage of development that they are in with the skill they have chosen, describe how they have determined their stage of development, and list the implications for practice.
3. Develop a six-week practice schedule for the skill they have chosen that is consistent with the above ideas.
4. Implement the practice schedule.
5. Assess performance at the beginning and after several days without practice at the end of the project to determine the degree of improvement that has taken place.

The teacher should assess and approve the first three steps before students begin practice.

---

you most likely will learn it incorrectly. The type of skill to be learned and the skill level of the learner will determine what type of practice is appropriate.

Organizing Practice

Several different terms are used to describe how practice is organized. The terms "blocked practice" and "variable practice" refer to the degree of drill-like repetition in the practice. The terms "distributed practice" and "massed practice" refer to how practice is organized over time. In the initial stages of learning a motor skill, blocked practice (repeating the same skill in the same way) has merit. Stage 1 learners are trying to get the idea of the skill. There is value in repetition because it helps develop consistency. For example, there may be merit in practicing the movement of the tennis forehand until the process characteristics that describe good performance become part of the action.

Example 6

Webbing a Concept into the Curriculum
Elementary School Example: Second Grade

Concept/Principle: External feedback that informs the learner on how to improve performance is usually the best kind of feedback.

The teacher has decided to teach students how to give good feedback as an important concept. She also has decided it is important for students to experience the concept in a variety of settings. She has, therefore, webbed the concept of transfer to work during the next several days in ball handling skills, gymnastics, and dance. For each lesson, students will work in pairs and the focus will be on giving their partner good feedback.

The first lesson is on throwing, something the students have worked on previously. The teacher provides each student with a checklist of the cues that they have been using, and has several students demonstrate for the group while the others assess their performances. After each demonstrator has performed his or her overhand throw, the teacher asks the other students to determine what the performer needs to do to improve the performance and how they would say it to this person if this person were their partner. The teacher stresses positive feedback—information about what the performer can do to improve. The teacher then sends the students off to work with their partners. At the end of the class, students discuss their feelings about the quality of the feedback they were given by their partners.

The teacher does the same thing in subsequent lessons in gymnastics and dance. She uses skills the students have been working on so they can focus on the feedback they are receiving. After the series of lessons on giving good feedback, the teacher turns to other parts of the curriculum. The teacher uses peers to give feedback to students on a regular basis, and continuously reinforces this work.

Blocked practice:
Repetitive practice of the same skill during a period of time.

After the initial stages of learning, open skills should be practiced under variable conditions (same skill, different conditions) that gradually take on the characteristics of the conditions of the game or performance (e.g., dribbling stationary, dribbling with other players, dribbling with a passive defense, dribbling with an active defense). The intent is to encourage processing during the learning stages. Rote drill does not encourage processing, and it is not effective for movements that must be adapted to continuously changing environments. Good practice involves getting a high degree of learner engagement. Drill-like and repetitive practice discourages high levels of learner engagement. This means that, even for closed skills, extended drill under the same conditions should be avoided.

Random practice of different skills may have merit for more advanced learners. Random practice in volleyball might include the forearm pass, the serve, and the overhead pass or spike in random order; or, random small sets of those skills. Small sets of practice under a variety of conditions (resembling the way the skill will be used) should facilitate learning.

Random practice:
Changing the skill and the order of the skill that is practiced during a practice session.

Transfer of Practice

Transfer of practice is the degree to which practice in one situation will be helpful in another situation. The manner in which a skill is practiced should relate as closely as possible to the manner in which it will be used in a game or performance. Skills that are practiced in simple conditions and then used in a complex game are likely to break down because there is no transfer from the practice to the setting in which they are used.

Variable practice:
Practicing the same skill in different conditions.

A typical example of lack of transfer is the volleyball forearm pass that is practiced from a light partner toss which then must be used in a game where the ball is coming with a great deal of force. In a game, the forearm pass is executed from a serve, usually coming at great speed and height. The passer must redirect the ball to a setter and not send the ball back in the same direction. Practice from a partner toss may be a good initial step for a beginning learner, but it only begins to approach the game conditions to which the player must eventually adjust.

Whole Versus Part Practice

A critical practice decision concerns whether it is better to practice a skill as a whole or to break the skill into its component
parts. Most skills should be practiced as a whole when possible.
This is particularly true of skills that have a great deal of rhythm
or flow quality, or those that are normally performed at fast
speeds (e.g., back handspring). When it is important to practice a part (such as the toss for the tennis serve), the whole skill
should be put together as soon as possible and the parts should
be practiced in a progressive manner. Very complex skills (e.g.,
tennis serve), and dangerous skills (e.g., giant swing on the
high bar) may benefit from practice of parts in initial stages.
However, they should be practiced as a whole as soon as possible.

Amount of Practice

Generally speaking, the more a person practices the better he
or she will become at a motor skill. This is particularly true if
the practice is good. Good practice encourages students to process what they are doing, to be highly engaged in what they are
doing, and to have an accurate plan for how to execute the
skill. However, learning can occur in practice even when performance has decreased. This means that learning can occur
even though the performer may be tired. Open skills take longer
to develop than closed skills; therefore, they require more practice as well as practice under varied conditions.

Speed-Accuracy Trade-Off

There are many skills that require both speed and accuracy to
be performed effectively. The tennis serve, for example, must
be placed in the opponent's court accurately. It also is more
effective if it is done at a high rate of speed. For most skills,
however, accuracy decreases as speed increases—particularly for
beginning learners. If good performance requires both speed
and accuracy, there may be merit in slowing the skill initially.

You don't want to put learners in a situation where you are
encouraging the practice of poor form. However, it is important to provide opportunities for practicing skills at high levels
of force and an appropriate level of speed. The demand for
accuracy can then be increased gradually. If too much pressure
for high levels of accuracy is put on beginning players they will

Massed Practice: The continuous practice a skill for a long period of time.

Distributed practice: Spreading practice time across several shorter practice sessions.

not develop the skills necessary to produce high levels of speed. They also are likely to change their form.

Kinesthetic Awareness

Calling attention to the feeling of a movement and learning to attend to its different stimuli can help develop internal feedback for a movement. Kinesthetic awareness plays a significant role in closed skills (e.g., gymnastics, swimming, ballet, diving, golf). It can be a major contributor to consistent levels of performance. The performer who has developed a high level of kinesthetic awareness of a skill can learn to detect errors and will have immediate access to internal feedback.

Skills Requiring Balance

Establishing a visual focal point during a skill requiring balance can improve the skill. This is most evident in balance beam events in gymnastics, where the end of the beam serves as a visual focus. Establishing a visual focus point also is useful in skills such as spins and turns in dance or skating.

Attention and Arousal Issues

Arousal is a term that refers to the general state of excitability of a person (Magill, 2001). If a person's arousal level is too high or too low the ability to attend to what is required for the performance will be diminished (see Figure 1). Readiness to perform, alertness, and the arousal level of the performer are related to the attention a performer is paying to a movement response. (Alert performers can respond more quickly.) The degree of arousal is affected by a performer's cognitive, emotional, and physiological involvement in a movement response.

Most motor learning theorists acknowledge that performance will be affected if a performer does not have a high enough level of arousal. It also is true that too high a level of arousal can negatively affect a performance. When the psychological arousal level for a performer produces both psychological and physical discomfort, the performer is said to be experiencing anxiety. Finding the optimum level of arousal for a particular individual and helping that performer exert some control over his or her state of arousal is an important function of teaching and coaching.

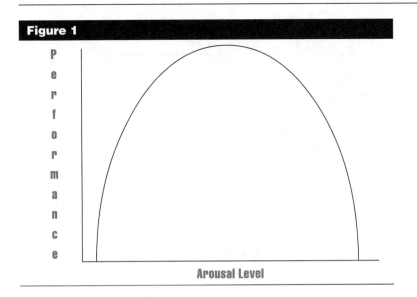

Figure 1

Performance (vertical axis)

Arousal Level

Different activities require different arousal levels. For example, a complex eye-hand coordination task (e.g., shooting a basket, walking on the high rope of a ropes course) may require more attention than a gross motor skill (e.g., jumping). The kind of motor skill that is being performed and the ability level of the performer also can affect the level of arousal. To a point, an increased arousal level can improve the performance of gross motor skills that are executed quickly.

Skills that require finer motor control or a high degree of decision making are adversely affected by high arousal. Beginners are adversely affected by anxiety in most motor performance situations. Sport psychologists have spent a great deal of time working with the idea of arousal, particularly as it relates to the elite performer.

Feedback
Information on feedback comes from both the motor learning literature and the literature on working with learners in more applied settings, such as teaching. Feedback is usually divided into knowledge of results (KR—e.g., what happened to the object/how far he or she jumped) and knowledge of performance (KP—e.g., the process characteristics of the movement). Feedback can be external (e.g., feedback from the teacher or feedback from seeing the basket go in or not go in) or internal

(e.g., kinesthetic). Learners who are denied access to knowledge of results are more apt to focus on knowledge of performance. In some cases, teachers and coaches have prevented knowledge of results (hitting into a net in golf, bowling without pins) to help students focus on knowledge of performance.

Although a strong relationship between feedback and performance has not been established in the motor learning literature, the pedagogy literature has found a weak but positive relationship between feedback and performance. Most of the time, the feedback a teacher gives is reinforcing. Prescriptive feedback (feedback that informs the learner about how to change in order to improve performance) is generally preferable to negative feedback (feedback that gives information on what not to do).

Beginning learners who have not established consistent motor skills probably cannot use specific teacher feedback to improve performance unless their errors have become consistent. Learners at more advanced stages can use more specific feedback intended to refine aspects of their performance. When feedback is used, it is best to keep it specific. For example, if a learner is asked to focus on the step into a throw, the initial feedback should focus on the step into the throw.

The importance of practice to learning a motor skill is perhaps the most important idea in motor learning. Concepts related to what kind of practice facilitates learning are described below. They are organized by grade level.

Concepts/Principles

Kindergarten: *The more practice the more learning.* Very young children first need to understand that more is better. They should be encouraged to practice more, both in and out of physical education.

Second Grade: *Feedback provides information on your performance and can enhance the quality of practice.* Students should begin to understand the impact of information on their performance—information from peers and the teacher (external), and information they get by seeing the results of their performance.

Second Grade: *External feedback that informs the learner on how to improve performance is usually the best kind of feedback.* As students begin to give feedback to their peers they should be helped to understand the importance of giving feedback that projects what the learner should do rather than what the learner has done wrong.

Fourth Grade: *Where you look during a performance has a lot to do with skillfulness. Visual focus during a skill is an important aspect of the skill.* Teachers should give, and students should be helped to seek, information on where they should be visually focused during performance. Skills requiring balance can be improved with a visual focal point. Visual focus during most skills is specific to the skill, and may change according to the conditions of that skill.

Sixth Grade: *Practice that promotes processing of how to do the skill is good practice.* This concept has to do with encouraging students to understand that "going through the motions" of practice is not as good as practicing at a high level of engagement and paying attention to what you are doing.

Sixth Grade: *Skills should be practiced in conditions that are game-like and performance-like as much as possible.* Older students can understand the importance of participating in and designing their own practice that is more gamelike. However, some game analysis skills are necessary to begin to understand the full implications of this concept.

Eighth Grade: *Most skills should be practiced as a whole so that you maintain the rhythm of the skill. If you practice parts, they should not be practiced for too long a period before they are put back into the whole.* Students can understand the issues of whole/part practice in the context of complex skills, skills that are highly rhythmic, and skills where safety is an issue.

Eighth Grade: *There is a speed-accuracy trade-off in many striking/throwing skills.* If too much stress is put on accuracy during practice, performers are likely to change their form and reduce the speed of the action (e.g., the chop serve in tennis). Students need to understand that they should not change the skill in their attempt to be accurate.

Tenth Grade: *Distributed practice is better than massed practice.* Students need to understand that they are better off practicing many times for short periods of time than they are practicing for one long period of time.

Tenth Grade: *You can increase your performance by improving the physical and motor abilities that play a major role in the skill to be learned.* This is a similar concept to a previous one in another theme. The importance in relation to practice is that students can be helped to identify the physical components of an activity, and can be helped to include in their practice the development of these physical components, as they develop practice schedules.

Twelfth Grade: *Mental practice can increase performance, particularly at higher skill levels.* Students can be taught the value of and limitations of "rehearsing" their performance without actually doing it.

Will Learning One Motor Skill Help a Person Learn Another Motor Skill?

Motor learning theorists refer to the transfer of learning from one skill to another as skill-to-skill transfer. Such transfers can be either positive or negative. The closer one skill is to another, the more likelihood there is of transfer. For example, there are some aspects of tennis that transfer positively to racquetball (ball tracking, anticipating the rebound of the ball, etc.), and some aspects that do not transfer positively (e.g., wrist action). Transfer can be facilitated by directing attention to similar skills and to what you want to transfer (e.g., ready position, force production).

There is no such thing as general motor ability; however, there is a set of perceptual motor abilities that is thought to be a factor in performance across skills such as manual dexterity, multi-limb coordination, and reaction time. These factors are thought to impose limits on the level of performance that can be achieved by an individual. However, since most physical education programs are designed to develop participants in an activity and not world-class athletes, these factors play a limited role in helping us understand differences in learning between students.

Concepts/Principles

Kindergarten: *Some skills are used in many different activities (e.g., throwing).* Students need to be introduced early to the idea that there are fundamental skills that are used across a variety of activities. This is the first step in building the idea of transfer.

Second Grade: *Striking with an implement has many similarities to striking with your hand.* Students should begin to identify the similarities among a few basic skills at beginning stages. This is facilitated if teachers draw attention to the similarities, and if they use a consistent vocabulary to describe aspects of the skills.

Fourth Grade: *Throwing a large ball has some characteristics that are similar to throwing a small ball and some that are different.* Transfer is not only dependent upon determining similarities between skills and the use of skills; it also is dependent on determining differences. Students also may begin to explore issues of why there may be differences (context issues) when similar skills are used differently.

Sixth Grade: *The more closely related one skill is to another, the more likely the transfer of learning (e.g., throwing a variety of objects).* This is the official introduction to the formal notion of and the principle of transfer. It should result in the student understanding the idea of "identical elements" and understanding why some skills are more likely to transfer and some are not. This requires the ability to identify differences between how a skill is used in practice and how it is used in a game.

Eighth Grade: *Transfer from practice to the game is subject to the same "identical elements" issues of transfer.* Students can be helped to understand the notion of transfer as a general principle with applications not only to transfer of skills but also to transfer from skills to games.

Tenth Grade: *Knowing how one skill is the same as and different from another skill (or game) will facilitate transfer from one skill to another.* Skill analysis will facilitate the application of the concept of transfer. Older students should be encouraged to and should be able to analyze skills in terms of similarities and differences.

Twelfth Grade: *Although there is no such thing as a general motor ability, there is a set of perceptual motor abilities related to performance of different motor skills. Those abilities may impose limits on individual performance and may account for why some students seem to be good at "many skills."* Advanced students can begin to identify the perceptual motor abilities that play a role in learning and performance of motor skills and begin to associate those abilities with the skills they are trying to learn.

Placing Motor Learning Concepts in the Curriculum

If motor learning concepts are to be integrated into the physical education program, decisions must be made about where those concepts should be placed. Throughout this chapter, concepts appropriate for different grade levels are identified for each theme. The grade levels were chosen to be consistent

Example 7

The Immersion (Project) Approach to Teaching Motor Learning Concepts
Elementary School Example: Fifth Grade

Concepts/Principles:

Some skills are used in many different activities (e.g., throwing).

Striking with an implement has many similarities to striking with your hand.

Throwing a large ball has some characteristics that are similar to throwing a small ball and some that are different.

The teacher has decided that these concepts are important for students in the elementary grades to learn before they deal with the important discriminations involved in open and closed skills. The teacher has chosen a project approach. Students are to take a fundamental locomotor or manipulative skill and demonstrate how that skill changes in different environments.

Students may choose from several options:

1. Cut out pictures of people using the skill and describe what characteristics the skill would have in this environment (walking with another person, walking on the beach, and walking in a crowd; or, throwing a ball to a person who is close and throwing a ball to a person who is far away).
2. Videotape him or herself or another person using the skill in different environments and describe how the skill changes in those environments.
3. Describe different environments in which he or she thinks the skill is used and what is important in that environment.

with the grade levels used in the National Standards. The concepts are designed to be consistent with National Standard 2 (Applies movement concepts and principles to the learning and development of motor skills), as this standard relates to motor learning. The motor learning concepts are placed by grade level to correspond with the benchmarks and emphases described in National Standard 1 (Demonstrates competency in many movement forms and proficiency in a few movement forms).

The twelfth grade exit goal is for students to be able to apply these concepts independently to the learning of motor skills. Students must have many examples of a concept in order to develop it to this level. If concepts are developed experientially throughout the entire program, students will be more likely to use them independently.

Integrating Motor Learning Concepts into Instruction

The first responsibility a teacher has is to determine what concepts will be included in the curriculum and at what grade levels they will be taught. The second responsibility of the teacher is to determine how the concepts will be included in the program. It also is important that the teacher model good practice and provide specific learning experiences.

One of the best ways that teachers can reinforce motor learning concepts is to explain the concepts in relation to the learning experiences provided for students. For example, a teacher might say, "I am asking you to do 10 good trials of this skill. I want you to really focus on what you are doing, because good practice requires your best effort and full attention." If teachers use these principles in their selection of tasks for students, they need only share with students the "why" to reinforce the principles throughout the program.

The last chapter of this text looks at ideas related to integrating physical education content into other academic areas. This discussion draws heavily on the types of integration identified by Fogarty (1991) and reviewed in Chapter 1. Fogarty's work also is useful for conceptualizing ways in which teachers can integrate motor learning concepts into their physical education instruction. Threading, webbing, sequencing, and immersion all are integration methods.

Threading the Concepts into Your Existing Framework

Using a threaded method of integration, the teacher determines which concept(s) should be integrated into the existing curriculum (see Examples 1 and 2). Threading does not require the teacher to add more units, and it does not require a great deal of program time. It does require a long-term perspective and careful integration of content. The more similar concepts are reinforced by threading them throughout the curriculum, the more likely it is that they will be used. Most of the concepts identified in this chapter can benefit from being threaded into a succession of units.

Teachers determine when students have learned a concept by assessing the degree to which they use it in their independent work. This means that if students are free to design their own practice, and the practice does not use the concepts identified, they have not yet learned them to the necessary level.

Webbing Content Around a Concept

Another useful way to integrate motor learning concepts into the curriculum is to use a variety of activities to teach them, or to build content around a concept like a spider web. Figure 2 illustrates a potential web for the concept that there are similarities and differences in motor skills. Knowing the similarities will help students learn new skills that have similar fundamentals.

Examples 3 and 6 provide an elementary and a secondary example of webbing. In each of these examples, the teacher has identified a concept that he or she believes is critical to learning how to learn motor skills, and has developed opportunities to use and practice that concept across the physical education curriculum. Experiencing the concept across different skills and activities (in these cases many sports) serves to reinforce the idea that the concept can be generalized. It also increases the possibility that it will be used in new experiences.

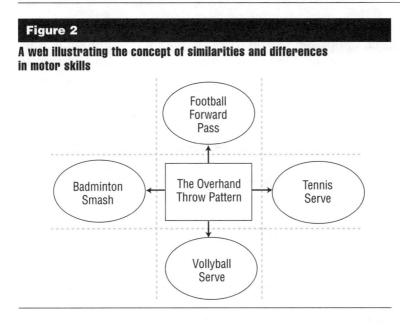

Figure 2

A web illustrating the concept of similarities and differences in motor skills

Sequencing Content To Teach a Concept

Sequencing content to teach a concept involves identifying those content areas that can best be taught in close proximity to each other to ensure transfer of the concept from one content area to another (e.g., teaching racket sports as a unit or sequence of units). Another example would be teaching several invasion games in sequential units (e.g., soccer, basketball, lacrosse) and emphasizing the related concepts.

Elementary teachers who discuss the principle of "giving" to receive an object and then teach catching, landing from heights, trapping, and collecting skills with objects are using sequencing. If they also draw their students' attention to how information about one skill can be used to learn another they are teaching the concept of transfer as well.

The Immersion (Project) Approach to Concept Development

The immersion approach (Fogarty, 1991) is more commonly known as the project approach. Teachers design a project that requires students to explore a given concept during an extended period of time. Examples 4, 5, and 7 illustrate how the immersion approach can be used at both the elementary and the secondary levels. The technique capitalizes on student interests and incorporates other skills in developing a project. The drawback of this approach is that it is quite time consuming. And, because projects are individualized, they are more difficult to assess.

Assessing Student Learning of Motor Learning Concepts

When students can use motor learning concepts in class to improve their performance—and out of class to learn new skills—the curriculum has been effective in teaching motor learning concepts. If students can answer the following questions appropriately when they leave high school, a physical education program has been effective. Students can be considered to be physically educated people.

You want to learn how to play a new sport or activity and have obtained a book on how to play the sport. For the sport or activity of your choice, identify:

A. What is good performance for this sport?
B. What stages are you likely to go through as you learn this sport?
C. What kind of practice for this sport will make you better?
D. What potential do you have for good performance in this sport?
E. What other sports or activities are likely to require the same kinds of skills as this activity and, therefore, be positively influenced by your learning this sport?

It is important for teachers to use assessment techniques and instructional process throughout the curriculum to assess the degree to which motor learning concepts have been learned. Many of these assessment techniques are described in detail in *Moving into the Future: National Standards for Physical Education* (NASPE, 1995) in Standard 2, and more generally in the reference section of this chapter.

Checking for Understanding

If the teacher wants to get some feedback on the extent to which the group as a whole understands a concept, one of the most useful methods is to ask the group and check the responses of several students.

Example: What kind of skill is this? What does that mean for the kind of practice we should be doing?

Thirty-Second Wonders
If it is important to obtain information about the understanding of individual students, a teacher can have each student write the answer to a quick question on a piece of paper. (Paper and pencils can be arranged on the side of the gym or work area.)

Example: This is the first time you have practiced this skill. What does that mean you should be trying to do?

Notebook Assessment
Many teachers have students keep notebooks in which they can record information at the end of a lesson. Teachers can use these notebooks to obtain information about student understanding of concepts or to help students reflect on their personal experience leaning a skill.

Example: What other sport activities that you enjoy are likely to be affected positively by learning what we did today?

Self-Assessment–Peer Assessment
Students can use specific criteria to assess their own performance. Peer observation requires one student to make a judgment about the performance of another. Peer observation is particularly useful for assessing the degree to which students use cues and concepts of practice to improve their performance.

Example: As your partner is playing, assess the degree to which he or she makes good choices about what to do. For now, do not worry about whether or not your partner is able to execute those choices effectively.

Student Logs and Journals
Student logs and journals are useful methods to individualize instruction and to involve students in their personal learning processes. They are usually kept for a long period of time. Student logs ask students to keep a record of performance.

Example: Ask students to record in their log on a daily basis their performance in archery. Toward the end of the unit, graph the performance and discuss learning curves with the students.

Student journals are useful for recording reflective experiences of students.

Example: Describe your performance on a daily basis and tell how you felt about your progress. The teacher can use these experiences to teach the critical role that success plays in motivation and enjoyment of the activity.

Student Projects and Group Projects
Student projects can be useful learning experiences and assessment techniques. They usually take more time to complete.

Example: Many programs encourage students to participate in activities outside of the school setting. The teacher can ask the students to choose a new skill to learn and to design a program, including practice schedules, for learning that skill.

Written Tests
The written test is a useful way to assess the degree of knowledge of a student about the subject. Written tests are an efficient method of assessing the knowledge base of students about concepts. Written tests should be designed to assess the level of knowledge that is desired. Assessing student knowledge of concepts at a declarative level (identifying a concept)—when in reality the teacher wants to know whether the student can apply the concept—only gives the teacher partial and incomplete information about student learning.

Example: Identify the three stages of learning a motor skill and describe what a learner is likely to look like at each stage.

Assessment Summary
Students should be able to use motor learning concepts in class to improve their performance and out of class to learn new skills. Students would be considered physically educated when

they leave high school if they know what constitutes good performance in a sport or activity of their choice and if they have some idea of how to approach learning from a "stages of learning" perspective for that sport or activity.

Concluding Comments

Many of the concepts described in this chapter may appear to physical educators to be common sense. That may not be the case with students and the public. Many adults continue to believe that sport ability is primarily a gift you are born with, and that they are not capable of learning a sport or activity to a level that would be enjoyable. Many adults continue to use rote practice for open skills. They give no thought to practicing skills in combinations. In short, they do not know how to approach their own learning.

Physical educators who teach motor learning concepts are providing students with learning that has the potential to affect the degree to which, as adults, those students are likely to take on the challenge of a new activity, and the degree to which they are likely to be successful in learning that activity. Never before have adults had so many opportunities to become involved in activity. Students who are prepared to learn have skills that are important for a lifetime of learning.

References

Fogarty, R. (1991). *The mindful school: How to integrate curricula*. Palentine, IL: IRI/Skylight.

Fitts, P., & Posner, M. (1967). *Human performance*. Belmont, CA: Brooks-Cole.

Magill, R. (2001). *Motor learning concepts and applications*. Champaign, IL: McGraw-Hill.

National Association for Sport and Physical Education. (1995). *Moving into the future: National physical education standards. A guide to content and assessment*. Reston, VA: Author.

Resources

Carr, N. J. (Ed.). (1987). *Basic stuff series II*. Reston, VA: AAHPERD.

Christina, R. N., & Corcus, P. M. (1988). *Coaches guide to teaching sport skill*. Champaign, IL: Human Kinetics.

Gould, D. (1992). The arousal athletic performance relationship: Current status and future directions. In T. S. Horn (Ed.), *Advances in sport psychology* (pp. 119-142). Champaign, IL: Human Kinetics.

Kneer, M. (Ed.). (1981). *Basic stuff series I*. Reston, VA: AAHPERD.

National Association for Sport and Physical Education. (1995). *Moving into the future: National physical education standards. A guide to content and assessment*. Reston, VA: Author.

Schmidt, R. (1991). *Motor learning and performance*. Champaign, IL: Human Kinetics.

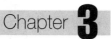

Chapter **3**

Motor Development

Kathleen Williams
Greg Payne

W *hy are some teenagers skilled while others are awkward? What is an appropriate age to start a child in organized sports? What are good activities to play with a four-year-old? Should I compare a four-year-old's motor performance to that of an older child? What are good activities for older people? The answers to all of these questions are rooted in the field of motor development. In this chapter, we will look at motor development concepts/principles that address both physical and cognitive development. These concepts/principles are an important part of the cognitive foundation for a physically educated person. An understanding of basic motor development concepts/principles can enhance the experience of acquiring or maintaining a physically active lifestyle.*

What Is Motor Development?

Motor development is the study of change in movement behavior across the life span and the processes underlying these changes. As a process, motor development includes both experience (such as practice and instruction) and an individual's current physical, cognitive, emotional, and social status. It encompasses changes across the entire lifespan. An important misconception about development is that change occurs automatically. Viewing changes in motor skills from a developmental perspective means that skills do not just appear; they do not simply mature at a certain age. There is a great deal of research showing that females, regardless of age, lag behind males in performance of skills such as throwing and kicking. We also know that males *practice* these skills more than females. Clearly, practice and experience are both important in moving the pro-

Motor development: A process that includes both experiences (such as practice and instruction) and an individual's current physical, cognitive, emotional, and social status. It leads to changes in motor behavior across the entire lifespan.

Developmental perspective:
A point of view that assumes learners are at different levels in their motor, cognitive, emotional, social, and physical development and that their developmental status will affect their ability to change.

cess of development forward. Although few people would say they think development just happens, many of us act as though that were the case.

Asking all the students in a class to perform the same skill or series of skills assumes that they are all the same. It implies that being in a particular grade or at a certain age results in having certain abilities and capabilities. Individuals differ developmentally, and developmental change does not occur automatically from maturation or biological change. Nor does it occur as errors in the way a person performs a movement. Performance differences are not performance errors. Change occurs as a result of the interplay between inherited potential, current status, and experiences that occur throughout our lives. Skill level is judged on a continuum, from least to most developmentally advanced, from least to most efficient. Where we fall on that continuum is a result of the interactive process called development.

Figure 1

Motor development involves a whole host of experiential and biological changes.

Used with permission
G.V. Payne 2002

Why Is Motor Development Important?

Strength: The ability to exert force against a resistance.

Understanding and accepting that change is developmental results in a different perspective from that often assumed by teachers and parents. Another chapter in this text outlines important concepts related to motor learning. Learning a motor skill focuses on practice and experience. But what happens when practice is not enough? A prepubertal boy may have insufficient arm strength to complete a series of push-ups. An inactive, postpubertal girl with poor eating habits may have gained excessive body fat, making it difficult to raise her trunk off the floor during curl-ups. Other youngsters may lack the motivation or cognitive sophistication to learn basic game strategies. Through the study of motor development, the physically educated person will understand that individuals develop at their own rate, and will allow themselves and those around them the time and practice opportunities they need to acquire new motor skills. They will learn that practice and physical maturation, taken together, are important.

Linking Motor Development to the National Standards

Motor development concepts are specifically targeted in Standard 2 (Applies movement concepts/principles to the learning and development of motor skills). However, motor development concepts/principles can be integrated with two other standards that relate to accepting that individuals are different:

National Standard 1: Demonstrates competency in many movement forms and proficiency in a few movement forms.
National Standard 6: Demonstrates understanding and respect for differences among people in physical activity settings.

Selected Motor Development Themes

The physically educated person needs to know about motor development in order to monitor his or her own change properly. Thus, motor development concepts/principles help the individual in becoming an independent learner of motor skills. Developmental information is organized around four themes:

- How quickly can motor performance improve?
- How does physical developmental influence motor performance?
- How does cognitive development influence motor performance?
- What happens to performance as people grow older?

Each of these themes is briefly developed in the next section. Critical student concepts that fall under each theme are developed in a K-12 format.

Developmental sequence: The series of changes that occurs from when a skill first emerges to when it reaches its most mechanically efficient state.

How Quickly Can Motor Performance Improve?

One very important characteristic of motor development is its sequential nature. The way most five-year-olds throw or kick is very different from the more advanced and mechanically efficient patterns we commonly observe in high school students or adults who play recreationally. The change from the five-year-old's performance to that of the adult occurs in many small, sequential steps over many years.

Developmental sequences describe those specific sequential steps that occur from when a skill first emerges to when it reaches its most mechanically efficient state. Descriptions for many fundamental movements skills are available in motor development textbooks (Haywood & Getchell, 2001; Payne & Isaacs, 2002). Sample developmental sequences for running and catching include:

Running (leg action) –

Step 1: The stride is short with little knee flexion.

Step 2: The stride is longer with increased knee flexion in the restraining phase and greater flexion in the swing position.

Step 3: The stride length continues to increase as the swing may reach flexion as great as 90 degrees.

Step 4: The swing leg may flex until the foot is nearly in contact with the buttocks during the recovery phase.

Catching (arm action) –

Step 1: Little active arm response; little to no adaptation to ball's flight; ball usually trapped against chest.

Step 2: Arms are extended sideways to hug the ball to chest.

Step 3: Arms are extended forward to scoop under the ball; ball is trapped against the chest.

Step 4: Arms give with the incoming toss extending to meet the flight of the ball. Ball is caught in the hand.

Regardless of when the first step emerges, the learner will progress through each step until the skill reaches its most advanced, or mechanically efficient, form. The speed at which change occurs varies dramatically from person to person, based on biological makeup and movement experiences. Because of this, some learners will never attain the most developmentally advanced pattern.

Fundamental skills are the building blocks of more complex actions such as sport–specific skills. Throwing is a fundamental skill that is incorporated into the sport-specific overhand throw used in softball and the lacrosse throw. Fundamental skills are of primary interest to physical education teachers and sport instructors and to physical therapists or physicians in rehabilitation settings. These same developmental sequences give therapists and physicians a set of expectations regarding the pattern of change patients may exhibit throughout their rehabilitation process. Physical education classes, rehabilitation settings, and family activities should be structured to challenge students to improve their motor skills developmentally, since there is ample research evidence to show that individuals who feel competent in their physical skills will remain active throughout their lives.

Fundamental movement skills: Include walk, run, hop, skip, jump, leap, slide, gallop, throw, catch, kick, and strike.

Example 1

Elementary School Example: Second Grade

Concept/Principle: Change in motor skills occurs gradually over many years.

Teachers and other skill instructors model this concept by clearly acknowledging differences among their students without assigning values regarding the "correctness" of their skills. They also have individuals monitor their own motor skill performance over time. For example, using the overarm throw, students are assessed (by the teacher or a peer using a performance rubric) at the beginning of the school year, and once a month throughout the year. After each assessment, students review their progress (both form and outcome) in a discussion with several other class or teammates. The teacher steers students away from discussions that lean toward comparing one student to another. Students advance at their own rate. The important thing is self-improvement through practice over time.

It is interesting to note that it takes much longer to reach the most advanced levels of many motor skills than generally thought (Halverson, Roberton, & Langendorfer, 1982). Early texts that described changes in motor behavior suggested that many fundamental skills were established (Sinclair, 1973) or that children were skillful (Zaichkowsky, Zaichkowsky, & Martinek, 1980) by age five or six. Much of this research was based on quantitative aspects of the skill, such as how far a ball was thrown, or how fast a certain distance was covered. Little attention was paid to the process of performing the movement or what the movement looked like. It is clear today that it is better to focus on movement form, since better results will eventually follow.

Concepts/Principles

Kindergarten: *Getting better at motor skills requires a lot of practice.* Many young children assume that motor ability is a naturally occurring phenomenon. Thus, they do not recognize the benefits of repetition or practice of a carefully constructed, thoughtfully designed, movement activity.

Second Grade: *Changes in motor skills occur gradually over many years.* Like most of us, children desire and expect to improve in their motor skill abilities quickly. Nevertheless, increased maturation may require months or even years. The evolution is often so subtle that individual performers do not recognize they have actually become more advanced performers.

Fourth Grade: *Fundamental skills are the building blocks of more complex actions such as sport–specific skills.* More advanced movement activities, such as full-fledged baseball, basketball, or soccer are composed of fundamental movement patterns. What is baseball, anyway? It is running, throwing, catching, and striking (among other things). For one to achieve success in baseball, or softball at higher levels, advanced performance of the fundamental skills that make up that activity is imperative.

Fourth Grade: *More advanced form usually leads to more successful results.* Imagine Olympians racing down the track in the 100 meters holding their arms in the high guard position (arms up for balance) that we often see among the least advanced runners. This technique would impede performance. It would affect the runner's ability to generate sufficient leg force and hamper efforts to achieve the necessary balance and forward lean required to achieve fast running velocities.

Sixth Grade: *Experience in a variety of movement settings improves motor performance.* Catching ability, for example, can be enhanced by designing a variety of different kinds of catching activities for practice. Ideas for varying the catching environment might include using a variety of different kinds of balls projected across various distances, and at different heights, trajectories, and velocities.

Eighth Grade: *People pass through developmental sequences at different speeds.* Regardless of the amount of practice we have had, and no matter how hard we work to improve, others may acquire movement skill faster and with less effort. Movement skill acquisition is not just a function of hard work and determination; it is also a matter of physiological characteristics such as speed, strength, flexibility, and one's ability to coordinate the action of several body parts simultaneously. Although activities can be devised to improve all of these characteristics, some children arrive at the activity faster, stronger, more flexible, and more coordinated.

Tenth Grade: *There is a specific sequence of changes that people pass through to become better movers.* Although we all may strive to arrive at the end point immediately, observations of children's movement have revealed that a consistent sequence of change gradually emerges. For example, immature throwers typically take no step in throwing. Although the most advanced throwing form is characterized by taking a step with the leg opposite the throwing arm, intermediate level throwers typically take a step with the leg on the same side as the throwing arm.

Twelfth Grade: *Individuals who have had more practice and experience will have better skills than individuals who have less practice and experience.* The first individual to attain step one of a skill may not be the first to attain step three. Despite individual differences in physical capabilities among individual performers, those who have participated in appropriate practice experiences typically will develop more advanced technique, and will be more successful in the movement activity. For example, consider a golf chipping drill where students are instructed to practice striking a plastic golf ball in to a hoop 30 feet away. Those students who have practiced the skill will typically demonstrate greater success in chipping the ball in or near the hoop. In addition, students will progress at different rates. Although one student may have excelled at achieving initial chipping characteristics or techniques, that student may not be one of the first to arrive at more advanced levels of the skill.

How Does Physical Development Influence Motor Performance?

In the previous section, we described the importance of developmental sequences and allowing individuals the time to develop and acquire motor skills. But what are some of the physical characteristics that change during the course of childhood and adolescence? How do the physical changes that occur as we grow influence the way we perform? It is important to examine how these factors influence both the form and the outcome of our motor performance.

Example 2

Middle School Example: Eighth Grade

Concept/Principle: Physical abilities contribute to one's potential in motor ability and level of participation.

During a volleyball unit, teams meet to decide who will set and who will spike. Students discuss similarities and difference between players and which differences might be exploited to improve play. Throughout the discussion, students consider skill, strength, height, previous experience, and the desire to play a certain position. It is important for the teacher to explain that professional sports are full of examples of athletes who are successful despite their lack of certain attributes, such as size. For example, Mugsy Bogues was a successful basketball player and Doug Flutie was a very skillful quarterback. Both were considered too small to play their positions. Ask students, "What other attributes did they consider when making selections for playing positions?"

Body Proportion

Throughout our lives, we continually undergo internal and external physical and physiological change. One of the most dramatic of these changes is the way in which our body proportions evolve (see Figure 2). At birth, we have a relatively large head, representing approximately 25 percent of our total body length. In contrast, our legs make up only about one-third of that length, and the trunk accounts for the remaining 45 percent of our length.

No wonder babies do not walk! Their large heads, long bodies, and short legs make them ill suited for upright locomotion. By the time a child begins school, the head makes up about 15 percent of the total height, while the legs comprise nearly 40

Figure 2

Changes in body proportions from two months post-conception to 25 years

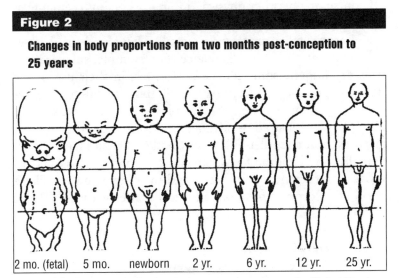

| 2 mo. (fetal) | 5 mo. | newborn | 2 yr. | 6 yr. | 12 yr. | 25 yr. |

Redrawn from H. Eckert (1987). *Motor Development*. Indianapolis, IN: Benchmark Press. Originally appeared in C. M. Jackson (1928). *Some aspects of form and growth.* In W. J. Robbins, S. Brody, A. G. Hogan, C. M. Jackson, & C. W. Green (Eds.), *Growth*. New Haven, CT: Yale University Press.

percent of that height. Although the proportions are not yet adult-like, a young child's body is much more suited to running, jumping, and throwing. Additional proportional changes continue throughout childhood and adolescence, although they are less dramatic. There is a spurt in leg length at adolescence, but most of the increase in height during late adolescence and early adulthood comes from growth in the length of the trunk.

There are few differences in the body proportions of boys and girls during childhood. This similarity before puberty supports the idea that children should not be separated by gender in physical activity during these years. There are clear differences in body proportions (and many other areas) following puberty, however. Then, young women have relatively longer trunks and shorter legs compared to young men of the same height. Of course, many other physical differences begin to emerge as well. In general, boys may develop larger hands, larger feet, or even become taller or stronger overall. These kinds of changes have implications for performance. For example, smaller hand size may impede some female performers in their use of the standard nine-inch diameter basketball–thus the shift to a smaller ball for women. Weaker, shorter performers may have more difficulty demonstrating advanced performance when shooting baskets at a regulation 10-foot basket. Studies have shown that allowing children to use smaller balls or lower baskets improves their chances of success, and may increase their likelihood of incorporating more advanced patterns earlier (Payne & Isaacs, 2002).

Skeletal Development

At birth, our skeleton consists largely of cartilage, the relatively flexible material that makes up the ears and nose. During the course of the next 20 years, the cartilage is gradually replaced with much harder, bony material. The process of laying down bony material is called ossification. It begins about two months after conception, when ossification centers appear within the shafts of long bones such as the humerus or femur.

Ossification: Beginning about two months after conception, the process of laying down bony material in the human body.

The first two years of life are a time of rapid growth. New growth centers appear at the ends of these bones, accounting for their increased length and the accompanying increase in stature. Although some children experience a mid-growth spurt during the elementary school years, growth typically begins to slow at that time compared to the first two years of life.

Toward the end of childhood or the beginning of adolescence, children will generally experience a 2.5 to three-year growth spurt that can account for as much as 20 percent of their eventual adult stature. Although considerable individual variation exists, this phenomenon most often occurs in girls at approximately 10.5 years of age, and in boys two years later. Most of the height growth gained during this period of time is a result of a lengthening of the trunk, not the legs. During early adolescence, many young teenagers experience a period known as "adolescent awkwardness." This period usually parallels the growth spurt and is characterized by a temporary disruption in motor performance. This may include balance ability or even a brief regression in performance on certain motor skills. Although this period is not universal, it appears in many adolescents, and it appears more commonly in boys. Motor assessments administered during this period should be considered carefully, as they may be influenced by adolescent awkwardness (Payne & Isaacs, 2002).

Typically, females also are ahead of males throughout adolescence in terms of skeletal age. For example, the growth plates in an adolescent female's humerus fuse at around 15.5 years; for males, growth does not cease until around 18 years (Haywood & Getchell, 2001). Once the growth plates fuse, the bone no longer increases in length. The longer period during which males grow contributes to their generally taller stature than females. This longer period of growth also has the potential to place males at greater risk for injury. Fortunately, breaks of the bone shaft generally heal rapidly. However, an injury to the area of the growth plate can be serious and can result in malformation or premature cessation of growth. These types of injuries are rare, but they can occur in contact sports such as football or with overuse such as what occurs in pitching baseballs. So, although the number of injuries to growing children and youth in sports situations is typically fewer than that for more advanced performers, the same injury in a child or youth can be more severe (Payne & Isaacs, 2002).

With the increased involvement of young women in high level competitive sport, scientists have begun to focus on the impact of training programs on the developing female body. In particular, investigators have identified a syndrome called the Female Athlete Triad, which involves disordered eating, amenorrhea, and osteoporosis (Khan et al., 2002). These characteristics appear to be especially prevalent among participants in sports emphasizing a specific body image, such as gymnastics and dance. However, they may occur whenever intense training is undertaken. These performers significantly restrict their caloric intake, even during strenuous exercise. Insufficient calcium intake during this period of typically rapid growth can result in compromised bone mineral density. It is unclear whether these athletes actually have osteoporosis, or are simply placing themselves at risk for an earlier onset of this disease. These athletes do have a higher incidence of stress fractures compared to other populations (Nattiv, 2000). Scientists suggest maximizing calcium nutrition and balancing caloric intake and energy expenditure during this period of rapid growth. Maximizing bone density early on can protect against later changes for all adolescents.

Increases in height cease for most individuals sometime between age 20 and 25. Later, particularly after age 40, many adults actually become shorter. These changes begin slowly and then accelerate to approximately one inch per decade, beginning around age 60. These changes evolve for a variety of reasons, including compression of spinal discs due to the increased incidence of diseases like osteoporosis that decrease calcification in the vertebral column. The rate of bone reabsorption is roughly equal to its replacement until women reach their 30s and men reach their 50s (Gabbard, 2000). Then, the rate of reabsorption exceeds the rate of bone replacement. Women tend to lose bone faster than men do. This loss is associated with declines in estrogen levels as women approach and pass through menopause. The loss of bone can be extensive and serious. Women tend to lose .75 to one percent of their bone mass per year after age 30. The rate of loss increases to two to three percent per year by menopause. By age 70, many women have lost 25 to 30 percent of their bone mass, while men have lost only 12 to 15 percent of their bone mass. Excessive bone loss is called osteoporosis, and it leads to increased risk of fractures. On average, women are at a four times greater risk of fractures after menopause than are men of the same age (Gabbard, 2000).

Treatment of osteoporosis traditionally has included hormone replacement therapy (HRT) for post-menopausal women, along with calcium supplements and weight bearing exercise. The latest information about the potential dangers of HRT must be discussed with one's physician. There is *no controversy*, however, about the benefits of weight bearing activities. Weight bearing exercise, such as walking or jogging, seems to stimulate the processes that help to maintain and even add to bone density. For older women, some sort of weight bearing activity is important for strengthening the head of the femur and the vertebrae of the spinal column. It is the head of the femur that often breaks, resulting in the need for hip replacement. Many older women also suffer small compression breaks of the vertebrae, which contribute to increased forward curvature of the thoracic spine (called kyphosis). Kyphosis can make twisting or turning movements more difficult. It also compresses the chest and lungs, making breathing more difficult.

Kyphosis: Increased forward curvature of the thoracic spine.

Muscular Development, Strength, and Flexibility

Most of the growth that occurs in muscle fibers is due to hypertrophy, an increase in the size of the muscle cells. Hypertrophy of muscle cells can occur as result of normal growth, but it also can be a function of physical training designed to enhance muscle size (Haywood & Getchell, 2001). As muscle fibers grow, they increase in length and diameter. During childhood, there are small gender differences in the characteristics of muscle that slightly favor boys. Differences are greater following adolescence, when muscle mass approaches 54 percent of a man's body weight, but only about 45 percent of a woman's body weight. Interestingly, gender differences are most marked in the upper body. They are much smaller in the legs. This can have obvious implications for the type of movement activities that attract males versus females. Males may feel perfectly comfortable in activities such as rope climbing, where upper body strength is at a premium, while females may feel more comfortable when they can rely on the strength of their lower body and legs.

Hypertrophy: An increase in size.

Strength is the ability to exert force against a resistance. The more something weighs, for example, the greater the force that must be applied in order to move it. Increased muscle mass often is associated positively with increased strength. While the size of the muscle is important, it is only one factor in determining the strength of an individual. Another aspect of strength is the ability to recruit motor units. A motor unit is the number of muscle fibers attached to a single motor neuron. Some motor units consist of a neuron and many fibers, as in the back. Where fine control of movement is necessary, motor units consist of a neuron and just a few fibers, as in the eyes or fingers. A person who is able to recruit more of the available motor units will be able to exert greater force than someone who recruits only a few. When assessing strength and changes in strength it is important to consider whether the changes are related to increased muscle mass, increased efficiency in recruitment, or both.

Considering the effects of strength in the performance of a movement activity also is important. For example, children may elicit immature movement characteristics as a result of having too little strength. Imagine a child or adolescent engaged in a striking activity with an implement (e.g., a bat) that is too heavy or too long. That individual may regress to an immature pattern when he or she is actually capable of demonstrating a more advanced level. However, if the time is taken to determine the most appropriate implement size for the child, optimal performance—both in terms of outcome and movement pattern—can occur.

Strength training programs for children and adolescents are increasingly popular. These groups can gain strength, primarily by learning to recruit muscle fibers more efficiently (Faigenbaum et al., 2001; Falk et al., 2002). Increased muscle mass is typically not observed until pubertal changes in sex hormones (androgens) occur. In a recent position paper, the Committee on Sports Medicine and Fitness of the American Academy of Pediatrics (2001) suggested that strength training for children and adolescents can be beneficial to performance of other strength-related activities, such as weight lifting and power lifting. However, strength training has little carryover value to other sport performance, such as football or basketball, and it does not seem to prevent injuries in children and adolescents. In addition, obese children seem to benefit less than children of normal weight from a progressive resistance program. Their results suggest that obese children might require different weight training guidelines than do other children (Falk et al., 2002). At the other end of the spectrum, muscular strength is important for older adults who need additional strength and balance for daily living (e.g., getting into and out of chairs or bed, walking short distances or up stairs), eliminating the need for a walking cane, and so on. Older adults can increase and maintain strength through a combination of increased muscle mass and more efficient recruitment (Fiatarone et al., 1990).

Flexibility is defined as the range of motion for a joint. Flexibility is very specific. Being flexible in one part of the body does not necessarily mean a person is flexible in other parts of the body. Despite this joint specific flexibility, the most widely used test is the backsaver sit-and-reach test of hamstring and lower back range of motion. This test is used because so many Americans suffer from chronic low back pain. In general, there are age-related improvements in flexibility, favoring females, across the childhood years. In a number of studies (reported in Payne & Isaacs, 2002), the improvements have been demonstrated to continue through late adolescence (between 15 and 18 years). Other studies, however, report declines beginning as early as age 10. The general consensus is that gradual decline continues throughout adulthood, and that osteoporosis may result in even less flexibility of the trunk, making twisting or turning movements more difficult. However, the decline does not have to be this rapid or start this early. Programs designed to increase and maintain flexibility are effective in offsetting the declines that are so common with increasing age. Yoga and other flexibility-related programs are becoming more popular activities for children and adults of all ages.

Cardiorespiratory Development

At birth, the left ventricle of the heart is smaller than the right ventricle. It grows very rapidly, however, and quickly attains adult proportions. Through the remainder of childhood the entire heart grows gradually until the adolescent growth spurt. There also are changes in heart rate and the oxygen carrying capacity of the blood. At birth, the average heart rate is approximately 140 beats per minute (bpm). This rate drops dramatically to around 100 bpm by year one, and it continues to decline throughout childhood. Slight gender differences appear at around age 10, when girls' heart rates remain three to five bpm higher than those of boys. By late adolescence, resting heart rates average 76 bpm for girls and 72 bpm for boys.

Oxygen carrying capacity of the blood is related to the number of red blood cells and the amount of hemoglobin those cells contain. Forty to 45 percent of an adult males' blood volume is composed of red blood cells; the figure is 38 to 42 percent for women. At birth, the blood is about half red blood cells, but this percentage declines rapidly after only a couple of months. Then, the percentage of red blood cells increases through adolescence for boys and through childhood for girls. The result of this gender difference is that boys have more red blood cells than girls and, therefore, greater oxygen carrying capacity. These differences have been attributed to differences in body mass and muscle mass (Malina & Bouchard, 1991).

Many investigations have demonstrated a nearly linear improvement in maximal oxygen uptake across childhood and adolescence. In fact, if changes in body weight (especially fat-free weight) are considered, there is virtually no change in maximal oxygen uptake during this period. This fact makes it difficult to determine if exercise programs that focus on cardiorespiratory fitness improve oxygen uptake. Thus, high intensity cardiorespiratory programs may not be appropriate for prepubescents. During childhood, a stronger focus should be placed on the teaching of motor skills, and on motivating children to seek regular participation in physical activity. In addition, the recommended method for calculating target heart rate zones was developed for adult populations. Evidence suggests lowering the predicted maximal heart rate for youth to a range of 195 to 200 bpm. (Buck, 2002; Rowland, 1992). Once children become pubescent, more rigorous forms of cardiorespiratory training may be appropriate (Payne & Morrow, 1993).

Body Composition
According to recent information reported in *Healthy People 2010* (U.S. Department of Health and Human Services

[USDHHS], 2000), only 65 percent of adolescents engage in the recommended amounts of physical activity (see Figure 3). The percentage decreases to 15 percent among adults, and 40 percent of adults engage in no leisure time physical activity at all! These numbers are important for a variety of reasons:

- Regular physical activity is highly associated with decreased risk of dying, even when one engages in moderate levels of activity.
- Regular physical activity is associated with increases in psychological well being, muscle and bone strength, and quantity of lean muscle.
- Regular physical activity is associated with reduced amounts of body fat.

Sedentary lifestyles often result in individuals who are overweight. This component of physical fitness is known as body composition. It is comprised of the relative proportions of fatty tissue and lean body mass (primarily muscle and bone). The relative proportion of lean body mass is important because of the positive relationship between it and high levels of physical fitness. Because of the problem with obesity, however, we often hear more about the relative proportion of fatty tissue in body composition. Although childhood physical inactivity and obesity are frequent topics for discussion, the older we are, the

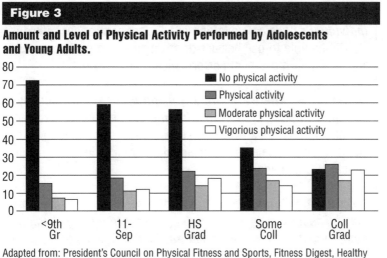

Figure 3

Amount and Level of Physical Activity Performed by Adolescents and Young Adults.

Legend:
- No physical activity
- Physical activity
- Moderate physical activity
- Vigorous physical activity

Categories: <9th Gr, 11-Sep, HS Grad, Some Coll, Coll Grad

Adapted from: President's Council on Physical Fitness and Sports, Fitness Digest, Healthy People 2010: Physical Activity and Fitness, 2001.

less physically active we become (USDHHS, 1996). This has clear implications for creeping obesity, the gradual increase of fat from year to year. Being overweight and obese increases the risk for diseases and conditions like Type 2 diabetes, high blood pressure, high cholesterol, heart disease and cerebrovascular disease, arthritis, some cancers, and decreased self-esteem (USDHHS, 2002). Although we may be relatively lean in childhood or early adulthood, it is common for adults to gradually gain weight to the point of becoming obese by later adulthood. However, for children and adults alike, maintaining a physically active lifestyle, in conjunction with appropriate nutritional decisions, can facilitate the maintenance of a healthy percentage of body fat.

Concepts/Principles

Kindergarten: *People may differ physically, even though they are the same age.* Children who are smaller or larger than their same aged peers typically need not be concerned about these differences—they (or their peers) will eventually catch up!

Second Grade: *Bigger, stronger people tend to perform physical skills better.* In these cases, an individual's size or strength may make up for developmental differences in form. The outcome of their performance may be similar to, or better than, more developmentally advanced peers.

Fourth Grade: *Equipment should be selected based on an individual's physical development.* Bigger or stronger individuals will be able to use heavier or stronger equipment to further enhance their movement performance.

Fourth Grade: *There are virtually no differences between boys and girls in body proportions throughout childhood.* Because average differences are so small between boys and girls, greater attention should be paid to individual differences in the selection of activities and equipment.

Sixth Grade: *During the adolescent growth spurt, more time may be necessary to adjust motor patterns to rapidly changing body dimensions and physical attributes.* Studies of children and older adults suggest that it is a combination of increased mass and the ability to recruit those fibers that results in increases in strength. Because peak weight velocity (a rough indicator of muscle mass increase) occurs six months to two years before peak strength gain, children need time to learn to coordinate the recruitment of muscle fibers beyond the period of maximum growth. This means there might be lag time between the adolescent growth spurt and improved performance of actions that require strength. People often talk about the awkwardness of adolescence. Perhaps the process of learning to effectively recruit muscles contributes to this condition.

Sixth Grade: *Some children begin puberty earlier than others, resulting in dramatic physical differences between same-aged individuals.* Any middle school class clearly illustrates this point. Some children will have completed their mid-growth spurt and have nearly attained their adult height, while others have barely begun. Some boys will already demonstrate the physical changes associated with puberty—including muscular growth—while others will remain small.

Eighth Grade: *Physical abilities contribute to one's potential in motor ability and level of participation.* People may be better suited for some activities or positions in an activity based on previous experience, size, agility, speed, coordination, balance, reaction time, and power.

Tenth Grade: *Females who participate in vigorous, regular physical activity can lessen the effects of age-related diseases.* The example of the Female Athlete Triad given earlier is an extreme example of an imbalance between important nutrients and changes in bone. Adolescent and young adult females who participate in vigorous physical activity can build strong bones to resist the later onset of osteoporosis.

Twelfth Grade: *Training (recommended after pubertal growth spurt) can help emphasize physical attributes.* After puberty, strength and cardiovascular training result in clear improvements in those characteristics. Individuals who learn to exploit their greater strength or cardiovascular fitness will demonstrate a clear advantage when compared with developmentally younger peers.

Example 3

Middle School Example: Grade 8

Concept/Principle: Practice with increasingly complex interactions among teammates and opponents can help individuals become better players.

Individual and small groups of players have been practicing the skills necessary for playing field games such as soccer. Players practice passing and reception skills in small groups, such as two vs. two or three vs. three. As larger groups are formed, teacher and students stop periodically to discuss the added complexity of four vs. four or even six vs. six. The teacher elicits verbal answers and motor demonstrations from students regarding passing to lead a teammate or how a defender begins to anticipate ball and player movement. As necessary, groups are broken down into the original smaller units for practice before recombining them. At the end of class, the teacher asks students about the benefits of practicing in increasingly complex situations. The teacher follows up with questions regarding the age at which someone should start practicing in increasingly complex game situations.

How Does Cognitive Development Influence Motor Performance?

Many changes occur in the ability to deal with cognitive information throughout the lifespan. Children learn to pay attention to relevant cues while ignoring things that are irrelevant. They process information more quickly so they can respond faster. They can interpret increasingly complex situations. How do these changes impact their motor development? To this point, most of the research has focused on the child's and the adolescents' abilities to incorporate increasingly complex strategies into their games and play.

Experienced players "see" more complex offensive and defensive situations, they can generate more possible solutions, and the skills that they attempt are more advanced than novice players. Experienced or expert players also spend more time practicing their activity. When the amount of experience is controlled, age-related differences in knowledge are often minimized or disappear altogether. While it is impossible to determine the precise contribution of experience versus maturational characteristics that accompany age, results of expert-novice investigations suggest that experience can overcome some limitations.

Certainly, experience involves more than the simple accumulation of time. Specific cues can assist children in picking out important aspects of a skill; with practice, their performances became more similar to the form observed in the model. However, focusing on too many cues at once can be overwhelming for children. Clearly, teachers and parents must pay careful attention to what performers are practicing and how they are interpreting our instructions!

Sequential Stages in Cognitive Development

The strong emphasis that has been placed on cognitive development throughout the years may be a result of work by Jean Piaget. Piaget (1952), originally a biologist, developed his clinical method of collecting data by observing his own children. He used a question and answer system to gain insight into how children think. Gradually, he composed the most carefully detailed and most widely known explanation of any aspect of human development (Payne & Isaacs, 2002).

Piaget observed four sequential stages in cognitive development:

1. Sensorimotor–birth to two years.
2. Preoperational–two to eight years.
3. Concrete Operational–eight to 11 years.
4. Formal Operational–11 to 12 years.

The ages Piaget set for each stage are intended to be guidelines. Nevertheless, most children are thought to follow the stages in order.

Sensorimotor Stage

Note that the word motor is imbedded in the name of this stage, indicating the importance that Piaget placed on human movement in intellectual development. In this stage, Piaget proclaimed that the infant "thinks by bodily movement." For example, initial efforts to reach out, grasp, and hold a toy provide opportunities for problem solving that facilitate cognition. Of particular importance in this stage is the child's interaction with the environment: It is instrumental in shaping cognitive function. Movements such as reaching, grasping, creeping, crawling, and eventually walking play a major role in the child's ability to experience, interact with, and learn about his or her environment.

Piaget also acknowledged the importance of reflexes during the first few months of life. While these movements are involuntary, infants initially learn to stimulate their own reflexes, creating a series of gratifying, repetitive movements. For example, the sucking reflex is generally observed during the first several weeks following birth. Babies may accidentally stimulate their own reflex and enjoy the feeling. After a few accidental touches, they learn to voluntarily stimulate their own sucking reflex. While the reflex remains involuntary, a new behavior has emerged.

As they progress through infancy, more and more voluntary movement evolves. Infants gradually learn to modify their movements through experimentation. Once a new behavior is created, the infant repeats it again and again, something Piaget referred to as a circular reaction. They also discover their hands and arms, and experiment with eye-hand coordination and early reaching and grasping. As the first year passes, infants gradually become more aware of their environment and expand their exploration. They also begin to combine movements to create completely new behaviors. Toward the latter part of the first year, they begin to apply past modes of behavior to new situations. This ability is enhanced by a rapidly expanding movement repertoire, including more efficient locomotion in the form of creeping, crawling, and then walking. The cognitive ability of anticipation also emerges. The infant begins to understand that when someone rolls a ball, he or she can roll it back.

During the first half of the second year, the young child actively explores and experiments. Locomotion plays an important role in helping the child explore the environment and learn from that exploration. Despite these new intellectual capabilities, the child still possesses limited ability to ponder future or upcoming events. Interacting with others becomes increasingly important as the child seeks help in problem solving. Piaget thought this indicated a child's increased understanding that people and things are separate from self. This awareness shows a clear relationship between cognitive and social development. Motor development is integral to this process, because movement is necessary to actively seek social interactions.

At this time, children also spend more time thinking about their own movement, a climax of Piaget's first stage of development. Throughout this first stage, the child's interaction with the environment has been facilitated by improving abilities in locomotion and manipulation. Concepts such as trajectory, velocity, direction, texture, and weight become increasingly clear intellectually as a result of the child's manipulation of objects. In short, this first stage is characterized by "thinking with the body." It is gradually replaced by "thinking with the mind." As a result, children can ponder the past via better recall capabilities and consider the future via better anticipation skills.

Preoperational Stage

Piaget's second major stage of cognitive development lasts from age two to eight, and is characterized by improved use of symbols, leading to improved language skill. Language skill is the most important characteristic of this stage of development. The rapid development of language skills may be related to similarly improving movement abilities. By this time, the child has well-developed locomotor skills. The increasing ability to move about results in increased opportunities to interact with the environment. Greater mobility plays a role in the emergence of many new cognitive skills.

Pretend play was another area of emphasis for Piaget. Children role play and use props as symbols for real life objects. They reconstruct past events or events they would like to see happen. This form of play contributes to social as well as cognitive development, and uses movement as a medium. Thus, once again, motor development is an important contributor to intellectual development.

The term "preoperations" was selected because most children are capable of limited logical thought at this time. Piaget believed the preoperational child's thinking was flawed in a number of other ways. For example, at this stage, children tend to think of inanimate objects as animate (e.g., trees may come to life or express emotions). They also tend to attribute cause and effect simply because two events happen simultaneously. Perhaps the most serious flaw in preoperational thinking is the child's narrow perspective. This narrow perspective and the child's inability to decenter thinking from one aspect of a problem to another hampers the ability to solve problems. These limitations also lead to an inability to conserve, a term Piaget attributed to knowing that specific properties of an object or a substance remain unchanged even when the appearance has been rearranged. A classic example of conservation is Piaget's ball of clay test. When a clay ball is rolled into a sausage shape, most preoperational children will say the clay weighs more, even though they saw that no clay was added. This is a result of the inability to focus on more than one aspect of a problem simultaneously, or to decenter attention.

The inability to decenter attention has obvious implications for motor development. Imagine the detailed problem solving or strategic abilities we expect of children at this age in youth sports. Many children have difficulty understanding that passing the ball to a teammate is a good way to score a goal. They focus primarily on how much fun it is to run and kick as they move down the field. Unfortunately, rather than understanding their intellectual limitations, we become frustrated because we expect too much too soon.

Concrete Operational Stage
The concrete operation stage lasts from about 8 to 11 years of age. Piaget thought this stage emerged with the improved ability to conserve and decenter attention. While the declining degree of egocentrism is important, there are still cognitive limitations. Children are unable to consider events that are unreal, unimaginable, or hypothetical.

Nevertheless, intellectual ability improves as children begin to demonstrate concepts such as reversibility or seriation. Reversibility is the ability to reverse a thought process. This is demonstrated by another of Piaget's classic tests: If a concrete operational child rolls three balls of different colors through a tube, he or she can predict the sequence of exit at the other end. If the child is then asked to roll the balls back through the tube without changing the order, the concrete operational child also can successfully predict the outcome. Preoperational children cannot do this.

Seriation is another skill that illustrates the improving cognitive ability found at this stage. Seriation is the ability to place objects or even concepts in a series based on such characteristics as length or size. It is the ability to understand the relationships between objects in a series. If a child is shown three colored balls of increasing size, he or she can explain that the red ball is bigger than the blue, and the blue is bigger than the green. From that information, the child also would know that the red ball is bigger than the green one. Seriation is another cognitive skill that appears to be influenced by a child's interaction with the environment, again reinforcing the importance of movement.

Formal Operational Stage

Piaget's final stage of cognitive development—formal operations—has its onset in early to mid-adolescence. Piaget noted that not all people achieve this level of cognitive ability, however. He believed formal operations to be domain or area specific. That is, you can exhibit formal operational qualities in one area and concrete operational thought in others. For example, a basketball player might be able to think abstractly about offensive or defensive floor positions, but may find singles tennis strategies problematic.

For those who reach the formal operations level, hypothetical thought emerges. They can consider propositions that are not based in reality. Furthermore, formal operators can understand and consider several aspects of a problem simultaneously. This has obvious implications for motor performance. Imagine the numerous decisions a quarterback makes when he prepares to receive a snap in football. To perform optimally, he must remember the snap count while carefully considering the defensive alignment in relationship to the play that he called. At the same time, he must check his team to ensure that they are all lined up properly, while remembering his responsibility when the ball is snapped. Clearly, anything less than formal operational thought would severely hamper the quarterback's ability to function.

Formal operators also are capable of what Piaget called hypothetical-deductive reasoning. This is a process of systematically thinking about a problem and its potential solutions. It is rational, logical, and abstract thinking that enables one to ponder hypothetical ideas. As Piaget noted, this form of thinking can have a dramatic emotional effect on young adolescents. They may become more idealistic as they think about perfect energy sources or world peace. Changing ideals can affect social interrelationships, decisions about peer group involvement, and, indirectly, choices concerning participation in movement activities. At this developmental level, an adolescent can begin to think about the positive consequences of lifelong physical activity and fitness.

Information Processing

Piagetian developmental stages are only one way that cognitive development can be viewed. Other researchers have looked at cognitive development from a different perspective, called information processing (Payne & Isaacs, 2002) They study what and how things are remembered across the lifespan. In one system, memory is divided into short- and long-term structures. Short-term memory is the ability to recall recently learned information (within the past few seconds or minutes). Long-term memory is the ability to recall information that was learned days or even years ago. Both forms of memory improve throughout childhood and adolescence, as children become more adept at employing strategies such as rehearsal and grouping. They can arrange, rearrange, and tag information for easy retrieval.

As we age, short- and long-term memory remains remarkably intact. This dispels the myth that general memory declines as senility develops during later adulthood (Payne & Isaacs, 2002). Another form of memory—secondary memory—shows some decline with increasing age. Secondary memory is similar to short-term memory, but differs in that a form of interference or distraction exists. For example, if you are introduced to a new person, then immediately diverted into a conversation, how well can you recall the person's name after a few seconds?

Information Retrieval Speed

A final examination of cognitive development looks at information retrieval speed. Children and older adults have been found to require more time to process information. Thus, certain types of problem solving may be more difficult, or may take longer for these groups than for younger adults. The reason for this phenomenon is still unclear, and probably differs for the two age groups. Young children may become more efficient in their search for information, while older adults may experience decline due to degeneration of the central nervous system. Declines in retrieval speed also may be related to increased amounts knowledge. The more knowledge one has to sort through, the longer it takes to find the desired information (Payne & Isaacs, 2002). Regardless of the cause, a slowing in mental processing can affect our ability to perform movement activities that require quick information retrieval and decision making. Thus, as intellectual ability declines, so may some forms of movement performance.

The relationship between movement and intellectual development also is illustrated in extensive research on reaction time and aging. While reaction time often is viewed as an indicator of movement ability, psychologists study it because of the role it plays as a marker for central nervous system integrity. Knowledge about reaction time and age can yield valuable information concerning our mental processing speed. Investigators have found that reaction times improve during the childhood years. We react fastest in our 20s, and then, beginning around age 40, a gradual decline begins.

Responding to a situation often involves making a decision about how to respond. The greater the number of potential responses, the longer people of all ages require to decide. More interesting, perhaps, is the research that has focused on the effect of consistent involvement in physical activity on the reaction time decline observed with aging. Researchers grouped older and younger participants by their level of physical activity. While younger adults still performed better on measures of reaction time, physical activity level appeared to be integral in reducing the amount of decline (Spirduso, 1995). These findings are supported by more current investigations that placed older adults in physical activity programs. Researchers found that increased activity levels prevented the slowing of reaction time. These results demonstrate the relationship between cognitive development and movement activity.

Concepts /Principles

Kindergarten: *People may differ cognitively even though they are the same age.* Cognitive development is governed by the same principles discussed for other areas of development. Just as children and adolescents will differ in their level of physical development, some will be more or less sophisticated in terms of cognitive development.

Second Grade: *People may understand instructions for performing motor skills differently.* Young children can focus on only one or two concepts at a time. Therefore, instructions for performing motor skills or practicing game strategies must be simple and concrete.

Fourth Grade: *Cognitive abilities influence complex skill performance.* Children and adolescents who have studied a sport or skill and have extensive practice can demonstrate the same level of performance as some adults.

Sixth Grade: *Preadolescents may need concrete instruction regarding how to perform specific skills or playing strategies.* Many children and adolescents will need to see a demonstration of a movement skill or game strategy. A verbal explanation or even a simple illustration will not be enough.

Eighth Grade: *Practice with increasingly complex interactions among teammates and opponents can help individuals become better players.* As individuals perform motor skills at more developmentally advanced levels, they are better able to incorporate them into increasingly complex situations. It is important that teachers, parents, and coaches increase task complexity gradually, however.

Tenth Grade: *As adolescents mature, they become capable of more advanced cognitive and motor skills.* As adolescents and young adults reach the formal operations level they can understand abstract and increasingly complex game situations and strategies. They can see relationships among several players at once as they play either offense or defense.

Twelfth Grade: *Increased activity levels reduce the slowing of reaction time in the elderly.* Cognitive activity plays a role in physical performance. Conversely, an increase in physical activity level can reduce reaction time in the elderly.

What Happens to Performance as People Grow Older?

We have looked at several biological aspects of aging in the other themes. From the examples, one might get the impression that we decline as we grow older, and there is little we can do about it. However, there are many things we can do to forestall or delay the effects of aging. There are even lifestyle changes that elementary and high school students can use to delay the effects of aging! Of course, most of them involve becoming and remaining physically active.

People are living longer than ever before (see Figure 4). At the turn of the 20th century, the average life expectancy was around 47 years, with females outliving males by approximately two years. By 1990, our life expectancy had increased to between 70 and 80 years. Now, the average man is expected to live to about 72 years, and the average woman to 79 years (National Center for Health Statistics, 2000). Life expectancy is expected to increase to 77 and 84 years, respectively, by 2050. Approximately 13 percent of the American population are older than 65 years of age. This older segment of the population will continue to grow rapidly as post-World War II baby boomers pass 50 and look toward retirement. By 2050, more than 20 percent of our population will be older than 65 years of age.

Example 4

High School Example: Grade 12

Concept/Principle: Accumulating at least 30 minutes of activity most days of the week can improve self-esteem; decrease stress, anxiety, and depression; and improve health.

As a class project, students interview older individuals regarding their life-long physical activity habits and their current health issues. During one class session, this information is compiled in order to determine if, in fact, regular physical activity can reduce the effects of age-related diseases.

Some older adults continue to participate in sport and fitness activities, and many perform extremely well. There are many examples of the physically elite elderly, such as the 87-year-old who completed the 2002 Boston Marathon in 5.5 hours. These individuals are the exception rather than the rule, however. For most older adults, maintaining an active lifestyle that enables them to live independently and participate in their community is a primary goal. Therefore, much of the research related to activity and aging has focused on helping older adults improve and maintain their quality of life. And, much of this research has focused on ways to control health care costs.

Balance has been studied extensively in older adults, because falling is an important health care concern. Even relatively healthy older adults often observe a decline in their balance abilities. Clinical balance tests, such as the functional reach (see Figure 5) and timed up and go (TUG), are used to document these declines. In the functional reach, participants stand with arms extended forward, and then lean as far as they can without taking a step. In the TUG, performers stand up from a chair, walk 8 to 10 feet, turn and return to their chair as quickly as possible. Tests can be administered easily and inexpensively by physicians or physical therapists. They provide information about balance ability that is roughly comparable to that pro-

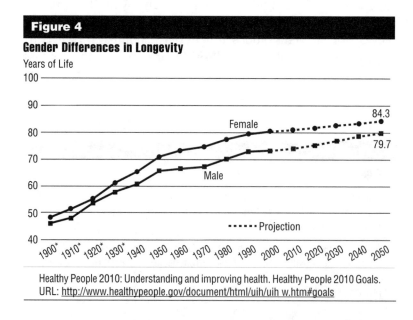

Figure 4

Gender Differences in Longevity

Healthy People 2010: Understanding and improving health. Healthy People 2010 Goals.
URL: http://www.healthypeople.gov/document/html/uih/uih w.htm#goals

Figure 5

Functional
Reach
testing

Used with permission
K. Williams 2002

vided by more technologically sophisticated techniques. Further, Rikli and Jones (2001) recently published age-graded norms for nine different clinical performance tests against which older adults, 60 to 95 years, may be compared. These instruments enable physicians, therapists, and other physical activity professionals to monitor critical changes among older adults. They also can assist older adults in setting baselines for the establishment of physical activity programs for themselves. This way, they can monitor levels of improvement during various periods of time. Older adults who are more physically active are more likely to maintain their ability to complete very important activities of daily living (ADLs)—e.g., sitting, standing, driving, reaching—and generally maintain an overall better quality of living.

Falls are a common outcome of compromised balance in older adults. Fall-related injuries and illnesses are the leading cause of death in persons older than 65 (Sattin, 1992). An estimated 300,000 hip fractures occur each year, most resulting from falls. Half of the 500,000 vertebral fractures every year occur as a result of falling. Approximately one-half of the individuals who suffer hip fractures do not regain their ability to walk independently. Falls are the leading cause of nursing home admission. As a result, falls and fall-related injuries result in billions of dollars of health care costs per year. Currently, there are many research groups studying intervention techniques aimed at preventing falls. Some techniques include a component of balance training. Participants may stand on one foot, with and without support, or perform heel-to-toe walking. Other training programs require individuals to walk on foam or uneven surfaces to simulate differences in terrain encountered in daily activities. Other investigators have examined the relationship between declines in strength and balance. In particular, weak ankle muscles have been found to contribute to increased risk of falling. Improvements in strength, such as those discussed previously, can lower this risk. Many intervention studies include some form of weight training as part of a fall prevention program. How improved strength affects balance is unclear. The research is consistent, however, in reporting a lowered risk of falling when strength training is provided.

Task complexity, especially when it involves a cognitive challenge, appears to influence the balance of older adults. One study observed older adults attempting to walk while carrying on a conversation (Lundin-Olsson et al., 1997). The researchers found that individuals with a history of falls tended to stop in order to talk. They could not complete these two tasks simultaneously! Current investigations have confirmed these observations and demonstrated that greater changes occur in movement tasks than in common speech. Taken together, it seems that even relatively healthy older adults are challenged by attempting to do two things at once. These findings should be taken into account when we interact with these individuals in professional and social situations.

According to a recent study (Schoenborn & Barnes, 2002), there is evidence of an association between leisure time physical activity, mortality (staying alive), and morbidity (staying healthy). Despite this, most older adults remain inactive (much like the rest of our population). Thus, increasing overall

Mortality:
An absence of life.

participation in leisure time physical activity has been consistently among the nation's health objectives. Nevertheless, as we get older our physical activity decreases. Young adults were almost twice as likely as older adults to engage in some leisure time physical activity, and nearly seven times more likely to engage in vigorous physical activity. Overall, nearly 40 percent of adults never engaged in any kind of leisure time physical activity. Interestingly, men (64.6 percent) were also more likely than women (59.1 percent) to pursue leisure time physical activity. White non-Hispanic adults (65.5 percent) and Asian/Pacific Islander non-Hispanic adults (61.8 percent) were more likely than black non-Hispanic adults (49.8 percent) and Hispanic adults (46.8 percent) to achieve some leisure time physical activity (Schoenborn & Barnes, 2002). There is evidence that physical activity can improve self-esteem and decrease stress, anxiety, and depression. Thus, a downward spiral can ensue for those who get too little physical activity. As we become even less active, more severe physiological changes such as heart disease, arthritis, osteoporosis, and other hypokinetic diseases become more prevalent.

Morbidity: An absence of health.

The tendency of many adults to be inactive seems to be influenced by socio-cultural factors. Three of the most influential factors often occur early in adulthood. For most Americans, we leave school, go to work, marry, and have children in our twenties. While these factors affect all adults differently, a common tendency is for us to become less physically active in conjunction with these events.

A number of other socio-cultural influences also occur throughout adulthood. These include empty nest syndrome (when children reach an age at which they are mature enough to leave home), retirement, and the death of a spouse. Most of us become increasingly sedentary with each successive event. For that reason, as we age we commonly see decreases in cardiac output, vital capacity, muscle mass, connective tissue elasticity, and nerve conductivity. We also see increases in physiological factors such as blood pressure, total blood cholesterol, and osteoporosis.

To further complicate the situation, our society holds low expectations for adults regarding their involvement in movement.

Even those adults who choose to maintain a physically active lifestyle may encounter some problems. Research results (O'Brien-Cousins & Janzen, 1998) indicate that barriers to exercise exist for the elderly: They are cautioned to be careful by their friends, their families, and even their physicians. These barriers may be greater than those inherent in sex stereotyping, and they are likely to contribute to a decline in participation.

The socio-cultural factors discussed in this section can have life-threatening consequences. As much as 50 percent of the physiological decline associated with aging may be related to lifestyle choices rather than to the aging process (Berger & McInman, 1993). In short, we can overcome much of the decline common in adulthood. For example, Barry, Rich, and Carlson (1993) studied frail elderly nursing home patients who were placed on an exercise program. They showed increased work and oxygen capacity, bone density, flexibility, muscle strength, and coordination. They also lowered their resting heart rates, total cholesterol, and blood pressure. Perhaps even more important, they improved their mental outlook while reducing loneliness, idle time, anxiety, depression, and appetite.

Concepts/Principles

Kindergarten: *Regular participation in physical activities is good for people of all ages.* The physical and mental benefits from physical activity have a positive influence on people of all ages.

Second Grade: *Learning many different motor skills gives people more choices for movement as they grow older.* Learning and practicing a range of movement skills and activities will help children and adolescents determine which activities they find most enjoyable. Enjoyment in movement and feelings of competence lead to persistence in physical activity. Children who practice movement skills and become proficient are more likely to maintain a high level of activity throughout their lives.

Fourth Grade: *Older adults have a difficult time performing two tasks simultaneously.* When interacting with grandparents it is important to keep this concept in mind.

Sixth Grade: *Regular participation in physical activity can help delay or minimize effects of age-related diseases.* Active adolescents are fighting the effects of aging by building strong bones. Most sixth graders may have only a vague awareness of diseases such as osteoporosis, particularly if they have a grandparent who suffers from it. Performing weight bearing activities (such as running and jumping) is a way to fight this disease, even early on.

Eighth Grade: *A variety of activities is necessary to maintain a high level of function throughout life.* Everyone can benefit from cardiorespiratory, muscular strength/endurance, and flexibility exercises, as well as physical activity in general.

Tenth Grade: *Physical activity patterns typically change throughout the lifespan.* As individuals grow older, their time is spent raising a family and pursuing a career, often with less time available for physical activity. However, this doesn't diminish the need for daily physical activity for physical and mental well being. Individuals need to schedule time for this important activity. Involving children *and* their parents is of benefit to all.

Twelfth Grade: *Accumulating at least 30-60 minutes of activity most days of the week can improve self-esteem; decrease stress, anxiety, and depression; and improve health.* Throughout this chapter, the importance of physical activity has been emphasized. Many professional organizations have suggested specific guidelines for the amount of activity that is necessary to gain and maintain physical fitness. Most recently, researchers and scholars have suggested that 30-60 minutes most days of the week is the gold standard that we should seek to follow.

Placing Motor Development Concepts in the Curriculum

If motor development concepts are to be integrated into the physical education program, decisions must be made about where those concepts should be placed. Throughout the chapter, placement of concepts appropriate for different grade levels are identified for each theme. The grade levels were chosen to be consistent with the grade levels used in the National Standards. The concepts are designed to be consistent with National Standard 2 (Applies movement concepts/principles to the learning and development of motor skills), as this standard relates to concepts of motor development. If concepts are developed experientially throughout the entire program, students are more likely to understand and use them to maintain a physically active lifestyle.

Integrating Motor Development into Instruction

It is one thing to determine the motor development content that is important for students. It is quite another for teachers to integrate that content into their instruction. The motor development concepts should be modeled during physical education instruction. Teachers need to acknowledge the developmental diversity in their classes and challenge all their students to meet their highest potential. Within one class, they will teach children who have had little opportunity or interest in being physically active or learning motor skills. Other children will participate in a wide range of activities outside their school day. In addition, the concepts should be taught directly as outlined in the lesson samples throughout the chapter.

Assessing Student Learning

The concepts outlined in the previous sections are aimed at helping individuals to improve their motor skills and to understand the lengthy (and sometimes frustrating) process of change in motor skill development. According to the National Standards, students should be able to apply the concepts described to their learning of motor skills. It is, therefore, important for teachers to actually check their students' learning of motor development concepts. Following are some ways that student knowledge might be assessed. This list is not intended to be exhaustive, and teachers are encouraged to add their own ideas.

Thirty-Second Wonders

At the end of class, students are asked to respond in writing to a question related to one or two main concepts covered during the class. Teachers use these summaries to assess student learning.

Examples:

1. How do differences in size and weight influence motor skill performance?
2. How much time should be spent daily on physical activity? Does this change throughout one's life?
3. How could you have included a younger sister or brother in your game today?
4. What is important to remember when playing with your grandparents?

Projects

Student projects are useful learning experiences and assessment techniques. However, they are very time consuming.

Example project:

Collect throwing for distance and running the 100-yard dash data on your classmates. Analyze the results–do boys or girls tend to do better on one or the other event? Do taller or shorter or lighter or heavier people do better on an event? Does age matter?

Research Reports

Motor development is an ideal area for research reports. Have students select a research topic or assign one of the following topics:

1. What effects (positive/negative) does exercise have on teenagers?
2. What is the average age for puberty in males and females, and what effect does this have on motor skill performance?
3. At what age should someone start to play organized football? Defend your answer.

Interviews

Students can perform a survey to determine levels and types of activity used by those around them. Students should keep a personal log of their activity for a week or a month. They should ask parents, grandparents, or older neighbors to maintain their own logs for the same time period. Students could interview these participants at the end for answers to questions such as:

- In what activities do you participate most frequently? Why?
- What barriers get in the way of your being active as much or as often as you would like?
- What enhances your ability to be active as much or as often as you would like?

Student groups then can compute the activity level of the participants and discuss what prevents and stimulates physical activity among individuals of different ages/life periods.

Written Tests
Written tests are an efficient method of assessing student knowledge about concepts. Written tests should be designed to assess the level of knowledge that is desired. For example, if asking a factual question, then a true/false question is appropriate; however, if asking an application question, then an open-ended question is a better choice.

Example: How do physical abilities influence performance? How would you include a visually impaired student in a softball game? What are the effects of cognitive development on motor skill performance?

Concluding Comments

Motor development consists of changes in motor behavior that occur across the lifespan and the processes that underlie and drive those changes. In this chapter, we have highlighted the important motor development concepts/principles. Physically educated adults should understand that individuals develop at their own rate, and should allow themselves and those around them the time and practice opportunities they need to acquire new motor skills. It is important to remember that change occurs as part of an interactive process between the current status of the individual and the environment in which he or she moves.

References

Alexander, N. B., Galecki, A. T., Grenier, M. L., Nyquist, L. V., Hofmeyer, M. R., Grunawalt, J. C., Medell, J. L., & Fry-Welch, D. (2001). Task-specific resistance training to improve the ability of activities of daily living-impaired older adults to rise from a bed and from a chair. *Journal of the American Geriatrics Society, 49,* 1418-1427.

Barry, H. C., Rich, B., & Carlson, R. T. (1993). How exercise can benefit older patients: A practical approach. *The Physician and Sportsmedicine, 21,* 124-140.

Berger, B. G., & Hecht, L. M. (1989). Exercise, aging, and psychological well-being: The mind-body question. In A. C. Ostrow (Ed.), *Aging and motor behavior.* Indianapolis: Benchmark.

Berger, B. G., & McInman, A. (1993). Exercise and the quality of life. In R. N. Singer, M. Murphy, & L. K. Tennant (Eds.), *Handbook of research on sports psychology.* New York: Macmillan.

Buck, M. M. (2002). *Assessing heart rate in physical education.* Reston, VA: NASPE.

Faigenbaum, A. D., Loud, R. L., O'Connell, J., Glover, S., O'Connell, J., & Westcott, W. L. (2001). Effects of different resistance training protocols on upper-body strength and endurance development in children. *Journal of Strength Conditioning Research, 15,* 459-465.

Falk, B., Sadres, E., Constantini, N., Zigel, L., Lidor, R., & Eliakim, A.(2002). The association between adiposity and the response to resistance training among pre- and early-pubertal boys. *Journal of Pediatric Endocrinological Metabolism, 15,* 597-606.

Fiatarone, M. A., Marks, E. C., et al. (1990). High-intensity strength training in nonagenarians: Effects on skeletal muscle. *Journal of the American Medical Association, 263,* 3029-34.

Gabbard, C. (2000). *Lifelong motor development* (3rd ed.). Needham Heights, MA: Allyn & Bacon.

Halverson, L. E., Roberton, M. A., & Langendorfer, S. (1982). Development of the overarm throw; movement and ball velocity changes by seventh grade. *Research Quarterly for Exercise and Sport, 53,* 198-205.

Khan, K. M., Liu-Ambrose, T., Sran, M. M., Ashe, M. C., Donaldson, M. G., & Wark, J. D. (2002). *British Journal of Sports Medicine, 36,* 10-13.

Lundin-Olsson L., Nyberg L., & Gustafson Y. (1997). "Stops walking when talking" as a predictor of falls in elderly people. *Lancet, 349,* 617.

Malina, R., & Bouchard, C. (1991). *Growth, maturation, and physical activity.* Champaign, IL: Human Kinetics.

Mandigout, S., Melin, A., Lecoq, A. M., Courteix, D., & Obert, P. (2002). Effect of two aerobic training regimens on the cardiorespiratory response of prepubertal boys and girls. *Acta Paediatrica, 91,* 403-408.

National Center for Health Statistics. (2000). *Advance data from vital and health statistics: Numbers 31–40.* Washington, DC: Author.

Nattiv, A. (2000). Stress fractures and bone health in track and field athletes. *Journal of Science and Medicine in Sport, 3,* 268-279.

Nevett, M. E., & French, K. (1997). The development of sport-specific planning, rehearsal, and updating of plans during defensive youth baseball game performance. *Research Quarterly for Exercise and Sport, 68,* 203-14.

O'Brien-Cousins, S., & Janzen, W. (1998). Older adult beliefs about exercise. In S. O'Brien-Cousins (Ed.), *Exercise, Aging & Health: Overcoming Barriers to an Active Old Age* (pp.71-96). Philadelphia: Taylor & Francis.

Payne, V. G., & Isaacs, L. D. (2002). *Human motor development: A lifespan approach.* Boston: McGraw-Hill.

Payne, V. G., & Morrow, J. (1993). Exercise and VO2 Max in children: A meta-analysis. *Research Quarterly for Exercise and Sport, 64,* 305-313.

Piaget, J. (1952). *The origins of intelligence in children* (Margaret Cook, Trans.). New York: International Universities Press.

Roberton, M. A., Halverson, L. E., & Harper, C. (1997). Visual/verbal modeling as a function of children's developmental levels of hopping. In J. Clark & J. Humphrey (Eds.), *Motor development: Research & Reviews* (Vol. 1). Reston, VA: AAHPERD.

Sattin, R. (1992). Falls among older persons: A public health perspective. *Annual Review of Public Health, 13,* 489-508.

Sinclair, C. (1973). *Movement of the young child: Ages two to six.* Columbus, OH: Merrill.

Spirduso, W. W. (1995). *Physical dimensions of aging.* Champaign, IL: Human Kinetics.

Trappe, S., Williamson, D., & Godard, M. (2002). Maintenance of whole muscle strength and size following resistance training in older men. *Journal of Gerontology: Biological Sciences, 57A,* B138-143.

VanSant, A. (1990). Life-span development in functional tasks. *Physical Therapy, 70,* 788-798.

Whitall, J. (1992). Elementary school physical fitness. *Teaching Elementary Physical Education, 3,* 14-15.

Zaichkowsky, L. D., Zaichkowsky, L. B., & Martinek, T. (1980). *Growth and development: The child and physical activity.* St. Louis: Mosby.

United States Department of Health and Human Services. (2000). *Healthy people 2010: Understanding and improving health.* Washington, DC: Author.

Resources

Centers for Disease Control. (2001). Youth risk behavior surveillance–United States, 2001. Retrieved from http://apps.nccd.cdc.gov/YRBSS/index.asp.

Committee on Sports Medicine and Fitness, American Academy of Pediatrics. (2001). Strength training by children and adolescents. *Pediatrics, 107,* 1470-1472.

Haywood, K., & Getchell, N. (2001). *Life Span Motor Development* (3rd ed.). Champaign, IL: Human Kinetics.

Rikli, R., & Jones, J. (2001). *Senior fitness test manual.* Champaign, IL: Human Kinetics.

Rowland, T. W. (1992). *Pediatric laboratory exercise testing: Clinical guidelines.* Champaign, IL: Human Kinetics.

Schoenborn, C. A., & Barnes, P. M. (2002). Leisure-time physical activity among adults: United States, 1997-98. *Advance Data from Vital and Health Statistics,* Department of Health and Human Services, Number 325, 1-24.

United States Department of Health and Human Services. (1996). *A report of the Surgeon General: Physical activity and health.* Washington, DC: Author.

Chapter 4

Biomechanics

Susan J. Hall
Gail G. Evans

At what angle of release should a ball be thrown for maximum distance? What movements can contribute to the development of lower back pain? Why does a properly thrown boomerang return to the thrower? Why are some people unable to float? The answers to all of these questions are rooted in the scientific field of biomechanics. In this chapter, we will look at biomechanical concepts as they relate to safe and effective movement in exercise, sport, dance, and daily living. These concepts are an important part of the cognitive foundation for a physically educated person. Further, an understanding of basic biomechanical principles can enhance the experience of acquiring or maintaining a physically active lifestyle.

What Is Biomechanics?

Force: A push or a pull in a linear direction.

Biomechanics is the application of mechanical principles in the study of human movement. It involves the analysis of force, including muscle force that produces movements and enables the throwing and kicking of balls. It also involves the analysis of impact force—such as catching or falling—that may cause injuries. Biomechanics explains why motor skills are performed in explicit ways in order to improve their efficiency and effectiveness.

Biomechanics, at the professional level, is a multidisciplinary field of study that involves biologists and zoologists; biomechanical and biomedical engineers; orthopedic, cardiac, and sports medicine physicians; dentists; physical therapists; exercise scientists; and physical educators. Researchers interested in human biomechanics have studied a wide variety of topics.

Using computer analysis of films or videotapes, biomechanists have studied performers who range in ability from physically challenged to elite. They have studied many movement forms—including dance, aquatics, gymnastics, individual and team sports, outdoor and leisure pursuits—as well as safety and rescue activities.

Sport biomechanists also are concerned with reducing the number of sport injuries by eliminating dangerous practices and improving sport equipment and apparel. And, there are important clinical applications for biomechanics research. Physical therapists regularly analyze the biomechanics of patients' walking gaits and other movements to monitor progress toward rehabilitation. Prosthetists work to improve the biomechanical aspects of artificial limbs and implants. Occupational biomechanics deals with preventing work-related injuries and improving working conditions and worker performance (Chaffin & Andersson, 1991).

Why Is Biomechanics Important?

A solid understanding of biomechanical concepts is important for the physical educator because it is intimately linked with effective teaching and learning of motor skills. And, a basic understanding of biomechanical principles is important for anyone interested in learning and improving movement skills. Adults who have a strong background in basic biomechanical concepts will be better prepared for an active life. They will be able to maximize their performance and efficiency while minimizing the chances of injury.

Linking Biomechanics to the National Standards

The biomechanical concepts are important cognitive components of the first two National Physical Education Standards developed by NASPE in 1995. They are:

- National Standard 1: Demonstrates competency in many movement forms and proficiency in a few movement forms.
- National Standard 2: Applies movement concepts/principles to the learning and development of motor skills.

An understanding of basic biomechanics is also relevant to several of the other National Standards, including:

- National Standard 3: Exhibits a physically active lifestyle.
- National Standard 4: Achieves and maintains a health-enhancing level of physical fitness.
- National Standard 6: Demonstrates understanding and respect for differences among people in physical activity settings.

Themes

It is important for physical education teachers to understand and be able to apply the information contained in the textbooks on biomechanics. While physically educated individuals do not need the same depth of understanding, it is important for students to grasp certain concepts if they are to be independent learners of motor skills. These ideas are organized around six major themes:

- What is force?
- How is force generated?
- How is force effectively matched to motor skill requirements?
- How is force effectively applied to projectiles?
- What external forces influence motion?
- What biomechanical concepts are important for safe participation in everyday physical activities?

Projectile: A body in free fall subject only to the forces of gravity and air resistance.

Each of these themes is briefly developed in the next section. Critical student concepts that relate to each theme are developed in a K-12 format.

What Is Force?

Where should a ball be hit when executing a floater serve in volleyball? What determines whether a push can cause a heavy piece of furniture to move? Why is it easier to open a door by pushing on the doorknob rather than in the center of the door? The answers to these questions all center around the nature of force. A force may be thought of simply as a push or a pull. Each force can be characterized by its magnitude or size, its direction, and the point at which it is applied. Although we tend to notice the forces acting on our bodies only in injury-

Friction: A force acting at the interface of bodies in contact that opposes the direction of motion.

Gravity:
A force accelerating all bodies vertically toward the surface of the earth at about 9.8 m/s^2.

related situations, forces act on us continually during daily activities. The forces of gravity and friction enable us to walk and manipulate objects in predictable ways when our muscles produce internal forces. When we participate in sports activities we apply force to balls, bats, racquets, and clubs. We absorb forces from impacts with balls when we catch them, and from impacts with the ground or floor when we walk and run.

The Effects of Force

There are two potential effects of force. The first is acceleration, or the change in velocity of the object to which the force is applied. The more massive or heavy the object, the smaller

Example 1

Elementary School Example: Kindergarten

Concept/Principle: More force must be applied to move heavy objects than light objects.

The kindergarten students are being oriented to the primary playground. During the lesson, the teacher has the students first push swings while they are unoccupied and then while they are occupied by another child. In each case the students let the swings stop on their own.

The teacher then asks the children: (1) In which case was it more difficult to get the swing going? (2) In which case was it more difficult to keep the swing going? (3) Why do they think one was more difficult than the other?

Example 2

Middle School Example: Sixth Grade

Concept/Principle: Spin occurs when a force is applied anywhere on the object except through the center of gravity.

During a racquet sports unit, students are paired for striking practice. As the students are striking the ball back and forth, the teacher asks the students as a group if they can:

1. Strike the ball without producing spin.
2. Strike the ball to produce forward (or top) spin.
3. Strike the ball to produce backward (or back) spin.
4. Strike the ball to produce right and left spin.

During closure, the teacher questions the group about how they struck the ball under each condition, and about the effects of spin on the ball's path. Students should determine that applying force off-center causes spin in the direction of the force deviation from center, and that the ball tends to rebound in the direction of the spin. For homework, students complete a worksheet illustrating where the ball must be struck to produce each type of spin. In subsequent lessons, the concept of spin is reinforced during applicable units of instruction (i.e., volleyball, golf).

the acceleration will be. The second effect is deformation, or change in shape. When a racquetball is struck with a racquet, the ball is both accelerated (put in motion in the direction of the racquet swing) and deformed (flattened on the side struck).

Figure 1

Net Force

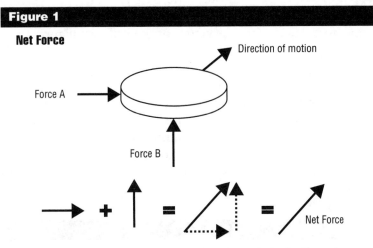

A hockey puck contacted simultaneously by 2 sticks will move in the direction and with the magnitude of the net force, which is the vector sum of the two original forces.

Net force:
The single force resulting from the vector addition of all forces acting on a body at a given time.

Center of gravity: A unique point around which a body's weight is balanced at a given time.

Net Force

Since a force rarely acts in isolation, it is important to recognize that what we see and feel are effects of what is called the net force. The net force is the vector sum of all the acting forces on a body (see Figure 1). Thus, it represents the size and direction of all acting forces. The magnitude and direction of the net force determines the speed and path of motion of the body that is experiencing the net force. When the forces acting on an object are balanced, or cancel each other out, there is no net force and no resulting motion. If two people simultaneously apply equal and opposite forces on the two sides of a swinging door, for example, the door will not move.

The effect of a net force on the resulting motion of a body depends not only on the size and direction of the force, but also on the point at which the force is applied. A body's center of gravity is the point around which its weight is balanced. When a pencil is balanced horizontally on an extended finger, the pencil's center of gravity is positioned directly above the finger. When a net force is directed through a body's center of gravity, the resulting motion of the body will be along a straight

Line of action: The straight line extending through the point of application and along the direction of the force.

line in the direction of the force. If a net force is directed through any point other than the body's center of gravity, the body will also rotate as it moves in the direction of the force. To execute a floater serve in volleyball with no spin, for example, the server applies force directly through the center of the ball, which is the ball's center of gravity. To produce spin on a ball, we would apply force away from the center of the ball (see Figure 2).

Torque

Torque, which may be thought of as rotational force, is the product of a force and its moment arm. A moment arm is the shortest distance between the force's line of action and the body's center of rotation (see Figure 2). The size of the force and the size of the moment arm contribute equally to torque. A heavy door can be pushed open with minimal effort by applying force at the farthest possible distance (moment arm) from the hinges.

Moment arm: The shortest distance between a force's line of action and the center of rotation of the body acted upon.

Torque: Rotary force.

Figure 2

Joint Torque

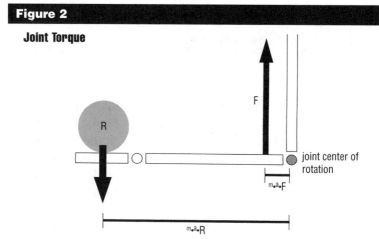

Schematic representation of the arm and hand, with the hand supporting a resistance. Muscle torque at the elbow is the product of muscle force (F) and muscle moment arm (m.a.F). Resistance torque at the elbow is the product of the resistance (R) and resistance moment arm (m.a.R). Motion at the joint is in the direction of the net torque.

Equilibrium

Equilibrium: A state involving a balance of all acting forces and torque; net force and net torque are zero.

When all acting forces and torque on a body are balanced (there is no net force or net torque acting), the body is said to be in a state of equilibrium. A body in equilibrium may either be motionless or moving at a constant speed along a straight path. A body's tendency to remain in equilibrium is known as its inertia. A body's inertia is proportional to its mass, with heavier objects having more inertia than lighter objects. For example, the more weight discs that are loaded onto a barbell positioned on the floor, the greater the barbell's inertia, and the more difficult it is to disturb its equilibrium.

Inertia: Resistance to change in state of motion.

Reaction Force

When one body exerts a force on a second body, the second body exerts a reaction force of equal size and opposite direction (Newton's Third Law). When we catch a ball, our hands apply a force to the ball that reduces its velocity to zero. During the catch, the ball applies a force of equal size to our hands. When we walk or run, our feet apply force to the ground and the ground applies reaction force to our feet.

Concepts/Principles

Kindergarten: *More force must be applied to move heavy objects than light objects.* Students should understand that they must push harder when trying to move heavy objects. Or, they may want to recruit a friend to help!

Reaction force: Force generated by a body in response to a force acting upon it, equal in size and opposite in direction to the original force.

Second Grade: *Force can cause both motion and change in shape of the body acted upon.* For example, when a red playground ball is hit really hard it will "squash" when it hits the ground. Then, it will travel in the opposite direction.

Second Grade: *Giving with the force gradually reduces its speed.* That's why you bend your knees when landing after a jump. By reducing your speed, there is less chance for injury.

Fourth Grade: *For every action there is an equal and opposite reaction.* When you walk, your foot applies a force to the floor, and the floor applies the same (this point is critical to the concept) force back in the opposite direction.

Sixth Grade: *Spin occurs when a force is applied anywhere on the object except through the center of gravity.* When the force is applied through the center of gravity of an object, it will travel in a relatively straight line.

Center of rotation: The point around which a body rotates.

Sixth Grade: *The longer the contact and the greater the area of absorption of a force, the less chance of injury.* When you catch a hard ball that is traveling very fast, you want to use a thick glove for greater absorption, and you want to bend your arms and "give" with the ball as much as possible.

Eighth Grade: *When more than one force acts on a body, the effect on the body is the result of the sum of the sizes and directions of the forces.* The force with the greatest magnitude will have the greatest effect.

Eighth Grade: *Both the size of the force and the distance of the force from the center of rotation contribute to torque.* The greater the magnitude of the force and the farther it is applied from the center of rotation, the greater the torque.

Tenth Grade: *A body's motion is determined by the net forces and torque acting upon it.* The forces and torque with the greatest magnitudes will ultimately determine the direction of motion and/or rotation.

Twelfth Grade: *A force's magnitude and moment arm contribute equally to the torque generated by the force at the body's center of rotation.* A diver on a springboard will generate greater torque the farther he or she is from the axis of the board, for example. Similarly, a heavier diver will usually generate more torque than a lighter one.

Twelfth Grade: *Equilibrium is a state of balanced forces and torque (a body in equilibrium can be stationary or moving at a constant speed in a given direction).* A gymnast executing a pose on the balance beam and a swimmer poised to take off from the starting block are both in a state of equilibrium.

How Is Force Effectively Generated?

Why do skilled tennis players position the serving arm so far behind the body during the "back scratch" or preparatory phase of the serve? Why are muscles "stronger" when the body is in certain positions? The answers to these questions are related to the body's ability to generate force.

Muscle Tension

There are approximately 434 muscles in the human body. About 150 of these muscles control body movements and posture. The others are responsible for activities such as eye control and swallowing. When a muscle produces force, it does so by developing tension—a pulling force. A tensed muscle pulls on the bones to which it is attached. Because each muscle can only apply force in one direction, muscles are arranged in functional pairs that pull on bones in opposite directions. For example, tension in the quadriceps muscle group on the anterior thigh extends (straightens) the knee, and tension in the hamstrings on the posterior thigh produces flexion (bending) at the knee.

Although muscles can only pull on bone, several things can happen when a muscle is tensed. When a tensed muscle shortens, the attached bones are moved closer together and there is motion of one or more body segments (i.e., forearms, thighs, hands, feet). Muscles also can develop tension without any change in length. When bodybuilders pose, they tense muscles on opposite sides of the body segments so the effects of the muscle forces are neutralized and no motion occurs. Finally, tensed muscles can lengthen. Lowering a barbell from shoul-

Example 3

High School Example: Tenth Grade

Concept/Principle: A change in the moment arms of the involved muscles or the resistance forces can increase or decrease the relative difficulty of an exercise.

This lesson is conducted during a weight training unit.

1. Have students hold a light dumbbell in their dominant hand with the arm horizontally extended to the point of fatigue while a partner times them with a stop watch.
2. Repeat the process with the same student holding the weight in the non-dominant hand, this time with the arm positioned horizontally and the elbow at a 90-degree angle.
3. Have the students switch roles and repeat.

This exercise is designed to illustrate the significance of the moment arm of a resistance. Even when using the nondominant arm, students should be able to hold the weight longer when the elbow is at a 90-degree angle, because the distance between the weight and the center of rotation at the shoulder is much shorter than when the arm is fully extended. This exercise can - be repeated with several different weights to show that both moment arm and weight magnitude contribute to the difficulty of the exercise.

At the end of the lesson, the teacher asks the students about the implications of this exercise for lifting and carrying a load. (The load should always be positioned as close to the trunk as possible to minimize the moment arm of the load with respect to the spine and thereby minimize the work that must be performed by the lower back muscles.)

Tension:
Pulling force.

der height to waist height involves lengthening of the elbow flexor muscles at the same time that tension is produced to control the movement of the barbell. The terms used to describe decrease, increase, and no change in the length of a tensed muscle are concentric, eccentric, and isometric.

Effects of Muscle Tension

Several factors influence the resulting effect of muscle tension on motion of the body segments. A major factor is the magnitude, or amount, of tension developed. We produce large magnitudes of muscle tension during a forceful motion. Because muscles that are larger in cross-section are stronger than muscles that are smaller in cross-section, we tend to use larger muscles and to recruit more muscles for tasks requiring large amounts of force. Thus, the large, powerful gastrocnemius is called to action during a maximal vertical jump. Only smaller muscles—such as the underlying soleus—are intermittently active to control postural sway when we stand.

Concentric:
Involving shortening of a tensed muscle.

An equally important influence on the outcome of muscle tension development is the moment arm of the muscle force (see Figure 2). Muscles within the human body produce torque at joints. This is the product of muscle force and muscle moment arm, or the distance from the muscle force's line of action to the center of rotation at the joint. Torque causes rotation of a body segment at a joint. A muscle's strength is essentially the amount of joint torque it can produce. As the angle at a joint such as the elbow changes, the moment arms of the muscles crossing the elbow also change. Change in muscle moment arm translates directly into change in the muscle's ability to generate joint torque. Isokinetic resistance machines are designed to provide variable resistance through a joint's range of motion that matches the changing torque—generating potential of the muscle groups involved.

Eccentric:
Involving lengthening of a tensed muscle.

Joint Movement

Whether movement occurs at a joint in response to torque produced by a muscle depends on the magnitude of the resistance torque at the joint (see Figure 2). Resistance torque is the product of a resistance force and its moment arm with respect to the joint center. Resistance forces can be applied by external loads, such as a weight held in the hand, the weight of the

Isometric:
Involving no change in the length of a tensed muscle.

body segments, and the opposing muscles. Motion at a joint occurs in the direction of the net torque. Because most of the muscles of the human body attach relatively close to the joints they cross, muscle forces must typically be much larger than resistance forces to generate a net joint torque that causes motion.

Effect of Muscle Stretch

Muscle length is another factor that influences the torque produced by a muscle at a joint. A muscle's ability to produce force increases when it is slightly stretched. Thus, a stretch fosters subsequent forceful shortening of the muscle. This phenomenon promotes effective muscular force development in many sport activities. For example, baseball pitchers, football quarterbacks, javelin throwers, and water polo players all place the anterior shoulder muscles in eccentric stretch during arm "cocking" immediately before forceful throwing. The same action occurs in muscle groups of the trunk and shoulders at the peak of the backswing of a golf club or a baseball bat, and during the "back scratch" position of the tennis serve or the badminton clear shot. During walking and running, the cyclic stretching of the gastrocnemius and the soft tissues of the arches of the foot also acts to store and return elastic energy.

Concepts/Principles

Kindergarten: *Muscles move the body.* If you tense your biceps, your elbow will automatically bend.

Second Grade: *Muscles move the body by producing force.* When your foot pushes against the floor it creates a force that allows you to walk forward.

Second Grade: *Muscles act by pulling on the bones to which they are attached.* Tendons from the hamstring muscles cross the back of the knee joint and attach to the bones in the lower leg. When the hamstring muscles contract the knee will flex.

Fourth Grade: *Large muscles can generate more force than smaller muscles.* Most people can kick a ball farther than they can throw one, because their leg muscles are larger than their arm muscles.

Sixth Grade: *Muscles are arranged in functional pairs that can move our body segments in opposite directions.* The biceps can cause flexion at the elbow and the triceps can cause extension at the elbow.

Sixth Grade: *When we tense both muscles in a functional pair equally, no body motion occurs.* This is called an isometric muscle contraction. For example, if the biceps and triceps produce equal force about the elbow, no motion will occur.

Eighth Grade: *Muscles with a larger cross-sectional area can produce more force than smaller muscles.* When you need to lift something very heavy, you should always bend your knees. You can use the strength from your larger leg muscles rather than risk straining your back or smaller arm muscles.

Tenth Grade: *Muscle forces and resistance forces combine to produce joint torque.* The direction of the torque will be determined by whichever is greater—the muscle force or the resistance force.

Tenth Grade: *Changing the moment arms of the involved muscles or the resistance forces can alter the difficulty of an exercise.* It is much harder to hold a heavy object away from the body than close to the body, for example, because the moment arm is longer.

Twelfth Grade: *Forcefully stretching a muscle immediately before a concentric contraction increases the force of that contraction.* This concept relates directly to plyometrics, as well as to stretching before exercising.

How Is Force Effectively Matched to Motor Skill Requirements?

Why do baseball players "choke up" on the bat to execute a bunt? Why do expert dart throwers move at just one joint during the throw? Why do elite gymnasts tend to be of short stature and slight build? Although muscular strength is an important asset for many sports, strength alone does not always translate into skillful performance. Effective movement during sport, exercise, dance, and daily activity also is dependent on factors such as movement speed, range of motion, the weight and length of the body segments, the number and coordination of the body segments involved, and the anthropometric characteristics of the body.

Movement Speed and Range of Motion

When an athlete swings a bat, club, or racquet, the faster the angular velocity of the swinging implement and the greater the amount of force that will be delivered to the ball at impact, when other factors are equal. The larger the range of motion—or distance through which the motion occurs—the greater the potential for building angular velocity. This is true for both swinging sport implements and moving human body segments. For example, a volleyball player uses a large range of arm motion to generate high angular velocity and deliver a large force to a spiked ball, but uses a much smaller range of motion and angular velocity to dink the ball over a block.

Weight and Length

Other factors to consider are the weight and length of the swinging bat, club, racquet, or body segment. If other related factors are the same, a heavier implement or body segment will produce more force than will a lighter version of the same implement or segment. The same is true for a longer implement in comparison to a shorter one. In brief, it is the distance between the center of rotation of the swinging implement and the point at which the ball is struck that influences the velocity of the struck ball. This distance between the center of rotation and a given point of interest on a rotating body is known as the radius of rotation (see Figure 3).

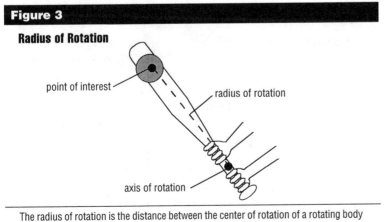

Figure 3

Radius of Rotation

point of interest

radius of rotation

axis of rotation

The radius of rotation is the distance between the center of rotation of a rotating body and a point of interest (in this case, the point of contact with a ball).

Example 4

Middle School Example: Sixth Grade

Concept/Principle: Increasing the range of motion through which body segments are rotated tends to increase the force generated.

At the beginning of a unit on object manipulation, the teacher has the students experiment with different methods for throwing and kicking a ball for maximum distance.

1. The teacher has the students experiment with kicking a ball from the ground for maximum distance with the following conditions:
   - Knee and hip in slight flexion but motionless; kicking motion involves ankle dorsiflexion only.
   - Ankle and hip stationary; kicking motion involves knee extension only.
   - Hip and thigh are stable; kicking motion involves knee extension and ankle dorsiflexion.
   - Knee and ankle are stable and leg is straight; kicking motion involves hip flexion only.

2. Then, the teacher has the students experiment with throwing a ball for maximum distance with some of the following conditions:
   - Using wrist motion only.
   - Using wrist and elbow motion; the upper arm remains stationary.
   - Using wrist, elbow, and shoulder motions; the trunk remains stationary.
   - Using all arm segments; trunk rotation encouraged.

For homework, the teacher has the students write a summary of their findings. Students should determine that an increase in swinging leg segment mass and in movement range of motion increases the distance the ball is kicked, and that, generally, using more joint action increases kick distance.

Example 5

Middle School Example: Eighth Grade

Concept/Principle: Extension of the joints of moving body segments increases the radius of rotation for throwing or striking motions.

The activity the teacher is working with is badminton. As part of the planned experiences for this unit, the teacher has the students working on the badminton clear for maximum distance.

During the lesson, the teacher has the students experiment with a badminton clear for maximum distance under some of the following conditions:

- Using shoulder motion only; the elbow and wrist remain firm.
- Using shoulder and elbow motion; the wrist remains firm.
- Using shoulder, elbow, and wrist motions; the trunk remains stationary.
- Using all arm segments; trunk rotation encouraged.

For homework, the teacher has the students write a summary of their findings. Students should determine that badminton clear distance is maximized by motion at all upper extremity joints.

Example 6

Middle School Example: Eighth Grade

Concept/Principle: The greater the distance between a bat, club, or racquet's center of rotation and contact point with a ball (radius of rotation), the greater the amount of force that tends to be delivered to the ball. The radius of rotation for a bat or club striking a ball should be adjusted in accordance with the force requirements of the activity.

The activity the teacher is working with is softball. As part of the planned experiences for this unit, the teacher has the students working on pitching and batting.

During the lesson, the teacher has the students work in pairs with one partner tossing easy softball pitches for the other partner to bat. After several minutes of practice, the teacher asks the students to experiment hitting the ball under the following conditions:

1. Using bats of different sizes (weights).
2. Swinging a given bat at different angular speeds.
3. Choking up on the bat.

For homework, the teacher has the students write a summary of their findings. Students should determine that if other relevant factors are equal, they can hit a ball farther with a heavier bat, a faster bat swing, and a larger radius of rotation. For some students, however, there may be a trade-off between bat weight and the angular speed at which the student can swing the bat. Students should determine that a bat that is too heavy places them at a disadvantage, since it may make it more difficult to make contact with pitched balls.

During subsequent lessons, the teacher reminds the students about the variables involved in hitting a ball farther.

Other factors being equal, the longer the radius of rotation for striking a ball, the greater the amount of force transferred to the ball. For this reason, we use longer clubs (woods) for longer shots in golf and shorter clubs (irons) for shorter ones. Likewise, we tailor the length of the radius of rotation of moving body segments to the force requirements of the activity. A water polo player uses an entire extended arm to throw a long pass, but may use only forearm motion for a short toss, for example. A skillful baseball pitcher uses considerable trunk rotation, making the spine, rather than the shoulder, the center of rotation in order to maximize the radius of rotation for delivery of the ball.

Radius of rotation: The distance from the center of rotation to a point of interest on the rotating body.

Number of Moving Segments and Coordination

The greater the force requirements of the motor skill, the larger the number of body segments that are likely to be involved.

This makes sense for two reasons: Increasing the number of moving segments increases the amount of body mass involved in force production, and the more segments that are involved, the longer the potential radius of rotation between the major joint center of rotation and the point of force application. To impart a large force to a ball, a server in tennis strikes the ball with the arm fully extended to maximize the ball's radius of rotation.

Motion of more than one body segment brings into consideration another important factor that affects delivery of force during motor skill execution. This is the timing and sequencing of joint motions, or coordination. Although coordination is a highly complex neuromuscular phenomenon, two general observations may be made about the coordination of skillful movements. Skillful execution of ballistic activities such as throwing and kicking involves a sequential progression of segment motions, beginning with the more proximal (and larger) segments and ending with the more distal (and smaller) segments. Alternatively, skillful execution of activities such as weight training, that require control of a heavy resistance object, tend to involve simultaneous joint motions.

Anthropometric Considerations and Body Position

People vary considerably in anthropometry (height, weight, the shapes of body segments, etc.). We typically associate basketball players with large stature, gymnasts with small stature and slight build, and football players with large body mass. Although diet and training certainly influence body weight and—to some extent—the shapes of the body segments, body size and shape are functions of genetic makeup. Although people of average anthropometric characteristics have the potential to participate in a wide range of sport, dance, and other physical activities, it is clear that some characteristics provide advantages for selected activities. As discussed previously, a body's inertia, or resistance to change in state of motion, is proportional to body mass. For this reason, people with large body mass tend to excel at activities where a large amount of stability is desirable (playing the offensive line in football is an example). Alternatively, the small body mass and short height of most gymnasts are assets, since both height and mass contribute to what is called moment of inertia, or resistance to rotation. Rotation is easier with both shorter height and smaller body mass.

Although most adults do not have the anthropometric charac- **Moment** teristics to excel at playing the line in football or doing gym- **of inertia:** nastics, we all can manipulate body position to our advantage Resistance in other sports. Other factors being equal, we can enhance body to rotational stability by lowering our center of gravity (bending the knees), motion. increasing the size of our base of support (widening the stance) in the direction of force resistance, and leaning in the opposite direction of any force to be resisted (leaning into an oncoming force or away from a pulling force). We also can improve our ability to rotate the body during a forward roll or a dive by assuming a tightly tucked position.

Fast movements of body segments can be facilitated by keeping them as close to the major center of rotation as possible. Good sprinters, for example, swing their legs forward with the knees in near maximum flexion, keeping the lower leg and foot as close to the center of rotation at the hip as possible. In throwing motions, a large amount of flexion at the elbow during the "cocking" phase allows forward motion with maximum speed, since the forearm and hand are positioned close to the center of rotation at the shoulder. Similarly, spins and twists executed by dancers, ice skaters, gymnasts, and divers are more efficient when the limbs are held close to the body's axis of rotation.

Concepts/Principles

Kindergarten: *Lowering the body's center of gravity (bending the knees), widening the base of support (stance), and leaning away from any force increases the ability to maintain balance (stability).* It is much easier to stay in a balanced position on your hands and knees than it is in a standing position.

Second Grade: *Faster movement produces greater force.* If you are running really fast your feet are pushing harder against the ground than if you are walking.

Fourth Grade: *Increasing the size, number, or speed of moving body segments tends to increase the force generated.* Movement speed and the number of moving body segments should be adjusted in accordance with the force requirements of the activity.

Fourth Grade: *Raising the body's center of gravity, narrowing the base of support, and leaning in the direction of movement allows for a quicker start.* Track athletes tend to lean forward in the starting blocks in order to get a faster start, for example.

Sixth Grade: *The larger the range of motion, the greater the potential for angular velocity and force production.* If you use your whole arm to throw a ball it should go farther than if you bend your wrist or your elbow.

Sixth Grade: *Longer or heavier bats and clubs tend to produce more force than shorter or lighter ones.* That's why "homerun hitters" usually want their bats to be as long and heavy as possible.

Eighth Grade: *The longer the distance between a bat, club, or racquet's center of rotation and the contact point with a ball (radius of rotation), the greater the amount of force that tends to be delivered to the ball.* The radius of rotation for a bat or club striking a ball should be adjusted in accordance with the force requirements of the activity. Because you don't need as much force, you can "choke up" on the bat when you want to bunt the ball.

Eighth Grade: *Extending the joints of moving body segments increases the radius of rotation for throwing or striking motions.* You will have the shortest radius of rotation if you bend your wrist while throwing, and the greatest if you keep your arm straight and throw from the shoulder, for example.

Tenth Grade: *Positioning moving body segments close to the major center of joint rotation facilitates faster movement.* An ice skater who pulls her arms in while executing a turn will spin faster than if she extends her arms, for example.

Tenth Grade: *Forces applied to a stationary object must overcome the mass of the object, so heavier people tend to be better at activities involving stability and shorter people tend to be better at activities involving body rotation.* On a football team, stability is most critical for the linemen, so they are usually the heaviest players.

> **Twelfth Grade:** *Movement speed, range of motion, joint extension, and the number of moving body segments should be adjusted in accordance with the force requirements of the activity.* In general, the greater the force required, the greater the speed, range of motion, joint extension, and number of moving body segments you will want to use.
>
> **Twelfth Grade:** *Body anthropometry can help or hinder skillful performance of some motor skills.* Equipment should be selected to match the anthropometric characteristics of the user. A larger ball player will usually be able to handle a heavier bat than a smaller one, for example.

How Is Force Effectively Applied to Projectiles?

What is the optimal angle of release for throwing a softball the maximum distance? Where along its flight path does a curve ball actually curve? How does spin affect the rebound of a ball served in tennis? The answers to these questions are related to the ways in which force is applied to the projected ball. A projectile is a body that is moving through the air and subject only to the forces of gravity and air resistance. Projectiles include not only balls, Frisbees, boomerangs, javelins, and falling acorns, but also human bodies during the performance of jumps or dives. In the absence of air resistance, the flight path or trajectory followed by a projectile is predetermined by the force of projection. When force is applied to project a body into the air, the magnitude, direction, and point of application of the applied force all exert potentially significant influences on the resulting flight path of the body.

Projection Speed

Typically of greatest importance is the magnitude of the applied force that influences projection speed. Other related factors being the same, it is the projection speed that determines the overall size of the trajectory. Successful shot, discus, javelin, and hammer throwers possess the muscle strength and power necessary to apply a great deal of force to the implement.

Projection Angle and Relative Projection Height

The angle at which a body is initially projected determines the shape of the trajectory in the absence of air resistance. The flight path of a body projected at an angle between 0 degrees and 90 degrees is a smooth, symmetrical curve, with left and right halves forming mirror images of one another when projection and landing heights are the same (see Figure 4).

When the goal of projection is to achieve maximum horizontal distance, the optimum projection angle varies with what is called the relative projection height. The relative projection height is the difference between projection and landing heights. A football punted from a height of four feet that falls to the playing field has a relative projection height of four feet. A soccer ball kicked from the field and landing on the same field has a relative projection height of zero. When the relative projection height is zero, the optimum angle of projection for achieving maximum horizontal distance is 45 degrees. When projection height is greater than landing height, however, the optimal angle for projecting something for maximum distance is less than 45 degrees.

Performance Considerations
It is important to recognize that human body biomechanics often require tradeoffs among projection speed, angle, and height. During a throw for maximum distance, for example, it is advantageous to maximize release height, since greater release height translates to longer flight time and greater dis-

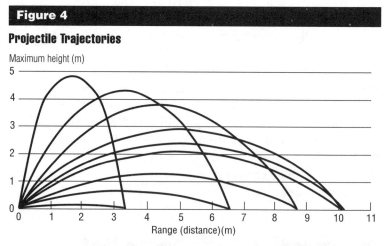

Figure 4

Projectile Trajectories

Maximum height (m)

Range (distance)(m)

Trajectories, or flight paths, for a ball projected at 10 m/s with projection angles of 10, 20, 30, 40, 45, 50 60, 70, 80, and 90 degrees.

tance. It would be a mistake, however, to release the ball at too large an angle of projection, since this would shorten the distance achieved. If all other factors are the same, release velocity will have the greatest impact on distance.

When the projectile is the human body during a jumping event, there also is a potential tradeoff between projection angle and projection speed. In the long jump, since takeoff and landing heights are the same, the theoretically optimum take off angle is 45 degrees. Yet the takeoff angles actually measured for elite long jumpers range from 18 to 27 degrees (Hay, 1986). This is because in order to achieve a 45 degree takeoff angle, researchers estimate that jumpers would decrease their horizontal speed going into the jump by about 50 percent, resulting in much poorer performance (Hay, 1986).

Concepts/Principles

Kindergarten: *The faster a ball is thrown or kicked, the farther it tends to go.* If you are running when you kick a ball it will tend to go farther than if you are standing still.

Second Grade: *The greater the angle at which a ball is thrown or kicked, the higher the projectile travels.* If you throw a ball straight up in the air it will tend to travel higher than if you let it go in front of your body.

Fourth Grade: *The speed and angle of an object when it is released, or a person jumping determines the flight path.* If there is no wind involved, the best angle of release for maximum horizontal distance is 45 degrees. The faster the speed at release (takeoff), the farther or higher the object will travel.

Sixth Grade: *The greater the height from which something is projected, the longer it tends to remain in the air.* If you throw a ball from above your head it will tend to be in the air longer than if you release it at waist height.

Eighth Grade: *If air resistance is absent, the trajectory (flight path) of a projectile is determined by the initial speed, angle, and height of projection.* Of these three elements, speed of release has the greatest effect on flight path.

Eighth Grade: *The optimum projection angle for maximum projection distance is 45 degrees when projection and landing heights are the same, but less than 45 degrees when projection height is greater than landing height.* You would want to release a javelin at a smaller angle than you would a football pass, in order to get maximum distance, for example

Tenth Grade: *Projection speed is usually the most important factor in achieving maximum horizontal distance.* The more body parts you can involve, the greater the speed.

Tenth Grade: *The shape of a projectile's trajectory is symmetrical in the absence of air resistance.* In other words, the body will take off and land at the same angle when there is no wind resistance.

Tenth Grade: *Increasing relative projection height tends to increase flight time.* A ball thrown overhead will tend to be airborne longer than a ball thrown underhand, for example.

Twelfth Grade: *When projection and landing heights are equal, a projectile's landing speed is the same as its projection speed.* This is only true if there is no air resistance.

Twelfth Grade: *There are tradeoffs among optimum projection speed, angle, and height when projecting for maximum horizontal distance when the human body is applying force to a projectile or serving as the projectile.* In general, the most influential factor is projection speed.

What External Forces Influence Motion?

Why is it difficult for some people to float? Why does a golf ball have dimples? How can a ballet dancer be perfectly balanced while standing on one toe? The answers to these questions have to do with the actions of external forces.

Gravity

Gravity is an external force that is always present on earth. The force of gravity accelerates all bodies vertically toward the surface of the earth at a constant rate of about 9.8 m/s^2. Our body weight is the product of our mass (physical matter) and gravitational acceleration. An astronaut on the surface of the moon experiences a much lighter body weight because, although his/her body mass is the same as on earth, there is less gravitational acceleration on the moon.

It is important to recognize that gravitational acceleration is constant and that it acts equally on all bodies, regardless of their size, shape, or mass. Neglecting aerodynamic factors, this means that objects dropped from the same height fall at the same speed.

Buoyancy and Floatation

Buoyancy is an external force that can counteract the force of gravity. Buoyant force acts vertically upward. The size of the buoyant force acting on a body in the water is proportional to the amount of body volume submerged beneath the surface of the water. Of course, when a person is in the water, gravitational force continues to act. A person is able to float only if he or she has sufficient body volume to generate a buoyant force greater than or equal to body weight. (In the presence of these two opposing vertical forces, the action of the net force causes the body to either float or sink.) Individuals who have difficulty floating typically have high ratios of lean body mass to fat, or comparatively high body weight relative to their body size. One simple strategy for improving the ability to float is to hold a large breath of air in the lungs, thereby increasing body volume with a negligible addition of body weight.

Resistance Forces

Several types of external force act to slow the motion of moving bodies. One such force is friction, a force that acts against the direction of motion or intended motion at the interface between two surfaces in contact. Friction increases with the roughness or interactivity of the surfaces in contact and with the amount of force pressing the surfaces together (often the weight of an object sitting on a surface). The magnitude of friction varies, being greatest just before motion is initiated and least after motion occurs.

Although friction can sometimes be a nuisance, as when we are trying to rearrange heavy pieces of furniture in a room, it also can be very useful. Without friction, for example, our feet would slide out from under us each time we tried to take a step. A

Example 7

Middle School Example: Eighth Grade

Concept/Principle: Streamlined shapes and smooth surfaces reduce air and water resistance on a moving body.

During a bicycling unit, or as a homework assignment, the teacher has students on bicycles change quickly from a traditional crouched seating position for cycling to a fully upright seated position and then back again while going down a hill at a relatively fast speed.

Note: Make sure that this experiment is carried out under safe conditions. There should be no vehicular traffic, and cyclists should be spread out. This activity also can be done with students on roller skates, inline skates, ice skates, or skis.

For homework, the teacher has the students write a summary of their findings and explain the "why" behind their findings. Students should indicate dramatic changes in speed, with drag slowing them down in the upright position.

---

great deal of sports equipment is designed to optimize the amount of friction generated. This is true not only of athletic shoes designed for specific sports—and even for different playing surfaces—but also for racquet, bat, and club grips; for the gloves used in many sports; and for the tires used in different types of cycling competitions.

It is useful to remember that the nature of both surfaces affects the size of the frictional force. The friction between the soles of a pair of leather shoes and a sidewalk may provide excellent traction when the sidewalk is dry, but very poor traction when the sidewalk is icy. Likewise, whereas ballet shoes are constructed to provide the proper amount of friction for sliding and pivoting on a smooth wooden floor, they would not provide proper traction on surfaces such as concrete or asphalt.

Frictional force is dramatically reduced with rolling motions as compared with sliding motions, and when a layer of fluid is present between the contact surfaces. Within the human body, the layer of fluid present at synovial joints reduces the amount of friction present to only about 17–33 percent of that produced by a skate on ice under the same load (Brand, 1979).

A resistance force known as drag also opposes the movement of bodies through fluids and through air. Drag increases with factors such as the roughness and surface area of the body, the relative speed of the body moving through the fluid, and the density and viscosity of the fluid. Streamlining body shape, on the other hand, serves to reduce drag. In speed-related sports such as swimming, skiing, skating, and cycling, athletes wear tightly fitting apparel made of ultra-smooth fabrics. They also assume crouched (streamlined) body positions to reduce drag. The dimples on a golf ball are carefully designed to streamline the air flow around the ball during its flight. The generation of waves by a swimmer is also a source of drag, which increases with up and down motion of the body in the water. Swimming pool lane lines are engineered to dissipate wave action.

Lift and the Magnus Effect
Lift is another force that can affect the movement of bodies through air and water. Although the term suggests upward movement, lift is directed perpendicular to the relative fluid flow and can be oriented in any direction. Objects that are shaped like a foil are capable of generating lift (see Figure 5). The special shape of the foil creates a difference in pressure on the top and bottom that creates a force directed toward the foil's flat side. Lift increases with the velocity of the foil relative to the fluid, the fluid density, and the surface area of the flat side of the foil. A swimmer's hands resemble a foil shape when viewed from a lateral perspective. As the hands slice rapidly through the water, they generate lift forces directed toward the palm. Lift is an important contributor to propulsion in a number of swimming strokes, particularly the breaststroke (Schleihauf, 1979).

Drag: A force that acts to slow the motion of a body moving through a fluid.

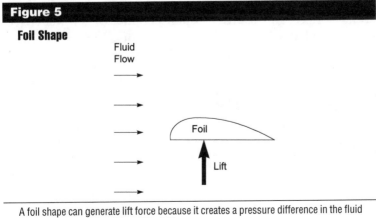

Figure 5

Foil Shape

Fluid Flow

Foil

Lift

A foil shape can generate lift force because it creates a pressure difference in the fluid on the curved and flat sides of the foil.

Figure 6

Magnus Effect

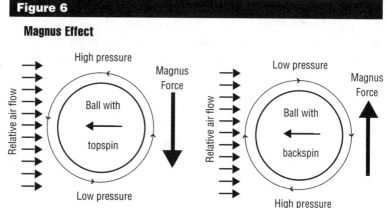

A boundry layer of air spins with a ball. On one side the boundry layer collides with the air flow, ceating high pressure, and on the other side it accelerates the airflow, creating low pressure. The force directed from the high pressure zone to the low pressure zone is called the Magnus Force. The Magnus Force causes a spinning ball to deviate from its flight path in the direction of the spin.

When a projectile is shaped and oriented such that it generates lift, the result is a longer trajectory and greater horizontal distance. The shapes of the discus, football, flying disc, and boomerang are sufficiently foil-like that they generate lift when properly oriented with respect to the relative flow of air.

Balls can generate lift by spinning. Like lift generated by a foil, the spinning action of a ball creates a difference in pressure on opposite sides that produces a force in the direction in which the spin was imparted. This force, known as the Magnus effect, is what causes curve balls to curve and tennis serves hit with topspin to drop. The path of a spinning ball is a smooth arc. The Magnus effect also has an impact on rebound from a horizontal surface. A ball with topspin rebounds on a lower trajectory, and a ball with backspin rebounds on a higher trajectory, as compared with the same ball without spin.

Concepts/Principles

Kindergarten: *It is easier to float in water while holding a big breath.* This is because when you fill your lungs with air, it takes up lots of space with very little weight.

Second Grade: *It is harder to push heavier objects across a table or floor surface than it is to push lighter objects.* Heavier objects create more friction than lighter objects.

Fourth Grade: *Increases in weight or surface roughness increase the friction between a moving body and the surface underneath it.* It's much easier to walk in tennis shoes on a gym floor than it is on an ice skating rink!

Sixth Grade: *Increases in contact force or surface roughness produce more friction between the two objects in contact.* Often, baseball or softball pitchers will use a sticky substance (rosin) to create more friction between their hands and the ball, in order to put spin on the ball.

Sixth Grade: *Gravity causes objects dropped from the same height to fall at the same speed (discounting air resistance).* If there were no air resistance and you dropped a bowling ball and a golf ball from three feet above the ground, they would both land at the same moment.

Eighth Grade: *Streamlined shapes and smooth surfaces reduce air and water resistance on a moving body.* This is why some swimmers shave their heads in order to create a "smooth" surface in the water. Some swimmers even shave their arms and legs!

Eighth Grade: *A ball with topspin rebounds on a lower trajectory and a ball with backspin rebounds on a higher trajectory than the same ball without spin.* Tennis players often use the backspin lob in order to get the ball to bounce above their opponent's head.

Tenth Grade: *Whether a body sinks or floats depends on whether the weight of the water displaced by the body is greater or less than body weight.* Bodies that are less dense will have a greater tendency to float than those that are more dense. Muscle and bone have a greater density than adipose tissue.

Tenth Grade: *Lift is a force produced by a foil shape or a spin that alters the path of a body moving through air or water.* Airplane wings are designed to create lift.

> **Twelfth Grade:** *Fluid forces increase with the density and viscosity of the fluid.* Because salt water is more dense than fresh water, fluid forces will be greater in salt water.
>
> **Twelfth Grade:** *Buoyancy increases with the volume/weight ratio of the submerged body.* Taking the air into your lungs will increase volume and therefore will increase buoyancy.
>
> **Twelfth Grade:** *Friction is reduced by a layer of fluid between two surfaces in contact.* You will get a better grip on an object if you first wipe the sweat off your hands!

What Biomechanical Concepts Are Important for Safe Participation in Everyday Activities?

Why is the old adage, "lift with your legs and not with your back," not necessarily good advice? Should exercises that are taxing to the lower back muscles be avoided? When is it appropriate to perform fast, ballistic exercises? The answers to these questions are based on biomechanical concepts.

Lifting and Carrying

Because lifting and carrying even light objects can place an added load on the spine, understanding the biomechanical factors that contribute to spinal loading can help prevent back pain or injury. When the body is in an upright position, body weight, the weight of any load held in the hands, and tension in the spinal ligaments and muscles all contribute to compression on the spine.

Tension in the spinal muscles increases when a load is held in front of the body. These muscles must produce enough torque to balance the torque generated by the load to prevent the body from toppling forward. To minimize the work that must be performed by the back muscles during lifting and carrying, the load should be positioned close to the body.

For this same reason, workers have been advised to "lift with the legs and not with the back." This translates to maintaining the trunk in a relatively upright position when lifting an object from the floor. The benefit of this style of lifting is that it minimizes the flexor (forward leaning) torque generated by the trunk that must be counteracted by the spinal extensor muscles. Leg lifting is often impractical, however, because of the awkward nature of the task or simply because it is more physiologically taxing than back lifting (McGill & Norman, 1993).

It may, in fact, be more important during lifting to focus on biomechanical factors other than use of the legs. One alternative is to maintain a normal curve in the lower back, rather than allowing the lumbar spine to flex, or sag forward (McGill & Norman, 1993). This enables the lumbar extensor muscles to better control the load and helps to even the force distribution on the spine.

Other research-based advice includes avoiding lateral flexion— or side bending—and twisting during lifting. Other factors being equal, researchers have estimated that compression on the L4/ L5 vertebral joint is nearly doubled with side bending, and more than tripled with twisting as compared to flexion (McGill & Norman, 1993). Asymmetrical left-right loading of the trunk also should be avoided due to the increased load on the spine resulting from side bending torque (Drury et al., 1989; Mital & Kromodihardjo, 1986). It is important to remember that protection of the back is maximized when motion occurs in only one plane.

Another factor that has been shown to affect spinal loading is speed of body movement. Lifting in a very rapid or jerking fashion dramatically increases the force acting on the spine, as well as tension in the spinal muscles (Hall, 1985). This is one of the reasons that resistance training exercises should normally be performed in a slow, controlled fashion.

Exercising
Protecting the lower back should be a priority when exercising. This does not imply, however, that the back muscles should not be exercised. In fact, weakened back and abdominal muscles are known to be predisposing factors for lower back pain.

It is particularly important that back exercises be performed in a slow, controlled fashion to avoid injury. Exercises involving lumbar hyperextension should be stopped before the end of the range of motion is reached (Liemohn, 1993). Curl-up type exercises should always be performed with the hips and knees in flexion, with the trunk elevated no more than approximately 30 degrees. This ensures that the abdominal muscles are exercised without involving the hip flexors. Overdevelopment of the powerful hip flexor muscles can promote exaggerated lumbar lordosis, which predisposes the individual to lower back pain.

All exercises performed for strength development should be done in a slow and controlled fashion. This minimizes the momentum of the resistance, thus promoting involvement of the working muscles throughout the range of motion. It also minimizes the likelihood of injury derived from accidentally exceeding a joint's normal range of motion.

In accordance with the principle of specificity of training, however, athletes who are training to increase movement speed or develop muscle power should exercise with quick, ballistic type movements. To avoid injuries, it is important for these athletes to develop an adequate strength base prior to engaging in exercises that are more challenging to the musculoskeletal system.

One popular and relatively inexpensive form of resistance training involves the use of free weights. Proponents of free weights point to the fact that the user must control the motion of the weight while at the same time maintaining balance. A disadvantage of free weights is that if the load is jerked at the beginning of the lift, the weight's momentum can carry it along its path of motion with little contribution from the working muscles. Proper technique when using free weights includes not arching the back and avoiding full knee flexion. It also is important to use a spotter when working with heavy weights.

A variety of resistance machines and devices are available. They range from large, heavy, expensive machines to portable, "fold-up" equipment designed for use in the home. The resistance can be provided by weights, hydraulic or air compression cylinders, springs, or elastic cables. Although resistance for legitimate exercises can be provided by different means, beware of products advertised to provide exercise benefits with minimal effort on the part of the user. Research has shown that some popular exercise devices provide absolutely no benefit to the user (Ross et al., 1993).

Concepts/Principles

Kindergarten: *When lifting or carrying something, it is important to hold it close to your body.* This makes the object seem lighter and it will be easier to carry.

Second Grade: *When lifting something, it is important to bend your knees.* Bending your knees means you are using your leg muscles to lift. They are bigger and stronger than your arm muscles.

Fourth Grade: *When lifting something, it is important to bend your knees and not let your back slump.* Keeping your back straight decreases the chance of injuring it.

Sixth Grade: *Perform lifts and exercises in a slow and controlled fashion.* This reduces the likelihood of injuring muscles and joints.

Eighth Grade: *Always face the object you are lifting so you do not have to twist or bend to the side.* When you twist and lift at the same time there is a greater chance of injuring your back.

Tenth Grade: *For safety purposes, always use a spotter when exercising with heavy free weights.*

Twelfth Grade: *Perform exercises in a slow and controlled fashion unless training for muscular power development.* Slow movements tend to increase muscular strength, whereas faster movements tend to increase power.

Twelfth Grade: *To minimize spinal load when lifting, avoid bending or twisting, keep the trunk erect, and hold the load close to the body.* The back is one of the most vulnerable parts of the body in terms of injury. To reduce this risk of injury, keep the back straight while lifting.

Placing Biomechanics Concepts in the Curriculum

Learning takes place most effectively when the learner is ready to learn. Throughout this chapter, concepts appropriate for different grade levels are identified for each theme. The benchmarks and emphases described for National Standard 2 (Applies movement concepts/principles to the learning and development of motor skills), as well as National Standard 1 (Demonstrates competency in many movement forms and proficiency in a few movement forms), were used as guides for matching concepts with grade levels. By the end of the twelfth grade, students should be able to apply these biomechanics concepts presented in learning new motor skills.

Integrating Biomechanics into Instruction

This section suggests ways in which teachers can incorporate biomechanics concepts into instruction. Although the examples provided can be incorporated into class instruction, they also can trigger ideas for other activities appropriate to particular grade levels, class sizes, and student backgrounds and skill levels. In all cases, reinforcement of these concepts through appropriate questioning following the activity will facilitate student understanding and retention of the concepts.

It is also good practice for the teacher to explain the "why" behind the correct technique for a movement skill when it is introduced or reviewed. For example, when introducing the headstand, teachers can remind students that a wider base of support offers more stability, so increasing (to an optimal point) the distance between the head and hands in a triangular formation will allow the students to be more successful with the skill. In this way, the concepts are taught in relation to the learning experiences provided.

Assessing Student Learning

Students should be able to use biomechanics concepts in class to improve their own performance and out of class to refine their motor skills. Many of the techniques teachers can use to assess learning are described in detail in the discussion of Standard 2 in *Moving into the Future: National Standards for Physical Education* (NASPE, 1995). There is a more general discussion in Chapter 1 of this book.

Thirty-Second Wonders

Student understanding of biomechanics concepts is perhaps best assessed on a lesson-by-lesson basis through thoughtful questioning. Students can jot down their answer(s) on a piece of paper or a 3x5 card.

Example: Once students can describe the characteristics of a skillful performance, an effective follow-up question for the teacher to ask is, "Why?" For example: "Why do batters choke up on the bat in order to bunt a ball?" or, "Why do skilled gymnasts tend to be short?"

Written Tests

Periodic written examinations can be constructed to more formally assess student understanding. Be sure to match the level of the question with the level of knowledge that is desired. For example, the "why" questions allow students to demonstrate a greater depth of knowledge, whereas the "what" question is at the recall level.

Example: "Why does holding air in the lungs make it easier to float?" "Why are muscles stronger when the body is in some positions as compared with other positions?" and, "What is the optimal angle of release for throwing a softball for maximum distance?"

Peer Observation/Self-Assessment

Students use videotape to conduct qualitative observations of other students and of themselves. Once students have achieved some level of familiarity with a new motor skill, and common errors have been discussed, performance may benefit from careful qualitative observations followed by appropriate peer feedback. Students can work in pairs, with one student practicing the skill while the other carefully observes for errors. Following are some hints for maximizing the effectiveness of peer observations:

1. If possible, select a setting that is well lit and free of distractions.
2. Choose a viewing angle and distance that will provide an optimal perspective.
3. Observe several executions of a skill before formulating a diagnosis.

4. Pay attention to auditory as well as visual information.

5. Try to focus on performance execution as well as performance outcome.

6. Provide feedback to the performer that is specific, factual, and nonjudgmental.

7. Avoid offering too much feedback at one time.

Example: Watch your partner attempt to apply topspin to the ball during a volleyball serve. Provide feedback as to the point of force application.

Group Projects

Group projects are very beneficial for assessing student learning related to biomechanics concepts. However, be aware that they often require more time to complete than do other assessment tools.

Example: Students work in small groups to write an analysis of their videotaped performances. Use of videotape has several advantages: the performer can view and analyze the performance along with others, and a taped performance can be frozen at critical points, played in slow motion, or replayed repeatedly.

Concluding Comments

Biomechanical concepts provide a basis for understanding the ways in which human movements in exercise, sport, dance, and daily living activities can be executed safely and skillfully. An understanding of biomechanical concepts and their applications is an important part of the cognitive foundation for a physically educated person. Understanding why human movement mechanics differ from person to person and from performance to performance can enhance the experience of acquiring or maintaining a physically active lifestyle and facilitate lifelong learning.

References

Brand, R. A. (1979). Joint lubrication. In J. A. Albright & R. A. Brand (Eds.), *The scientific basis of orthopedics.* New York: Appleton-Century-Crofts.

Buchanan, A. M., Martin, E., Childress, R., Howard, C., Williams, L., Bedsole, B., & Ferry, M. (2002). Integrating elementary physical and science: A cooperative problem-solving approach. *Journal of Physical Education, Recreation Dance*, *73*(2), 31-36.

Chaffin, D. B., & Andersson, G. B. J. (1991). Occupational biomechanics (2nd ed.). New York: John Wiley & Sons.

Drury, C. G. et al. (1989). Symmetric and asymmetric manual materials handling. Part 2: Biomechanics. *Ergonomics, 32,* 565-583.

Hall, S. J. (1985). Effect of attempted lifting speed on forces and torque exerted on the lumbar spine. *Medicine and Science in Sports and Exercise, 17,* 440-444.

Hay, J. G. (1986). The biomechanics of the long jump. *Exercise and Sport Science Reviews, 14,* 401–446.

Liemohn, W. (1993). Exercise considerations for the back. In J. L. Durstein, A. C. King, P. L. Painter, J. L. Roitman, L. D. Zwiren, & W. L. Kenney (Eds.). ACSM's resource manual for guidelines for exercise testing and prescription (2nd ed.), pp. 48-58.

McGill, S. M. (1992). A myoelectrically based dynamic three-dimensional model to predict loads on lumbar spine tissues during lateral bending. *Journal of Biomechanics, 25,* 395-414.

McGill, S. M., & Norman, R. W. (1993). Low back biomechanics in industry: The prevention of injury through safer lifting. In M. D. Grabiner (Ed.), *Current issues in biomechanics.* Champaign, IL: Human Kinetics.

Mital, A., & Kromodihardjo, S. (1986). Kinetic analysis of manual lifting activities: Part II. Biomechanical analysis of task variables. *International Journal of Industrial Ergonomics, 1,* 91–97.

National Association for Sport and Physical Education. (1995). *Moving into the future: National physical education standards. A guide to content and assessment.* Reston, VA: Author.

Ross, M., Hall, S. J., Breit, N., & Britten, S. (1993). Effect of a lumbar support device on muscle activity during abdominal exercise. *Journal of Strength and Conditioning Research, 7*(4), 219-223.

Schleihauf, R. E. (1979). A hydrodynamic analysis of swimming propulsion. In J. Terauds & E. Bedingfield (Eds.), *Swimming III.* Baltimore: University Park.

Resources

Grabiner, M. D. (Ed.). (1993). *Current issues in biomechanics.* Champaign, IL: Human Kinetics.

Hall, S. J. (2000). *Basic biomechanics (4th ed.).* St. Louis: WCB/McGraw-Hill.

Hay, J. G. (1993). *The biomechanics of sports techniques (4th ed.).* Englewood Cliffs, NJ: Prentice Hall.

Hudson, J. L. (1995, May-June). Core concepts of kinesiology. *Journal of Physical Education, Recreation Dance,* pp. 54-60.

Humphries, C. (2002). Elementary physical education and the National Standards. *Journal of Physical Education, Recreation, and Dance, 73*(5), 24-25.

Schrier, E. W., & Allman, W. F. (Eds.). (1984). *Newton at the bat.* New York: Macmillan/Charles Scribner's Sons.

Spindt, G.B., Monti, W.H., & Hennessy, B. (1991). *Moving for life.* Dubuque, IA: Kendall/Hunt.

_____. 2002a. *Moving as a team.* Dubuque, IA: Kendall/Hunt.

_____. 2002b. *Moving as a team physical education portfolio.* Dubuque, IA: Kendall/Hunt.

_____. 2002c. *Moving with confidence.* Dubuque, IA: Kendall/Hunt.

_____. 2002d. *Moving with confidence physical education portfolio.* Dubuque, IA: Kendall/Hunt.

_____. 2002e. *Moving with skill.* Dubuque, IA: Kendall/Hunt.

_____. 2002f. *Moving with skill physical education portfolio.* Dubuque, IA: Kendall/Hunt.

Multimedia Resources

ESPN Sport Figures. Video series from ESPN, http://www.espn.com

Biomechanics Made Easy. Software from Bonnie's Fitware, Inc. http://www.pesoftware.com

Chapter **5**

Exercise Physiology

Judith B. Alter

H*ow often should I exercise? What are the specific benefits of exercise? How can I get stronger? Why do I need to stretch my muscles? Experts in the field of study known as exercise physiology are working to answer these questions. This chapter focuses on how concepts in exercise physiology relate to developing and sustaining adequate fitness levels. These important concepts help provide the cognitive foundation for a physically educated person. An understanding of these concepts can enhance the experience of acquiring or maintaining a physically active lifestyle.*

What Is Exercise Physiology?

Exercise physiology is the study of how the bodily systems of human beings react and function during exercise and rest. Exercise physiology, a subdiscipline of physiology, incorporates information from other disciplines such as chemistry, physics, anatomy, and kinesiology. Exercise physiologists combine what they learn from looking under the microscope in their laboratories (*in vitro*) with actual experiences of thousands of people they have studied (*in vivo*). Information from exercise physiology includes the structure and chemical activity of human cells, tissues, systems, and—most importantly—how the components in these systems interact in the human body during exercise.

Why Is Exercise Physiology Important?

Giving students knowledge about exercise physiology and fitness provides them with the tools they need for a lifetime of physical activity and health. For many years, exercise physiologists have correlated regular physical activity with health, well-

Aerobic:
Exercise that requires oxygen to produce energy.

being, and longevity. In the 1996 report, *Physical Activity and Health,* the Surgeon General emphasized the vital importance of physical activity. In that report he decried the fact that "Nearly half of American youth 12-21 years of age are not vigorously active on a regular basis. Moreover, physical activity declines dramatically during adolescence" (p. 10).

Physical educators have watched this decline for several decades. This report verifies the necessity for implementing regular physical fitness programs in schools, teaching exercise physiology/ fitness concepts in grades K-12 (Sallis, 1994), and convincing youths to participate in these life-enhancing activities.

Power:
Allows muscles to hold, lift, and control weight rapidly.

Knowledge about how the cells and tissues of the moving body work enables people to prepare correctly for any physical exercise: to warm-up properly, to identify possible problems, and to find solutions when problems arise. These solutions range from physical ones such as undertaking an aerobic training program to help overcome excessive fatigue to nutritional ones such as eating more complex carbohydrates and less sugar to diminish excess weight gain. This kind of knowledge also has helped athletes improve their performance and set new records.

Cardio:
Heart.

Linking Exercise Physiology to The National Standards

Exercise physiology concepts/principles can stand by themselves as content for physical education. In fact, they often do at the high school level in states that require a physical fitness course. Standards 3 (Exhibits a physically active lifestyle) and 4 (Achieves and maintains a health-enhancing level of physical fitness) specifically target exercise physiology concepts. These two standards aim at countering the increasingly inactive lifestyle of many Americans. The standards align with the benefits, information, and national guidelines that experts have advocated

Respiratory:
Function of the lungs in breathing.

for many years, including the recognition that regular physical activity prolongs life, reduces stress, diminishes the threat of serious and even life-threatening diseases such as cardiovascular disease, colon cancer, noninsulin-dependent diabetes, mellitus, osteoarthritis, osteoporosis, and diseases related to obesity (USDHHS, 1996).

Selected Exercise Physiology Themes

Strength:
The ability of a muscle or group of muscles to exert force against a resistance.

Physical education teachers must understand and apply the information contained in the textbooks on exercise physiology and fitness. While physically educated individuals do not need the same depth of understanding, it is important for students to understand the main components of health-related fitness (cardiorespiratory capacity, muscular endurance, muscular strength, muscular flexibility, and body composition) and learn information about anatomical structures and physiological functions. These ideas are organized around four major themes:

1. What factors contribute to an appropriate cardiorespiratory fitness program?
2. How does the structure and function of human anatomy contribute to and restrict the development of lifetime fitness?
3. What characterizes a safe and appropriate muscular strengthening and stretching program?
4. How do body composition and nutrition interrelate to develop and maintain lifetime fitness?

The next section contains brief explanations of each of these themes. Critical student concepts that relate to each theme follow in a K-12 format.

What Factors Contribute to an Appropriate Cardiorespiratory Fitness Program?

Most people with access to contemporary media know something about how they can develop and maintain cardiorespiratory health. "Cardio" means heart and "respiration" describes the function of the lungs in breathing. When people build and maintain the fitness capacity of their heart and lungs, they gain

Sit in a chair with your back firmly supported. With both legs bent at right angles, place your feet on floor. Slowly, to the count of eight, straighten, (extend) one leg so the lower leg is now parallel to the floor. Do not lock your knee. Now slowly, to a count of eight, lower your lower leg (flexing it) and return it to the beginning position. Repeat this sequence four to eight times or until your thigh muscle group on the front of your thigh, the quadriceps, feels tired. Then, carefully, do the exercise one more time for the overload effect. Repeat this sequence using the other leg. After a two-minute rest, repeat this sequence.

Example 1

Elementary School Example: Grade 2
Concept/Principle: Vigorous activities that make the heart beat faster also make the heart stronger.

From a group discussion, teachers can compile a list of daily physical activities in which their students participate. They can label them as easy, moderate, and vigorous. Young students can keep a list of daily activities and the time they spend during different periods of their day—physical activity, school activity, recreational activity, and sleep—for several days. This record will show them how they use their time and how much time they spend engaged in vigorous physical activity. Then, teachers can challenge students to increase their daily vigorous activity and observe any changes they experience after this increase. For example, during physical education periods for several weeks, students can practice the one-minute run. After practicing the one-minute run each day, they can correlate their increased distance with their training heart rate to see and experience how working their hearts faster gives them greater capacity than before.

Example 2

High School Example: Grade 10
Concept/Principle: Maintaining and benefiting from a regular physical fitness program requires preparation, dedication, and updated information.

When students are in middle school and high school, they may consider devoting a large portion of their time to a challenging physical activity or to a fitness program. As part of their personal preparation to undertake this activity and understand what time, energy, and social sacrifices this dedication may require, young people can interview a friend who jogs or bicycles for fitness, or who participates regularly in dance, ice skating, competitive gymnastics, or on a varsity sports team, to learn about his or her sacrifices and rewards. In the interview, students can ask about what drives, inspires, or discourages the person; from where he or she learns the latest and best information about it; and how he or she handles homework and friends. Students can present reports of their interviews in class and compare their findings.

Example 3

High School Example: Grade 12
Concept/Principle: Regular aerobic activity releases endorphins that allow people to enjoy and sustain commitment to their fitness programs.

Have students commit themselves to a regular fitness program—four to five days a week for three months. As part of the program, have them keep a log of their moods and energy levels before and after their regular workout for the entire period. At the end of each month, and at the end of the three months, have the students analyze their log to find patterns in their endurance level, moods, and overall sense of well-being.

endurance–the ability to continue a vigorous activity, like running, for longer and longer periods of time without undue fatigue. Experts call this kind of endurance "cardiovascular" or "aerobic" fitness. The term "cardiorespiratory" emphasizes the cooperation between the heart and lungs, the term "cardiovascular" emphasizes the heart function, and "aerobic" describes the kind of physical activity that builds cardiorespiratory, or cardiovascular fitness.

The heart and lungs work together to supply oxygen-rich blood to the muscles and tissues of the internal organs in the body. Blood flows through the right half of the heart by means of the pulmonary arteries and into the lungs, where it receives fresh oxygen. The oxygen-rich blood exits the pulmonary veins into the left half of the heart, which pumps it throughout the rest of the body by means of the systemic arteries. The oxygen-poor blood flows back to the heart through the systemic veins.

Benefits of Aerobic Exercise
Dr. Kenneth Cooper and members of his fitness institute have discovered important facts about the value of fitness. For instance, people in automobile accidents often suffer heart attacks caused by that sudden shock to their system. In this extremely stressful circumstance, the autonomic "fight or flight" emergency reaction of the body floods the bloodstream with adrenaline. A well-conditioned heart can circulate this emergency chemical quickly, and the high level of adrenaline can help the body handle the trauma (Cooper Institute 1994). When a heart is in poor condition and unable to circulate blood rapidly enough, this large amount of adrenaline can cause a heart attack (Cooper, 1982). Researchers have also discovered that when people undertake and maintain a regular aerobic training program, they can more readily recover from several hypokinetic diseases such as adult onset diabetes, asthma, high blood pressure, obesity, and even nervous tension.

People gain an added mood-altering benefit from engaging in regular aerobic programs: They feel better psychologically after the workout than when they begin it. Increased aerobic activity releases neurotransmitters called endorphins. Endorphins act like tranquilizers that the brain releases naturally, the same way it does when people smile and give and receive hugs.

Thus, proponents of aerobic activity recommended it as a major mechanism to reduce stress.

Many factors act as barriers to establishing and maintaining a regular exercise regimen. Although the mechanical and technological conveniences available in contemporary society make life easier than in the past they also require less bodily and muscular exertion. Students ride in cars or on buses instead of walking or bicycling to school and to after-school activities. They engage in many passive or low-energy recreational activities, such as watching television and playing computer games. They live in communities designed more for cars than for people. They find fewer sidewalks, playgrounds, and empty lots in which to play, skate, hike, and even walk than in the past. Communities often spend public funds on safety and policing rather than on recreational facilities, hiking trails, and bike paths. Private fitness centers charge high membership fees that many students cannot afford to pay, or they work after school to support themselves, their families, or their car expenses. Stories about sports heroes in the media emphasize exceptional achievements rather than the regular, repetitious, and fitness-centered work those achievements require.

Intensity: How hard a person exercises (i.e., overload for strength; speed of aerobic activity).

Warm-up

Before engaging in any exercise—aerobic, strength training, or to increase muscle stretch—people need to warm up. Warm-up has two purposes. It prepares the muscles (the muscular/skeletal system) and the heart and lungs (the cardiorespiratory system) for the activity itself. Although experts in different physical activities debate how to warm up, all agree that warm-up must raise the body's core temperature above its "resting state." They define resting state as a person's temperature when he or she first wakes up from a night of sleep.

Physical education classes only last 30-50 minutes, so teachers must use a short, three-to-five-minute aerobic warm-up plus basic stretches tailored for the activity of the day. In addition, they must encourage students to begin their activity slowly, and gradually work up to the required speed and intensity. Whenever possible, however, teachers should tell students that the appropriate length of a warm-up of light aerobic activity lasts five to 10 minutes, and is followed by the stretching of all muscles to be used in the activity.

Cool-Down

A cool-down, consisting of five to 10 minutes of light to moderate activity, is as beneficial as the warm-up, because it maintains blood pressure, helps enhance venous return, and prevents it from pooling in the muscles. Most people end their activity with a moderate to slow jog around the field or gym. As part of their cool-down, most students need to get into the habit of stretching the major muscle groups that they just used. The cool down period is actually the best time to stretch the muscles.

Anatomists describe muscle, tendon, and ligament tissue as plastic. When warm, these tissues become pliable. When they cool down, they become firm. A few extra minutes of stretching will help prevent students' muscles from feeling stiff later, and those muscles may feel less tight the next time they stretch because they will have cooled in their lengthened state.

Aerobic Activity

Jogging has received much publicity since the early 1970s, when Dr. Kenneth Cooper, an Air Force physician, publicized the worrisome facts about the large numbers of 18-year-old recruits in the armed services who had inadequate endurance. These recruits could not run for long distances or engage in heavy training exercises. Because their diets included high quantities of saturated fat, their arteries resembled those of much older adults. Dr. Cooper devised an effective training regime that has become known as aerobic exercise.

Aerobics literally means, "utilizing oxygen." It applies to exercise that introduces sufficient oxygen into the body—processed by the lungs and pumped by the heart—to develop and then maintain an identified level of endurance. Jogging at a steady,

Figure 1

Common Forms of Aerobic Exercise

• Walking	• Aerobic dancing
• Running	• Jumping rope
• Jogging	• Roller or ice skating
• Bicycling	• Stair climbing
• Rowing	• Swimming
• Cross-country skiing	

Source: Cooper, K. H. (1982).

Anaerobic:
High intensity, short duration activities that do not utilize oxygen for energy.

comfortable, yet challenging pace for 20 to 30 minutes three to five times a week in the target heart rate zone, or engaging in other activities (see Figure 1) such as walking, bicycling, swimming, tennis, or handball will increase and then maintain aerobic fitness.

Exercise physiologists label some forms of exercise anaerobic, or literally "without oxygen." The high intensity of these activities limits oxygen delivery. People engage in anaerobic exercise for short periods of time up, to two minutes in duration (Hoeger & Hoeger, 1992). This kind of exercise puts more stress on the heart and lungs than aerobic exercise does. Though anaerobic activities such as a 100 meter dash build the body's capacity for speed, they do not exercise the heart and lungs in the way that aerobic exercises do. Anaerobic exercises, such as strength training, do, however, improve muscle strength that, in turn, enables people to increase and maintain their cardiorespiratory capacity.

Frequency:
How often a person exercises (sessions per week).

Cardiorespiratory Training

To gain and maintain fitness, exercisers must apply the principles of overload, individual differences, specificity, progression, and regularity. The acronym FITT (frequency, intensity, time [duration], and type [mode]), applied to each area of health-related fitness, synthesizes these directions into exercise principles for lifetime fitness (see Figure 2).

Individual Differences:
Adapting a program to fit an individual's starting and developmental levels.

Cooper realized that the heart and lungs, although organs, work like muscles. The more they contract and release in exercise, the better their shape. Regular exercise makes the heart and lungs work hard; therefore, it conditions them to work well all the time and respond to emergencies without being overtaxed. Aerobic activity achieves this goal by raising the heart rate to the training level appropriate for the age group and maintaining it at that level or better. As children's bodies grow and mature, their physical capabilities also grow and mature. Experts do not offer specific guidelines for children until the age of 10, although they recommend a minimum of 10 to 15 minutes a day of vigorous activity for all children. For adults, they recommend engaging in some kind of aerobic activity three to five days a week.

Mode:
Different kinds of exercise for training, such as running, walking, bicycling.

Measuring heart rate during exercise helps to determine aerobic fitness and ensure that the exerciser reaches a level high enough to challenge the heart and lungs. To determine the appropriate level, take the nonexercise pulse rate (resting heart rate - RHR) preferably at the wrist by counting the number of beats in 10 seconds and then multiplying that number by six. Do not take the pulse at the carotid artery of the neck, because if pressed too hard, it can cause dizziness and even fainting. Then, determine the maximum heart rate (MHR) by subtracting age from the number 220 (e.g., for a 20-year-old it would be 220-20=200).

Overload:
The load or amount of resistance for each exercise, providing a greater stress, or load, on the muscle group than it usually handles to increase fitness.

After determining the resting heart rate and maximum heart rate, calculate the target (or training) heart rate zone. Experts use two formulas. The first calculates the upper end of the zone, and the second calculates the lower end of the zone (AAHPERD, 1999c).

Progression:
The gradual increase in either frequency, intensity, or time or a combination of all three.

- Formula 1: $((MHR - RHR)*60)+RHR$
- Formula 2: $((MHR-RHR)*.75)+RHR$

Figure 2

Training Principles Applied to Aerobic Fitness, Based on Fitness Goals

	Base health-related fitness	Intermediate health-related fitness	Athletic performance fitness
Frequency	3 times per week	3–5 times per week	5–6 times per week
Intensity	50–60% maxHR	60–75% maxHR	65–90% maxHR
Time	30 min total, accumulated*	40–60 min total, accumulated*	60–120 min total, accumulated*
Type	Walking, jogging, dancing, games, and activities that require minimal equipment demands**	Jogging, running, fitness-based games and activities, intramural and local league sports***	Training programs, running, aerobics, interscholastic, and community sports programs
Overload	Not necessary to bring child to overload during base level.	Be creative with activity to increase tempo or decrease rest period; 1–3 times per week.	Program design should stress variable intensities and durations to bring student into overload; 2–3 times per week.
Progression and specificity	Let student "get the idea" of movement. Progression is minimal.	Introduce program design and incorporate variation.	Specific sets, repetitions, and exercises to meet desired outcomes

*Activity can be accumulated throughout the day in segments of at least 10 minutes each (for students in grades three and above).
**Refer to *Physical Best Activity Guide — Elementary Level.*
***Refer to *Physical Best Activity Guide — Elementary Level* and *Physical Best Activity Guide — Secondary Level.*

Reprinted by permission, from AAPHERD (1999). Physical educaiton for lifelong fitness, the physical best teacher's guide. (Champaign, IL, Human Kinetics).

Regularity:
Engaging in activity on a routine schedule.

This recommended method for calculating target heart rate zones applies to adult populations. Experts recommend lowering the predicted maximum heart rate for youth to a range of 195-200 beats per minute (Buck, 2002; Rowland, 1992). In *Teaching Strategies for Improving Youth Fitness*, Corbin and Pangrazi (1994) provide the following guidelines for elementary school children and beginners:

- If the resting heart rate (RHR) is 60 or less, then the training heart rate (THR) should be 150.
- If RHR is 60-64, then THR should be 151,
- If RHR is 65-69, then THR should be 153,
- If RHR is 70-74, then THR should be 155,
- If RHR is 75-79, then THR should be 157,
- If RHR is 80-84, then THR should be 159,
- If RHR is 85-89, then THR should be 161,
- If RHR is 90+, then THR should be 163.

During aerobic activity, exercisers should take their pulse again to determine if they are achieving their target heart rate zone. To facilitate the monitoring of heart rate, exercisers might use a rate heart monitor. The recommended type uses a wireless transmitter attached to a chest strap (Mohnsen, 2001).

Other Kinds of Physical Activity

Specificity:
The type of exercise that increases fitness in each of the five specific areas (cardiorespiratory endurance, muscular strength, muscular endurance, muscular flexibility, and body composition).

As discussed in the previous section, one way to engage in aerobic exercise is to do an exercise continuously for a set amount of time, such as 15 to 20 minutes a session while in the target heart rate zone. Another way is to interrupt the time by walking, then jogging, and then running fast (interval training). This form of aerobic exercise intersperses set periods of activity with set intervals of rest. Continuous aerobic activity demands steady work by the heart and lungs, whereas interval training requires the heart and lungs to adapt rapidly to the change of exercise intensity, conditioning the body to train harder and faster. This adaptability enables people in good condition to maintain and increase their training level. Circuit training, a third type of aerobic activity, has participants move through a series of different kinds of anaerobic and aerobic exercises, increasing fitness and providing variety.

Any exercise is better than no exercise. The Surgeon General recommends at least "30 minutes or more of moderate intensity physical activity on all or most days of the week" (USDHHS, 1996, p.11). Researchers have found that when people just walk for a half hour during their lunchtime, they increase their endurance and metabolism and may even reduce their body fat.

Time: The duration of the exercise.

In the school setting, elementary aged students daily need a wide variety of age- and developmentally-appropriate physical activities, with at least 10 to 15 minutes of it being moderate to vigorous. The variety enables students to succeed no matter what their skill level, and vigorous activity builds basic endurance. Elementary aged students should accumulate 30 to 60 minutes of activity during each week. For students 13 years and older, their daily moderate to vigorous activity should last 20 minutes or more, with their total daily tally going beyond an hour, when possible (Corbin & Pangrazi, 1998).

Many young people, as well as adults, do not follow the cardiorespiratory guidelines. The Surgeon General (USDHHS, 1996), along with Moorhouse and Gross in *Total Fitness in 30 Minutes a Week* (1975), suggest several easy ways for people to increase their endurance if they have too little time to schedule regular aerobic activity:

Type: Refers to the specific physical activity chosen to improve a component of health-related fitness.

- Walk or bicycle to work or school.
- Climb the stairs instead of taking an elevator or escalator.
- Jog or walk quickly down the halls or stairs of buildings when they are not too crowded.
- Park the car a block from the destination and walk.

These minor lifestyle changes increase muscle use, challenge the lungs and heart to do a little more work than usual, and help people improve the condition of their bodies. The bottom line: Do it!

Over Exercising

Can aerobic exercisers get too much of a good thing? Moderation is the key when engaging in aerobic exercise. The acute injuries that result from too much exercise range from muscle, ligament, and tendon sprains and strains to less severe injuries

Joint: Where two bones meet.

such as bruises (Watkins & Peabody, 1986). Physicians have identified serious chronic injuries where young athletes have damaged the articular cartilage and the epiphyseal and apophyseal growth plates in their leg joints (Watkins & Peabody, 1996). If individuals over exercise and limit their food intake, they may also exhibit other kinds of symptoms such as apathy, sleeplessness, increased resting heart rate, and a depressed immune system. (See the section on Body Composition that appears later in this chapter.)

Concepts/Principles

Kindergarten: *Moderate physical activity contributes to a healthy body.* All parts of the body require activity to develop and mature because life's activities depend on movement. Fitness and strength, which result from moderate physical activity, help create and maintain a healthy body. Neurophysiologists now understand how gross motor physical activity helps develop children's capacity to learn school subjects, most of which use fine motor skills.

Kindergarten: *Moderate physical exercise makes the heart beat faster and the lungs work harder.* Different intensities of exercise provide immediate information about the cooperation and operation of the heart and lungs. Students can identify how their heart beats change and monitor the way their lungs work during and after they play vigorous games.

Second Grade: *Cardiorespiratory endurance; muscular strength, endurance, and flexibility; and body composition are the major components of health-related fitness.* Health-related fitness combines how the body uses air, food, and muscles in different kinds of activities. Food fuels the body and helps determine body composition; strong and adequately stretched muscles enable the body to move freely; and many different vigorous activities develop cardiorespiratory endurance where these health-related components coordinate.

Second Grade: *Vigorous activities that make the heart beat faster also make the heart stronger.* Students can observe how the capacity of their hearts increases—working fast for longer and longer periods of time—when they engage in vigorous activities during the course of a school year. They see that vigorous activities become easier than when they started doing them. These experiences give them evidence of their hearts' increased strength.

Fourth Grade: *Aerobic exercise provides people with many personal benefits—both physical and mental.* Not only can each individual engage in a variety of aerobic activities, but he or she can also identify and enjoy their many benefits. The physical ones range from improved cardiorespiratory fitness, diminished fatigue, and lower excess fat. The mental ones include lowered stress and tension levels, knowledge of improved endurance, and pleasure gained from the endorphin release.

Fourth Grade: *Aerobic activity should be performed for at least 10 to 15 minutes, three times per week.* Elementary school students should be physically active on a daily basis. Specifically, they should engage in aerobic activity for 10 to 15 minutes, three times per week.

Sixth Grade: *Personal preferences, skills, and talents influence students' choices, successes, and pleasure when engaging in vigorous physical activity.* Gardner's theory of multiple intelligences helps students and teachers understand why students prefer different vigorous physical activities. Some enjoy solo activities, while others prefer group ones. Some prefer activities that utilize a wide variety of skills and strategies (such as basketball or soccer), while some prefer to perfect one skill with more subtle strategies (such as cross country running or swimming). Some like quiet activities and others prefer loud ones. Some prefer visually simple activities, and others enjoy complex ones. Early exposure and encouragement also influence choices, as do physical maturity and changing interests.

Sixth Grade: *The principles of a cardiorespiratory fitness program include frequency, intensity, time, and type (FITT).* The FITT principles provide guidelines rather than rigid rules. Students must overcome the inertia of inactivity before they begin to vary how often, how hard, how long, and what kind of aerobic activity they engage in. Since variety makes most activities enjoyable, these FITT principles become logical and natural to follow.

Eighth Grade: *Regular vigorous physical activity and proper nutrition contribute to physical and mental health.* Proper nutrition, which means eating a wide variety of many kinds of nonprocessed foods and not overeating foods with empty or excess calories, fuels and determines the level of physical and mental well-being. Each system of the body requires nutrients from this wide variety of food. Then, the body systems work optimally in vigorous activity with the resultant mental payoff of pleasure, success, and well-being.

Eighth Grade: *The FITT guidelines for a cardiorespiratory fitness program include exercising a minimum of 20 to 30 minutes, three days per week, to a maximum of 50 to 60 minutes every other day, within one's target heart rate range.* At the end of middle school, students reach the level of physical and mental development where they gain the capacity for increased aerobic activity. They can safely increase the time and frequency of their aerobic programs and observe the benefits in this process. Varying the activities can influence the students' lifetime commitment to aerobic activity.

Tenth Grade: *Physical, emotional, and social growth influence individual needs and results of a regular physical fitness program.* As students mature, they can understand the benefits of becoming fit and maintaining that level of fitness. Personal appearance and social acceptance become an ever increasing part of motivation, for better or worse. Family and academic pressures also affect commitment to a fitness program. Emphasizing how the health benefits of fitness influence the other aspects of students' lives may help students remain committed to this process of lifelong self-care.

Tenth Grade: *Maintaining and benefiting from a regular physical fitness program requires preparation, dedication, and updated information.* An ongoing fitness program challenges exercisers to make a time commitment. Preparation requires appropriate clothing and shoes, proper stretching, and going to a safe location. Finally, exercisers should keep abreast of new developments in the field, especially in relation to the safety and efficacy of various protocols.

Twelfth Grade: *Family, school, and community attitudes toward vigorous physical activity influence an individual's commitment to that fitness program.* Since the family stimulates and nurtures individuals' value systems, the cultural, social, and physical context of the family plays a large part in how individuals integrate what they learn in school. The larger community context of a school also creates incentives or barriers to individuals' attitudes toward and affinity for undertaking and maintaining a fitness program. Families generate financial, nutritional, and recreational values from present and past geographic and ancestral communities. A complex web of factors influences individuals' attitudes toward undertaking and maintaining fitness programs.

Twelfth Grade: *Regular aerobic activity releases endorphins that allow people to enjoy and sustain commitment to their fitness programs.* Once people experience the internal sense of pleasure and well-being that endorphins trigger from engaging in fitness activities, they want to repeat that experience. Since it provides a kind of bonus to the physical health benefits, teachers can emphasize the safety of this stimulus of pleasure compared to the harmful effects of drugs and alcohol. When exercisers feel how a fitness workout can diminish sadness or depression, they can choose this form of "therapy" regularly.

How Does the Structure and Function of Human Anatomy Contribute to and Restrict the Development of Lifetime Fitness?

A brief anatomical overview of the human body will provide the context for understanding the importance of muscle strengthening and stretching. Approximately 206 bones make up the human skeleton. Ligaments hold most of these bones together. Tendons attach most muscles to bones, and muscles move the bones at their joints. Bones, ligaments, tendons, and muscles function interdependently; they make up a system that enables the entire body or separate parts to move. Metabolized

Ligaments:
Tissues that hold bones together.

food provides the energy for the body's movements. The heart pumps blood and circulates oxygen, which is processed by the lungs, throughout the system. The brain and the autonomic nervous system direct the entire process. All these processes working together enable the body to move.

Skeletal System

Bones, like steel girders in a building, serve as the framework of the body. Bones not only support the body, but some—such as the skull for the brain or the rib cage for the heart, lungs, and other internal organs—provide protection. The marrow of bones, like a central factory, produces red blood cells.

The skeleton, which is made up of bones bound together by ligaments, cannot stand by itself (see Figure 3). Muscles both move the body and enable the body to stand upright by means of their structure, size, function, and location. This explains why most of the largest and strongest muscles of the body—except for the quadriceps at the front of the thigh—are located in the back of the lower half of the skeleton. These include the gluteal muscles (gluteus maximus, medius, and minimus) at the back of the pelvis, the hamstrings (biceps femoris, semitendinosus, and semimembranosus) at the back of the thigh bone or the femur, and the calf muscles (gastrocnemius and soleus) at the back of the lower leg bones (the tibia and fibula) (Lutgens & Wells, 1982).

Joints

The places where different bones meet are called articulations, or joints. Their names describe their designs. Fibrous joints hold together immovable joints (e.g., where the bones of the

Tendons:
Tissues that attach muscles to bones.

Example 4

Elementary School Example: Grade 4

Concept/Principle: People inherit their ligament, tendon, and bone structure.

Have students measure their joints—shoulder, elbow, hip, knee, ankle—and their Achilles tendon to identify if they have normal, tight, or lax ligaments and tendons. Then, have them measure their parents' and their siblings' joints and tendons and compare their structures to other members of their family. If parents have accurate records or memories of their height at the same age as the student they can make a height comparison as well.

Figure 3

Skeletal System

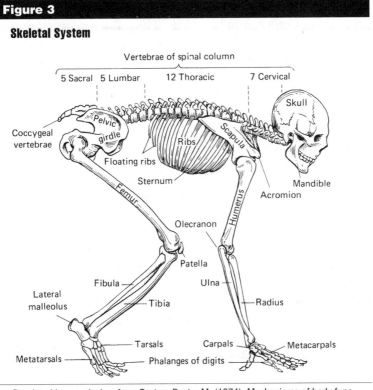

Vertebrae of spinal column

5 Sacral 5 Lumbar 12 Thoracic 7 Cervical

Skull

Coccygeal
vertebrae

Pelvic
girdle

Ribs

Scapula

Floating ribs

Sternum

Femur

Mandible
Acromion

Humerus

Olecranon

Patella

Fibula

Ulna

Lateral
malleolus

Tibia

Radius

Tarsals

Carpals

Metacarpals

Metatarsals

Phalanges of digits

Reprinted by permission, from Easton, Dexter M. (1974). Mechanisms of body function. (Upper Saddle River, NJ, Prentice-Hall, Inc.)

skull meet). Cartilaginous joints hold together slightly movable bones, such as those in between the spinal vertebrae. Synovial joints, which hold together most of the other bones of the body, connect bones that move freely (the knee, elbow, hip, and shoulder, for example). A capsule encases this type of joint. A synovial membrane lines the capsule and secretes fluid to lubricate the joint. A thin layer of articular cartilage covers the bony surfaces of these joints to lessen the friction and provide a weight-bearing cushion. Many of these joints contain little sacs lined with synovial membrane and filled with fluid, called bursa, that reduce friction between moving structures such as tendon and bone or muscle and bone. They swell when injured and, in that state, serve a secondary function to limit the mobility of the injured tissues.

Ligaments act like hinges in synovial joints, where they connect free-moving bones. The names of these synovial joints describe their function or appearance (see Figure 4). Nonaxial joints do not move around an axis. They simply meet or, in the case of vertebral joints, glide. Uniaxial joints either move in one axis like the hinge joint at the elbow, or pivot like the axis and atlas joint at the top of the neck, just below where the skull and spine join. Biaxial joints allow movement in two planes (e.g., the radio-carpal joint at wrist and the saddle joint of the thumb). Triaxial joints allow movement in three planes. They facilitate the widest range of movement. They include the shoulder and hip joints, which are known as ball and socket joints.

The similar range of movement in many of these joints (see Figure 5) makes understanding them fairly simple. Feet and hands have similar joint structures because they move and can function in similar ways, except that the big toe cannot move as freely as the thumb. Elbow and knee hinge joints only bend and straighten, flex and extend, in the same limited way. The entire arm and leg can rotate in an almost complete circle because of the ball and socket joints at the hip and shoulder. The

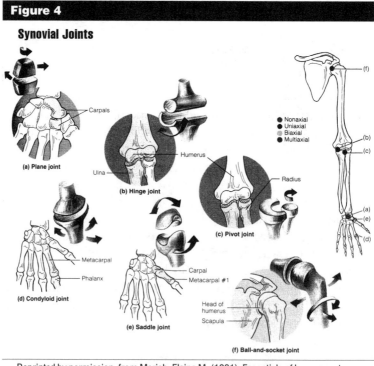

Figure 4

Synovial Joints

(a) Plane joint
Carpals

(b) Hinge joint
Humerus
Ulna

(c) Pivot joint
Radius

Nonaxial
Uniaxial
Biaxial
Multiaxial

(f)
(b)
(c)
(a)
(e)
(d)

(d) Condyloid joint
Metacarpal
Phalanx

(e) Saddle joint
Carpal
Metacarpal #1

(f) Ball-and-socket joint
Head of humerus
Scapula

Reprinted by permission, from Marieb, Elaine M. (1991). Essentials of human anatomy and physiology. (The Benjamin Cummins Publishing Co., Inc.)

Range of Motion

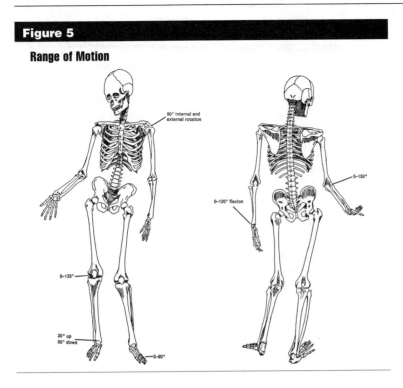

trunk, centered by the spine, moves forward and back, side to side, and rotates around its vertical axis, much like the head.

Muscles

The muscles work in groups. They move the bones in the directions allowed for by the design of the joints. Like the names of joints, the names of muscles often describe their function and the location on the bone to which they attach. Some of the muscles on the upper and lower areas of the body have similar names because they attach to and move limbs that have similar functions (see Figure 6).

In addition to their similar names and functions, all muscles act in one way: They contract (see Figure 7). To relax, extend, or repeat a movement, the muscles on the opposite side of the limb or body part, must contract and thereby cause the other set of muscles to extend. An example will help clarify this concept.

Bend your head forward and down to look at your waist. The muscles in the front of your neck contract while they also pull on the muscles in back of your neck to lower your head into position. To return your head to its upright position, the muscles on the back of your neck contract. If you look up at the ceiling, those same muscles must contract even further, pulling the muscles on the front of your neck into a stretched position. (When doing this head movement, do not drop your head back passively, but perform the action with your muscles.)

Neurons

In the above example, as with all movements, the body parts respond to the many commands they receive from the brain. The chemical reactions of potassium and sodium in cells called neurons enable the brain to give and receive signals to and from the vital internal organs and muscles. Calcium facilitates these signal transmissions. Neurons typically have dendrites, which receive the messages, called nerve impulses; cell bodies that contain all the standard parts of a cell, which can also receive messages; and axons, which conduct nerve impulses.

Figure 6

Major muscles

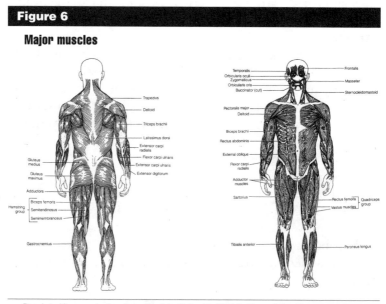

Reprinted by permission, from Marieb, Elaine M. (1991). Essentials of human anatomy and physiology. (The Benjamin Cummins Publishing Co., Inc.)

Figure 7

Muscle contraction

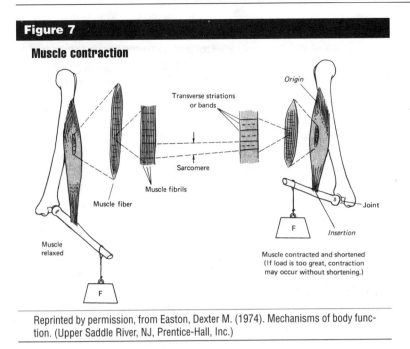

Reprinted by permission, from Easton, Dexter M. (1974). Mechanisms of body function. (Upper Saddle River, NJ, Prentice-Hall, Inc.)

Three kinds of nerves enable all the body's systems to function: sensory neurons communicate to the sense receptors; somatic motor neurons transmit messages to the skeletal muscles, skin, and fascia; and autonomic motor neurons connect to the organs. These neurons function in three modes: conducting messages from the periphery of the body to the central nervous system (afferent neurons); conducting messages from the central nervous system to the periphery of the body (efferent neurons); and a combination of these, which form a network of interconnecting neurons (interneurons). Interneurons enable the transfer of efferent and afferent messages. Nerves send all the movement messages of the body to and from the brain, from the largest jump to the smallest fleeting thought.

Concepts/Principles

Kindergarten: *Every activity in life requires movement.* Small movements such as the blink of an eye or a muscle twitch, and large ones such as a big jump or a "giant" step, require muscles controlled by the brain to create those actions. The lack of movement in the lungs and heart signal that life has stopped. Human infants share with other mammals some instinctive movements at birth that help them survive. But human beings learn most of their movement behaviors and live their lives with movement. Even while sleeping, many internal movements continue: lungs inhale and exhale, the heart beats, peristalsis of digestion continues.

Second Grade: *A coordinated system of bones, joints, and muscles moves the body.* Muscles move bones at their joints. Once the brain has initiated the movement, all human activity happens this way. Bones, joints with their ligaments, and muscles with their tendons carry out separate but related functions. They work as a unit; they cannot work separately.

Fourth Grade: *People inherit their ligament, tendon, and bone structure.* Like eye and hair color, people inherit the structure of their bodies. They possess loose or tight ligaments, flexible or tight tendons, and large, medium, or small bones. Each individual's structure comes from his or her mother's and father's families; thus, body structures vary widely.

Sixth Grade: *Because muscles only contract, they are typically found in functional pairs.* Muscles, which work in groups, move bones by contracting (shortening). They do not stretch on their own. The muscle group on the opposite side of a bone contracts to move the bone back to its starting position or to the next place it needs to move. For instance, in walking, the quadriceps on the front of the femur (thigh bone) contracts to move the leg forward in a step. The hamstrings on the back of the femur then contract to straighten the thigh at the knee to finish the forward step. These pairs function to balance each other and allow continuous movement.

Sixth Grade: *Most of the largest and strongest muscles of the body—the gluteus group, hamstring group, and calf muscles—are located in the back lower half of the skeleton to help hold it up.* Anatomists, in studying how the muscles function to maintain the body's upright balance, found that even when standing still, the muscles at the back of the hip— the gluteus group— and hamstrings and calf muscles down the back of the leg continue to contract in mini-contractions to maintain the body in its vertical position. These strong muscles counterbalance the weight of the trunk, where the rib cage, abdominal muscles, and pelvis contain the internal organs.

Eighth Grade: *Flexion, extension, abduction, adduction, and rotation of muscles at their joints provide the body's range of motion.* Anatomists use the words flexion (bring bones closer to each other) and extension (straighten and open them up from their bent position) in the forward-backward directions; abduction (move the limb to the side, away from the central line of the body); adduction (return the limb to the neutral position at the side of the body); and rotation (move the limb in a circular path) to describe how muscles move bones at their joints. The joints allow or limit the range of motion of each body part.

Eighth Grade: *Different synovial joints (nonaxial, uniaxial, pivot, biaxial, and triaxial) have different functions.* As discussed above, the names of joints describe how they allow or limit movement of the bones they join. The structures of these five types of joints also demonstrate the amazingly coordinated and varied ways they stabilize, limit, or facilitate movement of the body or body parts.

Tenth Grade: *Muscles, joints, and range of motion of the arms and legs are similar.* The arms and legs of human beings evolved from the prehistoric time when early homo sapiens walked on four limbs, not two. In fact, arms and legs coordinate well for climbing; they both have their greatest strength at or near a 90-degree angle. As described above, hands and feet, elbows and knees, and shoulders and hips have similar bone structure, joints, and range of motion.

Twelfth *Grade: People need to adjust their fitness activity as they age and mature.* The information about achieving and maintaining fitness learned in school applies to people throughout their lives. Many factors will influence and change as people grow older: needs, time, health, space, facilities, and interests are a few obvious ones. People should neither expect nor need to engage in the same fitness activities at the age of 60 that they did at the age of 16. They do, however, need to continue some reasonable and comfortable form of activity to remain in good, age-appropriate condition.

Twelfth Grade: *Neurons enable the brain to send and receive signals to and from the muscles and organs.* The study of how the nervous system works helps students appreciate the interaction of metabolized nutrients, biochemicals, and electrical impulses with the intricate structure of the spinal cord and brain in coordinating the body's ongoing daily activities. They can understand that neurons facilitate all physical activities, from thinking to running.

What Characterizes a Safe and Appropriate Muscular Strengthening and Stretching Program?

Proper stretching and strengthening can ready the body for activity and lessen the possibility of muscular stress and strain. For muscles to do their job, they must be strong. They also must be stretched to allow bones their range of motion.

Three Types of Muscular Strength

Experts define strength in several ways. Corbin and Lindsay (1993) simply say it "is the amount of force your muscles can produce" (p. 3). Dominguez and Gajda, in their discussion of muscular strength distinguish among strength, stamina, and power in their book, *Total Body Training* (1982). These ways of describing strength identify how each kind functions. Moving any amount of weight at all requires strength, and this kind

---

Example 5

High School Example: Grade 12

Concept/Principle: Design strength-training programs for individuals based on body composition, current strength, and the specific requirements of the activity.

In the light of their academic study of the physiology of strength and anaerobic exercise, students analyze their own physical strength and decide on an activity for which they will develop a strength training program. They should record their current body composition, resting and training heart rate, and level of muscular strength taken, perhaps, from their Fitnessgram scores. After consulting guidebooks and an instructor, students will engage in muscular endurance and strength training for four to six weeks, carefully monitoring their progress. At the end, students and instructors can evaluate the success of the program by comparing the beginning data with the results of the program.

of strength underlies the other two kinds. Stamina, also called muscular endurance, enables muscles to continue contracting for long periods of time without excess or overwhelming fatigue, such as climbing several flights of stairs while carrying a bag of groceries. Strength for power allows muscles to hold, lift, and control weight rapidly: "the faster you can move a resisting object, the more power you have" (Dominguez & Gajda, 1982, p.46).

Training for strength or endurance usually requires task specific training whereas all major muscle groups need basic strength training that transfers to all activities and other kinds of strength. Muscles require all three kinds of strength in daily activity as well as during vigorous physical activity. According Corbin and Lindsay (1997a), the power gained by sensible strength training for basic strength is vital to both physical fitness and health.

Types of Muscular Strength Training

People can best accomplish muscular strength (the ability of a muscle group to lift and hold weight) and muscular endurance, or stamina, (the ability for muscles to endure long periods of activity) in the context of the specific activity, such as repeatedly dribbling the ball with the feet as in soccer, or sprinting for short distances and stopping quickly to change direction for any number of other games.

The three types of strength training include isotonic, isometric, and isokinetic. Isotonic exercises involve moving the muscles of the limb or body part up and down or down and up, with control, against gravity along the line of pull of that muscle group until it feels tired. Then once or twice again, carefully move the limb up and down to achieve an overload. The resistance selected should be enough to elicit the overload principle, but not so much to sacrifice to technique and form. Overload describes the effect on the muscles when they become fatigued and reach their usual strength capacity. Going beyond this point, overloading the muscles, increases their capacity to lift and control weight. This type of strengthening increases capacity along the entire length of the muscle and can be done with or without free weights or special equipment. Controlled movement in basic strength training prevents momentum from

Concentric: Coming together or shortening (in a description of a muscle contraction).

Eccentric: Moving apart or lengthening (in a description of a muscle contraction).

Resistance: The amount of weight that is lifted in strength training.

Line of Pull: The direction of the muscle where it attaches to the bones.

Isotonic: Same resistance.

Isokinetic:
Variable resistance.

taking over the work the muscles need to do to become functionally strong. Physical therapists often prescribe a basic strengthening exercise (see Highlight Box 1) for people recuperating from knee injuries. This example, which everyone can do, demonstrates the effectiveness of slow movement in an isotonic strengthening exercise. Controlling the weight prevents momentum from doing the majority of the lifting and lowering. Isotonic strength training uses both concentric and eccentric contractions.

Isokinetic strength training utilizes special equipment with variable resistance. Hoeger and Hoeger (1992, p. 66) explain that, "the speed of the muscle contraction is kept constant because the machine provides a resistance to match the user's force through the range of motion." The guideline for slow speed and the principle of overload described for isotonic training applies for isokinetic training when beginning this kind of exercise session. The equipment, however, allows the exerciser gradually to increase the speed.

Isometric:
Contraction without movement.

Isometric strengthening uses a static contraction. This means contracting the muscle without moving any part of the body, (e.g., pushing against a wall), or not changing the position of parts of the body (e.g., holding in the abdominal muscles). Isometric strengthening is not as effective as dynamic (isotonic) strength training, except when specific static strength is required, such as for some positions in gymnastics or in a cast.

Training Guidelines

Coaches in many sports and directors of dance companies have added weight lifting for muscular strength and endurance to their regular training regimens with positive results. Readily available books with FITT specifications for individualized weight training programs contain programs applicable to many activities. The guidelines usually help exercisers pretest basic muscle strength and then specify the number of times (sets) they should repeat each exercise (usually 10 to 12); how long they should rest between sets (usually two minutes); how many sets they should do during the first training period (usually two); and how many they should do thereafter as muscular strength and endurance increases (usually 15 to 20 repetitions per set, and three sets). The specific muscular strength and muscular endurance protocol (mode, resistance, sets, and fre-

Sets:
Number of groups of repetitions in which a resistance exercise is done.

quency of training) depends on the individual's age, the activity for which he or she is training, and current basic muscular strength. Lifting very heavy weights one or two times a session does not create muscular endurance.

A major criterion by which to judge the safety as well as the value of the many available weight training guidelines centers on how well they follow the principles of sound training. Guidelines must recommend that participants tailor each program to their individual strength level, training experience, and the specific sport or activity in question. They must advise careful calibration when determining how much weight to lift, how many repetitions and how many sets of repetitions to do, and how much weight to add when participants increase their strength to maintain the overload principle.

Muscle Stretching

People use the term "flexibility" in two ways that can lead to confusion. Muscle flexibility can refer to the result people achieve after they do some stretching exercises. People also use flexibility in reference to individuals with loose joints, whom they often refer to as being double jointed. These people inherit excessively flexible joints; that is, their ligaments are extra

Flexibility: Description of the range of motion of joints and their ligament and tendon structure such as lax or tight, often confused with muscle flexibility that refers to the ready elasticity of muscles to contract, as in flexibility or stretching exercises. See *stretching.*

Stretching: Increasing the range of motion. Muscle tissue contracts and extends because of its elasticity. Stretching produces elastic elongation that increases the extensibility of muscles. Proper stretching exercises to lengthen muscles and maintain their elasticity allow muscles to move bones at their joints easily through their range of motion. See *flexibility.*

Figure 8	
Training Principles Applied to Muscular Stretching, Based on Fitness Goals. (Adapted from Corbin & Lindsay, 1993, p.111.)	
Purpose	Applies to basic, intermediate health-related, and athletic performance fitness.
Method	Use static stretch methods and gently and steadily pull with hands when possible.
Frequency	Stretch each muscle group, daily, if possible, but at least three days a week. Stretch before and after workouts.
Intensity	Stretch muscles beyond their normal length. Feel stretch sensation in the muscles and not it the joints.
Time	Hold each stretch 30-60 seconds to feel the tightness release. Stretch one side, then the other before stretching both together, if that is necessary.

Reprinted, by permission, from AAHPERD, 1999, Physical education for lifelong fitness: the physical best teacher's guide, (Champaign, IL: Human Kinetics), 88.

long or lax. Physicians, especially in sports medicine, consider lax ligaments to be a disability. These people injure at a 75 percent greater rate than people with normal joints do (Nicholas, 1970). In athletic and dance activities, they have a hard time adequately stretching. Their muscles often remain excessively tight and, therefore, they have less control of their limbs than people with normal joints do. Joint flexibility is a disadvantage, whereas muscle flexibility is an advantage. This section describes muscle stretching, and not muscle flexibility, to avoid any confusion.

Strengthening only gives muscles half the preparation that they require. They need proper stretching. Since muscles do not stretch on their own—(they only contract) they often remain in a semi-contracted state after an aerobic training session, a game, or a physically demanding activity. Students should stretch properly (see Figure 8) before and after each weight training session, game, or practice. In general, participants should hold stretch positions for 30 seconds to one minute—longer, if necessary, depending on the tightness of the muscles in that group. Proper stretch requires a minimum of 30 seconds for deepening a stretch position because it takes that amount of time for the neurological process of stretch to register in the muscle cells and nerve endings that signal tightness and release. People should feel the stretching as a gradual softening or diminishing of the tight sensation compared to when they began to stretch. Follow this pattern: one leg, then the other; one arm, then the other; one side then the other to stretch muscle groups. Stretching both limbs or sides at once feels too strong and the sides of the body parts are not equally strong. In some cases, after stretching each side, or one limb at a time, then stretch both. For example, right handed people are usually stronger and tighter on that side. People should hold the stretch positions longer on the tight side. Remember to feel the sensation of stretch in the long surface of the muscles, but never in the joints. When training for general sport or physical activity, stretch at least three times a week (frequency) and more often if possible.

Active people commonly use three kinds of stretching techniques to help lengthen and enable muscles to contract effectively. Static stretching involves placing the body part in a position to allow the weight of the body, with the assistance of gravity, to lengthen the muscles and requires holding that position for a period of time. Ballistic stretching uses bouncing or pulsing that can harm muscles. It does not stretch them effectively. It requires the muscles to contract and release in rapid succession. The third kind of stretching, proprioceptive neuromuscular facilitation (PNF), uses a three-second contraction of the muscle group followed by a static stretch of it. People often do this sequence with a partner but it can also be done alone. PNF uses the flexor reflex, which enables body parts to respond to an emergency. When a situation requires a rapid contraction, the opposite muscle group automatically relaxes to facilitate this emergency response.

The most effective form of stretch combines static stretching with modified PNF. Before stretching a muscle group, first contract it with an isotonic strengthening exercise. Then put the body part in the position where gravity can help to lengthen the muscle and actively and gently pull the body part for 30 to 60 seconds. For example:

Hold your arms out to the sides at shoulder height. Make four circles about 10 inches around, taking 10 to 12 slow counts for each circle. Afterward, grasp your hands behind the back and lift them up. Bend over at the waist and rotate one shoulder down toward the floor so that you feel the stretching sensation in the one shoulder that is toward the ceiling. Hold that stretch for 30 to 60 seconds and continue gradually to lift up your arms. Take care not to lock your elbows, and do not to let your shoulders roll forward. Then, rotate your stretched shoulder down toward the floor and your other one up and repeat the active stretching. After you have stretched both shoulders separately, lift them both at the same time. After first fatiguing your shoulder muscles and then stretching them, you should experience strong stretching in the front of your shoulders. At the end, this sequence should increase the height you can lift up your arms behind your back. When you bring your arms down into their normal position your shoulders should feel less tight and should not be rolled forward as much as they may have been before doing the exercise.

In some activities, students stretch each other in pairs. This kind of stretching can cause serious and sudden harm. Teachers must discourage this kind of stretching. The most common paired stretch involves students sitting opposite each other with their legs spread wide and their feet touching. They hold each other's hands and one pulls the other's upper body down to increase the stretch along the inner thighs. The student pulling cannot feel when the pull becomes too much, and the student being stretched may not say "stop" quickly enough. Avoid paired or partner stretches!

Injury Prevention

When exercising, stretching, or strengthening, participants must give special care to their knees and lower back (see Figure 9). Students must take care to feel no sensation in the knee—front, sides, or behind it—when stretching. The knee, along with the ankle and back, is one of the most vulnerable and most frequently injured joints in all sports and dance activities. It only bends one way, but it can wiggle sideways a little when it is flexed at a 90-degree angle. At that time it becomes most vulnerable to injury; most knee injuries occur in this position.

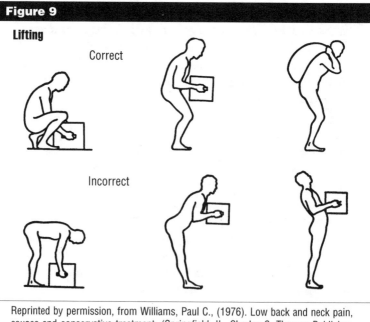

Figure 9

Lifting

Correct

Incorrect

Reprinted by permission, from Williams, Paul C., (1976). Low back and neck pain, causes and conservative treatment. (Springfield, IL, Charles C. Thomas Publisher, Ltd.)

Exercisers need to learn how to protect their knees from injury. If, during activity, exercisers use their toe muscles fully by pressing the toes down firmly (not gripping or squeezing), they can keep the knee aligned over the foot. This will protect the knee joint, because the toe muscles attach to the lower leg bones and serve to stabilize them at the knee joint. Exercisers can further protect their knees by keeping the muscles above (quadriceps and hamstrings) and below (calf muscles) adequately stretched. People constantly use their leg muscles, but they rarely stretch them properly. If exercisers safely and adequately stretch these muscles, they can help prevent knee injuries (Cooper, 1982).

Medical specialists in back care agree that, among adults in the Western world, the lower back continues to be the most frequently injured area of the body. These experts reiterate that 8 out of 10 adults will, at some time in their lives, experience severe back pain or injury. Back experts identify the main reasons for the back's vulnerability as poor structure, weak or improperly used abdominal muscles, hyperextended knees with associated tight calf and hamstrings, and the lack of pain-sensi-

Figure 10

Postural alignment

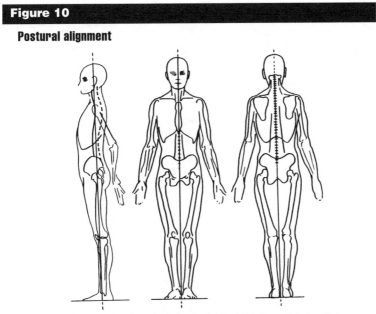

Reprinted with permission from Arnheim, Daniel D., 1991, Dance injuries: their prevention & care, (Princeton Book Co.) 23

tive nerve endings in the tissues that encase the intervertebral discs where the injuries tend to occur (Cailliet, 1981). Without pain, people receive no initial warning when they overstress or injure their lower back. Even people with very strong abdominal muscles can injure their backs.

Like the knee, the muscles around the spinal column (see Figure 10) require a balance of flexibility and strength. The abdominal muscles require regular strengthening because they remain passive during many daily activities (this passivity comes from their relaxed state). The muscles above the spine in the neck and shoulder and below the spine in the buttocks and leg muscles need stretching because they remain in contracted states to keep the entire body in its vertical position. The key idea here is balance! Stretch the muscles that the activity will primarily contract, and strengthen the ones that the activity will stretch.

Figure 11

Slump position

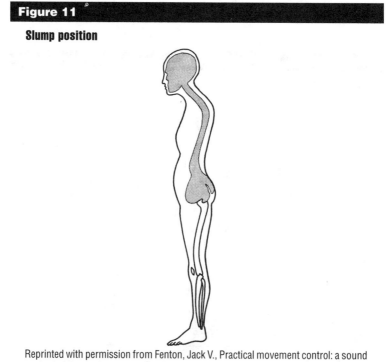

Reprinted with permission from Fenton, Jack V., Practical movement control: a sound method of developing good habits of body movement control & poise in young people, (MacDonald Evans LTD, Boston, MA) 1973

Three areas of the body do not need deliberate stretching: the abdominal muscles, the front of the neck, and the back top of the shoulders (Wells, 1967). Because students often settle for passive lifestyles and poor posture, the resulting weak abdominal muscles will need strengthening before or after activity. Because people frequently reach or slump (see Figure 11) their heads forward during normal daily activity, the weight of the head pulls the back top of the shoulder area into a rounded position and the muscles in the front of the neck relax. Finally, when people feel fatigue, they allow their shoulders to roll forward, their heads to sink forward and down, and their abdominal muscles to relax. These areas require constant monitoring of posture as well as daily strengthening.

Seven "don'ts" provide guidelines for safe strengthening and stretching exercises (J. Alter, 1990a, 1990b). Don't bounce, don't swing, don't do stretching or strengthening fast, don't lock (hyperextend), don't over-bend, don't arch the lumbar and cervical spine in any situation or exercise, and don't click (or pop) any joints. The reasons for these cautions follow:

- Bouncing, or even gentle pulsing (called ballistic stretching) initiates the stretch reflex and thus causes a contraction. Bouncing damages the microscopic fibers of muscle sheaths and makes them sore. Some people continue to bounce to stretch their muscles, even when information about more efficient and less harmful ways to stretch have been disseminated for more than 30 years. Because the action of a bounce combines one brief second of stretch followed by a brief second of contraction, the contraction cancels out the stretch. At the same time, the microscopically fine cross fibers that hold each of the longitudinal muscle fibers to one another tear because of the percussive mini-trauma that bouncing causes. The body secretes protein laden fluid to heal these tears, and the increase of fluid in the tissues causes the soreness (Hoeger & Hoeger, 1992).

- Swinging to warm up the muscles and joints depends mainly on momentum, not muscle strength. Swinging can also cause injury—especially when the swinging limbs go back and forth from one side of the body to the other, as in waist twists.

■ Fast stretching is bouncing, and it uses momentum, as does fast strengthening. Participants should hold stretches for 30 to 60 seconds. Strengthening requires controlled movement, down and up against gravity.

■ Locking a joint severely strains the ligaments and cartilage in the joints that have them, and can misalign the bones, as in hyperextending the knees (Cailliet, 1973; Micheli, 1983).

■ Over-bending is the opposite of locking. This action stretches ligaments, and they do not unstretch. Just like locking, over-bending progressively weakens the bindings of the joint. Deep knee bends usually over-bend the knee joint. When participants do push-ups too quickly they can over-bend the elbow if the exerciser goes down too low (Dominguez & Gajda, 1982).

■ Arching is what people do when they do a backbend or drop their heads back so much so that they can no longer talk. Muscles in the front of the neck or the abdominal muscles in the front of the lumbar spine can no longer hold (stabilize) the spine. In this position, participants can easily and permanently injure their discs (ACSM, 1992).

■ Clicking or popping sounds occur in joints such as the ankle, hip socket, and neck. Ligaments or tendons rolling over each other and/or bones suddenly sliding back into place from their slight misalignment cause the sound. Although the sudden corrected alignment feels better, participants can do the action slowly with only muscles controlling the realignment and prevent the sound and rubbing from occurring. In time, this rubbing can cause wear and tear and arthritis-like symptoms.

Harmful Exercises

Substitute modified versions of stretching and strengthening exercises for the following commonly used warm up exercises that can cause harm or are inefficient. These traditional exercises contain the causes of harm described above. Many people do not like doing exercises that hurt when they do them, and—

in most cases—they are correct to respond to the pain signal. Follow the most important guideline: Stop if it hurts!

- Head circles. These arch the neck, risking damage to the intervertebral discs. They use momentum and actually contract the neck muscles, achieving the opposite goal of stretching and relaxing these tight muscles. When done fast, they cause sore neck muscles. To correct, with one hand gently pull down on the top of the head, keeping the neck vertebrae aligned and never letting the chin touch the chest. Hold for 30 to 60 seconds. Then, pull and hold the aligned head, sideways, over each shoulder, in turn.

- Arm swings or circles. These use momentum, are mostly passive, and do not adequately stretch or strengthen any muscles. If people feel any sensation, it is in the shoulder joint and this may signal joint irritation and lead to injury. To correct, after aligning the shoulder blades, the scapula, slow down these circles, take 12 to 16 slow counts to make one circle and then reverse the direction of the circle. Repeat six to eight times or until fatigued.

- Waist twists. The swing action uses momentum and puts intervertebral discs of the lumbar spine in a vulnerable position (when that part of the spine rotates, it also slides slightly sideways and when it bends to the side it also rotates slightly). To correct, with knees relaxed (slightly bent) and arms extended overhead, pull up as much as possible and then more. Hold to feel the tight muscles in the upper back and rib cage release. In the same position, pull to the high right and then left diagonal where the wall meets the ceiling and hold as before.

- Side bends. These stretch the side abdominal muscles, making the waistline wider. They can cause similar harm to the lumbar discs as waist twists (Cailliet, 1981). People often bounce them as well, causing the soreness that can result from bouncing. Side abdominal muscles need strengthening, not stretching.

■ Back bends. This is the name of the acrobatic stunt that uses lumbar back arching. (See the explanation of arch, above, for the severe and often permanent harm these can cause.) There is no correct way to arch the lumbar spine. In a high chest arch, with the lumbar spine held in a vertical position by strongly contracted abdominal muscles, the rib cage can tip back, sideways, and forward. These positions and movements require great strength and control.

■ Prone arch or trunk lift. People use this exercise to strengthen the upper back muscles. In the position of lying on the floor, however, they severely arch their lumbar spine whether or not they lift their upper back or legs or both. This can cause the same injury to the intervertebral discs of the lumbar spine as backbends. Place a small pillow under the abdominal area to help protect the lumbar spine, but another position such as standing with knees bent enough to align the pelvis over the thighs (back parallel to the floor) and then slowly lifting and lowering in sequence the rib cage, neck, head, and arms, can adequately strengthen these upper back muscles (ACSM Fitness Book, 1992).

■ Fast, straight-legged sit-ups. These use momentum, strengthen the hip flexors (usually already strong and tight), and can hurt the lumbar spine, because often people do them by pushing out their abdominal muscles (Dominguez & Gajda, 1982; ACSM Fitness Book, 1992). Curl-downs provide the most effective dynamic abdominal muscle exercise.

■ Crunches. Instructors have substituted this way of strengthening the abdominal muscles for fast, straight-legged sit-ups and double leg lifts. Although crunches may lessen the risk of back injury somewhat, participants often do crunches fast, using momentum. They also use their arm muscles to do most of the dynamic work. Crunches only mildly strengthen the upper third of the rectus abdominus muscle while the other two abdominal muscles only stabilize the trunk (isometrically). The exercise does not lift and lower weight along the entire length of the abdominal muscles. And, even when it adds a twist of the rib cage, the exercise does not challenge the side abdominal muscles—the internal and external obliques—to go down and up against gravity (ACSM Fitness Book, 1992). To correct this, begin in the curled up position of crunches with most of the pelvis on the floor and the rib cage rounded forward with the neck and head aligned. Keep the rectus abdominus firmly held in and arms crossed on the chest, slowly lower the ribcage three to four counts, and then come up three to four counts to the original curled position. In this curled position, tip the entire body sideways to an angle where one buttock lifts off the floor and then uncurl down three to four counts toward the floor, and curl up in that same side-tipped position three to four counts. Repeat to the other side, and then repeat the entire sequence (center, side, side) two more times. To add overload, increase the counts to six to eight going down and six to eight coming up. Then add a fourth set. This curl-down is a very challenging strengthening exercise (ACSM Fitness Book, 1992).

■ Double leg lifts. This exercise causes the same harm as fast, straight-legged sit-ups, with the additional serious risk to the lumbar spine and potential separation of the abdominal muscle attachments from the linia alba, the long cartilage that reaches from the pubic bone at one end and to the bottom of the sternum at the other (Gajda, 1982; ACSM Fitness Book, 1992). It uses the abdominal muscles to stabilize the upper body and primarily strengthens the hip flexors, a group of muscles that usually remain too tight. To correct, use curl-downs instead.

■ Deep knee bends and squat thrusts. These over-bend the knee joint and require momentum to push the body percussively up from the deepest dropped position. They can cause torn cartilage and ruptured ligaments. If they do not actually damage it, they can seriously weaken the joint. Sports medicine experts (ACSM Fitness Book, 1992; Dominguez & Gajda, 1982) reduced knee injuries on football teams when they removed these exercises from the warm-up. To correct, simply lower the body slowly to the point above where the body drops below the control of the muscles. Where this place is depends on muscle strength, calf stretch, and the leg length of each individual (ACSM Fitness Book, 1992). Come up slowly, four to six counts in each direction.

■ Hurdler's stretch. People often use this position to bounce in a hamstring stretch. It can hyperextend the knee, put severe stress on the lumbar spine, and cause sore hamstring muscles if the student actually can stretch them in this position. It also can jeopardize the bent knee if it is placed on the floor at a right angle. Several very effective alternative ways exist to stretch the hamstrings. (See below.)

■ Straight-legged toe touch. People often bounce (potentially causing sore muscles) when doing these; they also lock back (hyperextend) their knee joints (weakening the knee joint). They forcefully round their lumbar spines; thus, with passive abdominal muscles, their lumbar spine becomes vulnerable to injury. To correct, bend the knees, fold the entire upper body down so the pelvis and rib cage touch the thighs. Drop the head and arms, placing the hands on the ground. Gradually unbend one leg at a time while keeping the upper body touching the thighs. Feel the stretch sensation in the back of the thigh only. Hold for 8 to 10 counts. Bend the first leg and repeat with the other. Repeat this sequence four to six times, or hold the stretched position longer each time.

The commonly used exercises listed above do not effectively accomplish their intended goals and they severely stress the vulnerable joints they should protect. As noted, instructors can modify most of these exercises or substitute safe and effective alternative exercises. Judy Alter (1990a, 1990b) provides more details about the corrections.

Other Safety Factors
Even with proper stretching, strengthening, and cardiorespiratory fitness training, accidents can occur. Accidental injuries most frequently occur at the beginning of the school term when participants are out of shape, and at the end of the term when they have become excessively fatigued. This knowledge can help

everyone concerned take extra precautions during these times and arrange practice and playing schedules accordingly.

Poorly cared for or slippery playing surfaces, severe weather conditions, and inadequate or worn out playing equipment also can contribute to accidents. Constant surveillance and repair of these environmental causes can help diminish the risks they present.

Clothing and shoes can affect health and safety. The manufacturers of sports clothing and shoes may appear to have the players' interests at heart, but since they intend to make a profit, instructors need to consider sensible nonmarket-driven guidelines. Natural fabrics made of cotton or wool allow the skin to breathe and they absorb sweat more effectively than do artificial fabrics, even mesh. If artificial fabrics fit too snugly, they increase the problem of improper air circulation for the skin.

Though young people are style conscious, designers do not make anatomically sensible decisions when creating their new styles. An example of poor design in sportswear is the high, top plastic or leather basketball shoe. Designers made the high top so inflexible that most teenagers wear them untied because, when tied, the back of the shoe puts too much pressure on the top of their Achilles tendon. The cloth high-top gym shoe that students wore in the 1940s, 1950s, and 1960s has returned to shoe stores and, again, is in style. The flexible cloth fabric allows the ankle to bend when laced up, but, compared to the more recently designed running shoes, the insufficient cushioning of the soles provides inadequate shock absorption.

Concepts/Principles

Kindergarten: *Exercising muscles makes them stronger.* Kindergarten students can learn the meaning of the saying, "Use it or lose it." The more a student jumps—with a jumping rope, for instance—the greater the number of jumps he or she can do because the leg muscles and the heart gain basic strength and muscular endurance. The more often a students lifts and carries boxes of books to help rearrange the classroom, for instance, the easier that task becomes because the arm and back muscles gain strength. Direct experience with everyday tasks helps students grasp the concept of gaining strength. And, if they stop those activities for a few weeks, they can experience the loss of their strength.

Second Grade: *Exercising muscles in many activities (such as jumping rope, playing tag, shooting baskets) makes them stronger in different ways.* Jumping rope, playing tag, and shooting baskets strengthen the legs, arms, and heart differently because they require various kinds of coordination, speed, and muscle use. Jumping rope and playing tag exercise the heart much more than shooting baskets does. Shooting baskets requires skilled use of arm muscles coordinated with the leg muscles, whereas playing tag or jumping rope do not require such controlled strength in the arms.

Second Grade: *Muscles need safe stretching to be ready to exercise.* Muscles work like balloons. Before blowing up a balloon, students learn to stretch the balloon gently a few times because it is easier than trying to blow it up without first stretching it. Sometimes, if someone manages to blow up an unstretched balloon, it pops with a little too much air in it. This happens less often with prestretched balloons. Muscles work the same way. Because muscles only contract on their own, they need stretching to prepare them to contract easily, efficiently, and repeatedly. Safe stretching involves gentle holding positions that lengthen muscles. The strong feel of stretching diminishes as the muscle lengthens.

Fourth Grade: *Regular monitoring of progress in gaining muscular strength, endurance, and flexibility demonstrates the benefits of engaging in and adding variety to a fitness program.* After monitoring progress toward muscular fitness, the idea that "nothing succeeds like success," becomes self-evident. Even students who make small gains become motivated to improve their abilities. The process of student record keeping also builds in the discipline and may diminish feelings of competition, since students follow their own success. Varying ways to improve muscle fitness allows students to determine their preferences and increase their range of abilities.

Sixth Grade: *For vigorous physical activity, proper stretching exercises serve to warm up and cool down muscles and maintain their contracting function.* For muscles to contract comfortably, they must begin their actions in their natural lengthened state. Therefore, proper stretching prepares them to contract. After playing, muscles become tighter and the tissues become more viscous (warmed) than before activity. Stretching muscles in this state allows them to cool down in their lengthened state and then helps ready them for their next use.

Sixth Grade: *The principles of muscle strength, endurance, and flexibility (adequate stretch) include overload, individual differences, progression, regularity, and specificity.* Individual differences override the other principles here, since exercisers begin their programs at different levels, with varying motivations, and with a range of abilities. When exercisers adapt these principles to their specific needs, they can remain motivated to continue their programs.

Sixth Grade: *Performing isotonic, isometric, or isokinetic exercises every other day improves muscular strength.* These three ways to strengthen muscles serve different functions. Isotonic strengthening—the most available and useful one—builds basic strength and muscular endurance without much equipment, whereas isokinetic strengthening requires properly adjusted machines. Strengthening every other day allows the muscles to rest and repair if necessary. Isometric strengthening can be done daily, because it does not challenge the muscles in as strenuous a way as the other kinds of strengthening exercises do.

Eighth Grade: *Hold stretches for major muscle groups for 30 to 60 seconds.* Often, exercisers do not hold their stretch positions for a sufficiently long time; their muscles, therefore, do not benefit from the stretching. The recommended time of 30 to 60 seconds becomes only a rough guideline, because muscles on the dominant side, or ones that the activity has just contracted, may require more time to release adequately. Exercisers must feel the stretching-lengthening sensation in their muscles and take the time necessary for that to occur.

Eighth Grade: *The FITT principles of strength training include frequency of training (F), intensity—amount of weight (I), time—sets of repetitions (T), and type of exercise (T)—using body weight, free weights, or weight machines.* The use of different ways to accomplish strength training when applying the FITT principles gives variety to a potentially uninteresting activity. As important, not all exercisers, schools, or facilities have all forms of equipment. If possible, exercisers should learn the correct body positions for all three ways of strengthening.

Tenth Grade: *Bouncing, swinging, over-stretching, strengthening fast, locking, over-bending, arching, and clicking the joints are harmful aspects of some exercises.* Exercisers can modify most exercises and remove the harmful aspects of them. Hold and gently pull in stretching instead of bouncing; move slowly instead of swinging, clicking, or strengthening fast; relax joints to unlock them; and do not arch the low back or neck. Sudden and sharp pain in the joints signals the harm exercises can cause. Stop the pain and stop the potential harm.

Tenth Grade: *Specific dangerous exercises that people should avoid include neck circles, hurdler's stretch, deep knee bends, back arching, and double leg lifts.* The list of harmful exercises contains clues to causes of their harm. They strain the spine and knee joints and do not work muscles safely or correctly. They also give exercisers a signal of their harm because they frequently cause sharp pain when doing them or after doing them. Exercisers can correct all but back arching.

Twelfth Grade: *Design strength training programs for individuals based on body composition, current strength, and the specific requirements of the activity.* By the end of high school, most young people reach their adult body composition. Thus, the strength training program can reflect this level of maturity. The design must fit, challenge, and interest the individual, because the program serves as a model for adult fitness activity. This program should coordinate with proper cardiorespiratory activity, careful stretching, and good nutrition.

Twelfth Grade: *Setting goals and recording progress in a stretching and strengthening program enable students to overcome barriers to continued participation.* When exercisers take responsibility for their fitness activities—including stretching and strengthening—by goal setting and recording their progress, they help themselves take control of their own well-being. Using the tool of self-monitoring, when it becomes a habit, provides a model for other behaviors that require commitment and devotion.

How Do Body Composition and Nutrition Interrelate to Develop and Maintain Lifetime Fitness?

Food provides the body with sufficient nutrients to maintain its energy, repair its parts, and support the immune system. In most circumstances, any informed person can eat a balanced diet. Proper nutritional guidelines in relation to body composition follow the discussion of metabolism.

Adenosine triphosphate (ATP): Major molecule in which living cells store energy.

Metabolism
Think of the body as a machine with the bones as the supports, the joints as the hinges of the moving parts, the nerves as the electrical wiring, and the muscles moving the bones. The only thing missing here is the energy to fuel this living machine. This energy, of course, comes from the processes of digestion

Example 6

Elementary School Example: Grade 4

Concept/Principle: Carbohydrates, proteins, and fats should be eaten every day.

From a group discussion, teachers can compile a list of foods their students eat and label the foods as carbohydrates (fruit, vegetable, and starch); proteins (animal and vegetable); and fats. Students can use this list to record and group the foods they eat for a week. They can use the food pyramid to see how their diet compares with the recommended amounts of these food groups. This will show students how their diet contributes to their nutritional needs and how they might modify their intake in a beneficial way. During the next week, they can modify their food intake (if possible) to meet the nutritional recommendations in the food pyramid and monitor how they feel with these changes.

and metabolism that transform food into usable energy. Digestion is the mechanical and chemical breaking down of food in the digestive track. Metabolism occurs in the cells that break down food molecules into chemical compounds that are absorbed into the bloodstream and distributed to the muscles, the brain, and the organs. If the body does not use this energy for its essential functions, it releases it as heat or stores it in the liver or in fat cells for use at a later time.

Example 7

Middle School Example: Grade 6

Concept/Principle: Inherited, familial, and cultural factors influence the size and shape of people's bodies

When students study body composition they can focus on describing their own body type and those of family members. Students can interview family members about their childhood patterns of eating, recreation, and physical activity and inquire about the inherited anatomical and structural characteristics such as height, bone structure, and body composition. They can study family photographs to trace inherited resemblances and changes from generation to generation. They can then compare their family inheritance to those of their friends from the same and different ancestry to see how ancestral background influences what characteristics they value in body size and shape.

Example 8

Middle School Example: Grade 8

Concept/Principle: Family, school, community, and commercial information about proper nutrition influence an individual's commitment to his or her physical fitness program.

Have students interview a schoolmate whose family has recently moved to the U.S. from another country. They can ask about eating, recreational, and activity patterns in that country and how they have changed or not in this country. They can ask if advertising and the large selection of food in supermarkets influence their food choices. This interview will help students appreciate the diversity of attitudes and practices in their own community and understand that adults may work such long hours that they cannot eat properly or undertake a fitness program. Students can present reports on these interviews to compare their findings. Then, have students interview an adult who regularly works out at a gym or does aerobic activity. Students can ask about motivation, rewards, drawbacks, and changes in metabolism and nutritional needs that occur with long-term physical training. The students can present their reports to the class and compare their findings to see how committed people maintain their fitness and nutritional programs in spite of all the conflicting commercial information broadcast in the media.

Food generates the chemical compound adenosine triphosphate, known as ATP, the prime energy source stored by living cells. The main source of ATP is glucose that comes from the food groups: carbohydrates (grains, vegetables, fruits), proteins (animal products such as meat, fish, and eggs; and vegetable sources such as beans and seeds), and fats (from animal and plant sources). Though carbohydrates provide the most readily available glucose, the liver also produces glucose from proteins and fats (Kapit, Macey, & Meisami, 1987).

Carbohydrates are the main component of starches such as bread, rice, and potatoes. They supply about half of Western society's dietary needs. Fruit and vegetables also contain carbohydrates, but they contain much more water than starches. Fruit and vegetables also supply the body with essential vitamins, minerals (different from the ones supplied by starches), and natural complex unrefined sugars.

The U.S. Department of Agriculture food pyramid (see Figure 12) recommends the following number of daily servings of these food groups: six to 11 servings of starches such as bread, cereal, rice, and pasta; three to five servings of vegetables; two to four fruit servings; two to three servings of protein (four to six ounces each); and fats, oils, and sweets eaten sparingly.

Figure 12

Food Pyramid U.S. Dept. of Agriculture

The Food Guide Pyramid

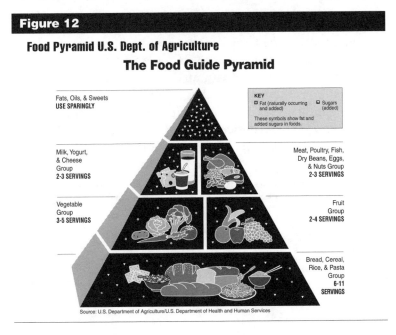

Fats, Oils, & Sweets
USE SPARINGLY

KEY
Fat (naturally occurring and added)   Sugars (added)
These symbols show fat and added sugars in foods.

Milk, Yogurt, & Cheese Group
2-3 SERVINGS

Meat, Poultry, Fish, Dry Beans, Eggs, & Nuts Group
2-3 SERVINGS

Vegetable Group
3-5 SERVINGS

Fruit Group
2-4 SERVINGS

Bread, Cereal, Rice, & Pasta Group
6-11 SERVINGS

Source: U.S. Department of Agriculture/U.S. Department of Health and Human Services

The refined starches so popular among young people (French fried potatoes, pasta, white bread, donuts, pretzels, and white rice) do not supply the body with the necessary trace minerals to maintain it in its optimal readiness state for physical activity. For instance, the skin of the potato, the bran of whole grain wheat, and the bran of brown rice contain high quantities of magnesium, which the body requires for the synthesis and use of energy rich compounds and the maintenance of membrane properties of cells. The refined starches young people commonly eat do not supply enough magnesium, especially if they do not eat ample amounts of magnesium rich, dark green leafy vegetables.

Nuts, animal products, and vegetables such as beans and seeds contain protein. Although they also supply the body with glucose, fats, and energy, proteins primarily supply the body with the essential amino acids the body does not manufacture itself. The body needs amino acids to maintain, build, and repair cells, tissue, and bodily structures that enable the body to function effectively. The liver, again, plays a major role in combining and separating amino acids and proteins for its own use as well as for the rest of the body. The daily diet should contain 12 to 15 percent protein, preferably of the low fat and vegetable or fish variety.

Here again, the proteins popular with young people, such as hamburgers and fried chicken, tend to be high in animal fat. Even when students choose to follow a vegetarian diet, they often eat large amounts of saturated fat from cheese, ice cream, and eggs. They fill up on starches made of refined wheat flour. Because eating a vegetarian diet without careful guidance and detailed knowledge is difficult, young vegetarians often become deficient in iron. Eating iron rich foods does not necessarily correct this deficiency. For the body to absorb iron, people need to combine high iron foods such as oats with other foods containing Vitamin C and minerals such as magnesium. Teachers should clarify what eating a balanced regular or vegetarian diet means: eating a wide variety of fruits, vegetables, grains, and low fat proteins.

In spite of the bad press that fats have received in the past 20 or 30 years, the human body requires them. They supply and store

Figure 13

Body Fat

Males Skinfolds (mm): 5 10 15 20 25 30 35 40 45 50 55 60

Very Low | Low | Optimal Range | Mod. High | High | Very High

% Fat: 6 10 13 17 20 24 28 31 35 38 42

Fitness Rating	% Fat (Males)
Too Little Fat	6 or less
High Performance	7–9
Good	10–19
Marginal	20–24
Too Much Fat	25 or more

Females Skinfolds (mm): 5 10 15 20 25 30 35 40 45 50 55 60

Very Low | Low | Optimal Range | Mod. High | High | Very High

% Fat: 7 11 14 18 21 25 29 32 36 39 43

Fitness Rating	% Fat (Females)
Too Little Fat	11 or less
High Performance	12–14
Good	15–24
Marginal	25–29
Too Much Fat	30 or more

Reprinted by permission, from C.B. Corbin & R. Lindsey, 2002, Fitness for life, Updated 4th Ed., (Champaign, IL: Human Kinetics), 94.

Calorie: Amount of energy it takes to raise the temperature of one gram of water one degree.

fuel, and they furnish insulation. This insulation provides both warmth and electrical conduction, and it makes up part of the structure of cell membranes. Fats also enable the body to transport oil soluble vitamins, such as Vitamin E. Fats have received bad press for two major reasons: their contribution to arteriosclerosis—the hardening of the arteries that contributes to the hypokinetic diseases such as heart disease—and obesity. Experts define obesity as weighing at least 30 percent more than the recommended normal weight. Normal weight depends on and is calculated in relation to one's height, age, and gender (see Figure 13). No more than 30 percent of the daily food intake should contain fat, with only 10 percent animal fat.

People associate the serious problems associated with cholesterol—the fatty substance found only in animal tissues—with fat. Human bodies need cholesterol and utilize it in essential ways: in fat digestion, in some hormone building, in the skin, in tissues of nerves, and in membranes of cells. Recently, researchers have questioned the causal relationship of dietary intake of high cholesterol foods in arteriosclerosis. However, the issue may relate more to how the liver breaks down, transports, and distributes the cholesterol in the body in relation to high sugar and alcohol consumption than it does to fat intake.

Researchers do agree that people should choose more polyunsaturated fats than saturated ones, because in the liver saturated fat interferes with the regulation of the cholesterol level in the blood. Polyunsaturated fatty acids, the technical way of describing these fats, are found in the liquid form of vegetable oil. These do not interfere with the liver's ability to regulate the blood level of cholesterol (Kapit, Macy, & Meisami, 1987).

People often choose crisp and salty snack foods, such as potato chips. These snacks have two disadvantages. They have little food value (essential vitamins and minerals), and they add extra fat and calories to the diet. And, eating something salty often stimulates people to eat something sweet afterward (Kempner, Newborg, Peschel, & Skyler, 1975). Young people commonly reach for refined sugar-filled carbonated drinks or candy bars to fill this need. These sweets contain little food value and add empty calories to the diet.

Empty calories contain few essential vitamins. They only add energy, often at the expense of a balanced metabolism. Refined sugar enters the bloodstream without much processing by the digestive system. When this extra sugar suddenly floods the system, it throws off the balance of glucose released into the bloodstream by the liver. To correct this imbalance, the liver stores the glucose it is processing. In the meantime, the person who just ate the candy or drank the soda experiences a rush of energy. Then, about a half hour later, a feeling of fatigue occurs, because it takes time before the liver resumes its function of glucose distribution. To satisfy their yen for something sweet, students can reach for sweet whole foods such as bananas, or dates, or raisins, or less sweet fruit such as apples or oranges. The body metabolizes these sweet complex carbohydrates as it does other unrefined sugars. Then, the liver can maintain the even flow of glucose.

The habit young people have of eating frequently (snacking) may be physiologically driven. In our society, people eat three meals a day, although advertisers offer many choices for snacks and suggestions for when to eat them between meals. Some researchers now recommend that, to maintain a steady supply of energy, people should eat six small, balanced meals during the day, rather than the traditional three large ones. The eating habits of teenagers, then, may prove more sensible than they would seem. They do need to modify their snacking habits, however, and reach for low-fat proteins such as yogurt, and low-fat carbohydrates such as whole grain bagels, or fresh fruits such as bananas, apples, or grapes.

Body Composition

Body composition refers to the relative amounts of muscle, fat, bone, and other tissues. Teachers can help young people monitor and keep track of their body fat by using the skin fold measure at the center (posterior midline) of the triceps muscle of the upper arm and the inside (medial) of the widest part of the calf. The sum of these two measurements helps determine the level of body fat in relation to the total percentage of body fat.

Corbin and Lindsay (1992) published tables of the relationships between this skin fold test sum and total body fat. They identify the optimal range for males as a total skin fold sum of 10 to 25 mm. That indicates the total percentage of body fat ranges between 10 and 20 percent. Their optimal range for females is between 17 to 30 mm for total skin fold, which indicates between 16 and 25 percent total body fat. If students have body fat beyond that range, they should increase their physical activity by using FITT principles and reduce their intake of empty calories— fat, sugar, and alcohol (if applicable).

It is important to de-emphasize weight reduction diets while focusing on lifetime eating habits. Because fat cells store potential energy for the body, dieting can disrupt the normal functioning of fat cells. An automatic feast or famine response takes over when a person diets. When that person completes the weight reduction diet, the cells will automatically replenish their stores of energy. The common and frustrating bodily result of dieting, then, is that the dieter gains back the weight. The cells continue to store fat rather than resume their normal function, especially if the person does not engage in regular physical activity.

In today's society, the media influences people with double-edged, loaded, and contradictory messages about body composition. The challenge for teachers is to inform students about real body composition facts and help them understand that one size does not fit all. Next, teachers can help students recognize the potentially harmful double messages conveyed in snack food and beverage advertisements. The diet industry and the related media messages provide teachers an important tool to use in teaching their students how to analyze and see through the inaccurate, ill-advised, and deceptive commercial information available today.

Inherited, familial, and cultural factors influence the size and shape of people's bodies. Not everyone can be tall, thin, and blonde—although advertisers would have consumers believe otherwise. Many people find this reality difficult to accept. They also find it difficult to accept that they cannot control all their body's features. While exceptions occur, familial tendencies operate automatically as young people grow toward their adult shape and size. If, beginning in the elementary grades, teachers help young people to understand the difference between internal and external beauty, while they study the infinite variety of human features, sizes, and preferences that exist in the world, then perhaps they will enter adolescence with an increased sense of self-acceptance.

An opposite problem to obesity exists. When young women train excessively for any kind of activity—be it running, gymnastics, or dancing—and they do not maintain 15 to 18 percent body fat, their bodies cannot naturally progress into puberty. As a result, their reproductive systems may sustain permanent damage (Vincent, 1989; Warren, 1991). Women may also experience increased fatigue, susceptibility to infection, delayed healing and recovery from injury, anemia, electrolyte imbalances, cardiovascular changes, endocrine abnormalities, and osteoporosis. Some young women and a few young men—who focus unnecessarily on their excess or apparent excess body fat—use inordinate amounts of aerobic exercise (three to four hours a day) to lose fat.

These unfortunate over-exercising young people may suffer from the disease known as anorexia nervosa. They combine excess aerobic exercise with consuming as little food as possible. Their physical state can become so weakened that they require hospitalization and constant supervision to prevent them from starving. These young people became overly susceptible to the contemporary emphasis on slimness that pervades the media. Teachers need to respond to early symptoms that excess physical activity reveals.

Ergogenics: A food or nutritional product thought to enhance performance

Nutrition and Health

How do the physiological components of nutrition affect safety and health? To answer this question, again think about the image of the body as a machine. When the machine uses proper fuel, it remains in good working condition. And, when kept in good running condition, it can do almost anything and go almost anywhere. Human beings, however, are not machines. They need more than just proper fuel to keep their bodies in good condition. Growing young people need sufficient rest and water, and a balanced variety of activities with supportive people. Psychological well-being and the resulting positive sense of self that physical health produces can enable youngsters to cope with the many difficult and unpredictable events they will encounter during the transition from adolescence to adulthood. Young people face one of the most dangerous and difficult choices: whether or not to experiment with or use legal and illegal drugs, alcohol, cigarettes or even nutritional ergogenics such as extra amino acids or large doses of Vitamin B12. Researchers such as Melvin H. Williams, Director of the Human Performance Laboratory at Old Dominion University in Norfolk, Virginia, have studied the effect of drugs, nutrients, chemicals, and so-called performance enhancers. They report that most make no difference in athletic performance. Officials in the Olympic Games and professional and college sports teams forbid some drugs such as steroids. Although they do enhance performance, they also can cause serious and even permanent harm and possibly death to those who use them.

People of all ages have a strong drive to find ways to achieve a state of euphoria, and some people will take extreme risks to achieve it. In studies of elite athletes, sports psychologists have identified the characteristics of what they call peak performance. Psychologist Mihaly Csikszentmihalyi (1990) has studied this state, which he calls "flow," in people all over the world. He defines flow as the euphoric state of unselfconscious concentration in an activity where time seems irrelevant, where ease seems to substitute for effort, and where work feels like play. Flow gives people such a high level of enjoyment that they will engage in the activity over and over again for its own sake. Mountain climbers, dancers, musicians, marathon runners, and young people playing basketball all describe this state.

Young people seek flow in their recreational and social activities, and because they do not realize that they need skilled concentration to create this experience naturally, they turn to artificial means such as drugs and alcohol. Physiologically, these flow activities all stimulate brain-secreted endorphins, the built-in tranquilizers to which all humans have access. Educators can help young people turn to these positive flow activities.

Unfortunately many young people do not make wise decisions about food, sleep, clothing, recreational activities, and so forth. Their stage of development makes these decisions difficult to counteract. Young people have little understanding of the future and believe that, in some magical way, they will be fine no matter what happens. When adults suggest that they exercise caution, the message has little meaning. Unfortunately, it takes a serious incident before some young people begin to make wiser decisions.

Concepts/Principles

Kindergarten: *Food provides the body with energy for daily life and vigorous physical activity.* Students easily understand that food provides their bodies with energy, since the innate sensations of hunger and fatigue have enabled them to survive since their births. They also have first hand knowledge about this concept from feeling hungry after they come in from playing. Fortunately, school authorities provide eligible students with breakfast and lunch, because students cannot concentrate adequately in school if they remain hungry.

Second Grade: *Breads, crackers, and muffins made of whole grain provide better sources of energy than those made with only refined white flour and lots of sugar.* This concept easily combines with a science lesson. Students can study the structure of whole grains and then grasp the difference between refined and unrefined grains and flours made from them. Breakfast cereals also serve as sources for study. Comparing the vitamin, mineral, and fiber content of refined and unrefined grains also will prove interesting and help students understand the problems associated with eating foods made with unrefined grains and lots of sugar.

Fourth Grade: *Carbohydrates, proteins, and fats should be eaten every day.* The Department of Agriculture's food pyramid illustrates how people need to eat a varied and balanced diet. The pyramid provides a visual image to explain what "balanced" and "varied" mean. The guide also shows the kinds of carbohydrates—fruits, vegetables, starches, proteins (animal and vegetable) and fats (mono and polyunsaturated, trans, and saturated).

Fourth Grade: *Body composition refers to lean and fat components of the human body; both affect and are affected by vigorous physical activity.* The idea of body composition gives students a unifying understanding of their bodies and de-emphasizes the notions of "overweight" or "skinny." Bodies contain differing amounts of fat, muscle, and bone that change as students grow, develop, and become more or less physically active. Although students can control some parts of their body composition, such as muscle mass and extra fat, they inherit other parts, such as bone size and ligament structure. This understanding can give students information about what they can and cannot control for themselves.

Sixth Grade: *Regular monitoring of changes in body composition demonstrates the benefits of engaging in a fitness program.* Keeping track of muscle mass and extra fat can provide students with information about their progress, especially in an encouraging and nonpunitive atmosphere, where these records remain private. This long-term undertaking can help motivate reluctant exercisers, especially when their fitness program reflects their current tolerance for and interest in self-challenging activity.

Sixth Grade: *Inherited, familial, and cultural factors influence the size and shape of peoples' bodies.* Only since World War II has "thin" become the standard for body size. Up until that time, thin represented unhealthy. People in many cultures still believe heavy bodies are beautiful. Children often see their parents as models of beauty and behavior. In turn, parents reflect their ancestral values as well as those in which they currently live. These factors may conflict, but they still play a part in how people view the size and shape of their own and others' bodies.

Eighth *Grade: Family, school, community, and commercial information about proper nutrition influence an individual's commitment to his or her physical fitness program.* Conflicting messages about food consumption surround exercisers. These messages encourage leisure and super challenge, abundance and restraint, belonging to the crowd and individuality, consumption and recycling. Family traditions may contrast with school instruction; community values may or may not follow suggestions made by commercial interests. Careful analysis of these conflicts can help students sort them out and make intelligent decisions for themselves.

Eighth Grade: *Proper nutrition contributes to physical and mental health, while excess sugar, starch, fat, alcohol, and food supplements impede performance of physical activities and can cause permanent harm.* Scientific information about nutrition can guide students to make wise decisions about how and what to eat or use when they want to improve and benefit from physical fitness. Media reports also provide notice about extreme events such as, death from binge drinking or the harm of steroids. These reports serve to warn students about unwise and harmful choices.

Tenth Grade: *Body composition and nutritional needs interact and change as students grow, engage in different physical activities, increase their fitness levels, and commit to ongoing after-school obligations.* High school students often commit to regular team activities such as track, wrestling, or soccer. The regular training for these activities requires many adjustments in time use, nutritious food consumption, daily rest, and adequate sleep while maintaining academic achievement and focus. As students get stronger and in shape for their activities, their food and rest requirements will change. Careful attention to what changes and what remains the same will help them achieve success in fulfilling these new obligations.

Twelfth Grade: *Nutritional and exercise needs change and people must adapt them to various stages of life.* Students know family members and friends who have changed their nutritional needs and activity levels during college, after taking an office job, on vacations, after injury or sickness, and even in later years. Some of these people have managed to eat healthy meals and remain fit with a simple jogging and weight lifting program, while others have changed their activities because of the new circumstances in their lives. They also know people who have stopped and then started their nutritional and fitness programs again. The various ways people adapt their nutritional and exercise needs to their changing lives illustrate the challenge of remaining fit and eating properly.

Twelfth Grade: *Health experts can treat the potentially life threatening eating disorders, such as anorexia nervosa and bulimia.* When physicians began to identify eating disorders as diseases, they also began finding medical and psychological explanations and interventions for parents, teachers, coaches, and patients themselves to use. This research coincides with increased understanding about addictions of all kinds. Although difficult, physicians can treat these disorders. Recovered former patients have helped physicians and psychologists establish support groups for families and patients and have created a national support network to help people recover from these potentially devastating eating disorders.

The Placement of Exercise Physiology Concepts in the Curriculum

To integrate exercise physiology concepts/principles into the physical education program, instructors must decide where to place those concepts/principles. Throughout the chapter, concepts/principles appropriate for different grade levels develop each theme. National Standards 3 and 4 serve as the guide for the age appropriate sequential concepts.

If students in the earlier grades have not previously had age appropriate activities and have not learned the necessary information, then teachers might consider giving assignments listed for younger students to the older ones before moving on to more advanced study and experiences. The ultimate goal is to develop physically educated adults who can make informed decisions about their health, fitness, and physical activity levels.

Integrating Exercise Physiology Concepts into Instruction

As an integrated subject, exercise physiology combines many sources of knowledge from the laboratory to the playing field. Teachers can integrate exercise physiology concepts into their programs on a daily basis. They also can model a few of these concepts by teaching safety in their daily warm up exercises. They can provide grade level learning experiences in which students can understand and apply these concepts directly. Throughout these suggested lessons, whenever possible, include developmental, geographical, social, psychological, familial, and communal issues and their interrelationships.

Assessing Student Learning

Teachers can use a variety of assessment techniques to determine student progress in the applications of exercise physiology. *Moving into the Future: National Standards for Physical Education* (NASPE, 1995) contains many of these. They are described in detail under Standards 3 and 4, and more generally in the reference section of that book.

Checking for Understanding

The teacher can get useful feedback on the extent to which the group as a whole understands a concept by asking a question and then checking the responses of several students.

Example: Where do you feel this stretch exercise? What is your resting heart rate and your training heart rate? What kind of strength does jogging build?

Written Tests

The written test is a useful and efficient way to assess the degree of knowledge a student has about the subject. Questions can include multiple choice, short answer, and essay. The type of question should match the level of knowledge desired.

Example: FitSmart (Zhu, Safrit, & Cohen, 1999) is a national health-related physical fitness knowledge test for high school students. In addition, most of the textbook series–*Fitness for Life* by Corbin & Lindsay(1997b), *Personal Fitness: Looking Good, Feeling Good* by Williams, Harageones, Johnson, & Smith (1998)—contain sample written tests.

Student Journals and Logs

Because fitness programs are student centered and do not involve competition, the process of self-study is inherent in them. Students in all grades should keep an ongoing record of their progress in sports, games, and activities that they enjoy. This record will provide them with a history of their fitness development and clues to potential lifelong involvement in some of these activities. The record also serves as a central assessment tool.

Example: What did I learn today about my fitness level? What should I work on next time? What amount of time did I spend in moderate and vigorous physical activity today? What is my weekly total number of hours and minutes? How do I feel after engaging in aerobic exercise?

Observation

Teacher observation of students participating in vigorous physical activity remains the primary way to assess achievement in Standards 3 and 4 for engaging in a physically active lifestyle and maintaining a life-enhancing level of physical fitness. The authors of the National Standards recommend using the Cooper Institute Fitnessgram (mentioned earlier) beginning in the fourth grade, because it provides for an ongoing record of student progress in body composition (percent of body fat), aerobic capacity, muscle strength, endurance (for the abdominal, upper arm, and upper back muscles), and flexibility. The Fitnessgram is especially useful for helping students set goals, keep track of their fitness status, and see the results of their commitment for themselves. In assessing student progress in this area, the teacher serves as monitor and supporter, not as judge or critic.

Student Projects

Although student projects provide useful learning experiences, they often require a lot of time.

Example: Students can create and implement a fitness plan that includes cardiorespiratory, muscular strength and endurance, and stretching exercises, as well as dietary goals. This program serves as an authentic assessment tool for determining student understanding of and ability to apply the concepts related to exercise physiology. The detail of this plan can become more specific and challenging as the student advances from one grade level to the next.

Concluding Comments

The main concepts in exercise physiology center around how the internal systems in the human body function and how people can help themselves continue to function in an optimal way. The study of the heart and lungs; nutrition, metabolism, and body composition; and muscles—their strength, endurance, and flexibility—can inform students about how best to care for their bodies now and in the future.

References

Alter, J. (1990a). *Stretch and strengthen* (rev. ed.). Boston: Houghton Mifflin.

_____ (1990b). *Surviving exercise.* (rev. ed.). Boston: Houghton Mifflin.

American Alliance for Health, Physical Education, Recreation and Dance. (1999a). *Physical best activity guide: Secondary level.* Reston, VA: Author.

_____. (1999b). *Physical best activity guide: Elementary level.* Reston, VA: Author.

_____. (1999c). *Physical education for lifelong fitness: The physical best teacher's guide.* Reston, VA: Author.

American College of Sports Medicine. (1992) *Fitness Book: The most practical fitness book, written by the most respected fitness organization in the world.* Champaign, IL: Leisure.

Buck, M. M. (2002). *Assessing heart rate in physical education.* Reston, VA: National Association for Sport and Physical Education.

Cailliet, R. (1981). *Low back pain syndrome.* Philadelphia: F.A. Davis.

Clarkson, P. M. (1995, February). *Micro-nutrients and exercise: Antioxidants and minerals.* Paper presented at the International Scientific Consensus Conference on Nutrition in Athletics, Monaco.

Cooper Institute. (1994). *The Prudential Fitnessgram, test administration manual*. Dallas: The Cooper Institute for Aerobics Research.

Cooper, K. H. (1982). *The aerobics program for total well-being: Exercise, diet, emotional balance*. New York: Bantam.

Corbin, C., & Pangrazi, R. P. (1994). *Teaching strategies for improving youth fitness*. Reston, VA: AAHPERD.

Corbin, C. B., & Pangrazi, R. P. (1998). *Physical activity for children: A statement of guidelines*. Reston, VA: NASPE.

Corbin, C. B., & Lindsay, R. (1997a). *Concepts of fitness and wellness with laboratories*. Madison, WI: Brown and Benchmark.

Corbin, C. B., & Lindsay, R. (1993). *Fitness for life. Teacher's Annotated Edition*. Glenview, IL: Scott, Foresman and Company.

Csikszentmihalyi, M. (1990). *Flow: The psychology of optimal experience*. New York: Harper Collins.

Dominguez, R. H., & Gajda, R. (1982). *Total body training: A proven program for improving sports performance, rehabilitating injuries, and maintaining all-over fitness*. New York: Warner Books.

Falk, B., & Tennenbaum, G. (1996). The effectiveness of resistance training in children. *Journal of Sports Medicine, 20*(3) 176-186.

Freide, A. (Ed.). (1997). *CDC prevention guidelines: A guide for action*. Baltimore: Wilkins & Williams.

Kapit, W., Macey, R. I., & Meisami, E. (1987). *The physiology coloring book*. Cambridge: Harper Collins.

Kapit, W., & Elson, L. M. (1977). *The anatomy coloring book*. New York: Harper and Row.

Kempner, W., Newborg, B. C., Peschel, R. C., & Skyler, J. S. (1975). Treatment of massive obesity with rice/reduction diet program. An analysis of 106 patients with at least 45 kilo weight loss. *Archives of Internal Medicine, 135*(12), 1575-84.

Luttgens, K., & Wells, K. (1982). *Kinesiology: The scientific basis of human movement*. (7th ed.). Philadelphia: W. B. Saunders.

Micheli, L. J. (1983). Overuse injuries in children's sports: The growth factor. *Orthopedic Clinics of North America, 14*(2), 337-360.

Mohnsen, B. S. (2001). *Using technology in physical education*. Cerritos, CA: Bonnie's Fitware.

Morehouse, L. E., & Gross, L. (1975). *Total fitness in 30 minutes a week*. New York: Pocket Books.

NASPE (1995). *Moving into the future: National Standards for Physical Education, A guide to content and assessment*. St. Louis: Mosby.

Nicholas, J. A.(1970, June 29). Injuries to knee ligaments: Relationship of looseness and tightness in football players. *Journal of the American Medical Association*.

Rowland, T. (1994). Effect of prolonged inactivity on aerobic fitness of children. *Journal of Sports Medicine and Physical Fitness, 34*(2), 147-155.

_____ (1992). *Pediatric laboratory exercise testing: Clinical guidelines*. Champaign, IL: Human Kinetics.

Sallis, J. (1994). Determinants of physical activity behavior in children. In R. Pate & R. Hohn (Eds.), *Health and Fitness Through Physical Education*. Champaign, IL: Human Kinetics.

U. S. Department of Health and Human Services. (1996). *Physical activity and health: A report of the Surgeon General*. Rockville, MD: Author.

Vincent, L. M. (1989). *Competing with the sylph: The quest for the perfect dance body* (2nd. Ed.). Princeton, NJ: Princeton Book Company.

Warren, M. P. (1991). Exercise in women: Effects on reproductive system and pregnancy. *Clinics in Sports Medicine 10*(11),131-139.

Watkins, J., & Peabody, P. (1996). Sports injuries in children and adolescents treated at a sports injury clinic. *Journal of Sports Medicine and Physical Fitness, 36*(1), 43-48.

Wells, K. (1978). *Kinesiology: The scientific basis of human movement*. (4th ed.). Philadelphia: W. B. Saunders.

Williams, C. (1995, February). *Macro-nutrients and performance*. Paper presented at the International Scientific Consensus Conference on Nutrition in Athletics, Monaco.

Williams, M. H. (1995, February). *Nutritional ergogenics in athletics*. Paper presented at the International Scientific Consensus Conference on Nutrition in Athletics, Monaco.

Resources

Bailey, C. (1994). *Smart exercise: Burning fat, getting fit*. Boston: Houghton Mifflin.

Greenberg, J. S., & Pargman, D. (1989). *Physical fitness: A wellness approach* (2nd ed.). Englewood, Cliffs, NJ: Prentice Hall.

Hoeger, W. K., & Hoeger, S. A. (1992). *Lifetime physical fitness and wellness: A personalized program* (3rd ed.). Englewood, CO: Morton.

Stokes, R., Moore, C., & Schultz, S. L. (1996). *Personal fitness and you*. Winston-Salem, NC: Hunter Textbooks.

United States Department of Health and Human Services. (1999). *Promoting physical activity: A guide for community action*. Champaign, IL: Human Kinetics.

Williams, C. S., Harageones, E. G., Johnson, D. J., & Smith, C. D. (1998). *Personal fitness: Looking good, feeling good*. Dubuque, IA: Kendall/Hunt.

Zhu, W., Safrit, M., & Cohen, A. (1999). *The national health-related physical fitness knowledge test: FitSmart test user manual: High school*. Champaign, IL: Human Kinetics.

Web Sites

Agricultural Library: http://www.nal.usda.gov/fnic

American Heart Association: http://www.americanheart.org

American Journal of Sports Medicine: http://www.sportsmed.org

Center for Disease Control and Prevention: http://www.hhs.gov/cdc

Cooper Institute: http://www.cooperinst.org
Food and Drug Administration: http://www.hhs.gov/fda
National Institute of Health: http://www.nih.gov
U. S. Department of Health and Human Services: http://www.hhs.gov

Chapter 6

Historical Perspectives

Jan Patterson

O*nce I learn a new sport, do I have to worry about the rules changing? Why were so many of our team sports invented in the late 1800s? What are some sports and dances I can teach to help my children develop an appreciation for our culture? What is the role of physical education in the 21st century? Physical activity and physical education have a remarkable history that affects each and every one of us today. This chapter provides insight into present day occurrences and how they have been shaped by historical events related to physical education, sport and physical activity, exercise and training, and the Olympics. These significant events, along with the concepts/principles they express, are an important part of the cognitive foundation for a physically educated person.*

What Is an Historical Perspective?

Historical perspective is the study of people, events, and changes that shaped the past within the social context of the time. It includes an examination of how these events have affected attitudes and practices of the present. Mechikoff and Estes (2002) note that, through the study of history, people learn how they are similar to civilizations of the past. By learning about the differences among people, we can better understand the opinions and behaviors unique to different cultures and civilizations. By studying the past, we gain greater insights into how and why today's events occur and how the past can influence the future.

Why Is an Historical Perspective in Physical Education Important?

Historical perspectives of physical education explain why the discipline has undergone changes that include, but are not limited to health and wellness, military training, sports and physical activity, dance, and a professional instructional discipline. We must learn from the past in order to appreciate the present and plan for the future. Historical perspective is a process by which we can learn to improve ourselves individually and collectively. Through the historical study of physical education, students will learn why present practices have emerged and why they may change with new knowledge. Physically educated individuals also will be able to predict future best practices in the discipline and personal best practices for lifelong health and wellness.

Linking Historical Perspectives to the National Standards

Historical perspectives concepts/principles are specifically targeted in Standard 6 (Demonstrates understanding and respect for differences among people in physical activity settings). The study of historical perspectives in physical education highlights the influences of many different cultures and times. It explains the origin of sport, exercise, recreation, dance, and instruction.

Selected Historical Themes

It is important for physical education teachers to understand and be able to integrate historical information in their teaching. While physically educated individuals do not need the same depth of understanding, it is important for students to grasp certain concepts/principles in order to fully appreciate individual movement and multicultural activities. These concepts/principles are organized around four major themes:

- The history of the Olympics from ancient Greece to modern times.
- The history of exercise and training.
- The history of physical activity and sport.
- The history of physical education.

Each of these themes is developed briefly in the next section. Critical student concepts/principles that fall under each theme are developed in a K-12 format.

The History of the Olympics from Ancient Greece to Modern Times

The Olympic Games began in ancient Greece. Although there is a limited connection to what is seen in today's Olympics, the concept of the games has been carried forward. The ancient games were held for several hundred years, until they were abolished during the early Christian era. The primary purpose of the ancient Olympics was to honor the gods. In addition to athletic events, they included competitions in music and oratory, and theatrical performances. The purpose of the modern Olympics is to acknowledge the athletic abilities, and to some extent, the superiority, of participants from around the world.

Ancient Times (2500 B.C.–500 A.D.)

It is believed that the ancient Olympic Festival originated sometime around 776 B.C. The first 13 Olympic games had only one event, the stade, which was a race of about 200 meters. No records were kept of the competitors' actual scores; however, Coroibus of Elis was the first recorded champion. In subsequent games, additional events were added. First came the longer running races, then wrestling, a pentathlon (running, jumping, spear-javelin throwing, discus throwing, and wrestling), boxing, and chariot racing. One of the most unusual

Stade: A foot race that measured the length of the stadium in which it was run; generally, the length was about 200 meters.

Example 1

Secondary School Example: Grade 12

Concept/Principle: Each year new events (e.g., baseball, softball) are added to the modern Olympics. The host country may choose one demonstration sport for inclusions.

Students research the demonstration sports that have appeared in the Olympics during the last 20 years. They work in groups of four, and do in-depth research on one demonstration sport from another country. The groups then present their findings to the rest of the class. During the presentation, each group should discuss the origin and social importance of the sport, and then compare it to something that may be similar in the United States. In order to perform this task, students may be required to read nonfiction novels, essays, and journals related to the sport or country of origin. At the conclusion of all the reports, the class should discuss how accepting cultural differences has changed the history of the Olympics.

Pankration:
An event in which a competitor used any means to force his opponent to give up, including boxing with bare hands, twisting an arm, and kicking in the stomach.

events was the pankration, which was a combined effort of upright wrestling and kicking.

The Olympic Festival, held in the Valley of Olympia, was a time of truce between warring city states. For several months prior to the events, athletes would train before game officials, who could disqualify individuals who lacked sufficient physical ability. Even in those times, athletes were required to assure the judges that they had adhered strictly to the rules of training.

In 146 B.C., the games were moved to Rome after Greece was conquered and made part of the Roman Empire. By 632 B.C., the games had been extended to include five days of competition every four years. Winners of the events were crowned with olive leaves. A herald would call out the person's name, the name of his father, and the place from which he came. Girls and women were not allowed to participate or watch the games. However, eventually the Herannic Games, in honor of Hera (wife of Zeus), were established for girls and women. These games were held regularly, two years after each Olympics. In 394 A.D., Emperor Theodosius I declared the event unchristian. The concept of the games seems to have remained dormant until the 19th century.

Pentathlon:
A five-event contest in which the competitors participated in running, jumping, throwing the discus, spear/javelin throwing, and wrestling.

The 19th, 20th and 21st Centuries

In 1850, Dr. William Penny Brooks, a physician and surgeon established the first Wenlock Olympics in England. This event was comprised of local sports such as quoits and cricket as well as track and field events. Dr. Brooks was motivated by the ideals of the ancient Greeks, who emphasized mind and body development along with the development of the spirit. Typically, local athletes participated; however, people from all of Britain eventually came to be involved. Around the same time, the Zappa family of Greece expressed an interested in reviving the Olympic Games. While both Dr. Brooks and the Zappas were in contact, the two factions could not seem to reconcile their visions. So, the Zappas attempted to restart the Olympic Games in Greece, limiting participation to Greek citizens

In France, a man by the name of Pierre de Coubertin also was contemplating the resurrection of the Olympic Games. However, he had a slightly different vision for the event. He wanted to develop a forum that would foster peace as well as national pride. In 1896, the first modern Olympics were held. Representatives from 13 countries met to compete in nine events: cycling, fencing, gymnastics, lawn tennis, shooting, swimming, track and field, weight lifting, and wrestling. In 1924, the first winter Olympics were held in Chamonix, France.

The modern Olympics have often been a venue for social changes. Women first competed in the Olympics in 1900. By the 1912 Olympics, 57 women athletes from 11 countries competed (Mechikoff & Estes, 2002). In 1968, the first Special Olympic Games were held.

In addition, World events and political pressures have affected the Games. In 1916, 1940, and 1944, the games were suspended due to war. At the 1936 Olympics in Berlin, Adolph Hitler advocated for Aryan supremacy. However, Jesse Owens, through his remarkable performance, sent his own message to the world refuting Hitler's political and social propaganda. In 1968, African American medal winners Tommie Smith and John Carlos garnered worldwide attention with their award ceremony protest of racial discrimination in the United States. And, in 1972, terrorism struck the Olympics when 11 Israeli athletes were killed by Palestinian guerrillas. Continued concerns regarding possible terrorist attacks have heightened security measures at Olympic Games in recent years for participants and spectators.

Political boycotts also have had their impact on the Olympics. In 1956, Iraq, Egypt, and Lebanon boycotted the Melbourne games to protest the Anglo-French seizure of the Suez Canal. The Netherlands, Switzerland, and Spain boycotted to protest the Soviet invasion of Hungary. In 1976, in Montreal, 33 African nations boycotted the games to protest apartheid in South Africa. The 1980 boycott of the Moscow Olympics by the United States was in protest of the Soviet invasion of Afghanistan. In response, the Soviets boycotted the 1984 Olympics in Los Angeles.

Several traditions highlight the Olympic Games, including the opening and closing ceremonies, the Olympic rings, the Olympic oath, the Olympic motto, the Olympic torch, and the Olympic medals. The Olympic motto, "Citius, Altius, Fortius," translates to "Swifter, Higher, Stronger." It was written by Father Henri Didion, headmaster of the Aucueil School near Paris, France, to represent the athletic ideal of the games. The Olympic Oath, "In the name of all competitors, I promise that we shall take part in these Olympic Games, respecting and abiding by the rules which govern them, in the true spirit of sportsmanship, for the glory of sport and the honor of our teams," is taken by all Olympic athletes at the opening ceremony.

Also during the Opening Ceremony is the lighting of the torch. This tradition dates back to the ancient games, when priests placed sacrifices on an altar and prepared to set them on fire. From 200 meters away, young boys waited for the sign to start their race. The winner seized the flaming torch from the priest and lit the fire. Replacing the laurel wreath of the ancient games are the gold, silver, and bronze medals that represent first, second, and third place. Finally, the five rings serve as the Olympic symbol representing the five major continents of the world: North America, South America, Europe, Asia, and Africa.

The idea of amateur status for Olympic athletes has been an ongoing controversy in different nations. In 1912, Jim Thorpe, an American gold medalist, lost his medals because he had played on a semiprofessional baseball team. In 1925, the International Olympic Committee attempted to define the concept of amateurism. However, what emerged was a definition of a professional as the receipt of payment while participating in a sport. The debate ensued as to whether providing accommodations for athletes during training meant they were being paid. The IOC finally decided that an athlete could be compensated for any loss of salary. In some Eastern European countries, sports are a very serious business. Children are required to participate, and the most promising athletes are groomed for world events such as the Olympics. Because of this, they are fully subsidized throughout the years while they train and compete in the Olympics. It is now at the point, however, where professional athletes are competing in the Olympics. Looking at the Olympic basketball teams, for example, it is apparent that the majority of players make their living playing the sport.

Being selected to host the Olympics brings myriad consider-ations related to the athletic competition. It can bring tremen-dous economic benefits to the city/state/country putting on the games. The money brought into the area from the indi-viduals attending the Olympics is a boon to the economy. How-ever, the effects are far reaching. Host cities must build world class facilities that use the latest technology. In Salt Lake City, the venue for the speed skaters utilized new technology to make the ice as dry, cold, and hard as possible to ensure faster times. In addition to the immediate effect on the event or sport, the host country gains worldwide recognition as a result of the media attention. Finally, the Olympic site and surrounding ven-ues create jobs, merchandise for the event, and opportunities for people to volunteer. Just to watch the individuals involved in the opening ceremonies is testimony to thousands of hours spent in creating, practicing, and performing the show.

The History of Exercise and Training

The history of exercise and training can be traced to the dawn of humankind. Hunting and gathering food for survival pro-vided primitive beings (pre-10,000 B.C.) with their first physi-cal activity (Anderson, 1985). The Neolithic Agricultural Revo-lution (10,000-8,000 B.C.), on the other hand, marked the beginning of a more sedentary lifestyle, as humankind reduced the time spent hunting and gathering in exchange for farming (Garnsey, 1999). At this point, people had to look for other reasons to be physically active.

Example 2

Secondary School Example: Grade 12

Concept/Principle: Research has improved the way people exercise and the equipment they use.

Students interview adults about the way they exercised when they were in elementary or high school. They then research new forms of these exer-cises. Finally, they write an essay comparing the older form to the newer form and explain why the new form is safer.

Concepts/Principles

Kindergarten: *The Olympic Games began a long time ago.*

Second Grade: *Summer Olympics are now held during the summer every four years.*

Second Grade: *Winter Olympics are now held during the winter every four years.*

Fourth Grade: *New venues (e.g., gymnasiums, pools) are built by the country hosting the Olympics.*

Fourth Grade: *There are many traditions associated with the Olympic Games.*

Sixth Grade: *The first Olympics had only one event (stade), but in subsequent years, new events were added (i.e., pentathlon, wrestling, chariot races, boxing).*

Sixth Grade: *The ancient Olympics were both a sport and a religious festival.*

Eighth Grade: *The modern Olympics (revived by Pierre de Coubertin in 1896, and held in Athens, Greece) aimed to further the cause of world peace, highlight athletes from different parts of the world, and prepare individuals to become highly trained athletes.*

Tenth Grade: *The country hosting the Olympics receives many benefits.*

Tenth Grade: *The meaning of amateur status in the Olympics has changed throughout the years.*

Twelfth Grade: *There have been many political events (i.e., war in 1916, 1940, 1944; boycotts in 1956, 1976, 1980, and 1984; terrorism in 1972; and racial conflict in 1936 and 1968) that have affected the Olympics.*

Twelfth Grade: *The host country also may choose one demonstration sport for inclusion in the Olympics.*

Ancient Times (2500 B.C.–476 A.D.)

In China, the philosophical teachings of Confucius encouraged regular physical activity (Matthews, 1969). The Chinese recognized that certain diseases were preventable with regular exercise. Cong Fu, the exercise program of the time, consisted of various stances and movements characterized by separate foot positions and imitations of different animal fighting styles (Dalleck & Kravitz, 2002). Today, this program is known as Kung Fu.

In India, the religious beliefs of Buddhism and Hinduism discouraged the pursuit of fitness. However, Hindu priests were able to pursue yoga as a way of bringing the body, mind, and spirit together. One of the most commonly known forms of yoga today is hatha yoga. It grew out of the original form developed more than 5,000 years ago. Hatha yoga utilizes a series of exercises meant to assist the individual with relaxation, meditation, and flexibility for lifetime wellness. These exercises are called asanas, or held poses. There are two types: cultural asanas increase muscle tone and positively affect the nervous, endocrine, and circulatory systems; meditative asanas provide for the elimination of the physiological side effects of stress. Today, more than 12 million individuals in the United States participate regularly in yoga.

Asanas: Held poses or positions.

Assyria, Babylonia, Egypt, Palestine, Persia, and Syria pursued fitness activities as a way to improve the performance of their military forces (Green, 1989). Persian leaders demanded a rigid fitness training program from their people that consisted of marching, hunting, riding, and javelin throwing (Wuest & Bucher, 1995). However, after the political and military leaders became wealthy and corrupt, the emphasis on fitness declined and the Persian Empire collapsed.

The Greek appreciation for the beauty of the body and the importance of health and fitness throughout Greek society is unmatched in history (Dalleck & Kravitz, 2002). The Greeks believed in the development of the body and mind; in fact the Greek term for exercise, *ascesis*, means body and mind exercises. Hippocrates and Herodicus, medical practitioners of the time, prescribed exercise regimens to assist in strengthening weakened muscles, weight loss, and health maintenance. Some

Ascesis: Greek term for exercise.

of these exercises included a type of weight lifting with objects that resembles modern day dumbbells.

The Spartans (Northern Greece) also valued fitness, primarily for military purposes. At the age of six, boys were required to begin special fitness programs designed to produce highly fit adult soldiers. Females also were required to be physically fit so that they could produce strong offspring (Barrow & Brown, 1988).

The Roman Empire emphasized vigorous exercise programs for its warriors. Military training consisted of marching, jumping, running, and discus and javelin throwing. The program was reported to be so rigorous that anyone found unfit was excluded from the ranks of the gladiators or soldiers. However, as the military conquered most of the western world, the general population was able to focus on garnering wealth and enjoying entertainment. The fitness levels of the general population began to decline, resulting in the fall of the Roman Empire to the physically superior Barbarian tribes from Northern Europe (Harris, 1972).

The Middle Ages and the Renaissance (476 A.D.–1600 A.D.)

Despite the cultural setbacks that occurred with the fall of the Roman Empire, fitness experienced a revival during the Dark (476 A.D.-1000 A.D.) and Middle Ages (900 A.D.-1400 A.D.). This was due to the fact that the Barbarian tribes lived much like primitive people, spending their time hunting, gathering food, and tending to cattle (Randers-Pehrson, 1993). Fitness had again become a requirement for survival.

During the Renaissance (1400 A.D.–1600 A.D.) there was a renewed interest in the human body. Leonardo Da Vinci (1452-1519) studied the human body and its internal workings by identifying and illustrating specific muscle groups and skeletal structures and their interactions. Many individuals of time, including Martin Luther (religious leader), John Locke (philosopher), and Vittorino da Feltra (the first modern schoolmaster) maintained that high fitness levels enhanced intellectual learning. (Dalleck & Kravitz, 2002).

In 1535, Leonard Fuchs, a professor and physician, studied the exercise teachings of the Greeks and Romans and developed his own theory of the art of exercise. He described two types of exercise—basic, simple exercise, and exercise with work. During this same time an Italian professor, Hieronymus Mercurialis, wrote a book on therapeutic exercise entitled *De Arte Gymnastica*. After numerous translations, it was determined by John Basmajian (1978) that the following ideals were held at the time for medical exercise:

- Each exercise should preserve the existing healthy state.
- Exercise should not disturb the harmony among the principal humors.
- Exercises should be suited to each part of the body.
- All healthy people should take exercise regularly.
- Sick people should not be given exercises that might exacerbate existing conditions.
- Special exercises should be prescribed for convalescent patients on an individual basis.
- Persons who lead a sedentary life urgently need exercise.

The 17th and 18th Centuries

During the 17th and 18th centuries, exercise again came into vogue as various countries established schools or training places, particularly for men. Their common function was to train men in strength, agility, and physical fitness. In Germany, Sweden, and Denmark these schools were meant to train soldiers to be better fighters. The premise was to keep the military strong at all times. In Colonial America, the lifestyle of plowing, hunting, and herding (Keller, 1971) provided sufficient levels of physical activity.

Several scholars and physicians during this period studied and wrote about the effects of exercise for the common individual. George Cheyne, a Scottish physician, wrote in 1724 about longevity and exercise. He promoted walking as a healthful and beneficial activity. Frederich Hoffman, a professor at the University of Halle in Germany, wrote a treatise about the differences among exercise, movement, and work (which he called gymnasium, kinesis, and ponos). Hoffman also discussed the benefits of muscle motion on cardiovascular circulation. In 1723, Nicolas Andry, considered to be grandfather of orthopaedics, presented a paper to the Paris Medical Faculty. It was entitled, *Is Exercise the Best Means of Preserving Health?* Later in his career, Andry developed rules of exercise for correcting postural anomalies. Additionally, Joseph-Clement Tissot, in 1780, recommended ambulation of surgical patients as soon as possible. He went on to become a founder of occupational therapy. He also added to the body of knowledge regarding respiratory exercise.

Enlightenment: A period during the 1700s when individuals believed they became more aware of the infinite world and hence more intelligent.

As society entered the Age of Enlightenment (18th century), Jean Jacques Rousseau, a French philosopher, revolutionized education when he placed health at the forefront of the needs of the fully developed citizen. In his treatise on education, entitled *Emile*, Rousseau wrote about the need for children to mature in harmony with nature. Rousseau believed that the body was strengthened through exercise guided by nature, and that in order to learn, individuals must exercise the body, senses, and organs. Unlike Plato, who touted a strong mind, spirit, and body primarily for warriors, Rousseau's philosophy dictated that a strong mind was developed through strengthening the body. This was the first time a link had been made between health and wellness for everyone. Many of these same ideas and beliefs were restated in the writings of Rene Descartes, John Locke, and John Dewey.

The 19th, 20th and 21st Centuries

In the years between the early 1800s and the onset of World War I, Georg Hegel, a professor of philosophy at the University of Heidelberg, and Karl Marx, an economic and political philosopher, argued that the mind controls the body. These men believed that an individual needed to become physically strong through exercise in order to be a contributing member of society. They further believed that a person's state of being (mental attitude) could guide the selection of a physical activity and the subsequent determination of how hard to perform that activity. Hegel concluded that the mind controlled the body, and therefore operated separately; that is, an intellectual rationale could be made for participation in physical activity (Mechikoff & Estes, 2002). This type of thinking, according to Hegel's philosophy, led to a higher order human being.

In the mid 1800s, the field of medicine broke into specialty groups. Physical education was one of them. George Barker Windship (1834-1876) was a key figure in this movement. While his name is not commonly known, he had a tremendous impact on the field of exercise physiology. Windship was particularly interested in developing personal strength because of his own slight stature. Windship entered Harvard Medical School, where he studied physiology and anatomy. He was so intrigued with this area that upon graduation, he typically prescribed exercise to cure the ills of his patients. From experiments conducted by Windship, a modern weight lifting system emerged (see Figure 1). He invented a system of graduated dumbbells for strength building. As a result of Windship's experimentation and prescription of exercise, he emerged as a pioneer for his day in strength and heath reform.

With a renewed emphasis on fitness and exercise, researchers in the late 1800s began to study the effects of strength training and how to measure increases in fitness. They also began to study various types of fitness testing. These studies set the stage for future physical fitness testing for the military and for educa-

Figure 1

George Barker Windship's Atmospheric Lifter and Strength Tester, patented February 20, 1872.

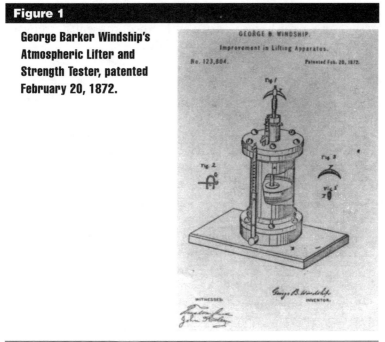

U.S. Department of Commerce, Patent & Trademark Office

tion. In many states, fitness testing is currently mandated as part of the curriculum at various grade levels.

With the arrival of World War I and the high level of war related injuries came an increase in the need for physical rehabilitation programs. Thus, the field physical therapy was founded as another medical strand of physical education. This strand echoed the early Chinese belief that through exercise the body could, to some degree, be restored.

During both world wars, a concern was expressed about the large number of men failing the fitness test for entrance into the military. During World War I one out of every three drafted individuals was unfit for combat, and many of those drafted were highly unfit prior to military training (Wuest & Bucher, 1995; Barrow & Brown, 1988). By World War II, nearly half of all draftees were rejected or given noncombat positions due to their poor levels of fitness (Rice, Hutchinson, & Lee, 1958).

In the 1940s, Dr. Thomas K. Cureton, from the University of Illinois, introduced the application of research to fitness. He studied questions such as: How much exercise is healthy? What types of exercise are most effective? How can physical fitness best be measured within an individual? He also developed fitness tests for cardiorespiratory endurance, muscular strength, and flexibility (Dalleck & Kravitz, 2002).

During the mid-50s, fitness concerns escalated as the Kraus-Weber Test, administered by Kraus and Hirschland (1954, as referenced in Patterson & Hallberg, 1966) to elementary school children in Europe and the United States, showed that American children compared poorly to European children. In fact, close to 60 percent of American children, and only nine percent of the European children, failed at least one test. The test battery measured abdominal strength, upper back strength, lower back strength, and hamstring flexibility. As a result, President Dwight Eisenhower became a strong advocate for the development of fitness throughout the United States. He held a White House Conference in June of 1956. This was followed by the formation of the President's Council on Youth Fitness and the appointment of the President's Citizens Advisory Committee on the Fitness of American Youth (Dalleck & Kravitz,

2002). As a result of the conference, the American Alliance for Health, Physical Education and Recreation (AAHPER) created the first national youth fitness test in 1958. It was comprised of eight test items: 50-yard dash, pull-ups (boys) flex arm hang (girls), sit-ups that were straight leg, shuttle run, standing broad jump, softball throw for distance, and 600-yard run/walk.

President John F. Kennedy also was a proponent of fitness and its benefits for the American people. He advanced the President's Council, renaming it the President's Council on Physical Fitness. Kennedy pushed the federal government to become more involved in national fitness promotion and started a pilot fitness program for youths that later became the President's Fitness Challenge.

Youth fitness tests designed by both the President's Council on Physical Fitness and the American Alliance for Health, Physical Education, Recreation and Dance (AAHPERD) have been updated numerous times. However, the tide definitely began to turn in the 1970s, when the test was criticized because it was viewed as a measure of athletic ability rather than general fitness. By the mid-1970s, a growing body of research supported the value of regular vigorous activity for the promotion of health. This led to the replacement of the youth fitness test with a health-related fitness test in 1980. An early researcher in this area was Dr. Kenneth Cooper, who without a doubt had a significant impact on the development of health-related fitness guidelines and health-related fitness testing.

In addition to improvements in fitness testing, there have been improvements in the body of knowledge related to the forms of exercise. From the early 1940s until the 1970s, ballistic stretching was the preferred warm-up method, and a cool-down was rarely mentioned. Hyperextension of neck, back, and knees also was considered standard stretching practice. The level of knowledge that exists today includes not only how to stretch and exercise, but also why one stretches and exercises and how to do so safely.

Research continues to support the role of health-related fitness as a way to lower risk factors for coronary heart disease and enhance the quality of life. Most recently, the Surgeon General's Report on Physical Activity (USDHHS, 1996) noted that adults need 30 minutes of moderate activity on most days of the week. In addition, Corbin and Pangrazi (1998), note that elementary school children should accumulate at least 30 to 60 minutes of age and developmentally appropriate physical activity from a variety of physical activities on all or most days of the week. In fact, an accumulation of more than 60 minutes, and up to several hours per day of developmentally appropriate activity is encouraged for elementary school children.

Today, rapid changes in technology are having a tremendous impact on the fitness industry. Exercise equipment such as treadmills, rowers, climbers, and cross-country skiing devices feature heart-monitoring devices. Some of these devices not only provide the participant with immediate feedback about heart rate during the exercise period, they also store the data, analyze it, and at the end of the workout provide the participant with information related to the next workout period. It seems that exercising regularly is being made less complicated through the use of technology. One can only speculate about the advances that will occur in exercise equipment and monitoring systems in the next 10 to 20 years.

Concepts/Principles

Kindergarten: *Throughout history, people have exercised.*

Second Grade: *Throughout history, there have been many reasons why people exercise.*

Fourth Grade: *Throughout history, there have been many reasons why people exercise. These include religious, military, and health reasons.*

Fourth Grade: *Throughout history, people have performed exercises that are potentially harmful.*

Sixth Grade: *Each of the ancient civilizations (Chinese, Indian, Near Eastern, Greek, and Roman) had different reasons for participating in exercise.*

Sixth Grade: *During the Dark Ages and Middle Ages, fitness was a requirement for survival.*

Sixth Grade: *During the Renaissance there was a renewed interest in studying the human body and related health issues.*

Eighth Grade: *The late 1800s marked a time when researchers studied strength training and fitness testing.*

Tenth Grade: *Fitness tests are currently conducted in most schools. They are changed regularly to conform to research findings.*

Tenth Grade: *The results of early fitness tests such as the Kraus-Weber test indicated a need to focus on the fitness of American youth.*

Tenth Grade: *There is currently an emphasis on health-related fitness and moderate physical activity directed toward health enhancement.*

Tenth Grade: *The poor fitness levels of WWI and WWII draftees heightened the public's awareness of the need for exercise programs.*

Twelfth Grade: *After a war is fought and won, there is a tendency for a society to exercise less.*

Twelfth Grade: *Research has improved the way people exercise and the equipment they use.*

The History of Physical Activity and Sport

People have participated in some form of play, dance, and physical activity throughout history. In a translation of *The Dance: Ancient and Modern*, Arabella Moore (1900) writes that primitive humans were known to dance, joining hands as they spun around. She believes that primitive people danced to avoid boredom, and that this turning motion began slowly at first, then increased with excitement.

Example 3

Middle School Example: Grade 6

Concept/Principle: During medieval times, jesters, squires, and knights participated in different activities. The knights and squires were preparing for combat; the jesters were entertainers.

This is an interdisciplinary learning experience held in conjunction with the medieval unit offered by the history/social science teacher. At the beginning of this unit, the students are taught the activities of the jesters—including juggling, stilt walking, and loop and stick. During the middle part of the unit, the students are taught the activities of the squires—including basic tumbling and self-defense. Finally, toward the end of the unit, the students are taught the activities of the knights—including melee, jousting, and long bow. This unit concludes with a Medieval Festival, where some of the students are jesters, some are squires, and some are knights participating in tournaments. Other festival activities will depend on what is taught by the history/social science teacher. Finally, students conduct their own research on medieval activities and write a newspaper article about them.

Herbert Spencer (1820-1903), a British philosopher and sociologist, believed that play was a natural instinct and that humans engaged in play for their personal well being and development as well as for sheer pleasure. Karl Goos, a play theorist in the late 1890s, believed that people played as a way to develop life skills; children watched the movements of adults and imitated them in their play and activity. G. Stanley Hall, a play theorist and professor at Clark University, Massachusetts, popularized the phrase, "ontogeny recapitulates phylogeny." His premise was that people were merely replaying the history of their ancestors. Luther Gulick (1865-1918), a prominent physical educator of the time, philosophized that through play, one would develop a social conscience that would bring order and sense to modern people and times. John Dewey (1859-1952), renowned educator, philosopher, and psychologist, believed that play had a purpose; that it was directed by the interest of the individual, thus suggesting a cognitive aspect to physical activity.

Jean Piaget (1966) from Patterson and Hallberg (1966), a child psychologist, described physical activity in the developing child as the fulfillment of the need to play. He outlined a developmental hierarchy of skill building from play as enjoyment, to play as a sense of accomplishment and control, to play as a socially interactive activity. In his treatise on interpreting play,

Middle School Example: Grade 8

Concept/Principle: As leisure time increased, so did the interest in playing and watching sports.

Students work in groups of six to research the origin of team sports in America during the late 1800s. Each group is assigned one sport (e.g., volleyball, basketball, football, baseball) to examine. Students investigate the origin of the sport, the social importance of the sport, and the original rules and strategies of the sport. They explore the reasons why the sport was introduced during this particular time period. The groups then present their sport to the rest of the class. During the presentation, the group teaches the original version of the game and provides an opportunity for the class to play.

Piaget alludes to the notion that physical activity and play are essential in the lives of humans. He cautions that how one interacts in that social environment can determine how well one makes the transition from child's play to adult play. Piaget's belief that physical activity and play are an integral part of life provides an explanation of why so many different physical activities exist.

Many of today's physical activities and sports actually had their beginnings in ritual and religious activities. Guttmann (1978) notes six characteristics of physical activity that have transformed sports from their ritualistic, religious beginnings to what they are today:

Figure 4

Reprinted by permission, from PhotoDisc, Volume 10, 1993. (Seattle, WA).

Religious: Sporting events, such as the Olympic Festival and some Native American games, were originally held strictly for the purpose of evoking positive favor from the gods.

Equality: The notion that physical activity was for everyone and that competition among the contestants should be fair.

Specialization: The idea that those competing in sport should train full time, unencumbered by jobs or financial concerns; pointing to the days of the ancient Greek athletes who would train full time for the Olympic Festival, and to modern day athletes who earn scholarships because of their athletic prowess.

Rationalization: The belief that rules of competition are an integral part of any sport; citing the rules for competition from the Ancient Olympics to modern times.

Quantification: The view that there is a need to quantify success or failure related to sport; citing the Polynesians who kept score in their dart games, the Romans who measured distance and time, and today's measuring of batting averages.

Records: The idea that there should be a record of sport statistics for future reference.

In studying play, dance, physical activity, and sport around the world, it becomes apparent that almost every culture has contributed to the mix. While it is beyond the scope of this chapter to account for the development of every sport and dance, it is important to note that each sport and dance reflects its culture of origin and has a rich history of its own. Understanding history helps us understand similarities and differences among people and cultures.

Ancient Times (2500 B.C.–500 A.D.)
In ancient times, dances were used for religious purposes, while sports were probably used as preparation for war. Some of the first evidence of sports comes from the Sumarian civilization (3000 B.C.–1500 B.C.). These people participated in wrestling, boxing, swimming, and archery.

The ancient Chinese (2600 B.C.), in addition to Cong Fu gymnastics, participated in archery, dancing, fencing, and wrestling. The Persians were engaged in hunting, riding, and throwing the javelin. The early Greeks participated in throwing the discus or javelin, boxing, and wrestling. The Greeks also were especially fond of contests and games, including chariot racing, foot racing, and even funeral games.

While much has been mentioned about the sports in which men participated, the women of Sparta also participated in some sports. They were involved in foot races, wrestling, and discus throwing. In the first century A.D., Roman women were engaged in sporting events such as foot racing, swimming, and dancing. There is evidence that women participated as gladiators in the Roman Empire. The Roman men engaged in rigorous weight lifting and competed in chariot races and gladiator events. It is apparent that these activities were associated with preparation for war.

There is evidence from the Sumerian ruins that the children played board games and had other toys. The early Greek and Roman children were fond of spinning tops and swinging in swings. And, during the later part of this era, the Romans introduced the skill of kicking a ball. They were known to participate in ball games (similar to handball) that required throwing and catching skills

The Middle Ages and the Renaissance (476 A.D.–1600 A.D.)

In China, organized sport evolved at the beginning of the T'ang Dynasty (618-907 A.D.). Boxing emerged as a popular sport, and in 1070 A.D., Chio Yuan Shang Jen, a Chinese boxing teacher, wrote training rules for the sport. It is believed that the martial arts emerged from the ideas proposed by Jen.

During the Middle Ages (900 A.D.-1400 A.D.), knights engaged in tournaments in order to maintain a level of physical fitness for combat. They participated in melee(sword fighting, which began on horseback, then once off the horse became hand-to-hand sword fighting), jousting (see Figure 5), long bow (archery), and crossbow (see Figure 6). Jesters participated in juggling, stilt walking, and an activity called loop and

Jousting: An event in which two armored riders charge each other.

stick, where a stick was used to rotate a circular object on its side. The squires participated in what would be referred to in modern times as basic tumbling, and in self-defense moves, including hand-to-hand combat.

Recreational activities during the Middle Ages included hunting, handball, tennis, billiards, and shuffleboard. There also was a continued interest in ball games such as boule, which may have been the origin of modern day soccer, and in rounders, the precursor to baseball. Despite the seeming abundance of physical activity, however, physical activity actually decreased during this time. In fact, only music, games, and dancing were considered acceptable upper class pursuits. The common people of the Middle Ages participated in more violent games such as foot fighting and wrestling.

Figure 5

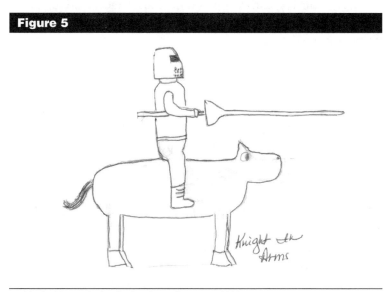

Used with permission Jordan James Patterson, 2002

The 17th and 18th Centuries

During these 200 years, games evolved from many different cultures and countries. As Europeans settled the Colonies and moved to other regions of North America, they brought their ideals, traditions, and games with them. Therefore, during this time, sport and play reflected the attitudes of the settlers. Even individuals such as Benjamin Franklin, Thomas Jefferson, and Noah Webster discussed the benefits of physical activity. In a letter to Oliver Neave, a friend, Benjamin Franklin touted the benefit of learning to swim (Patterson & Hallberg, 1966).

The Puritans, who settled the New England area, wanted physical activity to be more "Christian," without the violence or competition exhibited by many games. Therefore, nonfrivolous, useful activities such as fishing, hunting, and walking were encouraged within these communities. The Puritans believed that play was actually a poor use of time. It was only useful in assisting individuals in recovering from or preparing for work. From this philosophy came the term for recreation (re-creation).

The Quakers, who settled in the Mid-Atlantic area, enjoyed golf, tennis, bowling, and cricket. Like the Puritans, they preferred to be involved in physical activities that were less competitive in nature. During the winter months, they liked to ice skate and go on sleigh rides. Shooting matches and horseback riding also were acceptable activities to the Quakers.

In the southern regions of North America there was a slightly different outlook on sport. Horse racing for a quarter mile was a popular spectator sport, which had been introduced with slaves as the jockeys. People from the South also enjoyed fox hunting, dancing, fencing, fishing, rowing, lawn bowling, and boxing. Participants of this latter activity were called pugilists. Tom Molyneux, a slave, earned his freedom by boxing.

Just as the European settlers were important to the development of sport, so were the Native Americans. The Hurons played games that involved tossing a bladder type ball that was caught in a netlike object. This game was often played across great distances, involved more than 100 players, and lasted for several days. Lacrosse evolved from this Native American sport. Other contributions to American sport and physical activity by Native Americans included ball games, horse racing, and tribal dances.

The 19th, 20th and 21st Centuries
During the Industrial Revolution, the populations of cities increased and playgrounds along with other recreational facilities were developed. These facilities resulted from the growing concern about the poor health of children and the lack of space in

which they could play. In 1898, Joseph Lee created a model playground, the Columbia Avenue Playground in Boston, Massachusetts. Other cities across the United States used this concept to create space for children and adults to play.

In the late 1800s, there was an upsurge of new team sports in America. The assembly-line production of sporting goods and increased leisure made it possible, even during the 1800s, for more people to be involved in sports and activities. The YMCA, which originated in London, England, and was brought to America (Boston, Massachusetts) in 1851, was a popular recreation site.

Basketball was introduced in 1891, at what is now Springfield College in Springfield, Massachusetts. Created by James Naismith, a Canadian, the game originally used peach baskets and a soccer ball and combined the skills of football, hockey, and soccer. It was specifically designed for indoor play in small spaces during the extremely cold winter months. In 1901, A.G. Spaulding published the first basketball rulebook for women. Only three dribbles were allowed at a time, and then the ball had to be passed. In addition, each woman had to stay in a section of the basketball court, since running up and down the court was thought to be too strenuous.

Although basketball proved to be very popular, many businessmen complained that it was too demanding for a lunch break activity. So, in 1895, William Morgan invented volleyball for members of a businessmen's class at the YMCA. The original game involved striking the bladder of a basketball back and forth across a raised tennis net.

The influence of other countries is apparent in many of the games that were developed during the 19th century. For example, the British game of rounders was the forerunner of baseball. Rounders, in turn, was an offshoot of older games that may date back to the Egyptians. Football is another game whose roots date back many centuries; many related games involved kicking a ball, but the shape of the ball and the rules of the game varied.

As participation in sports continued to increase, so did spectatorship. After the Civil War, professional teams began to appear. For example, in 1871, the National Baseball League was organized. With the league came written rules, specialized roles, statistics, public information, and national competitions.

In the United States today, team sports such as baseball, basketball, and football are very popular spectator sports that also are played recreationally by the public. Other popular recreational activities include, walking, boating, fishing, bowling, bicycle riding, jogging, dance, tennis, and golf.

Ours is still a country of immigrants who bring their dances and sports with them. For example, with the increase in the number of Latin Americans and western Europeans in this country, we have seen an increase in the popularity of soccer. Knowing about the popular recreational activities in other countries can increase our understanding of these people and their cultures. In each case, the popularity can be linked to the geographic conditions (e.g., ice hockey in Canada) or the influence of immigrants or settlers (e.g., cricket brought to the South Pacific by the British settlers).

In this country in recent years, professional sports and community recreational programs have experienced tremendous growth in participation. There are women's teams, men's teams, and coed teams for sports, including softball, volleyball, field hockey, basketball and tennis. Along with the interest in sporting activities, there also has been a growing popularity in workout or fitness facilities. These range from private gyms, to programs run by city recreational departments, to programs run through the YMCA. Activities include aerobic workouts, racquetball, tennis, weight lifting, and swimming.

Concepts/Principles

Kindergarten: *Games that are played at school today may have looked different long ago.*

Second Grade: *There are reasons why games change.*

Second Grade: *The local climate influences the kinds of physical activity in which people participate.*

Fourth Grade: *Various cultures have had an impact on sports and recreational activities throughout different areas.*

Fourth Grade: *Many of today's physical activities, dances, and sports had their beginnings in ritual and religious activities.*

Sixth Grade: *The purpose of games, dance, and sport in the ancient world was to maintain the culture, train for combat, perform religious ceremonies, and to respond to a need for physical activity.*

Sixth Grade: *During medieval times, jesters, squires, and knights participated in different activities. The knights and squires were preparing for combat while the jesters were entertainers.*

Eighth Grade: *The Industrial Revolution was a catalyst for the development of playground and recreational facilities.*

Eighth Grade: *Many American sports and games have their roots in other countries. This accounts for many of the similarities between sports in different cultures.*

Eighth Grade: *As leisure time increased, so did the interest in playing and watching sports.*

Eighth Grade: *Professional sports (especially team sports) emerged after the Civil War.*

Tenth Grade: *Understanding the purpose and history of sport helps people make informed decisions regarding education and recreation.*

Tenth Grade: *Laws such as Title IX and Section 504 of the Rehabilitation Act have had an impact on who can participate in sports and physical education.*

Tenth Grade: *Sports rules are influenced by societal events; this is most noticeable in women's sports.*

Tenth Grade: *Women pioneers in athletics have paved the way for today's female athletes.*

Twelfth Grade: *Every game and sport we play has a history.*

Twelfth Grade: *Understanding the purpose and history of sport around the world helps people better understand different cultures and appreciate the contributions of different groups of people.*

Twelfth Grade: *The popularity of most sports can be linked to the geographic conditions or the influence of immigrants or settlers in the area.*

The History of Physical Education

In the western world, the study of physical education as a discipline can be traced back to the days of Plato and the concept of a sound mind in a sound body. Plato espoused the importance of maintaining physical health and conditioning in order to improve one's intellect. He also suggested that a balance between intellectual and physical education resulted in character training, which rendered an individual healthy in body and soul.

Ancient Times

Perhaps the earliest accounts of physical education can be found in the training of the Spartans. Spartan youth were instructed in swimming, running, fighting, wrestling, boxing, ball games, horsemanship, archery, discus and javelin throwing, and field marches. Each of these activities was designed to prepare them for military service. The training of youths in ancient Rome was also directed toward developing disciplined, obedient, and able warriors. Youths were taught jumping, running, swimming, horsemanship, wrestling, boxing, archery, and fencing.

In ancient Athens, music (meaning academics) and gymnastics were the two focuses of the curriculum. Students began their

Pancratium:
A combination of boxing and wrestling involving heavy and hard exercise.

education around the age of seven with physical conditioning. Gymnastics (or physical education) in Athens included boxing, wrestling, jumping, ball games, games with hoops, military skills, running, dancing, javelin and discus throwing, and the pancratium. Wealthy families in Athens hired a *paidotribe* (a physical education teacher who owned his own *palestra*, or wrestling center) to educate their sons. This seems to be very similar in concept to today's personal trainer or private health club. The women in Athens did not receive physical education instruction, although Spartan women participated in gymnastic exercise.

The Middle Ages and the Renaissance

During the Dark and Middle Ages, sporting activities and physical education seemed to have disappeared except for purely military activities. This may have been due, in part, to religious reasons and attitudes.

Paidotribe:
A physical education teacher who owned his own *palestra*.

During the Age of Science, physical education and sport again became accepted. Philosophers approved of the notion that creating a well-rounded individual through physical education was a prudent goal. One such philosopher, Vittorino Da Feltre (1378-1446), noted as the first modern schoolmaster, believed that part of the education of young men should include physical exercise instruction. Da Feltre stated that physical development through exercise would create a successful and educated individual. His students studied swimming, dancing, wrestling, running, leaping, fencing, climbing, walking, riding, hunting, playing ball, and shooting. There was a renewed interest in hygiene along with swimming and water safety. These areas were included in physical instruction for all students, but primarily for boys.

The 17th and 18th Centuries

In the 18th century, Johann Christoph Friedrick Guts-Muths (1759-1839) of Germany developed a training program in which athletes could work on strength, agility, and fitness skills. His athletes combined locomotion and nonlocomotion skills with posture and balance to prepare for both war and competition. At the same time, scholars and trainers in Sweden and Denmark began to develop training programs and schools for gymnastics and fencing. These programs were a manifestation

Palestra: A center for wrestling activity.

of the resurgence of nationalism, and the desire of many countries to develop strong men to fight wars.

Nationalism: A keen sense of pride in one's own country.

In 1774, Johann Bernhard Basedow founded the Philanthropinium in Germany on the educational philosophy of Rousseau. Combining Rousseau's ideology along with that of Francis Bacon and John Comenius, Basedow created an educational environment that offered physical education instruction. In Basedow's outline for learning, half the instruction was devoted to intellectual activities, while the other half included physical and recreational activities. Included in these activities were running, wrestling, throwing, and jumping. This was similar to the Greek *palestra*. It is believed that the individual responsible for instruction was the precursor to the modern day physical educator.

In Colonial America, education in general was left to the parents. Health and physical education were not valued, and therefore were not taught. This attitude probably stemmed from the lifestyle of the time, which was geared toward basic survival. Farming was a common occupation, and most children were expected to assist in the physical challenges of that occupation.

However, in 1790, Noah Webster voiced his views on physical education. He reviewed the statements of ancient philosophers about the value of a sound mind and body. Webster's ideas provided a stimulus for a renewed interest in the worthiness of physical education.

The 19th to 21st Centuries

Within Europe, schools had been an important medium for spreading the understanding of the need for fitness through physical education programs. However, in the United States, the educational process focused primarily on reading, writing, and arithmetic. Physical education remained absent from public education for the early part of the 19th century (Dalleck & Kravitz, 2002).

In the early 1800s, education in general varied with the area in which children lived. For example, on the western frontier, many families lived on ranches. For the wealthy, tutors came to the home to provide instruction. In this instance, physical education consisted of horseback riding and other challenges peculiar to the rural life.

Between 1830 and 1860, there were three major influences on physical education programs in the United States. These were Swedish calisthenics, which emphasized participation in a series of exercises performed on command; German gymnastics, which included vaulting, high jumping, wrestling, and pole vaulting; and English sports and games.

Catherine Beecher became one of the outstanding leaders in furthering the cause of education for women in the 1830s. She stressed the need for exercise, and because of this developed a system of calisthenics for young women. The Beecher System consisted of 26 lessons based on light exercises that were sometimes performed with light weights. The system was designed to exercise all of the muscles and to exercise them all equally. Beecher believed that this program would not only result in a strong and beautiful body, but also would remediate postural distortions such as scoliosis. In 1837, Catherine Beecher founded the Western Female Institute in Cincinnati for her physical education program.

By the mid-1800s, public schools began to include physical education instruction. After the Civil War, the popularity of Swedish and German gymnastics grew along with the new gymnastics introduced by Dioclesian Lewis (Rice, Hutchinson, & Lee, 1958). At this time, there also was a greater emphasis on physical exercise as a way to improve and maintain a healthy body. During this period, many states passed laws governing physical education instruction and certification in public schools.

As a result of physical education in the public schools, teacher training and preparation for physical education began in the normal schools. These institutions focused solely on the preparation of teachers. Individuals interested in physical education attended a normal school and then enrolled in summer school courses that dealt with physical training, or they attended one of the few four-year universities. During the beginning stages of professional preparation programs, the study revolved around calisthenics, remedial exercise, and health. Medical professionals were generally the instructors and the decision makers about the course of study. One such doctor, Edward Hitchcock (1828-1911), was a professor of physical education and hygiene at Amherst College. He studied anthropometric measures, using them in his research, which involved physical examinations of all students. This research was used to form the foundation for his physical education program. Hitchcock's pioneer physical education program served as a conceptual model and beginning point for 20th century physical education.

Dudley Allen Sargent (1849-1924), another physician who greatly influenced the discipline of physical education, created one of the first teacher training colleges for physical educators, one specifically for women physical educators. As a youth, Sargent was committed to physical activity. As a man, he espoused the strong connection between strengthened muscles and strengthened morals. During Sargent's college career, he became extremely interested in the connection between health and medicine, and more specifically in the connection between physical training and the study of physiology and anatomy. Sargent eventually founded a private school for women at Harvard University, where he established a program that allowed physical educators to earn a professional teaching credential. Sargent then opened a gymnasium (a type of teacher training facility) in Cambridge, Massachusetts. Here, students were prepared to become wholesome and efficient as they entered the discipline of physical education instruction. Sargent's program stressed the connection between medicine and physical education that still exists today. By 1914, 24 colleges offered teacher training in physical education, including baccalaureate degrees in the discipline (Davenport, 1984).

During the early 1900s, while many physical educators were still debating the virtues of Swedish and German gymnastics, the English sport model was sweeping America. Many physical education classes began to focus on recreational activities, including golf, tennis, track and field, and basketball. By 1921, physical education was required in 28 states.

In the late 1930s, an educator by the name of Jesse Feiring Williams suggested that the benefits of physical education included not only improvements in muscular strength and en-

Anthropometrics: The study of body segment measurement, girth measurement, and length measurement.

durance, but also in social enlightenment and personal enjoyment. He encouraged participation in physical education purely for pleasure and happiness. Williams went on to discuss the benefits of participation in socially appropriate physical education, including the development of leadership skills. He felt that the activities should be sporting in nature, rather than focusing only on calisthenics. Williams further believed that physical education would eventually establish the basis for maintaining a healthy lifestyle. Many physical educators consider Jesse Feiring Williams to be the father of modern day physical education.

Other noted physical educators of the time included C. H. McCloy and Delbert Oberteuffer. McCloy is considered the first modern researcher in physical education. Oberteuffer emphasized the relationship between work, play, and physical education. He believed that any learning resulting from physical education was intellectual as well as physical, and that physical education was an academic discipline.

Since World War II, physical education has gone through a number of cycles, from an emphasis on physical fitness to an emphasis on movement education, lifetime activities, health-related fitness, and social skills. Currently, there seems to be an emphasis on the conceptual understanding of physical education through a variety of activities (i.e., dance, team sports, fitness, gymnastics, aquatics, outdoor education, individual and dual sports, and self-defense).

One major change in physical education occurred with the passage of Title IX in 1972. While primarily focused on equal participation for women in athletics, it became a catalyst for coeducational physical education. Similarly, Public Law 94-142 (1977), which mandated physical education for all individuals, led to physical education classes where many physically and mentally challenged individuals could participate alongside their nonchallenged peers.

Today, the need for physical education is even more compelling. The research of Caine and Caine (1994) supports the notion that learning coupled with physical activity is stored on the dendrites for recall and retention. Most recently, Jerry

Gabriel (BrainConnection.com, June 2001) has consolidated several studies done by researchers from Duke University, the Salk Institute, and Arizona State University. His work confirms that, "Running increases the genesis and survival of new cells in the hippocampus, a region important for learning and memory." In today's colleges and universities, physical education trends are reflected in teacher training programs that include the study of human body systems, as well as teaching methodology, curriculum development, and much more.

Concepts/Principles

Kindergarten: *Physical education is good for people, and that is why it is taught in school.*

Second Grade: *Physical education looked different long ago.*

Second Grade: *There is a difference between someone who pursues a single sport (an athlete) and someone who wants to stay healthy by becoming physically educated.*

Fourth Grade: *Many states have laws governing physical education instruction in both elementary and high school.*

Sixth Grade: *In ancient Athens, music and gymnastics were the two focuses of the curriculum.*

Sixth Grade: *During the Dark and Middle Ages, physical education was virtually nonexistent.*

Eighth Grade: *During the 19th century, three major programs (English sports and games, German gymnastics, and Swedish calisthenics) influenced American physical education.*

Eighth Grade: *Public schools begin to include physical education programs in the 1850s.*

Eighth Grade: *Medicine was very influential on early physical education.*

Eighth Grade: *Colleges and universities began training physical educators in the late 1800s.*

> Tenth Grade: *Physical education has emphasized different aspects (e.g., calisthenics, marching, recreation activities, fitness, movement, lifetime sports, social activities) of the field at different times during the last 100 years.*
>
> Tenth Grade: *In 1977, Public Law 94-142 stated that all children from ages 3 to 21 with a handicapping condition had the right to receive specialized physical education instruction.*
>
> Twelfth Grade: *There are programs and careers that are related to physical activity and sports in the United States and around the world.*
>
> Twelfth Grade: *During war times, fitness is emphasized in physical education programs.*

Placing Historical Perspectives in the Curriculum

If historical perspective concepts are to be integrated into the physical education program, decisions must be made about where those concepts should be placed. Throughout the chapter, placement of concepts appropriate for different grade levels are identified for each theme. The grade levels were chosen to be consistent with the grade levels used in the National Standards. The concepts were designed to be consistent with National Standard 6 (Demonstrates understanding and respect for differences among people in physical activity settings), as this standard relates to historical perspective concepts. These concepts also are aligned with the typical history/social science curriculum across the United States:

- Kindergarten: Study of oneself in time and space.
- Second Grade: Study of one's local community.
- Fourth Grade: Study of one's state.
- Sixth Grade: Study of ancient and/or medieval times.
- Eighth Grade: Study of the United States through the 19th century.
- Tenth Grade: Study of the United States in the 20thcentury.
- Twelfth Grade: Study of world history.

By the end of twelfth grade, students should have an understanding and appreciation for the history of sport, dance, physical activity, and physical education.

Integrating Historical Perspective Concepts into Instruction

Teachers must determine the best method for integrating historical concepts into their instructional program. This decision should be based on the individual needs of the school, grade level teaching approach, individual teaching style, and the learning needs of the students. Much research has been conducted on connecting new information with previous learning. It is probably most logical to begin this quest by looking at the history/social science curriculum, and then to align the study of the history of movement.

Assessing Student Learning

When students can use historical concepts in class to explain the importance of a physical activity to their country of origin or analyze the role of physical education and sport in American history, the curriculum has effectively taught historical concepts. It is important for teachers to use assessment techniques throughout the instructional process to assess student learning. Many of these assessment techniques are described more generally in Chapter 1 of this book.

Checking for Understanding

This assessment tool provides the teacher with a quick method of determining how well students understand the information being presented. The teacher poses a question and then calls on several students for their responses.

Examples: What is the history of basketball? What exercises did people perform during ancient times? When did the first modern Olympics take place?

Written Tests

The written test is an efficient way to assess student understanding, especially in highly cognitive areas such as historical perspective. Test questions can parallel the questions included in the checking for understanding section, as well as higher level questions.

Examples: Why were many team sports invented in the United States at the end of the 1800s? Why are many of the sports and games played in different countries so similar? Why is it important to understand the history of physical education? Describe the significance of sport in one culture we studied this year.

Student Projects

Student projects are another good technique to use when assessing the higher cognitive areas of physical education. Just be aware that projects—both individual and group—require more time than other assessments.

Examples: Prepare a presentation on the origin and history of a sport from another country. Design an ancient sports digest complete with pictures, interviews with ancient Olympians, and/or stories about things that occurred during the ancient Olympics. Create a brochure that shows how a piece of sporting equipment has changed during the past 200 years.

Figure 6

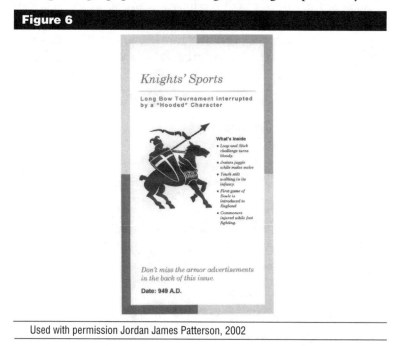

Used with permission Jordan James Patterson, 2002

Closing Comments

It is remarkable that the study of physical education dates back to at least 2700 B.C. The ancient Chinese, the ancient Greeks and Romans, and people from the Middle Ages into the 19th and 20th centuries all have had an impact on physical education as we know it today. The appreciation of this diversity and the uniqueness of people from different cultures as they participate in movement help students develop an historical perspective of physical education.

As Piaget (1966) noted, play and physical activity are a part of the human personality. If that is true, then a piece of all aspects of the world is in each of us when we play, dance, select a leisure activity, or perform any physical activity.

Sir Isaac Newton acknowledged his ancestors and their historic contributions to his life when he said, "I saw what I saw because I stood on the shoulders of giants." As we study physical education, let the history of the discipline be the shoulders of the giants in the field, and let us use their wisdom to see the future of physical education.

References

Anderson, J. K. (1985). *Hunting in the ancient world*. Berkeley, CA: University of California.

Barrow, H. M., & Brown, J. P. (1988). *Man and movement: Principles of physical education* (4th ed.). Philadelphia: Lea and Febiger.

Basmajian, J. V. (1978). *Therapeutic Exercise*. Baltimore: Waverly.

Caine, G., & Caine, R. (1994). *Making connections*. Alexandria, VA: Association for Supervision and Curriculum Development.

Corbin, C., & Pangrazi, R. P. (1998). *Physical activity for children: A statement of guidelines*. Reston, VA: National Association for Sport and Physical Education.

Cottrell, D. M. (1984). The Sargent school for physical education. *Journal of Health, Physical Education, Recreation & Dance, 65*(3), 32-37.

Dalleck, L. C. & Kravitz, L. (2002). The history of fitness. *IDEA Health and Fitness Source*, 26-33.

Davenport, J. (1984). The normal schools: Exploring our heritage. *Journal of Health, Physical Education, Recreation and Dance, 65*(3), 26-28.

Drury, B. J. (1965). *Posture and figure control through physical education*. Palo Alto, CA: The National Press.

Feuerstein, G. (2002). A short history of yoga. Yoga Research and Education Center. Retrieved from www.yrec.org/shorthistory.html.

Garnsey, P. (1999). *Food and society in classical antiquity.* New York: Cambridge University.

Green, P. (1989). *Classical bearings: Interpreting ancient history.* London: Thames and Hudson.

Guttmann, A. (1978). *From ritual to record.* New York: Columbia University.

Hardy, S. H. (1974). The medieval tournament: A functional sport of the upper class. *Journal of Sports History 1*(2), 91-105.

Harris, H. A. (1972). *Sport in Greece and Rome.* Ithaca, NY: Cornell University.

Henry, B. (1981). *An approved history of the Olympic Games.* Los Angeles: The Southern California Committee for the Olympic Games.

Keller, A. (1971). *Colonial America: A compact history.* New York: Hawthorn.

Matthews, D. O. (1969, January). A historical study of the aims, contents, and methods of Swedish, Danish, and German gymnastics. *Proceedings of the National College Physical Education Association for Men.*

McClam, E. (2002, April 7). 70% of American adults don't exercise regularly, study says. *San Diego Union-Tribune.*

Mechikoff, R. A., & Estes, S. G. (2002). *A history and philosophy of sport and physical education.* New York: McGraw-Hill.

Melograno, V. J. (1994). Portfolio assessment: Documenting authentic student learning. *Journal of Health, Physical Education, Recreation & Dance, 65*(8), 50-61.

Michaels, L. (1999). A is for activity, F for Sluggo. *ASU Research E-Magazine.* Retrieved fromResearchmag.asu.edu/stories/activity.html.

Moore, A. (1900). *The Dance, Ancient and Modern* (trans.). Philadelphia: Library of Congress.

Moran, R. (1999). Evaluation and treatment of childhood obesity. *American Family Physician.* Retrieved February 15, 1999, from www.aafp.org/afp/990215ap/861.html.

Patterson, A., & Hallberg, E. C. (1966). *Background readings for physical education.* New York: Holt, Rinehart and Winston.

Randers-Pehrson, J. D. (1993). *Barbarians and Romans. The birth struggle of Europe, A.D. 400-700.* Norman, OK: University of Oklahoma.

Rice, E. A., Hutchinson, J. L., & Lee. M. (1958). *A brief history of physical education.* New York: The Ronald Press.

San Diego County Office of Education. (1994). *California Region 9 sample physical education curriculum.* San Diego: Author.

United States Department of Health and Human Services, Public Health Service. (1996). *Physical activity and health: A report of the Surgeon General.* Atlanta, GA: Author.

Welch, P. D. (1996). *History of American physical education and sport* (2nd ed.). Springfield, IL: Charles C. Thomas.

Wuest, D. A., & Bucher, C. A. (1995). *Foundations of physical education and sport.* St Louis: Mosby.

Resources

Ashe, A. (1988). *A hard road to glory: A history of the African American athlete*. (Vols. 1–2). New York: Warner.

Bland, A. (1981). *The Royal Ballet*. New York: Doubleday.

Caerter, J. M. (1992). *Medieval games: Sports and recreation in feudal society*. New York: Greenwood.

Cook, J. J. (1978). *Famous firsts in tennis*. New York: G. P. Putnam's Sons.

Fisher, L. E. (1980). *Nineteenth century America: The sports*. New York: Holiday House.

Fradin, D. B. (1983). *A new true book: Olympics*. Chicago: Children's Press.

Frommer, H. (1988). *A hundred and fiftieth anniversary album of baseball*. New York: Watts.

Gulbok, S., & Tamarin, A. (1976). *Olympic games in ancient Greece*. New York: Harper & Row.

Guttmann, A. (1992). *The Olympics: A history of the modern games*. Chicago: University of Illinois.

Hackins, J. (1991). *Black dance in America*. New York: Watts.

Henry, B. (1981). *An approved history of the Olympic Games*. Los Angeles: Color Graphics.

HickockSports.com wwwhickocksports.com

Johnson, K. (1990). *The concise encyclopedia of sports*. New York: Crowell.

Kent, Z. (1992). *U.S. Olympians*. Chicago: Children's Press.

Lucas, J. A. (1992). *Future of the Olympic Games*. Champaign, IL: Human Kinetics.

Lyttle, R. B. (1982). *The games they played–Sports in history*. New York: McClelland & Stewart.

Merriam Webster editorial staff. (1976). *Webster's sports dictionary*. New York: Merriam-Webster, Inc.

Moldea, D. E. (1989). *Interference: How organized crime influences professional football*. New York: Morrow.

Nash, B., & Zullo, A. (1993). *The greatest sports stories never told*. New York: Simon & Schuster.

Paul, J. (1983). The health reformers: George Barker Windship and Boston's strength seekers. *Journal of Sports History, 10*(3), 41-55.

_____. (1985). Medieval sport. *Journal of Sport History, 12*(3), 286-287.

_____. (1986). George Barker Windship. *Journal of Health, Physical Education, Recreation & Dance, 57*(4), 29-31.

_____. (1999). Physical activity promotion and school physical education. *President's Council on Physical Fitness and Sports Research Digest*. Series 3, No. 7. Retrieved from www.fitness.gov/activity/activity2/digest_sep1999/digest_sep1999.html.

_____. (2000). Babe Didrikson Zaharias. *The Glass Ceiling Biographies*. Retrieved from www.theglassceiling.com/biographies/bio38.html.

Reidenbaugh, L. (1985.) *The sporting news: First hundred years 1886-1986*. New York: Sporting News.

United States Olympic Committee. (1995). *Curriculum guide to the Olympic games: Volume I*. Glendale, CA: Griffin.

_____. (1996). *Curriculum guide to the Olympic games: Volume II*. Glendale, CA: Griffin.

Wiggins, D. K. (1995). *Sport in America*. Champaign, IL: Human Kinetics.

Chapter **7**

Social Psychology

Rita Mercier
Gayle Hutchinson

H*ow can I resolve the conflicts I have with my team members? Why do some people adhere to exercise programs while others do not? What affects my own attitude/participation in physical activity? Why do people from different countries have different views about physical activity and exercise? Why do some people like to be active while others don't? What kinds of things should I do with my own children so that they develop good social skills? The answers to all of these questions are rooted in the field of study known as social psychology. In this chapter, we will look at social psychology concepts/principles as they relate to the development and enjoyment of physical activities. These concepts/ principles are an important part of the cognitive and affective foundation for a physically educated person, and an understanding of these concepts/principles can enhance the experience of a physically active lifestyle.*

What Is Social Psychology?

Sociology is the study of the attributes of social groups and their relationships to other social groups. Sociologists are concerned with patterns of conduct among groups of people— such as students; or among larger groups—such as schools, states, or whole societies (Hewitt, 1984). In physical education, sociology of sport is a subdiscipline that focuses specifically on sociological concepts/principles in sport and physical activity. Sociology of sport operates on the premise that sport is an integral aspect of society, and that it has a significant impact on the behaviors of individuals and groups. Sport sociologists typically investigate social structure, social relations, and

Sociology: The study of the characteristics of social groups and their relationships to other social groups.

Psychology:
The study of behaviors and mental processes.

Social psychology:
The study of how the thoughts, feelings, and behaviors of individuals are influenced by the presence of other people.

Self-concept:
One's perceptions of one's abilities, behavior, and personality.

Self-esteem:
Evaluation of oneself.

social problems as they relate to sport (McPherson, Curtis, & Loy, 1989).

Psychology is the study of behaviors and mental processes of the individual. Psychologists are primarily interested in what the individual does and the kinds of things that may or may not influence his or her behavior (Cox, 1994). Sport and exercise psychology applies psychological principles to sport and physical activity settings in order to understand how psychological factors affect individuals' physical performance, and to understand how participation in exercise and sport affects psychological development, health, and well-being. Many sport and exercise psychologists investigate the emotional and personality profiles of athletes, examine the effects of stress on performance, and help athletes reach their highest level of motor performance. Many other sport and exercise psychologists are concerned with children, seniors, people with disabilities, and adults who participate in a variety of physical activity settings such as physical education classes, activity classes, community events, and recreational leagues (Weinberg & Gould, 1995).

Social psychology, then, is the study of the social nature of the individual. The definition of social psychology is a combination of the working definitions of both sociology and psychology. It examines the influence of other human beings on the thoughts, feelings, and behaviors of individuals. Succinctly stated, social psychology of sport "is the field... that studies individuals' social interactions, relationships, perceptions, and attitudes" (Allen & Santrock, 1993, p. 490). The interrelationship of social psychology with sport and physical activity becomes clear. The individual participates in sport or physical activity, which is embedded in social context or the interactions with classmates, peers, teammates, teachers, coaches, officials, and spectators (Carron, 1980), that influence the individual's behavior.

Many sport sociologists, along with sport psychologists, spend a great deal of time examining the influence of sport and physical activity on human development. In fact, they are concerned with the "social psychological aspect of human enrichment" (Cox, 1994, p. 5). Sport sociologists and psychologists have explored many social psychological concepts/principles. Therefore, it is important to note that the concepts/principles reviewed in this chapter have been drawn from the disciplines of sociology, psychology, social psychology, sociology of sport, social psychology of sport, and sport and exercise psychology.

Why Is Social Psychology Important?

Today's population is increasingly culturally and ethnically diverse. Students also differ greatly in physical, social, and cognitive abilities; socioeconomic status; and basic values and beliefs. These differences can have a profound effect on student learning needs and social interactions. Unless careful and ongoing consideration is given to learning needs and the way in which students interact when curriculum and instruction are planned, schools can be enigmatic and sometimes intimidating places for students. The complex human interactions that occur in schools provide daily challenges, as well as opportunities, for students to develop their personal and social capabilities.

Interest in social psychological concepts/principles stems from our professional concern for the emotional and physical safety and well-being of all. Teachers are particularly interested in helping students interact cooperatively and respectfully, solve conflicts in constructive and peaceful ways, and feel safe in class and in school. The nature of physical activity and sport presents abundant opportunities for students to develop social psychological knowledge and skills. Thoughtful consideration to affective elements, including the continuous enhancement of teacher knowledge and skills, produces a learning climate that is conducive to building positive student self-concept and self-esteem. Social psychological concepts/principles provide the foundation for the successful teaching of all other concepts/ principles.

As students understand selected social psychological concepts/ principles that influence and potentially enhance their sense of self and well-being, they are more apt to engage in more meaningful practice of these concepts/principles. Understanding, coupled with meaningful practice, may help students adapt these concepts/principles and related skills to their daily lives in order to live more healthy, fulfilling, and active lifestyles. Physically educated adults who have practiced these skills from childhood are much more likely to continue to enjoy and participate in sport and physical activity.

Linking Social Psychology to the National Standards

The National Standards emphasize the importance of defining what a physically educated person should know and be able to do. Social psychology concepts/principles are specifically targeted in Standard 5 (Demonstrates responsible personal and social behavior in physical activity settings), but can be successfully integrated with all of the others. This is especially true of Standard 6 (Demonstrates understanding and respect for differences among people in physical activity settings), and Standard 7 (Understands that physical activity provides opportunities for enjoyment, challenge, self-expression, and social interaction). In Standard 5, the development of personal and social behaviors is emphasized through physical activity. Social responsibility and social interactions with people different from ourselves are the focus of Standard 6. The importance of aesthetics and enjoyment of physical activity for individuals as well as groups is highlighted in Standard 7. These standards guide teachers in their planning of appropriate personal and social development experiences for all students.

Selected Social Psychology Themes

The world changes more rapidly today than it did a decade or more ago. We engage in situations that may change on a daily basis. For instance, students may find themselves living in one town one day and a new town the next day. There may be a significant change in the family or neighborhood structure (i.e., divorce, neglect, violence, or drugs). Students encounter change at school as well. They learn new computer technologies, new curriculum for different subjects, and more. Life as we know it today changes from one moment to the next. Youth must learn to embrace the process of change as a way of life. Accepting the notion of change as a lifelong process means that students will learn to be lifelong learners. Physical education teachers can enable students to acquire these lifelong learning skills, in part by helping them learn social psychological concepts/principles.

Feeling good about ourselves and having a healthy sense of worth helps each of us develop to our potential and interact positively with those around us. Physical education classes serve as natural environments for helping students develop sense of self and positive interaction skills through physical activity and sport.

It is important to note that cognitive understanding does not occur without emotion. The brain uses emotion as a filter for cognition (Goleman, 1995). Every thought is attached to emotion. In the affective domain, thoughts, feelings, and actions are analogous. Arguably, a person can understand courtesy conceptually without practicing or demonstrating it. However, the knowledge of the concept of courtesy is embedded in the use of courtesy. For these reasons, the concepts/principles section of this chapter will take the following approach to the teaching and learning of social psychological concepts/principles through physical activity:

1. The presentation of social psychological concepts/principles is based on the belief that knowledge and understanding of concepts/principles in the affective domain is inextricably bound to the application of those concepts/principles. The concepts/principles in this chapter will be illustrated and discussed, at times, in terms of demonstrated student behaviors.

> **Social skills:** Those skills that help partners or groups complete a task and build positive feelings in the participants.

Figure 1

Reprinted, by permission, from C. Himberg, G.E. Hutchinson, and J.M. Roussell, 203, Teaching secondary physical education, (Champaign, IL: Human Kinetics).

Affiliation/belongingness: Feeling of acceptance by others; includes feelings of appreciation and respect.

2. Considerable attention will be focused on the teacher's role in influencing student understanding of social psychological concepts/principles. As students explore selected concepts/principles of social psychology, they will learn strategies for developing positive self-concept, self-esteem, coping skills, and prosocial behaviors.

The social psychological concepts/principles selected for this chapter are organized around six themes. The first three themes focus on the student and are titled "Self as an Individual." Themes 4, 5, and 6 address the students as he/she interacts with others, and are referred to as "Self in Relation to Others."

Competence: Relates directly to the achievement of goals and the recognition of success.

Self as an Individual

- **Theme 1:** How do people feel about themselves when participating in physical activity?
- **Theme 2:** How can people improve their sense of self through physical activity?
- **Theme 3:** How can people continue to develop toward their full potential through physical activity?

Self-determination: Freedom to choose one's course of aciton.

These first three themes are closely related, yet subtly different. For instance, in Theme 1, self-concept and self-esteem are defined. Seven concepts/principles (security, selfhood, affiliation/belongingness, purpose, competence, virtue, and self-determination) that lead to positive self-concept and self-esteem are explained. People need to comprehend these core concepts/principles in order to understand their own feelings and to move forward to Theme 2. Positive self-concept and self-esteem are directly related to one's achievements and beliefs about one's own potential. Goal setting, positive self-talk and self-assessment are concepts/principles and skills discussed in Theme 2 that people use to succeed in areas such as motor performance and social interactions. Understanding broad definitions of self-confidence set the foundation for Theme 3, where individuals strive toward self-actualization and self-efficacy.

Purpose: Positive reasons for living; leads individuals to a greater sense of self-empowerment.

Self in Relation to Others

- **Theme 4:** How do people learn to understand and respond to individual and group diversity in sports, games, and other physical activities?

■ **Theme 5:** What kinds of social skills must people learn in order to perform successfully with others in sports, games, and other physical activities?

■ **Theme 6:** How do people achieve the social skills needed to perform successfully with others in sports, games, and other physical activities?

Security: Feeling comfortable and safe in an environment.

Each of the last three themes address the individual as he or she interacts with others. Social concepts/principles and psychological concepts/principles are neither discrete, nor are they learned independently of one another. Therefore, some overlap will occur in the presentation. Each of these themes is briefly developed in the next section. Critical student concepts/principles that fall under each theme are developed in a K-12 format.

Figure 2

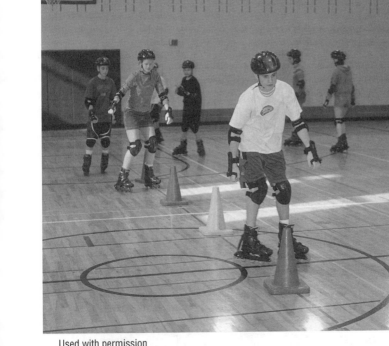

Selfhood: Developing one's sense of unique individualism.

Used with permission
Photo by Reade Bailey at www.deadlinecom.com

Virtue: Demonstration of behavior that is consistent with an established moral code for one's culture.

How Do People Feel About Themselves When Participating in Physical Activity?

Participating in physical activity can be enjoyable and exciting. Physical activity provides many opportunities for people to explore their bodies and their abilities. It is an ideal way to develop positive self-concept and self-esteem. Self-concept can be defined as how a person sees his or her own abilities, behavior, and personality. It is often recognized by the attitudes a person holds about him or herself (Gallahue, 1996). Self-esteem is one's evaluation of self, thus determining whether one is likeable or worthy. Together, self-concept and self-esteem create a complex foundation upon which people build their perceived sense of worthiness and competence.

Many researchers have found that physical activity significantly affects children's self-concept and self-esteem (Payne & Isaacs, 1995). Developmentally appropriate and student-centered physical education programs, physical activity experiences, and other forms of guided play provide excellent opportunities for students to develop positive self-concept and self-esteem. This is essential if students are to develop self-confidence and exhibit improved social behavior and school achievement (Borba, 1989). Researchers have identified seven factors that affect the development of positive self-concept and esteem. They are: security, selfhood, affiliation/belongingness, purpose, competence, virtue (Borba, 1989, Hellison, 1995, Gallahue, 1996), and self-determination (Ryan & Deci, 2000).

Security
Security is the feeling of comfort and safety within an environment. Individuals feel secure when they know what to expect from their surroundings. These feelings are enhanced when class rules and consequences are clear and consistent. The presence of reliable and dependable people (students and teachers) also enhances the sense of security. When people feel secure in their environment, they are more open to learning.

Selfhood
Selfhood is the development of one's sense of individualism. As individuals develop selfhood, they learn about their abilities

Example 1

Elementary School Example: Kindergarten

Concept/Principle: Learning how the body moves helps people feel positively about themselves.

Children at this age still engage in parallel play (playing side by side with minimum interaction) and strive to acquire body control while moving. The objective of this lesson is to help children learn that moving is fun and helps them feel good about themselves. One way to do so is to provide children with positive opportunities to explore moving their bodies safely and with control. In other words, children would move without bumping into others or putting others in danger of getting hurt.

Teaching children the concepts/principles of personal and general space is a good place to start. Personal space is that space immediately surrounding the body. General space is that space outside of one's own personal space. Children should explore their personal space before they explore general space. Many teachers place polyspots around the classroom, gymnasium, hard top, or field in order to help children identify their own personal space. As children come to understand the concept, the polyspots are no longer necessary.

Providing a series of suggestions or asking open-ended questions such as, "How tall can you get?" are appropriate ways to enable children to explore their own personal space. For instance, as children stand on their polyspots, the teacher suggests that they move their arms all around their bodies using different rates of speed at different levels (high, medium, and low). For example, the teacher may say, "Show me how you can slowly move your elbows to different places around your body." or, "Let's see you reach your hands high over your heads and stretch to a high level while standing on your tippy toes."

As children begin to understand the concept of personal space and exploring personal space with different body parts, the teacher can provide them with choices about moving in personal space. The teacher may suggest to children that they now choose a body part that they would like to explore and find different ways to move it around their bodies, using varied speeds and levels. From here, the teacher can encourage children to make shapes with their bodies, act out stories or songs, and/or simply explore further moving in their own space.

During this activity, it is most important to help children make the connection that moving their bodies is fun and helps them feel good. This can be done in a variety of ways. For example, the teacher may simply comment on the number of smiling faces (when culturally appropriate) that he or she sees during the lesson, and ask children to explain why they are smiling. Children may comment that they are having fun or that they feel good. Here, the teacher follows up by asking what is making them feel good, thus helping children realize that moving is fun and provides them with positive feelings.

Using other mediums to encourage discussion regarding this concept also is a good idea. For instance, the teacher can ask the children to draw pictures of themselves moving in their favorite ways. As children show their drawings, the teacher can ask them to explain how their favorite movements make them feel.

Acceptance:
To receive
with favor.

and their limitations, enabling them to understand themselves better.

Affiliation/Belongingness

Affiliation and belongingness means that individuals feel accepted by others. Acceptance involves feelings of appreciation and respect.

Purpose

Purpose is having a reason for living, something to strive for. Individuals with purpose are motivated to set and pursue goals. Purpose leads to a greater sense of self-empowerment.

Competence

Competence relates directly to the achievement of goals and to success. According to Harter (1978), individuals are intrinsically motivated to be competent in all aspects of their lives. Individuals typically develop competency through mastery of

Appreciation:
To greatly value
over time.

skills. Mastery of skills improves self-concept and self-esteem, and this relates directly to one's confidence in his or her ability to participate in regular physical activity, find enjoyment in physical activity, and develop positive beliefs concerning the benefits of physical activity (U.S. Department of Health and Human Services [USDHHS], 1996).

Virtue

Virtue is the demonstration of behavior that is consistent with an established moral code. In physical education, the moral code may encompass acceptance of diversity, fair play, conflict resolution, mutual respect, honesty, etc.

Self-Determination

Self-determination, or having choice or control of one's behavior, has been linked to the development of positive self-esteem. It serves as a critical factor for motivation and overall well-being (Ryan & Deci, 2000).

Concepts/Principles

Diversity:
Distinct
characteristics
of people.

Kindergarten: *Learning how the body moves helps people feel positively about themselves.* It helps people develop and gain competence in a variety of locomotor, manipulative, and nonlocomotor skills, such as skipping, throwing, and balancing. Improved skill levels help people gain control of themselves and their environment, therefore increasing their sense of security and independence. As people learn how their body moves, they come to understand its location in space. For kindergarten students, this is a perfect time to learn about personal space and the rights of others to move freely and safely through general space.

Second Grade: *Moving with personal control gives people a sense of self, purpose, and control.* It also helps people control mean behaviors toward themselves and others. Teachers can provide students with numerous opportunities to participate and play in self-space, as well as with others.

Fourth Grade: *Safe and appropriate physical activity helps people feel secure.* Safe environments encourage people to be open to learning new motor skills and concepts/principles, such as learning about the body and how it moves. Feeling safe while exploring movement assists with building a foundation where children feel positively about themselves and learn to enjoy movement. This critical concept should be practiced at all grade levels. Safe and appropriate physical activities are inclusive; they help people develop a sense of affiliation or belonging. Inclusive physical activities encourage students to work cooperatively and productively with partners and in small groups. Inclusive physical activities also help people realize their abilities and limitations (selfhood) in ways that are non-threatening. And, they teach respect for and acceptance of individual differences. In competitive settings, they help students demonstrate virtues associated with healthy play and competition such as fair play, honesty, and gracious behavior as winners and losers.

Sixth Grade: *Working productively in cooperative and competitive settings establishes purpose.* Sense of purpose is important to people, in that it gives them a reason for living and helps them set goals. Purpose also empowers people to take risks that are courageous and meaningful, therefore decreasing reckless and uncontrolled behaviors. Working productively includes solving problems and resolving conflicts and arguments. People benefit from learning conflict management and resolution strategies and applying them in cooperative and competitive physical activity settings.

Eighth Grade: *Identifying behaviors that are supportive and inclusive of others in physical activity builds people's sense of self.* Physical activities that are inclusive and propose a common problem to be solved or goal to be attained encourage people to work together in a supportive manner. They also provide an excellent way for people to practice virtues such as honesty, respect, fairness, understanding, and empathy. We suggest that teachers consider a variety of physical activities that not only promote cooperation, but that also challenge students' self-expression, social interaction, and aesthetic experience.

Tenth Grade: *Clarity and consistency in creating and following game rules give people a sense of security as well as purpose and competence.* Following rules implies knowledge of a game or activity. Appreciation for general rule structures of games and physical activities provides a template for students to follow as they work to create and determine rules for their own games and activities. By following the rules, students also demonstrate prosocial behaviors consistent with the established virtues of the class, such as respect, fair play, and honesty.

Tenth Grade: *Participating and succeeding in challenging and culturally diverse physical activities develops positive attitudes, openness, and a sense of accomplishment.* Challenge enables people to recognize personal abilities and limitations. It also helps people explore alternative solutions and work together to overcome or solve the challenge. When that happens, individuals feel a strong sense of purpose and accomplishment as well as a bond toward the group or class. Belonging to a group requires respect and openness for people who are different from ourselves. It also helps to build appreciation for other cultures, abilities, and skill levels, therefore deepening the level of acceptance for others.

Twelfth Grade: *Community service and cross-age projects develop a sense of purpose and belonging as well as* *competence for physical activity.* Community service such as volunteering for a Special Olympics track meet, or cross-age projects such as teaching first graders how to throw and catch, are purposeful acts that foster not only a feeling of belonging to a community, but also a purpose for learning and mastering physical activities. When high school students provide service to school and community, they reinforce and improve upon the seven core concepts of security, selfhood, affiliation/belongingness, purpose, competence, virtue, and self-determination. Our hope is that these projects will encourage students to be active for life and continue to volunteer their time to community efforts.

How Can People Improve Their Sense of Self Through Physical Activity?

To begin, we must examine what motivates people to participate in physical activity. Motivation is defined as the direction and intensity of one's efforts (Sage, 1977; Weinberg & Gould, 1995). Direction of effort is the type of situation to which a person is attracted. For example, students may be attracted to music class and band practice, and not attracted to physical education or after-school athletics. Intensity of effort means how much effort a person puts forth in a specific situation such as a particular physical education class (Weinberg & Gould, 1995). For example, it is interesting to observe how some students put more effort into a lacrosse unit than a swimming unit. For the purpose of this section, direction and intensity of effort are closely related when describing motivation.

It is not uncommon for teachers working with students who appear to lack motivation to assume that they are disinterested in learning, or that physical activity is just not a priority in their lives. On the other hand, there are times when teachers may simply assume that lack of motivation is based on the situation. For instance, students may be bored in class, or perhaps they don't like the particular unit they are in right now. Assumptions about the person or the situation may prove to be too narrowly focused if dealt with separately. Low or high motivation is typically a combination of both personal and situational

Challenge: A testing of one's abilities or resources in a demanding but stimulating undertaking.

Example 2

Elementary School Example: Grade 4

Concept/Principle: Positive self-talk increases self-confidence and one's ability to perform physical activities.

This lesson uses an inclusion style of teaching, meaning that everyone in class will have opportunities to experience success during the lesson. This strategy is helpful, particularly when teaching students to engage in positive self-talk, determine realistic goals, and take calculated risks. The inclusion style takes advance planning and good organization of the learning environment in order to ensure student success.

The lesson begins with the teacher stating the concepts/principles and objectives for the day. Next, the students are asked to give examples of self-encouraging words and phrases. They discuss the positive, kind, and supportive things they can say to themselves while they practice jump roping skills. Teachers should consider using a T-chart to help students create a list of encouraging phrases and words.

The teacher should have the students jump rope and determine which skills they can do and which skills they would like to improve. With an idea of which skills they would like to work on, students can determine individual learning goals by answering the following questions:

1. What would I like to be able to do?
2. How will I achieve this goal?
3. What is my timeline for achieving this goal?
4. If this challenge becomes too difficult or unrealistic, what smaller goals can I set in order to experience success and continue toward the bigger goal?
5. If this challenge becomes too easy, what other goals will I find more challenging?

In a jump rope unit, the teacher can provide examples of rope jumping skills through videotapes, demonstrations, written explanations, and diagrams. In the inclusion style, students are encouraged to begin with skills they know they can perform and then identify new goals or challenges. For example, the student who cannot turn a rope and jump it at the same time may choose to lay the rope on the ground and jump over it. While students practice, they must engage in positive self-talk. Teachers should design opportunities—like writing in a log, answering teacher questions, and interviewing peers—to allow students to assess whether or not they have been successful in achieving their goals.

As students achieve their goals, they should describe their success and how it made them feel before setting new goals. If they do not reach their goals, they must determine why and set more realistic goals. Not reaching a goal should be looked at as a positive learning experience. Students should be reminded to use positive self-talk in these situations.

The inclusion model requires students to spend a lot of time working independently. Teachers serve as facilitators in this process. They help students make the connection between motor skill practice and developing a positive sense of self. They can use individual, small group, or whole class discussions; journals and worksheets; and feedback to help students develop positive identities and take responsibility for their learning.

factors (Weinberg & Gould, 1995). As teachers, then, we must focus our attention on both. We must examine how they interact with one another. There are several guidelines described by Weinberg and Gould (1995) that teachers may use to understand motivation more clearly. First, people participate in physical activity and exercise for a number of reasons. Youth participating in organized sport report doing so to improve their skills, have fun, be with friends, experience excitement, achieve success, and develop fitness (Weinberg & Gould, 1995). Individuals who participate in exercise do so in pursuit of health, weight loss, fitness, self-challenge, enjoyment, activity, social engagement, and improved sense of well-being.

School-based physical education is often compulsory, meaning students must attend; they don't have a choice. Therefore, understanding student motivation is important. We can do this by asking students about the kinds of activities they like and dislike. We also can survey students' motives for participation in order to understand better their actions in class.

Second, understanding student motivation enables you to structure a physical education class to meet student needs. Since class sizes typically are large, the teacher must structure the environment to meet multiple needs and provide numerous opportunities for learning. That is why we strongly recommend a student-centered approach to teaching. Third, physical educators influence student participation in class, making them an integral part of the motivation environment (Weinberg & Gould, 1995). It is important for teachers to be enthusiastic, energetic, approachable, and fair. Everyone has a bad day, but a teacher's bad day may have a strong affect on student motivation and participation.

Now that we understand a broad definition of motivation, why is it that some students appear highly motivated and always striving for challenges and success, while others recede to the back of the gym with apparent lack of motivation? Sport and exercise psychologists term this concept achievement motivation, which means "to master a task, achieve excellence, overcome obstacles, perform better than others, and take pride in exercising talent" (Murray, 1938; Weinberg & Gould, 1995). Achievement motivation influences one's sense of self by influencing behavior, thoughts, and feelings such as choice of activity, effort to pursue goals, intensity of effort, and persistence to achieve through challenge and failure (Weinberg & Gould, 1995). Achievement motivation is believed to have three sequential development stages:

1. **Autonomous competence stage:** This stage is described as children's focus and effort to master their environment through self-testing. Generally, this stage occurs before children reach the age of four.
2. **Social comparison stage:** Here, children directly compare their abilities to the abilities of others. Their focus is on who is the strongest, fastest, biggest, funniest, and so on. Children generally enter this stage at the age of five.
3. **Integrated stage:** As the name implies, this stage integrates characteristics of the previous two stages. Individuals may enter this stage at any time. Involving both social comparisons and autonomous challenges, a person in this stage knows when to focus on self-challenge or to compete and compare his or her performance to that of others.

Understanding achievement motivation will help teachers understand student needs. In turn, you will be able to help students learn specific strategies to help them improve self-concept and self-worth. Some of these strategies include goal setting, positive self-talk, and self-assessment.

Goal Setting

Achieving goals helps people identify their own levels of competency and degrees of success. There are two major goal perspectives: task orientation and outcome orientation (Dweck & Elliott, 1983; Nicholls, 1984; Gill, 2000; Duda, Olson, & Templin, 1991). Task-oriented goals focus on personal improvement and mastery of skills. People with a task-oriented approach set self-referenced goals. They measure how much their performance on tasks and activities improves over past performances (criterion-referenced). People with an outcome orientation are more concerned with how their abilities compare with others (norm-referenced).

Task-oriented goals: Focus on personal improvement and mastery of skills.

Research has shown that individuals with task orientation tend to be persistent and unafraid of failure. They pursue mastery and choose moderately difficult challenges. Individuals operating from an outcome orientation may not be persistent. They are easily discouraged, withdraw from efforts when success is not ensured, and tend to choose tasks that are either too easy or too difficult.

Outcome orientation: Judging the success of one's performance by how it compares with the performances of others.

We must not be hasty in labeling people as task oriented or outcome oriented. Many sport and exercise psychologists have shifted their way of thinking about achievement motivation to achievement goal theory. In this theory, three factors interact to determine a person's motivation in a particular context. And, yes, motivation may vary depending on the situation. The three factors are achievement goals, perceived ability, and achievement behavior. Understanding students' achievement requires that we examine their achievement goals and how they perceive their ability or competence in order to attain those goals (Weinberg & Gould, 1995).

To help students take responsibility for their own achievement it is important to teach them principles for setting short and long-term, goals (Gill, 2000; O'Block & Evans, 1984; Cox, 1994; Weinberg & Gould, 1995). Here are a few guidelines:

1. Task-oriented goals focus on personal improvement and are more beneficial in helping people achieve success.
2. People must accept goals as worthwhile and achievable, and as their own.
3. Goals should be special and challenging.
4. Goals are more easily understood when they are described in behavioral terms.
5. Goals should be measurable so that progress can be determined.
6. Short-term goals set a natural progression toward realizing long-term goals.
7. It is important to determine specific strategies for attaining goals.
8. Goals should be monitored and assessed periodically in order to determine progress, success, and the need for any modifications.

Self-talk: A
cognitive
process
whereby
individuals
make
statements to
themselves,
both internally
and externally.

Self-Talk

Self-talk is a cognitive process. Individuals make statements to themselves that serve to direct their attention, judge themselves or others, and critique their ability to perform. Self-talk is a powerful tool that helps make perceptions and beliefs conscious and actions realized (Bunker, Williams, & Zinsser, 1993). Many elite athletes use positive self-talk during competition to heighten their focus, increase self-confidence, and reduce feelings of self-doubt (Williams & Leffingwell, 1996). People can use self-talk to encourage continuing effort in physical activity if they find themselves discouraged. They can use it to improve skill performance, focus attention, and increase and maintain self-confidence.

When using self-talk to improve skill performance, a person must emphasize desired actions and behaviors. Self-talk may range from a short description to one-word cues. For instance, students practicing dribbling in basketball may use cues such as, "Knees bent, eyes up, and dribble ball with fingertips." People engaging in a team building activity may say, "Always spot my partner, safety first, everyone participates."

People may use words and cues to help focus their attention on a task or activity. They might say such things as, "Listen and be alert for encouragement." "Look at group members' faces and pay attention." "That's the way." Cues for attention can help students stay on task or regain their focus during class.

Self-talk can have a positive or negative influence on an individual's self-confidence. Negative self-talk (e.g., "You're a stupid, loser! You can't do that.") is self-defeating. It replaces self-confidence with self-doubt.

Positive statements (e.g., "You can do that. Go ahead, try it. Taking safe risks is fun.") serve to increase self-confidence. People must become aware of the positive and negative statements they make. The paper clip exercise is one easy way to help develop student awareness. Have each student carry a handful of paper clips in a pocket. Each time a student makes a negative statement, he or she must transfer one paper clip to another pocket. During one class period, students will become aware of how often they make negative comments.

Encouragement is the ability to say positive things in order to support and stimulate self and others. Sometimes people find it difficult to encourage themselves; they may think of it as arrogance. It is important for youngsters to learn that self-encouragement is healthy. When teaching students how to give self-encouragement, begin small. Have them tell how they feel about doing physical activity. For instance, "When I threw the ball and hit the target, I felt happy and excited." Next, help students think of ways they can encourage themselves, such as looking at mistakes as possible learning experiences, or by engaging in positive and supportive self-talk. For instance, encourage them to say things like, "Good effort." "I tried my best that time." and, "I love trying new activities and sports."

Another good way to elicit self-praise is to have students answer this question: "What did I do well in this effort/performance?" Once students learn to encourage themselves, they will feel good, and they will be able to encourage others. (Encouraging others will be discussed further when we look at concepts/principles five and six.)

Self-Assessment

Assessing personal progress toward short and long-term goals is another important aspect of developing a positive sense of self. Feedback about performance is necessary for assessment to take place. Feedback occurs in many forms such as, but not limited to, teacher feedback, peer feedback, and self-feedback. Self-assessment allows individuals to reflect on or cognitively review their own progress toward established goals and desired performance levels. Consider the following points:

1. Self-assessment provides information about progress toward achieving goals.
2. Clearly stated goals that are measurable enable individuals to assess their behavior and motor performance accurately and consistently.
3. A number of strategies may be employed to help individuals collect information to use in assessing their own progress. These may include things such as task sheets, checklists, journals, and progress logs.
4. Open-ended questions such as, "What was my goal?" "How have I made progress toward my goal?" "What do I need to do to modify my goal?" "How do I need to

change my practice in order to achieve my goal?" "What have I done well?" and, "What do I need to improve on?" can provide the structure for quick self-assessments.

5. Students can develop a positive sense of self through student-centered instructional strategies. As the sense of self develops, teachers may guide student thinking toward continuous improvement of their knowledge and performance. As a result, students can attribute their success to their own abilities and not to luck or the easiness of tasks.

As students learn to evaluate their progress consistently and accurately, they also learn to recognize when goals have been achieved and when goals should be modified. Some individuals may find self-assessment a difficult thing to do initially, but as they learn to provide accurate self-talk and focus on authentic indicators of progress, they will enhance their ability to conduct self-assessments. Accurate self-assessment reinforces appropriate behaviors and aids in skill development. It is a powerful learning tool for encouraging individuals to look at mistakes and poor performances as opportunities for learning.

Concepts/Principles

Kindergarten: *Positive self-talk makes people feel pleased.* Many students will be in the autonomous competence stage. Some will be entering the social comparison stage. Teaching children positive self-talk is important. Using positive and kind statements (e.g., "Good effort!" "I like to move." "I try my best." "Look what I can do!" "I like to make up movement." "Moving makes me smile!" and, "Yea, I did it!") helps children feel good about themselves.

Second Grade: *Exploring a variety of movement skills and concepts enables people to develop motor skills and identify movements and activities they do and do not enjoy.* Many students in second grade will demonstrate behaviors associated with the social comparison and integrated stages. Students also begin to express their feelings more through physical activity. We find that students are more motivated to participate in movement forms they have found enjoyable. It is important to note that people often find activities that they do well enjoyable because they can ensure some level of success. When working with young children, it is important to provide a safe environment where new skills can be learned and experienced. Children should be encouraged to try new things. When they do, they experience joy in moving.

Fourth Grade: *Positive self-talk increases self-confidence and one's ability to perform physical activities.* So often, we have witnessed a child who attempts to practice a motor skill such as throwing to a target become disheartened when she missed, making the assumption that she failed. Afterward the disheartened child may say she "can't do it." Other times, a child may freeze in space, unable to move because he believes he will do the log roll incorrectly. His negative self-talk hampered his ability to even try. We can imagine our students' experience by reflecting upon our own experiences with self-doubt. How many times on the golf course or softball field have you talked yourself out of making the shot or hitting the ball? As much as people suffer from self-doubt through negative self-talk, they are rewarded with positive experiences and success through positive self-talk. Teaching students positive self-talk not only improves self-confidence and the ability to perform, but it adds enjoyment to the activity.

Sixth Grade: *Setting and achieving goals based on personal strengths and weaknesses creates a sense of personal responsibility for one's own learning.* With practice, students will be able to assess their abilities realistically. The next step is helping students learn how to set attainable goals. This takes time and practice. Goals need to be challenging, yet achievable. Goals set too low can decrease motivation and turn an activity into a boring event. Goals set too high can hurt motivation and lead to disinterest. Effective goal setting contributes to meaningful practice and productive work.

Eighth Grade: *Consistent use of short-term goals and self-evaluation when learning a new skill or activity makes it easier for people to recognize and appreciate the things that they are doing well.* Short-term goals also present a natural progression toward long-term goal setting and self-assessment, making it easier for people to strive for improved performance during periods of time that are longer than a typical physical education unit or academic year. In other words, it helps to prepare students for the future so they may determine long-term physical activity goals during adulthood. Satisfaction found through accomplishing goals will help students find enjoyment in physical activity and the motivation to continue outside of class.

Tenth Grade: *Pursuing multicultural and new activities and sports, alone and with others, gives people occasions to use self-encouragement and positive self-talk while discovering more about their own abilities.* Positive self-talk and self-confidence may lend itself to positive social interactions with individuals different from us. People learn a lot about themselves when interacting with others, particularly through activities that are new or unfamiliar. Social interactions provide opportunities for students to learn empathy (identifying with one's experience, emotion, or situation). Social interactions also provide individuals with information about how others perceive them and their actions. Diverse cultural experiences and new activities can promote positive interactions that include encouragement and compliments for others.

Twelfth Grade: *Developing numerous strategies for preparing to succeed in movement challenges (visualization, positive self-talk, or relaxation exercises) can help people become successful in any activity.* Practicing goal setting, positive self-talk, and self-assessment can prepare students to take control of their lives and responsibility for their health and wellness. Teachers can help by providing students with opportunities to assess, plan, and implement their own health-enhancing fitness and physical activity programs.

How Can People Continue To Develop Toward Their Full Potential Through Physical Activity?

Abraham Maslow (1954) introduced a hierarchy of needs that identified certain basic necessities—food, shelter, water, safety, belongingness, love, and positive sense of self—that must be realized before a higher need for self-actualization can be addressed. Teachers see examples of this daily: Students come to school hungry, thirsty, and tired. Some students are homeless or highly transient. In many areas, students fear physical violence at home, on the streets, and at school. When young people's fundamental needs are not met it is of little wonder that they have difficulty learning.

Self-actualization can be described as one's motivation to reach his or her fullest human potential. This is a lifelong process. Creating conditions that stimulate and promote thinking skills increases student cognition, enabling them to recognize and internalize concepts/principles, ideas, and understandings more readily. Increased cognitive ability contributes to student self-confidence, motivating them to set new goals and challenges, and to strive to reach their potential. When they have a positive, healthy, realistic sense of self, people intrinsically pursue opportunities to learn, explore, and create.

Teachers can motivate student desire by providing learning environments that promote risk taking, and by setting achievable challenges that stimulate personal growth and development. The following principles can be applied to the achievement of self-actualization:

1. Basic needs such as food, shelter, water, safety, belongingness, love, and positive sense of self must be addressed before progress toward self-actualization can take place.
2. Safe learning environments increase motivation toward self-actualization by providing a positive and secure structure for meeting students' basic needs.
3. Positive self-talk, goal setting, and self-assessment help improve self-concept and self-esteem, making work toward self-actualization possible.
4. When learning is perceived as meaningful, students become more motivated to learn, thus engaging in the process of self-actualization.
5. Ethical decision making involves the ability to choose the appropriate action and adhere to an established moral code. It promotes personal integrity and self-actualization.

Self-efficacy is a form of self-confidence that is situation specific. In other words, individuals' self-confidence is dependent on their belief that they are competent and able to do or per-

Example 3

Middle School Example: Grade 8

Concept/Principle: Relaxation techniques help relieve stress, improve attention and focus, and assist with impulse and anger control. Like any skill, relaxation techniques require practice.

Two common techniques that we have seen teachers use are breathing control and muscle relaxation. Breathing is central to achieving relaxation and focus. Have students recall times when they felt calm and in control of a situation. Ask them to think about how they were breathing. Chances are high that they found their breathing to be smooth. When students remember times when they were nervous or anxious they should also recall that their breathing was more rapid and shallow. If students have difficulty remembering their own experiences, have them think about times when they watched movies where the characters were afraid or stressed out over something or someone. When they have the movie scene in mind, ask them to describe the characters' breathing. Many athletes may find that their breathing is shallow, tense, and irregular when they perform under high pressure. Ask students to name times when they feel pressure or stress in their lives, then ask them to recall their breathing. Now, describe the benefits of breathing control.

We know from studies that breathing in and holding it increases muscle tension. We also know that breathing deeply, regularly, and smoothly decreases muscle tension. When you watch tennis on television and hear players grunt upon returning a volley, they are working to breathe regularly and not hold their breath. These athletes know that breathing during release will decrease muscle tension and enhance performance. The same is true while taking a test or asking a person out on a date. Breathing control needs to be practiced. Students can spend one day discussing the benefits of breathing and practicing controlled breathing. On other days, practicing breath control can and probably should occur during warm-ups and cool-downs.

Practice: Have students sit or stand comfortably by showing good posture. Students also may lie on their backs during this exercise. If sitting or standing, the back should be straight, the neck erect, and the head comfortably in line with the back and neck. Students should practice slow, deep breaths, striving to breathe from the diaphragm instead of the upper chest. As students breathe, encourage them to concentrate on their breathing and nothing else. Soft music in the background may help alleviate other distractions.

Application: Students must learn when to apply controlled breathing. Encourage students to apply it just before skill performance. For instance, in golf class, have students address the ball. Just before hitting it they should try controlled breathing as a means of centering their concentration on the ball and reducing muscle tension. You can ask students to apply this technique to other skill performance as well as to social interactions.

Muscle relaxation is another technique that helps relieve stress and improve concentration or focus. This may be practiced for the entire class period or during parts of class such as warm-up and cool-down. Some teachers enjoy

continued on next page

conducting relaxation exercises at the end of class in order to help students relax before they venture back to the regular routine of school. Other teachers feel students benefit from doing relaxation technique at the beginning of class as a way of letting go of hectic schedules and gathering focus for physical education. Either way, we encourage you to spend at least a minimum of 5s to 10 minutes at a time on muscle relaxation.

Practice: Discuss the benefits of muscle relaxation with students. Muscle relaxation includes relaxing and tensing and relaxing specific muscle groups throughout the body. When students enter class, ask them to find a quiet place and lie down in a comfortable position. Provide mats if possible. Dim the lights. Soft background music can help to drown out other distractions. Once students are comfortable ask them to listen to your voice and practice controlled breathing. Now, with a soft voice ask students to tense and relax one specific muscle group at a time. Teachers often begin with the toes and feet and work their way up to the head. Once you have asked students to relax neck, face, and head muscles, allow them to remain relaxed with controlled breathing. After several minutes, ask students to slowly join the class when they are ready by sitting up and opening their eyes.

Application: Encourage students to use this technique at home as a means of relaxing and reducing stress. You may ask students to brainstorm other times when this technique may be used. After students brainstorm out of class ways to use relaxation techniques, consider out of class assignments and projects that enable students to try these suggestions and report their experiences.

Integrity: Adherence to a strict moral or ethical code.

form successfully in a particular situation. Students with high self-efficacy are more inclined to seek challenges, try hard, and persist through difficult times. Low efficacious individuals will avoid challenges, give up, and become anxious or depressed with adverse situations (Gill, 2000). There are several factors that enhance self-efficacy; teachers should be aware of: skill mastery, modeling, verbal persuasion or encouragement, and emotional arousal.

Self-efficacy

Skill mastery or performance accomplishments have the most powerful effects on self-efficacy. Practicing correct skill form and mastering the form encourages the learner to perform that skill in future practice and game situations. Someone who is skilled in basketball is more apt to play basketball outside of physical education class. Someone who is not skilled at wrestling may not seek out opportunities to wrestle.

Self-efficacy increases when students observe the teacher, peer, athlete, or someone else accomplish a skill. This is called mod-

270

eling, and it is an integral part of physical education instruction. Encouragement, or verbal persuasion, is not as effective as skill mastery or modeling, but it contributes to the development of self-efficacy. Emotional arousal around performance may enhance or hinder performance. Emotional arousal is dependent on individual interpretation of a situation (Gill, 2000). Emotional arousal affects social interaction as well as motor performance. Individuals who notice such physiological responses as the heart pounding, knees shaking, or hands sweating may benefit from learning relaxation and stress management techniques.

Imagery

Imagery, or mental practice, is a technique used to focus the attention of the individual on a particular aspect of performance and help that individual use all the senses to cognitively create or recreate an experience (Gill, 2000). Imagery can be used to enhance practice and mastery of skills. It can be used to facilitate relaxation and curb emotional arousal that is detrimental to performance. Imagery also can be used to help students cognitively rehearse appropriate social behaviors.

Relaxation techniques such as breathing exercises, progressive tensing and relaxing of muscles, and meditation can be used to manage stress and directly affect physiological responses caused by emotional arousal. Use of relaxation techniques enhances student attention and focus to skill development and performance. It also can assist with impulse and anger control in social situations.

Concepts/Principles

Kindergarten: *Students learn best by doing and watching a model of the movement form.* They also may learn best using different modalities and situations—seeing, hearing, or doing; alone, with a partner, or in a group setting. Encouragement helps students stay focused on the task and keep trying. Teachers can provide children with many models of movement in order to encourage them to move and explore movement. Verbal encouragement from the teacher, peers, and self will enhance student participation.

Figure 3

Reprinted, by permission, from C. Himberg, G.E. Hutchinson, and J.M. Roussell, 2003, *Teaching secondary physical education*, (Champaign, IL: Human Kinetics).

Second Grade: *Encourage students to use imagery to think and recreate why a movement or social interaction was successful.* Imagery will help students develop movement and social skill mastery. Imagery also can be used to problem solve or create other movement forms and expression. For instance, a child learning to jump rope may imagine jumping over a straight rope lying on the floor. When encouraged to imagine other ways to jump over the rope, the child may discover jumping forward and backward, side to side, hopping on one foot over and back, or alternating feet with each hop.

Fourth Grade: *Working in small groups with peers enables students to practice giving appropriate feedback, verbal persuasion, and encouragement.* Feedback about skill performance and social skill interaction allows students to correct and improve motor performance and social interactions. Students must be taught how to observe and assess skill performance and social behavior. And, they must learn to deliver appropriate feedback. Checklists, task sheets, and "T" charts can be used to break down skill performance and social interactions into observable pieces. Verbal persuasion and encouragement can be used as a means for delivering accurate and constructive feedback to others.

Sixth Grade: *Achievement is directly related to the effort and motivation put forth.* Effort and motivation are related to self-efficacy, or one's confidence to do or perform successfully. Therefore, opportunities should be provided for students to practice and achieve success in order to progress to more difficult challenges. Achievement should not be confused with winning. Winning is only one form of achievement. Instead, we should view achievement broadly as success in attaining realistic goals for performance or social interaction that have been established by the teacher or student(s).

Eighth Grade: *Relaxation techniques help relieve stress, improve attention and focus, and assist with impulse and anger control.* As mentioned previously, emotional arousal may enhance or hinder skill performance and social interaction. Through relaxation techniques, students learn how to calm physiological responses such as rapid heartbeat and sweaty palms, and to temper emotions such as anger. They also learn to dissuade self-doubt with positive self-talk. These techniques work to enhance student focus and attention for learning, performance, and positive social interaction.

Tenth Grade: *Imitation of positive interactions with others, asking for feedback, and formulating goals enhance self-confidence and self-actualization.* First, students need to understand what positive social interactions look like. This is accomplished through modeling and through descriptions of positive social behaviors. Next, teachers can create environments and activities where students are expected to engage or imitate these behaviors. It is important to discuss the benefits of these positive social interactions with students so that they come to understand how prosocial behaviors make them and others around them feel. Understanding, practicing positive social behaviors, then reflecting on the benefits of these behaviors to self and others may help students choose to use them in situations outside of class.

Twelfth Grade: *Levels of self-efficacy may predict whether or not individuals function independently to pursue physical activity outside of high school.* By twelfth grade, students should have developed competence in a variety of movement forms, understand the health-related benefits of physical activity, and demonstrate the ability to assess and provide feedback to self and others in the areas of skill performance and social interactions. They should be able to set realistic goals for health-enhancing activity in the future and know what activities they like to do. These skills lend themselves to strong self-efficacy and the hope that students will pursue wellness activities and make healthy life choices beyond high school. Teachers can help by creating opportunities for students to plan their own wellness programs for the present and future.

How Do People Learn To Understand and Respond to Individual and Group Diversity in Sports, Games, and Other Physical Activities?

Distinct characteristics and qualities of people (e.g., culture, language, race, religion, ability, gender, family lifestyle, and beliefs) are known as diversity. Diversity among people creates the foundation for a rich array of thoughts, ideas, knowledge, spiritual beliefs, and civic contributions—contributions to the arts and recreation as well as personal growth experiences that embody the American culture. Along with the advantages of diversity come the responsibilities and challenges of living, playing, and working together with people who may have varied needs and wants. Acquiring insufficient or inappropriate information regarding others can create fear and misunderstanding. Stereotyping in this way inhibits one's ability to know and appreciate each individual for who he or she is.

Stereotyping: Using insufficient or inappropriate information to label groups of people.

Learning to understand and respond to the diverse needs of others is a complex process that can be enhanced continuously throughout your life. Learning the skills needed to respond appropriately to individual differences usually requires a willingness to learn about others as well as the ability to demonstrate empathy. In physical education, we practice these skills through play/sport. The skill of empathy involves identification with and understanding of another's situation, feelings, and motives. When you can feel what another person might be feeling, you are practicing empathy. A willingness to learn creates a much greater likelihood that you will learn.

Empathy: Identification with and understanding of another's situation, feelings, and motives.

Although understanding others is influenced by experiences acquired from every aspect of your life—including family, friends, community, and spiritual beliefs—physical education offers a unique and powerful opportunity to enhance these skills in ways no other content area can. The abundant interactive nature of physical activity lends itself to limitless opportunities for learning about the cultures of others, their abilities, thoughts and feelings, similarities and differences, learning styles, activity preferences, communication skills, needs, and wants. When

Example 4

High School Example: Grade 10

Concept/Principles: An increasing willingness to learn about others can include exploration of and participation in cultural and ethnic dances, games, and activities.

Constructing for meaning allows students to develop a learning task that embraces their culture, heritage, interests, and experience. It stimulates creative and critical thinking skills, and it may involve research on the part of the learner. The teacher's principal roles are to provide appropriate primary resources (equipment, time, instructional materials, etc.), and to facilitate learning.

Students may work alone, in pairs, or in a group. They select a historical period that is of interest to them (e.g., the civil rights movement, the roaring twenties, modern pop culture, ancient Egypt, etc.), and research the significant movement and recreational activities from that period as a homework assignment. Any number of products can result from this research:

• Students can create a game, dance, or movement activity from the time period and teach it to the class. The class can describe the nature of the interaction skills involved in the activity, how these skills are learned through the activity, and their significance in the context of the culture from which they originated.

• Students can adapt games learned in class to incorporate the cultural, historical, or philosophical perspectives of their time period.

• Students can invent their own game or activity that incorporates motor learning concepts/principles, biomechanics, exercise physiology, or social skills.

• Students can invent a game or activity based on predicting what a particular culture and lifestyle might be like in the future, focusing on the social nature of the activity. This kind of assignment lends itself to working together with the history or social studies teacher to develop a strategy for providing students with primary resources as well as helping them to develop their ideas. Teachers can decide together the kinds of outcomes they will require, the timelines and due dates, and what portions of the product will be used by and graded by each teacher.

you participate in physical education, you make active choices about the way you allow new knowledge and information to influence the way you interact with others. Choosing to allow continuous new knowledge regarding similarities and differences in people can create the capacity to grow in understanding of individual and group diversity for a lifetime. The ways that you demonstrate understanding can be thought of in levels. The first level is tolerance, which means to endure with patience. The second is acceptance, which means to receive with favor. Appreciation is the third level. It means to greatly value over time. The highest level of understanding is celebration, or an intense appreciation for diversity. It is not necessary to practice the highest level of acceptance every time. It is helpful to be conscious of choosing among these levels in all of your interactions with individuals who are different from you.

Understanding the kinds of skills needed to perform successfully with others begins with accepting that everyone can learn these skills. Avoid categorizing yourself or other students as good or bad. Social skills are skills that help you build positive feelings with others and perform successfully in pairs, teams, and groups. You can think of social skills in much the same way that you think of skills in other subjects. You may be very knowledgeable about some math skills, but not very knowledgeable

Figure 4

Reprinted, by permission, from C. Himberg, G.E. Hutchinson, and J.M. Roussell, 2003, Teaching secondary physical education, (Champaign, IL: Human Kinetics).

about science skills. Everyone has different levels and knowledge of a variety of social skills. Learning social skills involves your feelings to a greater degree than does learning academic skills. Social skills also are influenced greatly by how other people treat you, or how you perceive the way people treat you.

Concepts/Principles

Kindergarten: *Including everyone in activity makes learning fun for everyone.* Including others demonstrates that everyone has the right to participate in physical activity. In addition, when everyone feels like they belong, physical education class is safe and happy.

Second Grade: *Boys and girls can learn to be partners and respect each other.* Many people think that boys can only be friends with boys and girls can only be friends with girls. When you feel comfortable with both boys and girls, physical education class is a better place to learn. Being a respectful partner to both boys and girls allows you to learn better and have more fun.

Fourth Grade: *Respecting others means showing a willingness to consider their thoughts and feelings as you participate during games, activities, and sports.* Respecting others in this way helps make physical education class emotionally safe. Everyone deserves to feel safe when participating in physical activities. You show you care when you can participate positively with all kinds of people.

Sixth Grade: *Opportunities to practice inclusion of all kinds of differences and similarities in individuals helps your groups/teams function more effectively.* This skill greatly influences people's understanding and accommodation of similarities and differences among individuals. Multiple differences exist in the world. When you learn to understand and accommodate people's strengths and limitations you are better prepared for working and living in a diverse society.

Eighth Grade: *Practicing the use of empathy during physical activity with others will be especially helpful in developing* *effective communication skills.* Seeing an issue from the other person's point of view can give you great insight into the thoughts and needs of others. Empathy is a critical skill for developing the ability to include people with diverse needs and wants in games, sports, and physical activity. As you learn more about others, you can increase your level of respect toward individuals who are different from you.

Celebration:
Intense
appreciation.

Tenth Grade: *An increasing willingness to learn about others can include exploration of and participation in cultural and ethnic dances, games, and activities.* This kind of experience is invaluable in helping to develop the knowledge and ability to appreciate a wide variety of people. Increased knowledge of diverse peoples better prepares you to live and work with people who are different from you.

Tolerance:
The ability to
endure with
patience.

Twelfth Grade: *Community service projects involving physical activity provide opportunities to learn about the needs of others in a real life, meaningful way while also providing the opportunity to practice social skills.* Practicing responsible social behaviors through physical activity and emphasizing acceptance and appreciation maximizes understanding of others and enjoyment of the activity.

What Kinds of Social Skills Must People Learn in Order To Perform Successfully with Others in Sports, Games, and Other Physical Activities?

Empathy forms the basis for developing many other social skills. It is critical for developing constructive communication, which is a necessary skill for successfully interacting with others. Constructive communication includes active listening (the ability to demonstrate body language and facial expressions that indicate attention), paraphrasing (repeating what was said in one's own words), questioning (the ability to ask questions that indicate a context for what was previously said), and clarifying (asking questions to improve one's understanding). Providing specific feedback to partners and group members helps each student develop thinking and communicating skills. Taking turns in a variety of leadership roles (e.g., team leader, timer,

Active listening:
Ability to demonstrate body language and facial expressions that indicate attention.

facilitator, equipment monitor, warm-up leader, checker for individual and group understanding, encourager, feedback provider, recorder, and skills monitor) allows each person to contribute in a meaningful way as a group member while also developing social skills. Social skills such as encouraging, caring, courtesy, positive disagreement, complimenting, kindness, fairness, honesty, and integrity will contribute to the ability to perform successfully with others.

There are many skills that help people interact successfully with others. The choices about specific social skills that will be emphasized for teaching in schools, churches, and homes will depend on the collaborative efforts and input of students, par-

Clarifying:
Asking questions to improve one's understanding.

Paraphrasing:
Repeating what was said in one's own words.

Specific feedback:
Detailed, nonevaluative information about the performance, product, or outcome of a task or process.

Example 5

Elementary School Example: Grade 4

Concept/Principle: Using courtesy and complimenting in all games and activities makes the activities successful for everyone.

Ask your students to brainstorm about the meaning of courtesy. Their ideas should be recorded and posted where they are visible to all. Students will then be asked to move a ball in various ways to the cues of the teacher. After several minutes of practice, have students think of as many ways as possible to be courteous when choosing a partner. Allow students to work with a partner if they wish. After several minutes, ask students to share their responses. Their answers may include:

• Say "yes" with a smile when someone asks to be your partner.
• Be willing to be partners with someone other than your best friend.
• Say "thank you" and "please" to your partner.
• Don't leave anyone out, even if you have to make a group of three.

Next, have students select partners. Give each student a task card with the following set of instructions written on it:

1. Say "thank you" every time the equipment is handed to you.
2. Say "you're welcome" when your partner says "thank you."
3. Hand your partner the equipment when it falls.

Give each pair of students one ball to share. While one child is performing to the cues of the teacher, the other is observing and making encouraging statements. After a few minutes, have the students switch roles. After they have each had a turn, they should stop and ask each other if they remembered to use the courteous statements and behaviors listed on the task card. They should talk about how it felt, then they should repeat the activity while trying to maintain or improve their courteous behavior.

At the end of the lesson, have students talk to their partners about whether they had the opportunity to use any of the other courteous words and behaviors listed on the class chart.

ents, teachers, community leaders, and spiritual leaders. It is important for people to know themselves well enough to identify their social skills strengths and weaknesses. This self-knowledge can help individuals construct personal growth plans. There are many strategies for developing social skills. Some are practiced individually, but most are developed as a result of working with others. When student interaction is planned and organized to create nurturing experiences and encourage reflection on these experiences, students have a much greater probability of developing appropriate social skills.

Concepts/Principles

Kindergarten: *Using caring words and actions makes everyone feel good when playing in games and activities.* Caring words and actions are kind and thoughtful. When you are caring and kind to others they usually respond by being caring to you. This is what makes playing games and activities enjoyable for everybody.

Second Grade: *Listening means that you can say what you heard and ask questions to make sure you understand.* Listening is important to understanding another person's way of thinking. Listening is not automatic. It has to be learned. Practicing every day as you listen to your physical education teacher as well as other students will develop your listening skills.

Fourth Grade: *Using courtesy and complimenting in all games and activities makes the activities successful for everyone.* Courtesy is the ability to use polite language and actions with everyone during physical activity, even if the person is not your friend or is different from you. Complimenting others during physical activity means recognizing and saying when someone has done something well, or has improved in his or her skills. It is an important skill for helping all students feel encouraged to work to their ability and to provide a safe place for all students to try their best.

Sixth Grade: *Paraphrasing is the ability to restate something that another person said to you, to check for understanding and to demonstrate that you cared enough to listen well.* Listening without judgment, paraphrasing thoughts and feelings, and clarifying for mutual understanding enhances one's ability to understand and appreciate others. It is easy to misunderstand another person's intended meaning, especially if the person has different culture, language, gender, etc., from yours. The skill of stating back what you think was said is a critical life skill in helping to get along with all kinds of people. It even enhances the critical thinking ability of your brain.

Eighth Grade: *Providing specific feedback will enable you to develop communication skills, increase content knowledge, and improve oral speaking skills.* Providing specific feedback also provides an opportunity for reciprocal teaching experiences. Specific feedback is the description of what you see and hear as your partner or group performs specified skills. It is nonjudgmental, clear, precise, and thoughtful. Using specific feedback in a caring and considerate manner helps build a mutually nurturing environment for learning.

Tenth Grade: *Integrity is the ability to adhere to a strict moral code with others. It fosters cooperative efforts.* Integrity is the ability to be true to your own values and beliefs through your actions. In sports and physical activity, this is one of the most important ways to build positive relationships and gain the trust of your peers. Gaining the trust and respect of others is an important process, because it affects the way that others feel about participating in physical activities and sports with you. It also forms the basis for all relationships that you nurture throughout your life.

Tenth Grade: *Empathy enhances effective communication skills.* Using empathy when you are listening means that you can see the statement/issue/problem from the other person's perspective. This is a higher level extension of the skill of paraphrasing. It is taking that additional step beyond clarifying for meaning and putting yourself in the other person's position to try to see an issue the way that person sees it. The skill of empathy allows you to feel what the other person might be feeling. This is a necessary component in helping to determine the most appropriate way to respond.

Twelfth Grade: *Constructive communication (active listening, empathy, paraphrasing, questioning, and clarifying)* *builds shared understanding and an appreciation of diverse points of view.* Improved communication skills increase content knowledge, improve oral speaking skills, and empower students to be more successful personally, socially, and professionally.

Twelfth Grade: *Ethical decision making involves the attainment of a number of learned social skills, including empathy, respect for other persons/property, honesty, integrity, and self-discipline.* These skills, learned and practiced every day during physical activity, develop over time. They form the basis for the ability to make ethical decisions as you are faced with increasingly complex moral and ethical situations.

How Do People Achieve the Social, Moral, and Ethical Skills Needed To Perform Successfully with Others in Sports, Games, and Other Physical Activities?

Recent brain-based learning research has provided great insight into how the brain affects feelings, and how feelings affect behavior. Many of the thoughts, feelings, and emotional responses that people have come to believe are automatic can be controlled by understanding the processes in the brain that inhibit its full use, particularly in times of stress (MacLean, 1990). A person's understanding of basic brain processes and the way that the brain filters information can serve as an excellent tool for controlling and self-monitoring behavior. It also provides a basis for understanding the elements of effective communication.

The ability to communicate thoughts, feelings, and understandings effectively provides the foundation for identifying, monitoring, and processing social skills. Effective communication requires abundant practice as well as feedback about how clearly thoughts, feelings, and understandings are shared by others. Social skills are learned by identifying and defining the skills, understanding them, and practicing them with others. Students may acquire social skills through role-playing prior to practice, or through practice. Let's examine three frameworks—cooperative groups, competition, and conflict resolution—and the

ways they can influence the learning of social skill concepts/
principles and interaction skills.

Cooperative Groups

Cooperative groups have predetermined steps for identifying
the social skill to be practiced, ways for individuals to monitor
the skill, and a way to evaluate it to see how well it was learned.
One of the most effective strategies for practicing social skills
during physical activity is working with partners and cooperative groups. Working with a partner to solve problems and give
feedback provides for the practice of a variety of social skills
(e.g., active listening, paraphrasing, positive disagreement, caring, encouraging, and complimenting). Students' interactions
with teachers also provide occasions for practicing a rich variety of social skills, such as getting to class on time (punctual-
ity), being prepared (responsibility), listening attentively (active listening), and contributing to the success of the class (responsibility, caring, encouraging, courtesy). The social skills that
students develop during school will affect their interactions with
others in all areas of life.

Cooperative groups: Groups structured to promote positive interdependence and social skills acquisition.

Competition

While competitive experiences cause great anticipation for some,
they can produce apprehension and anxiety in others. The effect of competitive experience on social development has been
identified by some as a necessary and natural part of preparing
students for a competitive world. Qualities such as aggression
and single-minded self-interest were thought to create winners—individuals who could beat out others to be number one.

Alfie Kohn, in his book, *The Brighter Side of Human Nature:
Altruism and Empathy in Everyday Life* (1990), makes the case
for focusing on the side of human nature that is decent, caring,
and concerned for the well-being of others in social structures,
and particularly in schools.

Many teachers and coaches are concerned about how the moral
development of children is affected by their participation in
competitive sports and games. Darren Treasure's concern about
the moral development of youths in sports led him to conduct
a series of studies of male soccer players, ages 12 to 14. He
found there was a high correlation to a well-developed set of

Example 6

Middle School Example: Grade 6

Concept/Principle: Practicing the skills of conflict resolution help to resolve problems that occur naturally in games, sport, and physical activities.

The teacher divides students into heterogeneous groups of six, being careful to balance the groups with students having both higher and lower social skills proficiency. The students are given group identification names or numbers by a student monitor during warm-ups.

The teacher has a chart with the word ENCOURAGE written on the top, and HEAR/SEE underneath. After the teacher gives an example of a time when encouraging might be needed (e.g., a marathon runner is almost finished and can see the finish line but doesn't think that she can make it), the teacher asks students to identify some other situations where encouraging might be helpful. Students brainstorm as many encouraging statements as they can. These may be things like, "You can do it!" "Keep going!" "Don't stop!" "Nice try!" and, "Way to go!" The teacher writes all of the ideas on the chart.

Next, the students brainstorm encouraging actions. These answers may include clapping, smiling, cheering, patting on the back, or giving a thumbs up or high five. After the chart is completed, the students are told that they will be practicing encouragement in the next two activities. They are told to listen and watch for it in their groups so they can share what happened at the end of the class. The teacher and/or selected students will also monitor as the students are performing, writing down the encouraging things they say and do.

Each group of students creates two triads. In these triads, students perform the following tasks.

– One student will practice the overhand throw, another will catch, and the third will watch and monitor the throw by referring to a task card that lists the following three critical elements:

1. Step forward with opposite foot from throwing arm.
2. Trunk twist starts with hips facing sideways in the direction of the throwing arm and ends with hips facing forward toward the throw at the moment of release.
3. Hand snaps downward during the release of the ball.

The student who is observing performs three tasks: giving the practicing student specific feedback on the three elements listed on the card, giving encouraging comments, and keeping track of the number of throws. The student who is catching also does or says encouraging things.

After the practicing student throws six times, the students rotate. The activity continues until all three students have performed all three roles.

– After students have practiced in their triads for a designated period of time, they will be asked to develop several ideas for a six-person game that uses the overhand throw and encouraging. After each group of three has had an opportunity to develop several ideas, they join the other half of their original group, share their ideas, and create and play their new game.

After playing the game, students are given three minutes to process their understanding of how they developed the ability to encourage and their use of encouraging during the game. They should use the following questions:

1. What did you hear or see that demonstrated the skill of encouraging?
2. How did it feel to have someone encourage you?
3. How did it feel to encourage others?
4. What did you do that helped you understand what encouraging others means?
5. What would you do differently next time?

At this time, the teacher should share some of his or her observations.

morals among players who held a mastery-oriented approach to participation in competitive activities. These players were more inclined to fairness and doing what is right, and they were more conscious of the needs of others. This was in contrast to the performance-oriented approach that emphasizes a "winning at all costs" attitude. These players were more likely to intimidate others, risk injuring an opponent, and push the limits of the rules in order to win (Treasure, 2001) Another down side to strictly performance-oriented thinking is that students begin to drop out of sports in adolescence. They compare themselves to others and get discouraged, or they may have been more skilled than others up to that point and drop out because they can no longer dominate (Treasure & Roberts, 1995).

Joan Duda (1996) describes the different orientations to sport climates as task-oriented versus outcome-oriented. Outcome-oriented sports environments are those in which success is demonstrated only by superior ability. Success is the only thing that matters; personal goals and values do not consider the social environment. Task-orientated sport environments emphasize rewarding hard work and improvement. Goals and values are based on the social environment. Duda maintains that task-oriented sport environments bring out the best in all players, including those who are more naturally outcome-oriented. She believes that coaches/teachers create the orientation of the sports learning environment through the use of responses that emphasize effort.

Presumably, then, educators can change the nature of social expectations for individual success. They can place greater value on qualities such as fairness, improvement, altruism, and cooperation. There appears to be a growing body of evidence that supports the argument for a specific kind of approach to competition being of greater value in terms of moral development in children. The value of competition compared with other instructional strategies will continue to be debated for some time. However, when a teacher uses competition as a teaching strategy it is generally agreed that it is preferable to use it in combination with other teaching strategies.

Two examples that illustrate an appropriate method of focusing on social skill concepts/principles within the context of competitive experience are downplaying or eliminating the score and changing the scoring process to include points for appropriate use of social skills. Successful competition requires all students to be prepared to an appropriate level for the physical, cognitive, emotional, and motor demands of the activity. If students are adequately prepared and competition is producing anger, frustration, fear, name calling, aggression, cheating, or other forms of negative behavior, then additional instructional strategies may be required. These might include peer teaching, inclusion, and cooperative learning.

Creating an emotionally safe atmosphere that is conducive to prosocial behavior does not mean simply creating an environment where negative behavior is disallowed (such as having a no put downs rule). Safe competitive risks for all students can only occur in an environment where students nurture and care for one another. If the teacher pays daily attention to prosocial student interaction and models prosocial behavior, students will develop successful interaction skills.

Conflict Resolution
Routine practice of social skills increases the likelihood that the skills will be acquired. A process such as conflict resolution provides another way to enhance social skill acquisition. Understanding how to resolve conflict involves recognizing the nature of conflict in relation to one's own beliefs. A person's beliefs and attitudes about conflict determine how that person will react when conflict occurs. If students view conflict as an opportunity to develop problem solving strategies and communication skills and to learn more about themselves and others, it will be worthwhile. There are four situations in which conflict can occur: interpersonal (self), intrapersonal (between

two or more people), intergroup, and between groups (Community Board, 1993).

For the purpose of addressing resolution as a process, conflict is defined as two or more people who interact and perceive incompatible differences between, or threats to, their resources, needs, and values (Morton & Deutch, 1973). What students do in response to conflict can lead to a consequence that is either negative or positive. For example, they may complain to someone else, cry, make jokes, smile even if it hurts, become visibly angry, pretend nothing is wrong, give in, or go to an authority. The choices that students make are critical, because the consequences of those choices can make their beliefs about conflict even stronger (Morton & Deutch, 1973).

Fundamental to conflict resolution is the understanding that responses are conscious choices, and that individuals have complete control of them. Conflict will result in positive consequences and will de-escalate only if feelings are expressed rather than acted out. There is a decrease in emotion and perceived threat, disputants talk directly or use neutral third parties, and communication and problem-solving skills are employed (Morton & Deutch, 1973).

Major themes of conflict resolution programs include active listening (the ability to paraphrase or summarize what is said to ensure accurate comprehension), cooperation (one person speaks while the other listens without interruption), and creative problem solving (individually or together brainstorming solutions and selecting the one that best accommodates the needs of both disputants—the win/win concept).

One of the most important aspects of conflict resolution is the use of "I" statements. I statements focus on the needs and feelings of the person who has the problem. They provide a way for that person to communicate the consequences of a behavior, rather than just focusing on the behavior. I statements contain three parts:

1. I feel...
2. When you... or, when this happened...
3. Because...

I statements should be made in a nonthreatening tone of voice. Body posture and facial expressions should be open and caring. When people make "You" statements (e.g., "You always yell at me." and, "You make me mad.") they are not accepting ownership of the problem. Until each disputant owns the problem, it cannot be adequately resolved. Owning the problem is the ability of disputants to believe and say, "I did this..." and as a result, "this occurred." "I am responsible for my thoughts, actions, and feelings."

Another important skill in conflict resolution is the ability to paraphrase, or restate in one's own words, what the other person said. This can be practiced within all pair, group, and team-processing sessions. Teachers can model it when listening and responding to students.

The next step is reflection, or the ability of each person to state his or her understanding of how the other person feels. This skill can be practiced in partner activities that require students to depend on one another for safety and security. An example would be leading a student whose eyes are closed. After the pair walks for a period of time, they stop and the person who had the closed eyes describes how it felt to be led. The leader listens, then responds by describing the partner's feelings as he or she understood them.

In a real conflict situation, this skill is particularly critical to reaching the next step—validating the other person's issues and feelings while showing appreciation for his or her willingness to solve the problem. After validation, it is usually possible for disputants to generate several ideas for solving the problem and to agree on one.

Self-reflection is a critical component of monitoring one's behavior and interactions with others. It is beneficial to use positive self-reflection often, particularly when developing new social skills. Positively directed self-reflection focuses on what happened in the interaction that was worthwhile, while using any negative outcomes to determine what to do differently the next time. Self-reflection should not be used to dwell on mistakes or inabilities. This usually serves to decrease self-esteem and inhibit the growth of social skills (Bunker, Williams, & Zinsser, 1993).

Concepts/Principles

Kindergarten: *It is okay to make mistakes.* Mistakes are a good way to learn to do something a different way the next time. Learning from mistakes is what matters. When you are learning a new skill you may make a lot of mistakes, but you will only get better if you keep trying.

Kindergarten: *All of your actions are choices.* You can choose the way you act. Anger, sadness, fear, and excitement are all emotions. Emotions can be shared with others in many ways. You can learn to choose the ways that you show and share your feelings.

Second Grade: *Problem solving is a process that involves thinking about more than one possible way to do something and choosing the one that you think will work the best.* Thinking about many ways to solve a problem while participating in physical activity and choosing the best one makes your brain work better on future problems. When you problem solve with others it also helps you get along with different kinds of people.

Fourth Grade: *Collaboration happens when you are working together with someone or a team for different results, such as sharing equipment or space to make up separate games.* This is such an important skill to learn in physical activity because of the many daily challenges of sharing space, equipment, team members, and teacher attention. Collaboration involves thinking about helping all students get what they need to learn successfully.

Sixth Grade: *When students have abundant opportunities to alternate leadership roles, give feedback, practice social skills, and contribute to the success of the group, they learn to work successfully with people in any activity.* Developing a working knowledge of interacting effectively in groups requires regular, ongoing practice in all of these areas. Teacher support, modeling, and feedback are critical to students acquiring these skills.

Sixth Grade: *Practicing the skills of conflict resolution helps to resolve problems that occur naturally in games, sports, and physical activities.* It is useful to think of conflict as an opportunity to learn rather than an unfortunate consequence of human interaction. Regular application of the steps of conflict resolution enables students to explore options that they may not have thought about on their own. It can be an invaluable skill in working with others.

Eighth Grade: *Understanding of the brain (brain stem, limbic system, and neo-cortex) can help people understand why they react as they do during interactions with others.* The brain stem and limbic system form the basis of the way people respond to new knowledge and information. The neo-cortex is the center of thinking. Strengthening this part of the brain is critical to problem solving, learning, and developing effective ways to work with others.

Eighth Grade: *Moral and ethical interactions with others in physical activity include holding one's self accountable to rules and predetermined standards of behavior that affect the ability of all students to be successful.* It is important to understand that behavioral decisions do affect other students. It is imperative for each individual to consider the needs and wants of others as decisions are made regarding behavioral interactions.

Tenth Grade: *Keeping the importance of winning and losing in perspective during physical activities and sports helps maintain positive feelings about self and others.* When all social, collaborative, and cooperative skills are practiced on a regular basis, the student response to winning and losing is more likely to be kept in perspective. Placing a balanced importance on all aspects of behavior in interacting within activities allows students to feel a sense of achievement in making appropriate behavioral choices.

Tenth Grade: *Frequent self-reflection about interaction skills creates deeper understanding and development of those skills.* This reflection also can be shared with a partner or group to have the added benefit of other's perspectives. Taking the time to think about how you responded to others during physical activity can help you choose how to improve the interaction the next time (or to repeat it on a regular basis if it was successful). This is the same process used in the evaluation a particular motor skill.

Twelfth Grade: *Decisions about pursuing regular physical activity will be determined by a person's combined knowledge, experience, and attitudes about a wide variety of physical activities.* These attitudes are based primarily on the enjoyment level developed in relation to others in those activities. Creating maximum opportunities for positive interactions between individuals in physical activities will greatly influence their commitment to pursuing involvement in a variety of physical activities.

Twelfth Grade: *Distributed leadership allows the development of a sense of responsibility for self and others and the chance to be perceived as a meaningful member of the group.* Being a contributing member of a group in a variety of leadership roles give students the opportunity to positively influence the behavior of others on a regular basis, thereby contributing to the quality of their behavior. All students need to hold a position of responsibility on a regular basis to develop a sense of responsibility, not only to themselves, but to the group.

Placing Social Psychology Concepts/Principles in the Curriculum

Integrating social psychology concepts/principles into the physical education curriculum requires decisions about where to introduce aspects of each concept. In making placement decisions, it is important to remember that the concepts/principles and skills do not occur independently of one another. Student needs as well as the appropriateness for the age and grade level also should be considered. Throughout the chapter, placement of concepts/principles appropriate for different grade levels are identified for each theme. The grade levels were chosen to be consistent with the grade levels used in the National Standards. The concepts/principles are designed to be consistent with National Standards 5, 6, and 7. The ultimate outcome is for physically educated adults to demonstrate appropriate personal and social skills during physical activity and throughout all aspects of their lives.

Integrating Social Psychology Concepts/ Principles into Instruction

Establishing an environment conducive to learning, where students feel emotionally safe, is the first step in helping students develop personal and social skills. Traditional physical education classes have been places where teachers have determined the curriculum, designed unit plans, and conducted lessons. Delivering information to students has been the primary responsibility of the teacher. Instruction focused predominately on teacher explanation and demonstration of motor skills, sport skills, and game rules. Students were responsible for demonstrating basic sport skills and memorizing what is known as surface knowledge (Caine & Caine, 1995) for a variety of sports and games. The teacher assesses student learning through skills tests, knowledge tests, and fitness scores. This teacher-dominated approach requires students to learn on an inflexible schedule filled with many time constraints. This traditional model often doesn't include instruction conducive to student development of positive personal skills and appropriate social skills.

The alternative to a traditional model is one where teachers shift from rote practice of skills and memorization of facts to more meaningful learning. In other words, shift from a teacher-centered physical education program to a student-centered physical education program. In this setting, physical education teachers guide and facilitate student learning and help students make meaning of new information. In this setting, physical education teachers create opportunities for students to explore, discover, and practice what they learn. Together, teachers and students find experiential ways to link information and understanding. This kind of interactive setting is ideal for helping students understand and develop their self-concept, self-esteem, and self-confidence and the ability to interact positively with others.

Physical education teachers may use a number of teaching strategies such as positive discipline, thematic instruction, cooperative learning, reciprocal teaching, and meaning-centered cur-

Student-centered physical education: An interactive learning process for students; together, teachers and students find experiential ways to link information and understanding.

riculum to establish a student-centered physical education program (Mosston & Ashworth, 1994). The end result? Physical education teachers view students as involved and not merely busy, happy, and good (Placek, 1983). Students become more responsible for setting goals, assessing their progress, and monitoring their own learning. They feel more comfortable learning and taking safe risks. They grow personally and socially as they develop motor and cognitive skills. The lesson examples in this chapter illustrate a student-centered approach to structuring lessons.

Social psychological concepts/principles focus on the beliefs, attitudes, and perspectives of individuals and on the ways individuals interpret their interactions with others. In order to effectively instruct students and help them develop their own self and social skills, teachers are encouraged to first focus on themselves as individuals, and then on how they interact with students in their classes.

Modeling

The affective domain is unique in conceptual understanding and student proficiency; in fact, the teacher's ability to understand and apply the concepts/principles in daily interactions is critical to the learning and practice of affective concepts/principles by students. If, however, a teacher is teaching students to understand the concept of courtesy and does not demonstrate courtesy in his or her interactions with others, the meaning of this concept will be distorted. Social psychological concepts/principles are feeling/sensing in nature, making it difficult to separate the process of understanding them from actual practice.

Modeling appropriate social skills is more challenging than it sounds. When teachers participate in a process of self-reflection and make note of their own beliefs, thoughts, attitudes, and behaviors, they are better able to model appropriate social skills for students. Self-reflection helps teachers attain a clearer sense of personal identity. Personal identity is dynamic; that is, it has developed over time and continues to develop as one makes the journey through life. Identity is important because it helps to organize and guide interpretations and behaviors in all situations.

One's personal identity is influenced by a sense of commonality with others. Affiliations or group memberships provide a sense of belongingness. For instance, "I am a physical educator, and I have something in common with all physical educators," or, "I am a basketball coach and I belong to a coaches association." These group memberships influence one's perceptions about teaching. Awareness of social group memberships and how these memberships influence one's life is helpful in understanding personal identity and its influence on teaching.

Modeling also is affected by teachers' attitudes toward students. Attitudes can be influenced by stereotypes, impressions, observations, and experiences. When teachers judge students, regardless of whether or not these judgments are accurate, they create expectations. And, students tend to live up to the expectations that teachers hold for them. For example, if a student is working hard, willing to try new things, and helping others whenever possible, the teacher probably will behave positively toward the student and the student will fulfill the teacher's expectations. The same holds true for the student who is viewed as a troublemaker. Teachers are more likely to treat such a student in a way that represents this view. And, most often, the student will fulfill the teacher's expectations.

Teacher beliefs and expectations directly influence their ability to model social skills in class, and they profoundly impact their students' sense of self and behavior. Teachers often find modeling social skills more challenging with students they perceive as low achievers. High expectations can promote positive self-esteem and self-confidence, and can promote more positive and constructive social behaviors. When teachers have high expectations for all students, they are more likely to consistently model social skills.

Effective Teaching Strategies
Beyond modeling, teachers also must provide instruction on the concepts/principles outlined in the previous section. Teachers are encouraged to move away from the traditional teacher-dominated model for teaching and adopt a more interactive, student-centered approach. It also is critical to create a positive classroom atmosphere where students feel safe to take risks and

where mistakes are not feared, but are welcomed as opportunities to learn.

Cooperative Learning

Cooperative learning is a student-centered learning model that structures learner tasks in ways that allow self and social skills to be taught. It also encompasses higher order thinking skills. Cooperative learning is not simply higher skilled students teaching lower skilled students, and it is not the best or only way to teach. It is, however, the best way to teach some skills specific to social interaction. Five principles underlie successful cooperative groups (Deshon & O'Leary, 1984):

- Equal distribution of leadership responsibilities (distributed leadership).
- Heterogeneous grouping.
- Positive interdependence.
- Social skills acquisition.
- Group autonomy.

Distributed Leadership

No leader is assigned by the teacher or chosen by the group. The teacher allows students to determine important tasks and the contributions that each student will make to the success of the group. These roles are continuously rotated throughout the week, month, quarter, etc., so that every student has the opportunity to perform all tasks. Some examples may include timer, facilitator, equipment monitor, checker for group understanding, encourager, feedback provider, recorder, and skills monitor (both social and motor).

Heterogeneous Grouping

Groups are formed at random or assigned in advance by the teacher. Groups should include both genders and a mix of physical capabilities, cultural and socioeconomic backgrounds, language/verbal skills, and cognitive and social skills. This kind of group diversity best reflects the real world and allows students the opportunity to learn and practice the skills involved in tolerating, accepting, appreciating, and celebrating differences.

Positive Interdependence

This is the opportunity for students to take personal responsibility while working with a group toward a common goal. The teacher can use one or more of the following strategies to ensure that everyone is involved in the learning: group accountability, common tasks, limited and shared equipment, and group projects. These strategies are often referred to as providing individual accountability, since they ensure that the most gifted or motivated student does not complete the entire assignment or activity alone.

Social Skills Acquisition

Cooperative learning is a particularly effective method for teaching social skills if the teacher also models the skills being taught. Social skills instruction is ineffective if the teacher tends to believe that students are good or bad. Teachers may have expectations of how students are going to behave based on their appearance (e.g., tall and muscular, small and overweight), their race, their culture, a look, a feeling, who their parents are, socioeconomic status, gender, etc. Teachers also may listen to others who describe a student as bad, trouble, incorrigible, or unteachable. There is little mention of strategies to teach students social skills in undergraduate preparation. Therefore, whatever level of skill teachers have acquired has come from their own experiences with others, and primarily from their families. This creates two perceptions that can potentially inhibit social skills instruction: teachers may believe that their own behaviors/values are being questioned or criticized, or teachers may believe that families have the sole responsibility for teaching students to behave appropriately. Teachers who have these perceptions must address them before the process of teaching social skills can begin.

There are five steps to teaching social skills:
1. Introduce the social skill to be learned (e.g., caring, encouraging, courtesy) and provide a rationale for using it.
2. Role play what it is and (sometimes) what it is not.
3. Brainstorm the skill using a T-chart (students brainstorm what the skill looks like and sounds like).
4. Students and teacher monitor the social skill while students engage in a task that allows for performance of the skill.
5. Students and teacher process the skill and the task.

T-chart: A charting method of identifying a social skill and brainstorming the visual and verbal attributes of the skill.

Group Autonomy

The teacher allows students to fail and learn from their mistakes, instead of rescuing them by intervening at the first sign of trouble. Rescuing in this sense describes teacher behaviors such as getting students back on task, settling arguments, and offering solutions to student problems. It is important that the group members be given the chance to solve the problems that arise by themselves. They should be given a process to use and parameters in which to work out the issues before they ask for help. Teacher prompting and monitoring will encourage group self-sufficiency.

Each of the grade level examples focuses on one social psychological concept. Each one uses cooperative learning strategies coupled with selected models for integrating concepts/principles across the curriculum. Teachers are encouraged to make age-appropriate modifications in order to meet the needs of their students.

The examples emphasize social psychological concepts/principles, and therefore may reduce movement/motor learning time. These examples illustrate how the concepts/principles may be used in class. The overall curricular emphasis in physical education, however, should remain on maximizing movement time and motor learning practice.

The first part of the cooperative learning model—self-esteem building—was the primary instructional focus of the first lesson (see Figure 3). As mentioned earlier, self-concept and self-esteem comprise the foundation upon which self-confidence, improved social behavior, and achievement are built. The learning activity provides children with positive experiences that help build a positive sense of self. The feelings reinforced in this lesson that relate directly to positive self-esteem are:

1. **Security.** Children were given clear rules for participation and a clear definition of personal space. They knew what to expect and that it was safe.
2. **Selfhood.** Children were exploring their own space and moving in ways that felt comfortable to them. They were developing self-knowledge about the way their bodies move.

3. **Affiliation.** Each child saw that other children were working on the same thing, thus providing a sense of membership to the class.
4. **Purpose.** The purpose of the lesson was made clear. Children were practicing the concept of personal space and moving successfully. Not only did they come to realize that movement is fun and makes them feel good, but they also developed their own sense of self-empowerment.
5. **Competence.** Children gained a better understanding of how they move and a sense of accomplishment for moving appropriately in personal space.

Processing is the practice of evaluating what has occurred during the lesson or activity. It helps students to understand and internalize cause and effect, and it provides valuable feedback from peers and the teacher. Processing should not be used to provide a forum for blame when the group has not been successful, however. Students can be taught to use tactful statements, such as, "Our group did not complete the task because everyone didn't get a chance to share." Contrast this statement with, "Our group didn't work because Mary is so bossy." Processing is crucial to teaching social skills, and it also helps students to develop critical thinking skills.

Cooperative learning strategies are particularly effective because the learning occurs in the context of instruction, not as a separate unit, subject, or course. Teachers can select several social skills per year and teach a new skill every four to five weeks, along with the regular curriculum. Teachers are encouraged to display, as visible reminders, social skill signs and posters. Teachers will decide how much time to focus on each skill based on the needs of their students.

Assessing Student Learning

When assessing student use of social psychological concepts/principles, it is important to be clear and specific about what knowledge, behaviors, and actions will be appraised, as well as what assessment tools will be used. Teachers are encouraged to engage students in the assessment process as much as possible so they may bring application to their understanding of these skills. Several things should be considered:

1. What do you expect your students to know and be able to do as a result of the instruction?
2. How will you know it when you see it? What will the understandings/behaviors look and sound like at different grade levels? In different classes? What role will the teacher have in the assessment? What role will the students have in the assessment?
3. What criteria will be used for judging the students' knowledge, understanding, and use of the concepts/principles?
4. What kind of feedback are you expecting to receive in order to make adjustments to the curriculum?
5. Are you collecting information that can help provide insight into the effectiveness of your personal interactions with students?
6. Are both formative and cumulative methods used consistently?

Following are some examples of ways to assess student knowledge and abilities regarding the social psychological domain.

Pair Share

The teacher gives task cards to each set of partners to help them monitor their ability to develop and use a social skill, such as courtesy, during the activity. At the completion of the lesson, each partner has 30 seconds to describe his or her own ability to use the social skill on the task card. He or she then describes the other person's performance.

Rubric

Rubrics are a means by which students can rate their own social skills and those of their classmates. Students work in groups of six to complete a task such as creating a new game incorporating the overhand throw. Then, students are asked to rate their team performance based on a specific rating criteria, or rubric. The teacher fills out a separate rating form for each team using the same criteria. The two are compared and discussed.

Open-Ended Question Journal

Students keep a journal, or use paper distributed in class. The open-ended question journal enables students to reflect on self, social skills concepts/principles, and experiences during class. The teacher can leave time for writing in class or assign journal writing for homework. The teacher and/or the students should determine an open-ended question for each writing assignment. Questions should relate to self-reflection, social skills, and lesson experiences.

> *For example:* How would you describe your participation and contributions to the group in each of your assigned roles in today's activity? How did you feel about your contributions to the group? How would you modify your input in the future based on today's learning?

Group Project

Group projects provide wonderful opportunities for students to work cooperatively.

> *For example,* after several weeks of school and numerous hours of teaching students elements of physical and emotional safety, the teacher decides to have the students create their own safety project. The teacher tells the students that they are going to develop the expectations for a safe physical education class for the kindergartners. Students are given time to work in pairs to think of as many behaviors as they can that make learning in physical education safe. They will then be asked to describe how children learn these skills. After several minutes, the teacher asks partners to share their an-

Figure 5	
Sample Rubric	
3	All students gave input into creating the game.
	All students used encouraging statements at appropriate times.
	Feedback provided by each student in the group was specific and clear.
2	Most students gave input when creating the game.
	Most students used encouraging statements sometimes.
	Feedback provided by most students was specific and clear.
1	Only a few students gave input into creating the game.
	Few students used encouraging statements.
	Few students provided specific or clear feedback.

swers and records them on a chart. After everyone has had an opportunity to share, the teacher asks for clarification and consensus on the behaviors and methods of learning that the students have described. A group of students is assigned to redo the chart so that it is neat and clear. All students sign the chart and it is presented to the kindergarten class.

Checklist

As students are performing an assigned activity, they can be asked to self-assess, be observed by peers, or be observed by the teacher. Regardless of who does the assessment, a checklist is used. The observations work best if they are objective in nature and do not require any judgment on the part of the observer. Checklists can be modified to include specific behaviors.

Portfolio

Social psychological concepts/principles can be included as entries in comprehensive portfolios, or separate portfolios can be created specifically for social psychological concepts/principles. A portfolio for social psychological concepts/principles may document growth in understanding about social and/or interpersonal skills over time. Portfolios in the social psychological domain should reflect real life, challenging utilization of concept knowledge and application and/or synthesis of skills. Social psychological skills can be student self-selected, so that each portfolio contains skills specific to each student's developmental needs. What makes a portfolio different than a folder filled with completed assignments is the interactive process involved. When students create portfolios, they are actively engaged with content and their own learning. The steps for developing portfolios are quite specific, yet flexible, depending on student and teacher needs. The teacher, the teacher and the student, or the student may determine the details of each step stated below.

1. Determine the purpose of the portfolio (e.g., "Students will self-assess their understanding of how to develop social skills and their use of skills identified and taught throughout the unit, semester, or year.").
2. Determine what kind of student work will be included in the portfolio (e.g., "Students are to include a report that

chronicles the development of their ability to understand and apply the social skill of accepting personal differences to their interactions with others in each game, activity, or skill throughout the unit, semester, or year."). Teachers and students establish criteria for evaluating the work.

3. Create timelines for completing each piece of student work. Make these timelines reasonable (e.g., "One reflection per week will be turned in to the teacher.").

4. Design ways to evaluate and provide feedback for stu-

Figure 6

Sample Checklist Items

	OBSERVED		
	Frequently	Sometimes	Never
1. Student uses courtesy when asking for and returning equipment to others.			
2. Student listens and can repeat what he or she heard a partner or group member say.			
3. Student willingly chooses and welcomes partners of the opposite gender.			
4. Student willingly accepts and welcomes individuals who are differently abled, or who have limited physical or cognitive abilities.			
5. Student willingly invites and accepts partners and group members of different cultures and ethnic backgrounds.			
6. Student contributes as a member of the group in whatever capacity assigned.			
7. Student takes risks such as volunteering to demonstrate taking a turn when it is appropriate, answering questions, speaking in front of the class, finding own partner/group.			
8. Student offers to help others.			
9. Student is able to provide specific feedback in a caring and supportive manner to a partner or group member during an instructional task.			
10. Student practices active listening during teacher instruction.			

dent work, both during the process and upon completion. It is important to have checkpoints during the process where students can have their work reviewed and discussed so they can monitor their progress. Evaluation during the process and upon completion may be conducted by the student, by peers, and/or by the teacher. For example, each student might receive feedback from a peer every two to three weeks regarding reflections and new understandings. The teacher can become involved if it appears that a student is having difficulty acquiring and/or applying the skill.

5. Build in opportunities for students to make sense of the learning process and share their finished portfolio with others. For example, students might have the opportunity to share their reports orally in small groups and to discuss the learning they have used.

Concluding Comments

Every student in a physical education program has the potential to become a capable, caring contributor to the class, the school, and society as a whole. Why, then are some students unsuccessful? We know that interpersonal and intrapersonal characteristics are shaped by a multitude of factors. At times, it is tempting for educators to blame the environment, the family, the community, or society at large for challenging students. However, this view can prevent educators from embracing the challenge and taking responsibility for nurturing all students. All students deserve the right to develop to their full potential. And, an essential attribute for successful development is a positive sense of self.

Teachers must believe that they have the power to nurture the sense of self in all students. The question that remains, then, is, "How?" The teachers' role in providing thoughtful, well-organized environments where students feel physically and emotionally safe will depend largely on the amount of time, energy, resources, and self-reflection they are able to expend. Integrating social psychological concepts/principles across the physical education curriculum and into daily lessons invites the pursuit of personal and social lifelong learning for students and educators alike.

References

Allen, L., & Santrock, J. W. (1993). *Psychology: The contexts of behavior.* Madison, WI: WCB Brown & Benchmark.

Borba, M. (1989). *Self esteem builders resources.* Torrance, CA: Jalmar.

_____. (1995). *Strengthening at-risk students' achievement and behavior,* A resource handbook. Bellevue, WA: Bureau of Education and Research.

Brooks, M. G., and Brooks, J. G. (2000). *In Search of Understanding: The Case for Constructivist Classrooms.* Upper Saddle River, NJ: Prentice Hall.

Bunker, L. K., Williams, J. M., & Zinsser, N. (1993). Cognitive techniques for improving performance and building confidence. In J. M. Williams (Ed.), *Applied sport psychology: Personal growth to peak performance.* Mountain View, CA: Mayfield.

Caine, R. N., & Caine, G. (1995). Reinventing schools through brain-based learning. *Educational Leadership, 52*(7), 43-47.

Community Board Program, Inc. (1993). *Conflict resolution resources for schools and youth.* San Francisco: Author.

Cory, G., and Gardner, R. (2002). *The Evolutionary Neuroethology of Paul MacLean: Convergences and Frontiers (Human Evolution, Behavior, and Intelligence).* Westport, CT: Greenwood.

Costa, A. (1995). *Teaching for intelligent behavior-Outstanding strategies for strengthening your student's thinking skills, A resource handbook.* Bellevue, WA: Bureau of Education and Research.

Cox, R. H. (1994). *Sport psychology: Concepts and applications* (3rd ed.). Madison, WI: Brown & Benchmark.

Deshon, D., & O'Leary, P. W. (1984). *A guidebook for cooperative learning: A technique for creating more effective schools.* Holmes Beach, FL: Learning Publications.

Duda, J. L. (1996). Maximising motivation in sport and physical education among children and adolescents: The case for greater task involvement. *Quest, 48,* 290-302.

Duda, J. L., Olson, L. K., & Templin, T. J. (1991). The relationship of task and ego orientation to sportsmanship attitudes and the perceived legitimacy of injurious acts. *Research Quarterly for Exercise and Sport, 62*(1), 79-87.

Dweck, E., & Elliott, E. (1983). Achievement motivation. In E. M. Hetherington (Ed.), *Socialization, personality, and social development.* New York: Wiley.

Gallahue, D. L. (1996). *Developmental physical education for today's children* (3rd ed.). Madison, WI: WCB Brown & Benchmark.

Gill, D. (2000). *Psychological dynamics of sport and exercise* (2nd ed.). Champaign, IL: Human Kinetics.

Goleman, D. (1995). *Emotional intelligence.* New York: Bantam.

Gottman, J. M., & Declaire, J. (1998). *Raising an emotionally intelligent child.* New York: Simon & Schuster.

Harter, S. (1978). Effectance motivation reconsidered: Towards a developmental model. *Human Development, 21,* 34-64.

Hellison, D. (1995). *Teaching responsibility through physical activity.* Champaign, IL: Human Kinetics.

Hewitt, J. P. (1984). *Self society: A symbolic interaction in social psychology* (4th ed.). Boston: Allyn and Bacon.

Johnson, D. W., & Johnson, R. T. (1998). *Learning together and alone: Cooperative, competitive and individualistic learning* (5th ed.).Boston: Allyn and Bacon.

Kagan, S. (1997). *Cooperative learning.* San Clemente, CA: Kagan Cooperative.

Kohn, A. (1990). *The brighter side of human nature: Altruism and empathy in everyday life.* New York: Basic Books.

Kohn, A. (1997). *Beyond discipline: From compliance to community.* Alexandria, VA : Association for Supervision & Curriculum Development.

Mac Lean, P. (1990). *The triune brain in education.* New York: Plenum.

Maslow, A. H. (1954). *Motivation and personality.* New York: Harper.

McPherson, B. D., Curtis, J. E., & Loy, J. W. (1989). *The social significance of sport: An introduction of the sociology of sport.* Champaign, IL: Human Kinetics.

Morton, & Deutch. (1973). *Resolution of conflicts.* New Haven, CT: Yale University.

Mosston, M., & Ashworth, S. (1994). *Teaching physical education* (4th ed.). New York: Macmillan.

Murray, H. A. (1938). *Explorations in personality.* New York: Oxford University.

National Association for Sport and Physical Education. (1995). *Moving into the future: National physical education standards: A guide to content and assessment.* Reston, VA: Author.

Nicholls, J. G. (1984). Achievement motivation: Conceptions of ability, subjective experience, task choice, and performance. *Psychological Review, 91,* 328-346.

O'Block, F. R., & Evans, F. H. (1984). Goal-setting as a motivational technique. In J. M. Silva III & R. S. Weinberg (Eds.), *Psychological foundations of sport.* Champaign, IL: Human Kinetics.

Payne, V. G., & Isaacs, L. D. (1995). *Human motor development: A lifespan approach* (3rd ed.). Mountain View, CA: Mayfield.

Placek, J. (1983). Concepts of success in teaching: Happy, busy and good? In T. Templin & J. Olson (Eds.), *Teaching in physical education.* Champaign, IL: Human Kinetics.

Roberts, G. (2001). *Advances in motivation in sport and exercise.* Champaign, IL: Human Kinetics.

Ryan, R. M., & Deci, E. I. (2000). Self-determination theory and the facilitation of intrinsic motivation, social development, and well being. *American Psychologist, 55,* 68-78.

Sage, G. H. (1977). *Introduction to motor behavior: A neuropsychological approach* (2nd ed.). Reading, MA: Addison-Wesley.

Treasure, D. C., Duda, J. L., Hall, H. K., Roberts, G. C., Ames, C., & Maehr, M. L. (2001). Clarifying misconceptions and misrepresentations in achievement goal research in sport: A response to Harwood, Hardy, and Swain. *Journal of Sport and Exercise Psychology, 24,* 317-329.

Treasure, D. C., & Roberts, G. C. (2001). Students' perceptions of the motivational climate, achievement beliefs and satisfaction in physical education. *Research Quarterly for Exercise and Sport, 72,* 165-175.

Treasure, D. C., & Roberts, G. C. (1995). Applications of achievement goal theory to physical education: Implications for enhancing motivation. *Quest, 47,* 475-489.

United States Department of Health and Human Services. (1996). *Physical activity and health: A report of the Surgeon General.* Atlanta, GA: Author.

Weinberg, R. S., & Gould, D. (1995). *Foundations of Sport and Exercise Psychology.* Champaign, IL: Human Kinetics.

Williams, J. M., & Leffingwell, T. R. (1996). Cognitive strategies in sport and exercise psychology. In J. L. Van Raalte & B. W. Brewer (Eds.), *Exploring sport and exercise psychology.* Washington, DC: American Psychological Association.

Resources

Workshops

Attend the following kinds of workshops, within the context of physical education if possible:

- Cooperative Learning
- English Language Learners
- Conflict Resolution or Conflict Management
- Social Skills Instruction Management
- Reciprocal Teaching
- Constructivism or Meaning-Centered Teaching
- Multiple Intelligences
- Multicultural/Diversity
- Positive Discipline
- Project Respect: Don't Laugh at Me Curriculum
- Inclusion
- Authentic Assessment
- Tribes
- Class Meetings
- Critical Thinking/Higher Order Thinking Skills
- Developing a Positive Learning Climate
- Project Adventure or Other Initiatives Courses
- Brain Compatible Learning
- TESA-Teacher Expectations and Student Achievement
- Building Student Self-Esteem
- GESA-Generating Expectations for Student Achievement

Web sites
- About Homework Help/Sport and Exercise Psychology: http://psychology.about.com/cs/sport/
- Museum of Tolerance: http://www.wiesenthal.com/mot/
- Spreading Kindness: http://www.weinholds.org/kindness/index.htm

Books

Allen, A., & Gibbs, J. (1978). *Tribes-A process for peer involvement.* Lafayette, LA: Center for Human Development.

Bennett, B., Rolheiser, C., & Stevahn, L. (1991). *Cooperative learning where heart meets mind.* Bothell, WA: Professional Development Associates.

Gill, D. (2000). *Psychological dynamics of sport and exercise* (2nd ed.). Champaign, IL: Human Kinetics.

Glenn, S. H., & Nelsen, J. (1989). *Raising self-reliant children in a self-indulgent world.* Rocklin, CA: Prima.

Kuykendall, C. (1992). *From rage to hope, Strategies for reclaiming black and hispanic students.* Bloomington, IN: National Educational Service.

Lickona, T. (1991). *Educating for character: How our schools can teach respect and responsibility.* New York: Bantam.

Nelsen, J., Lott, L., & Glenn, S. (1993). *Positive discipline in the classroom.* Rocklin, CA: Prima.

Nicholls, J. G. (1989). *The competitive ethos and democratic education.* Cambridge, MA: Harvard University.

Rowan, F. F. (Ed.). (1994) *Programs with pizzazz: Ideas for elementary physical educators.* Reston, VA: AAHPERD.

Articles, Pamphlets, Reports, Papers, and Guides

Bredemeier, B., & Shields, D. (1984). Divergence in moral reasoning about sport and everyday life. *Sociology of Sport Journal, 1,* 348-357.

_____. (1986). Athletic aggression: An issue of contextual morality. *Sociology of Sport Journal, 3,* 15-28.

Bredemeier, B., Weiss, M., Shields, D., & Cooper, B. (1986). The relationship of sport involvement with children's moral reasoning and aggressive tendencies. *Journal of Sport Psychology, 8,* 304-318.

Deshon, D., & O'Leary, P. W. (1990). Social skills and processing in a nutshell, *Cooperative Learning, 10*(3), 35-36.

Duda, J. L. (1989). Goal perspectives and behavior in sport and exercise settings. In C. Ames & M. Haehr (Eds.), *Advances in motivation and achievement.* Greenwich, CT: JAI Press.

_____. (1989). The relationship between task and ego orientation and the perceived purpose of sport among male and female high school athletes. *Journal of Sport and Exercise Psychology, 11,* 318-335.

Hellison, D. (1993). The coaching club-teaching responsibility to inner-city students. *Journal of Health, Physical Education, Recreation & Dance*, *64* (5), 66-70.

McBride, R. (1995). *Conflict resolution resources for schools and youth*. San Francisco: Community Board Program.

Nicholls, J. G. (1984). Achievement motivation: Conceptions of ability, subjective experience, task choice, and performance. *Psychological Review*, *91*, 328-346.

Papaioannou, A. (1995). Motivation and goal perspectives in children's physical education. In S. J. H. Biddles (Ed.), *European perspectives on exercise and sport psychology*. Champaign IL: Human Kinetics.

Romance, T., Weiss, M. R., & Bockoven, J. (1986). A program to promote moral development through elementary school physical education. *Journal of Teaching Physical Education, 5*, 126-136.

Thill, E. E., & Brunel, P. (1995). Cognitive theories of motivation in sport. In S. J. H. Biddles (Ed.). *European perspectives on exercise and sport psychology*. Champaign IL: Human Kinetics.

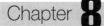

Chapter **8**

Aesthetic Experience

Judith B. Alter

W*hy do I watch one player on a field more than other players? How do judges decide who wins in gymnastics events? Why do I like to watch some tennis players while my friends prefer others? Why do the performances of outstanding players look so beautiful? Experts who study aesthetic experience in many fields such as education, anthropology, and the arts can answer these questions. This chapter examines basic concepts in aesthetic experience and how they fit into a physical education curriculum. Understanding these concepts can provide a physically educated person fundamental knowledge, and can enhance the experience of acquiring, maintaining, and appreciating a physically active lifestyle.*

What Is Aesthetic Experience in Physical Education?

The study of aesthetic experience focuses on the understanding and appreciation of beautiful form in all human activity. The root of the word "aesthetics" comes from the Greek word "aisthetikos," which means "of sense perception." To introduce the term aesthetic to students, substitute appreciation, or awe, or wonder when discussing it in movement activities.

The following example introduces the complex meaning of aesthetic experience. Imagine, for example, watching someone running in a race. Notice the person's running style, coordination, arm swing, and stride length. These features comprise part of the runner's technique or form. Or, notice the person's height, gender, hair color, running clothes, and facial expression. These features relate to the person's unique personal struc-

Aisthetikos: Greek word meaning "of sense perception."

Style: Established behavior recognized as unique and individual in structure and form.

Form: The shape of something, its outward or visible appearance; a fixed or usual method of doing something.

ture, or appearance. Notice the speed of the person's running, the distance in front of the other runners, and the anticipation felt (by you, the onlooker) about the outcome of the race. These observations relate to the person's accomplishment. Now, notice the elegant design in motion as he or she leaps speedily through space. This attention to the entirety of all the features, for the pleasure of this unified focus, constitutes the onlooker's aesthetic response to the runner running.

In the example above, the runner exhibits form, structure, and accomplishment. These elements also contain aesthetic properties. The features combine into a whole when the onlooker appreciates the beauty of an outstanding runner in action. Beauty is another term that describes exquisitely executed motor performance. Beauty refers to the design of the runner's agile body, running with grace, elegant control, and effortless speed. The overall impact of the entire event can produce a powerful aesthetic experience.

Now imagine the response of the runner after completing the race. That runner spent many hours practicing and training. The coach praises his or her outstanding stride and form on that day. The runner—recalling the experience of the race—agrees with the coach. The runner feels a rush of pleasure while contemplating how all the practiced components of running came together and united in that performance. That total recalled experience is also aesthetic; the totality of cognitive, physical/kinesthetic, and emotional appreciation became unified in that performance.

Aesthetic experience can be confusing because it is both a quality inherent in a person, action, or object—like the beauty of someone running—and it is also the special attitude people feel, like observers appreciating the beauty of the runner running. Said more simply, an object has aesthetic qualities and people use their aesthetic attitude to appreciate these qualities. When someone describes a special physical feat or achievement as "awesome," that response demonstrates an intuitive grasp of aesthetic experience.

Why Is Aesthetic Experience Important?

Aesthetic experience focuses on appreciating the liveliness of life—the central part of physical activity. Integrating the aesthetic dimension of physical education activities into the process of teaching other dimensions such as skills and rules helps students savor their aliveness and, thus, can increase their motivation for and pleasure in learning. Learning about the aesthetic qualities in movement activities helps students to distinguish a beautiful play from a well-executed one, whether or not it is successful.

When people focus on the most elegant, beautiful, brilliant, splendid, exceptional, or graceful way to carry out their physical activities, they become aware of the aesthetic component of an activity. This awareness helps them understand the goals for which they strive when participating in that activity. British artist and dance educator Elizabeth Watts in her *Towards Dance and Art* (1977), astutely points out that the word "kinesthetic" contains in its center the word "esthetic." The aesthetic quality of movement, she believes, stimulates good feelings and gives people the desire to repeat selected movements again and again to continue experiencing and prolonging these positive feelings. The kinesthetic sense—the muscle response—enables people not only to perceive physical activities in themselves but also to empathize with it in others. As children develop, they use their aesthetic impulse, which everyone has, to understand themselves and their capabilities. When students have felt the aesthetic features in their own movements they become sensitive to those qualities in others.

Linking Aesthetic Experience to the National Standards

The concepts for aesthetic experience connect to Standard 7 (Understand that physical activity provides the opportunity for enjoyment, challenge, self-expression, and communication). This standard includes some elements of aesthetic experience but does not address the central features of it: appreciation, awe, and comprehension of the total experience for itself. Enjoyment can come from meeting high aesthetic standards, as well as from the fun and play at the center of many physical activities. And, while students feel the challenge comes from surpassing their own previous performance, challenge also can relate to reaching aesthetic goals.

The concepts for aesthetic experience also connect to Standard 6 (Demonstrates understanding and respect for differences among people in physical activity settings). As members of a diverse culture, students must be able to see, experience, describe, and appreciate the differences and commonalties of culture, ethnicity, gender, body shape and size, and ability in relation to a variety of gestures, movement choices, and patterns.

Selected Aesthetic Themes

The next sections contain important concepts about aesthetic experience that students should understand. Throughout the chapter the terms "component," "feature," and "dimension" interchangeably describe the parts of aesthetic experience. Since human beings use movement to conduct all of life's activities, the following concepts concentrate on movement in general. The concepts highlight terminology that will enable students to analyze and discuss their aesthetic responses to all movement activities.

Five basic themes organize the concepts described here:

Theme 1. How do people learn to respond to aesthetic experience?

Theme 2. What are the aesthetic features of nonmoving objects and people in the environment?

Theme 3: What are the aesthetic components of movement?

Theme 4: What are the characteristics of movement patterns and how do they function?

Theme 5: What factors help determine criteria for judging the aesthetic quality of movement in one's own and other cultures?

The order of the themes follows a developmental sequence. The first one centers on the special attitude people access when they focus on aesthetic experience. The next three concern careful seeing, first of nonmoving objects and people, then when they are in motion, and then in patterned movement. Seeing patterns requires cognitive sophistication that middle and high school students can begin to pay attention to; this is difficult for elementary school children. The last theme, also advanced, centers on the criteria for evaluating the quality of aesthetic experience. This theme requires a synthesis of the others; therefore, accumulated practice enables students to approximate or achieve mastery.

How Do People Learn To Respond to Aesthetic Experience?

All human beings have aesthetic impulses and needs. People satisfy those needs when they organize or arrange their rooms, desks, purses, and briefcases; clothe themselves in special ways; choose furniture; seek out beautiful places in nature; play a musical instrument or listen to music; and participate in special ceremonies. Anthropologist Ellen Dissanayake, in her *Homo Aestheticus: Where Art Comes From and Why* (1992), describes this aesthetic impulse to put things in order as "making special" and "things done." Making special means to do something unusual with care and focus that goes beyond what is

Example 1

Early Elementary School Example: Kindergarten

Concept/Principle: People gain aesthetic awareness by seeing, hearing, touching, smelling, and tasting.

Have children describe, point to, or bring in an object they consider beautiful. The teacher can guide the children to use each of their senses and intelligences (Gardner, 1991) to explain their reasons for valuing the object. Students will see what they share and how they differ in their aesthetic appreciation of objects in their environment.

Example 2

Middle School Example: Grade 6

Concept/Principle: Shared receptive and generous feelings contribute to seeing and experiencing beautiful action.

After students attend a concert together or watch a film that contains special beautiful moments or actions, they can discuss how their group focus on appreciation helped each person shift their everyday attention to aesthetic experiencing. In this way, they can gain awareness of and write about the open and comfortable atmosphere that facilitates their aesthetic response.

Example 3

High School Example: Grade 10

Concept/Principle: Focusing on the unity of all the factors in a beautiful physical event develops aesthetic sensitivity.

After students work together on a class project or team effort, have them write a brief chronology of the steps they took from its beginning to its conclusion. Then, ask them to highlight the beautiful parts of that history. After all students have written and thought about these special moments, lead a discussion about what they wrote and finally, guide them in connecting the process and the result to help them appreciate the entirety of it.

Contrast:
Distinguishable differences.

necessary to accomplish the job. When students choose to wear colors in their clothes that contrast yet go well together, rather than just putting on the first garments they find, they are using their aesthetic taste. The extra thing done in that instance involves taking the time to choose, perhaps to hold up two or three combinations of shirts and pants to see which colors go best together. The aesthetic impulse, she explains, operates in most areas of people's lives and has done so throughout human history. This impulse helps people make order out of the world's apparent chaos, and appears to be innately satisfying and positive. The acts of making and doing something special aid in our attempt to organize unusual times and experiences in our lives.

All the senses serve as receptors for registering aesthetic experience of movement activities. When watching champion skiers, for instance, observers' eyes receive the image of each skier coming down the steep ski slope. At the same time that their eyes introduce these images into the brain, the muscles identify with the actions of the skier. Although the eyes provide one entry point for the kinesthetic sense (which registers touch and muscle knowledge), taste and smell enter the experience in a minor way. They trigger the memory of how excitement can lead to a dry mouth, and the smell of sweat that comes from extreme physical exertion. Although snow sports do not generate a great deal of noise, skiing makes its own subtle sounds, and these also contribute to how people appreciate the beauty and grace of the skiers. Students learn to describe aesthetic experiences in words or drawings. They pay attention to their taste—what they like and dislike—and explain their preferences.

Although many physically active people describe their outstanding performances in similar terms, each individual's personal aesthetic experience also has unique features. Each person may have a different mode of experiencing self-appreciation: a visual image, a rhythmic memory, a kinesthetic/physical recall, a spatial picture, or a combination of some or all of these. Students learn to apply their aesthetic attitude to their own performance and to appreciate their own experience aesthetically.

Guidelines exist to help teachers organize and sharpen the processes of aesthetic perception and reasoning. These broad guidelines apply to many activities, such as painting, dance, and film. They also work well for appreciating outstanding moments in physical activity. These guidelines serve as suggestions and jumping-off places for teachers and students to learn to appreciate their own and others aesthetic experience. David Perkins, co-director of Project Zero—basic research in the arts—at Harvard University has written a set of useful guidelines.

In *The Intelligent Eye: Learning To Think by Looking at Art* (1994), Perkins identifies six thinking dispositions that art and, by extension, other aesthetic experiences require and stimulate: sensory anchoring, instant access, personal engagement, dispositional atmosphere, wide-spectrum cognition, and multiconnectedness. In the first disposition, sensory anchoring, students encounter the activity with sensuous (of the senses) and imaginative perception. In physical education, the sensory anchor resides most often in the student-in-action (i.e., in running), or in a held position (i.e., landing a broad jump). Concentrated seeing with full attention and a receptive attitude of appreciation contribute to the kind of seeing Perkins encourages. This awareness centers on the particularity, the uniqueness of how beautifully the person carries out the activity.

Instant access—being able to capture the moment—is difficult to achieve when studying physical activity, because each instant goes by so quickly. Videotaping practice sessions of skill training and games can help preserve these instances. Continued repetition, so necessary in practice sessions, can provide access, although catching sight of the most outstanding action requires teachers and students to pay close attention.

Personal engagement requires special attention, focusing on the action to see it in its fullest way. Personal engagement requires students to reflect thoughtfully with a receptive attitude. This takes time and patience. When viewing the videotapes of practice sessions or games, students can look for this attitude in themselves and others. Personal engagement also requires teachers and students to experience and recognize authenticity of focus in physical activity. Students demonstrate authenticity in their energy level, intention, and clarity of action. They do not perform or execute activities in a blasé, passive, sloppy, or careless manner; they concentrate completely.

By dispositional atmosphere, Perkins means that the mindset of the class and teacher centers on appreciation. This, in turn, creates an atmosphere, an environment, for contemplation and acceptance. Paying attention to the aesthetic dimension of physical activity requires a generous and cooperative attitude along with the drive to do one's best. This mindset facilitates concentration, progress, and mindfulness since it helps focus students' attention on intrinsic action.

As an advanced skill in understanding aesthetic experience, wide-spectrum cognition helps students take in the unified whole, the entirety of the action, not just one or a few of its parts. Students use this ability when they watch marching bands and drill teams create designs on a football field, or when they see flocks of birds or squadrons of airplanes fly in formations. Wide-spectrum cognition enables students to deepen their aesthetic sensibility by becoming sensitive to the organization of patterns and forms. They learn to sense the innate order of what they perceive.

Perkins calls the final disposition that encourages aesthetic thinking multiconnectedness. He means that participants keep in mind all the parts of the event, such as: the student, the situation, the goals, the level of development, and the physical and mental atmosphere. The sense that everything just came together at that one moment reflects the height of multiconnectedness. Students and teachers should look for these moments and articulate them. By modeling them, teachers can introduce these dispositions to their students, and then use them in class.

Concepts/Principles

Kindergarten: *People gain aesthetic awareness by seeing, hearing, touching, smelling, and tasting.* Students use their eyes, ears, muscles, and even taste and smell when they learn new physical actions. They also use all their intelligences in these activities. When students pay attention to how their senses and intelligences help them learn, they can heighten their sensitivity to these experiences.

Second Grade: Special beautiful moments give sudden aesthetic pleasure. Students intuitively respond to beautiful or awful moments. The students' natural aesthetic impulse helps them distinguish between these kinds of moments, which often happen rapidly. Students need practice in seeing and describing these moments to help them recognize their special qualities.

Fourth Grade: Paying attention to aesthetic experience requires appreciative concentration and personal commitment. Aesthetic experience requires a shift in the kind of attention that students pay to their activities. Instead of focusing on skills or goals, students need to see and feel the quality of the movement, to appreciate it just for itself. For instance, students can look at flowers for their height, vitality, and variety, or they can focus on their beauty because of, or regardless of, the other factors. This special kind of attention takes practice and feels different from other kinds of attention.

Sixth Grade: Shared receptive and generous feelings contribute to seeing and experiencing beautiful action. When all members of the class together focus on appreciating beautiful action, individuals can more easily feel generous, receptive, imaginative, and involved. This openness to the wonder of the beautiful action enhances the experience and lets students feel safe in expressing their appreciation.

Eighth Grade: Recognizing and appreciating how all parts of a special physical moment fit together as a whole develops aesthetic perception. Learning physical education activities often involves paying attention to many details—separate actions, requirements, and rules. Aesthetic appreciation requires students to focus on how the parts fit together in the ongoing action, especially when the action is beautiful. When students and teachers take time to appreciate the special quality of this overall coordination of actions, they gain insight into the unique capabilities of human beings.

Tenth Grade: Focusing on the unity of all the factors in a beautiful physical event develops aesthetic sensitivity. Once students have achieved enough skill to participate in complex physical activities, they often pay more attention to strategies, nuances of skills, and high achievements than they do to the unity of the processes of learning and playing. If teachers point out how all the efforts and achievements of each player contribute to the unity of their special play, for instance, then students can practice multiconnected thinking.

Twelfth Grade: Understanding aesthetic experience in physical activities enhances pleasure for participants and observers. The net result of practicing how to see and experience physical activity with aesthetic sensitivity adds several dimensions to students' education. They appreciate and articulate the qualities in what they see beyond winning or losing. They understand the complexity of what they see and experience and can describe it. They can transfer this appreciative kind of thinking to other activities in their lives.

What Are the Aesthetic Features of Nonmoving Objects and People in the Environment?

The aesthetic features of nonmoving objects and people in the environment include shape, size, their relations in space—in the environment—and the point of view from which one sees these objects and people. Shape here refers to the outline or form a person or object takes (see Figure 1). Students identify the shape of things, organic or inorganic, apart from their function. Different shapes include square, rectangular, spherical, triangular, or cylindrical, or combinations of these (see Figures 2 and 3). Artists classify shapes in another way, as kinds of shapes: solid (i.e., rocks and fruit), containing (i.e., bowls and boxes), and reaching (i.e., trees and brushes) (see Figures 4 and 5). The shape of most natural objects combines several of the kinds of shapes listed here.

Figure 1

The Basic Elements of Shape.

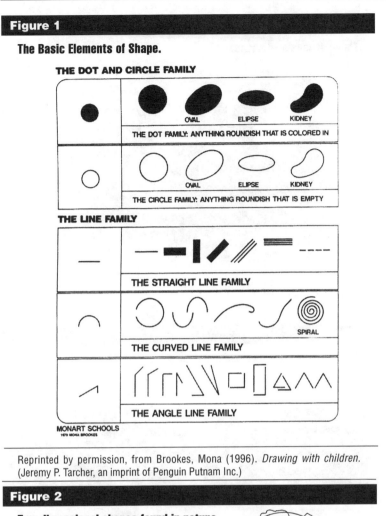

THE DOT AND CIRCLE FAMILY

THE DOT FAMILY: ANYTHING ROUNDISH THAT IS COLORED IN

OVAL   ELIPSE   KIDNEY

THE CIRCLE FAMILY: ANYTHING ROUNDISH THAT IS EMPTY

OVAL   ELIPSE   KIDNEY

THE LINE FAMILY

THE STRAIGHT LINE FAMILY

THE CURVED LINE FAMILY   SPIRAL

THE ANGLE LINE FAMILY

MONART SCHOOLS
1979 MONA BROOKES

Reprinted by permission, from Brookes, Mona (1996). *Drawing with children.* (Jeremy P. Tarcher, an imprint of Penguin Putnam Inc.)

Figure 2

Two dimensional shapes found in nature.

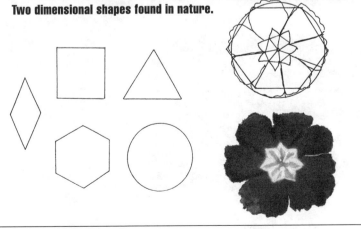

Courtesy of Anita Klebanoff.

Figure 3

Three dimensional shapes.

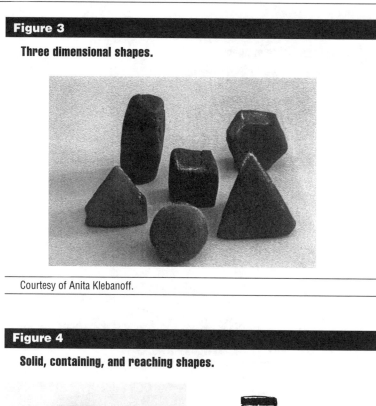

Courtesy of Anita Klebanoff.

Figure 4

Solid, containing, and reaching shapes.

Courtesy of Anita Klebanoff.

Reindeer head with: solid shape—the eye; containing shape—the ear; and reaching shape—the antlers.

Used with permission. Photograph by Judith M. Scalin.

The size of objects influences how people respond to them kinesthetically and aesthetically. Big mountains, huge buildings, and tall people can make children feel little in relation to them. Tiny objects, such as miniatures, create another aesthetic response—often of wonder, as well as feeling big. Large and small objects or people, near each other, cause another response because of their contrasting sizes.

The distance between the objects influences aesthetic responses. When things appear far away from each other, the distance can isolate them. Or, a small object can stand in front of a large one, giving another impression. The shapes of these objects in their locations in space also affect the onlooker's aesthetic response (see Figure 6).

Figure 6

Shapes close together and far away.
(Courtesy of Hollingsworth, p. 80.)

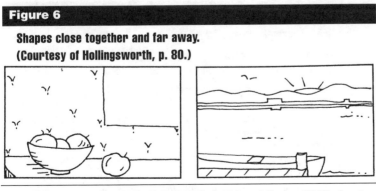

Reprinted by permission, from Hollingsworth, Patricia and Stephen (1989). *Smart art: Learning to classify and critique art.* (Zephyr Press, Tucson, AZ).

The point of view from which people see objects and people adds complexity to their study. People and objects may look different when seen from behind or above. If a person sees a table from underneath, it looks different than if that person stands next to it or on it. Looking down on a town or city from an airplane changes the apparent size, shape, and distance of the objects and people. These different viewpoints influence people's aesthetic responses.

Example 4

Early Elementary School Example: Kindergarten)

Concept/Principle: Naming the shapes of objects clarifies how they differ or compare to others.

Using guided discovery, children can name and imitate, from the environment shapes of things, such as tables, chairs, rocks, toys, plants, pencils, erasers, etc. These provide visual stimuli and source material for experiencing and understanding properties of nonmoving things that contribute to the aesthetic dimension of shape in daily life.

Example 5

Early Elementary School Example: Grade 2

Concept/Principle:. The size of an object influences people's aesthetic response to it.

Through guided discovery, children can imitate the shapes of objects in the environment. They can make the shapes very small and very large. Using movement, drawing, sounds, or words, students can explore or experiment with their responses to large and small shapes of objects and people in the environment.

Example 6

High School Example: Grade 10

Concept/Principle: Identifying and describing the aesthetic features of nonmoving objects and people facilitates understanding their complexity.

Students can study snapshots of themselves in action, photographs of sports activities, or drawings of moving objects to write descriptions of them in aesthetic terms. These reproductions of action capture the shape of stopped action. The students can study the shapes of the people and their active body parts, the size of the people or objects in relation to the background, the distances between the people or objects, and the point of view of the photo or drawing. This kind of written inventory will show students the aesthetic dimensions of reproductions of stopped action and give them practice in aesthetic observation.

Example 7

Elementary School Example: Grade 2

Concept/Principle: The rhythm of a movement along with meter and tempo affects its outcome; rhythm organizes movement.

Students can vary one rhythmic movement, such as skipping, by making it faster and slower. They can vary the rhythmic sequence of the step-hop step-hop by adding an extra step or hop with either the right or left foot or both. They can try to even out the rhythm. Students can watch, discuss, and write about each other's experiments to see how the rhythm controls the movement, even when they vary it.

Example 8

Elementary School Example: Grade 6

Concept/Principle: Movement qualities, or many ways of using energy, whether regular or irregular, contribute to the aesthetic dimension of physical activity.

Students can look for out-of-the-ordinary qualities that cause them to pay special attention to the dynamic action or unusual energy of actions. When students pay special attention and notice unusual qualities, they are developing aesthetic sensitivity. They can write about these qualities and imitate them to experience the various uses of energy they have observed. Then, students can identify both the obvious and more subtle movement qualities that help and hinder their own physical activities.

Example 9

High School Example: Grade 10

Concept/Principle: Shape, motion, time, space, energy, and flow interact differently across various movement activities.

Students can study and write about energy use, time, space, and flow of movement in different kinds of activities: ones they are learning in school, such as badminton, soccer, and dances such as the waltz or polka; ones they do everyday like brushing their teeth and climbing stairs; and ones they see at games, on TV, or in films. This analysis can help them identify which activities they prefer. Their preferences help students kinesthetically identify (have muscle empathy) with other activities that use similar features of movement. Once they have identified their preferences in these terms, they can either seek out similar activities or experiment with new ones that use these features differently.

Concepts/Principles

Kindergarten: Naming the shapes of objects clarifies how they differ or compare to others. Like many of the aesthetic dimensions of objects and people, shape is an abstract concept. When students identify blocks as square, and balls as spherical, they begin to see and describe these toy objects in a nonfunctional way. They can determine if the shapes they look at have two dimensions or three.

Second Grade: The size of an object influences people's aesthetic response to it. Students respond differently to simple shapes if they are large or small. Comparing relative size helps students understand this abstract idea and grasp that a circle remains a circle even if it is small or large.

Fourth Grade: Various distances between objects create differing aesthetic relationships among them. Things close together appear related, like trees in a forest. If they stand far apart they may appear disconnected, like widely spaced trees on a hillside. Variations in distance also can change the relative size of objects.

Sixth Grade: People's bodies combine different shapes and kinds of shapes. Studying the shapes that make up the human structure requires understanding variations of basic geometric shapes (for example, heads appear mostly oval, but sometimes they seem round) (see Figure 7). Beyond the shapes of the parts of the human body, people make a variety of shapes with their bodies as they go through their day, such as lying in bed stretched out or in the fetal position, sitting, bending over, standing, preparing to run. Photographs from magazines of these shapes let students see the wide variety of nonmoving shapes people make.

Eighth Grade: The size of nonmoving people and distances among them influence aesthetic responses to them. Like objects, the sizes of and distances between people influence the aesthetic impact they make on both onlookers and participants. The point of view will also influence the impact of groups of nonmoving people, such as in a stadium, at a bus stop, from the top of a hill, or from behind.

Tenth Grade: Identifying and describing the aesthetic features of nonmoving objects and people facilitates understanding their complexity. Describing the shape, size, distance, and point of view of nonmoving objects and people in words or pictures can help students compare and contrast the aesthetic features of what they see. The understanding of these aesthetic features can reveal a complex and rich appreciation of the world.

Twelfth Grade: How photographers, sculptors, and artists render objects and people shows their sensitivity to the aesthetic features they depict. Artists in many media focus on the beautiful form of objects and people. Their works show how these visual experts, throughout history, have captured the aesthetic dimensions of nonmoving objects and people in the environment.

What Are the Aesthetic Components of Movement?

The study of movement requires seeing how people and objects with their fixed or changing shapes behave in motion. Movement means both getting from one place to another or locomotion (e.g., a tired person dragging his or her feet walking home) and standing in one place while moving the entire body or separate body parts (e.g., the way the branches of a tree sway and its leaves rustle). Understanding the components of movement—space, time, effort, and flow—enables people to experience, describe, and analyze the aesthetic components of physical experience. By applying these concepts, students can focus on experiencing, seeing, and appreciating the shape or design of moving objects and people.

The first step in understanding shapes in motion focuses on their location in space. The concept of space includes immediate (narrow, one's own space bubble, or personal space) and larger (in the room, on the stage, on the playground) contexts. It also includes: levels—high (i.e., jumping), medium (i.e., standing), and low (i.e., bending over, kneeling, or lying down); directions—front (i.e., running forward), back (i.e., stepping

326

Pathway:
The pattern where a participant travels in space.

backward), side (i.e., reaching sideways to the right or left), up (i.e., jumping), down (i.e., landing from a high jump), diagonal (i.e., stepping in a zig-zag pattern), and around (i.e., spinning in one place or encircling a post); and pathway—the pattern of where in the room, stage, or playground the participants travel. People can see movement pathways when they watch a basketball player advance down the court toward the

Figure 7

Shapes made by active people.

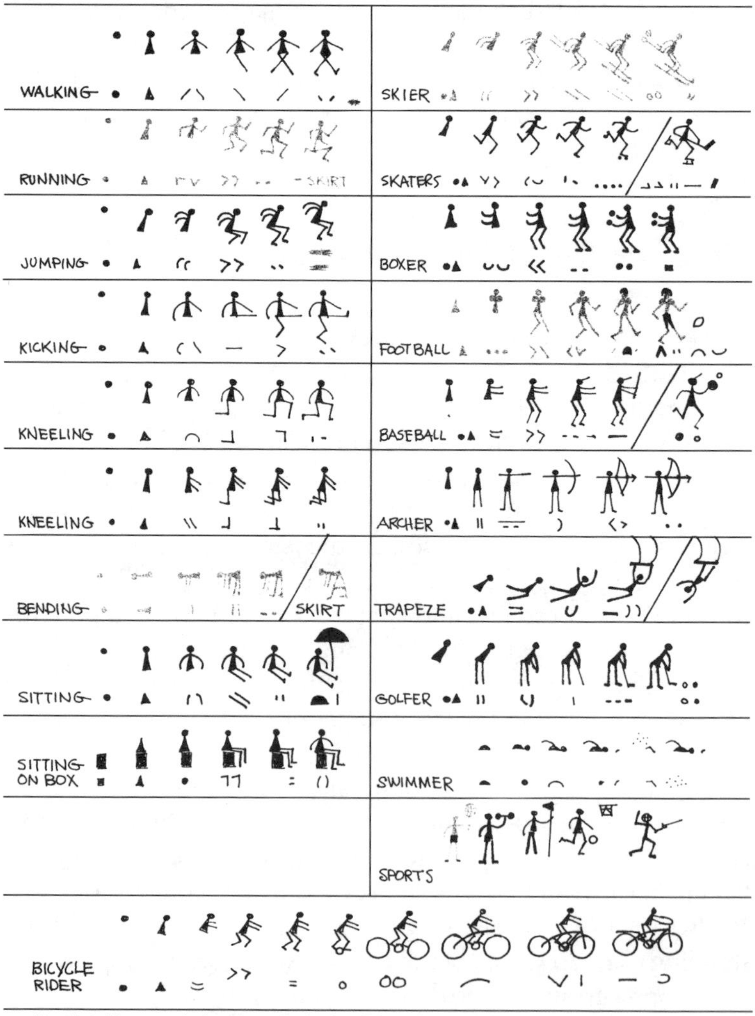

Reprinted by permission, from Emberley, Edward (1973). *Ed Emberley's drawing book: Make a world.* (Little, Brown and Company, New York, NY).

basket or an ice hockey player skate directly or indirectly toward the goal.

A more complex dimension of movement involves seeing, experiencing, and describing the concept of time in one's own movement and that of others. The term time means time on the clock. The features of time include meter—evenly timed repeated sounds, such as the clock ticking or feet walking or running evenly; rhythm—patterned and repeated sequences of sound, such as the heartbeat (tum, ta, tum, ta) or skipping (step-hop, step-hop); tempo—the speed of the sound/movement sequence, such as feet running evenly or skipping rhythmically at a slow, medium, or fast speed; accent—the sound that is emphasized more or is louder than others, such as the first syllable in the words **bas**-ket ball, or **soc**-cer, or the highest part of a jump; and sound/movement pattern—the overall design or sequence like a melody in music, such as the sound of the basketball dribbled, passed, dribbled, then the whoosh of it shot into the basket (see Figures 8, 9, 10, and 11).

Meter:
Evenly timed repeated sounds, such as the sounds of a clock ticking.

Rhythm:
Repeated uneven sequences of sound, such as the sound of a heart beating.

Sound pattern:
Overall design of the sound sequence.

Figure 8

Time and the rhythm of the heartbeat.

ACCENT
BEAT
UNIT

Accent:
Emphasis on sound, syllable, or part of a movement.

Figure 9

Two dimensional visual rhythm.

Courtesy of Anita Klebanoff.

Tempo:
Metered speed of an activity.

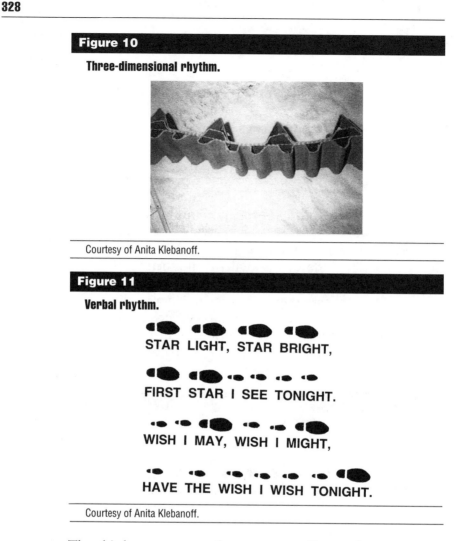

Figure 10

Three-dimensional rhythm.

Courtesy of Anita Klebanoff.

Figure 11

Verbal rhythm.

STAR LIGHT, STAR BRIGHT,

FIRST STAR I SEE TONIGHT.

WISH I MAY, WISH I MIGHT,

HAVE THE WISH I WISH TONIGHT.

Courtesy of Anita Klebanoff.

The third component of movement, effort, refers to experiencing, seeing, and identifying the variations of energy used in movement. Sometimes people call these variations movement qualities, such as swing (what arms do when people walk); shake (what a wet dog does); press (what a thumb and forefinger do to flatten a small ball of clay); clap (what hands do when applauding a good performance); and vibrate (what bodies do when they shiver with cold). Effort relates to the consistency and inconsistency in these, such as when the wet dog stops and starts shaking itself at regular intervals with the same intensity to get dry (with consistency), or when the applause gets louder or softer at irregular intervals (with inconsistency) during a slow baseball game (see Figure 12). Sometimes people use the term

Figure 12

Energy: movement qualities, called efforts, by movement theorist, Rudolph Laban.

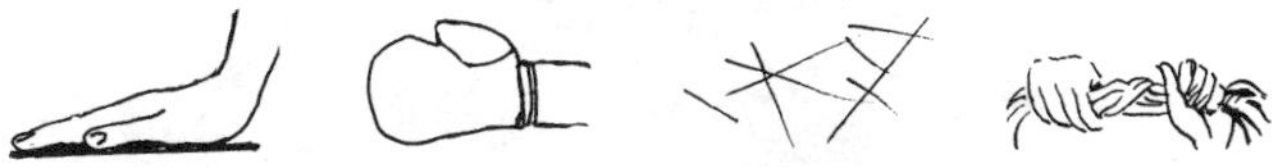

EFFORT:	**PRESS**	**PUNCH**	**SLASH**	**WRING**
Weight	firm	firm	firm	firm
Direction	direct	direct	flexible	flexible
Duration	sustained	sudden	sudden	sustained
Flow	controlled	controlled	abandoned	abandoned

EFFORT:	**GLIDE**	**FLOAT**	**DAB**	**FLICK**
Weight	light	light	light	light
Direction	direct	flexible	direct	flexible
Duration	sustained	sustained	sudden	sudden
Flow	controlled	abandoned	controlled	abandoned

Courtesy of Anita Klebanoff.

force instead of energy. When they coach students, teachers often use terms such as tension and ease, bound and free, smooth and choppy, strong or weak to describe movement qualities that can interfere with or aid the performance of many physical activities.

Ongoingness describes the flow of movement, like the water of a river rolling, or a bird flying (see Figure 13). Flow can be rhythmic (like the regular flapping of a bird's wings, or waves on a shore) or have no rhythm (like a hum, one note held on a flute, or a ball rolling before it stops). Flow characterizes the primary quality of ice skating, rollerblading, bicycle riding, swimming, and skiing. The ongoingness of those activities gives people a particular aesthetic experience when doing them and watching them. The energy people use when engaging in these ongoing activities may vary from intense to relaxed, the time (speed) used may change from fast to slow, the space covered may range from a lot to a limited amount. Some activities may use limited amounts of flow, such as the plays in a volleyball game, or hitting and pitching a softball.

Figure 13

Flow: patterns of moving water from Figure 23.

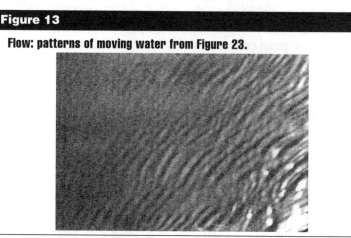

Used with permission. Photograph by Kwan Lam Wong.

Concepts/Principles

Kindergarten: *Naming movements of people or things begins the process of describing them in aesthetic terms.* Most movements have names, such as walking, running, skipping, hopping, sliding, jumping, and rolling. These locomotor movements travel through space, from one place to another (see Figures 7, 15, and 16). People or objects can move using axial or nonlocomotor movements, even though they do not travel. Many words describe axial movement: sway, swing, reach, twist, shake, throw, catch, etc. Children need to name the movements they do and see before they can understand how to describe them.

Second Grade: *Terms such as level, direction, range of personal space, and pathway identify how one moves in space.* The abstract notion of space contains several components, although children can easily explore and understand its parts. The range of personal space, or space bubble, includes the area around the child as far as he or she can reach. Children enjoy exploring a variety of levels and directions. Footprints in the sand help students see and follow a pathway, which is a more advanced idea (see Figure 17).

Fourth Grade: *The rhythm of a movement, along with meter and tempo, affects its outcome; rhythm organizes movement.* Once children understand how to tell time on a clock, they can explore the ideas related to time. Songs, poetry, and marches offer examples of rhythmic order and meter (see Figure 11). Slow motion replays of events in sports on television show how tempo influences action.

Sixth Grade: *Movement qualities, or many ways of using energy, whether regular or irregular, contribute to the aesthetic dimension of physical activity.* Once understood, the abstract idea of energy can help students identify their preferences for some activities over others. It also can clarify their aesthetic perception. When they begin to pay attention to it, they can feel variations of energy more easily than see them. Changes of energy offer immediate results in the experience of physical activities (see Figure 18).

Eighth Grade: *Space, time, and energy come together in flow (ongoingness) activities.* The aesthetic dimensions of stop-and-start activities differ considerably from those that contain large amounts of flow. Experience in many kinds of physical activity gives students, as participants and as observers, an opportunity to understand how these components of movement work together both physically and aesthetically.

Tenth Grade: Shape, motion, time, space, energy, and flow interact differently across various movement activities. This concept asks students to combine what they learned about nonmoving people and objects with the components of movement. An analysis of the components of movement (shape, motion, time, space, energy, and flow) reveals similarities and differences in movement activities. This complex multidimensioned study can add another layer of meaning to participating in and observing all physical activities.

Twelfth Grade: Artists and photographers utilize the components of movement (shape, motion, time, space, energy, and flow) in their different renditions of movement activities. The study of these artworks shows how artists utilize the components of movement to capture the dynamism of what they see in spite of the immobile limit of their media. Filmmakers also manipulate movement factors when they speed them up or slow them down to achieve their aesthetic goals, even in documentary films.

Dynamism: A sense of liveliness or active vigorous involvement.

Figure 14

Movement flow: simultaneous—all the body parts moving together in the running figure and successive—separate body parts following each other in the figure bending over.

Figure 15

Birds flying through the air (traveling). (Courtesy of Emberley, 1972, p. 16.)

Figure 16

Bird standing in one place while moving its head (axial movement). (Courtesy of Emberley, 1972, p. 16.)

Reprinted by permission, from Emberley, Edward (1973). *Ed Emberley's little drawing book of birds.* (Little, Brown and Company, New York, NY).

Example 10

Middle School Example: Grade 6

Concept/Principle: The combination of the basic elements of movement: shape, motion, time, space, energy, and flow create regular or irregular movement patterns.

Students can work together in pairs or trios to create movement variations on basic locomotor movements such as walking or sliding. They can change the body shape, the level and directions in space, and move quickly or slowly as part of the sequence they perform together. They can repeat each variation an equal number of times, creating a regular pattern. Then, they can make the pattern irregular by making the number of repetitions of each variation uneven, or by having one of the pair or trio perform the sequence faster or slower or with different numbers of variations. Making these regular and irregular patterns can help them recognize these kinds of patterns in other movement activities.

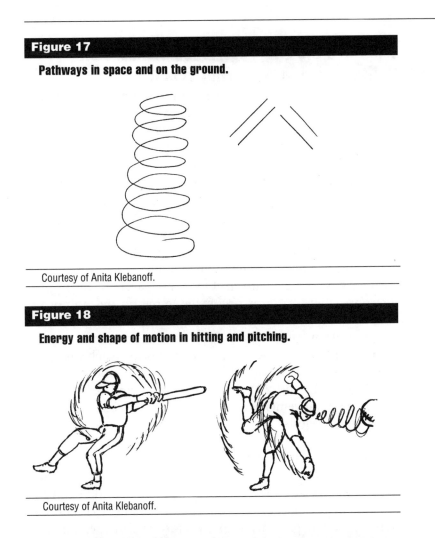

Figure 17

Pathways in space and on the ground.

Courtesy of Anita Klebanoff.

Figure 18

Energy and shape of motion in hitting and pitching.

Courtesy of Anita Klebanoff.

Example 11

Middle School Example: Grade 8

Concept/Principle: Aesthetically carried out movement becomes congruent with its goal when people achieve the goal directly, elegantly, and efficiently.

Watching, discussing, and writing about videotapes of physical education activities enables students to study the congruence of their own and teammates' movements in games, practices, and even warm-up activities. Watching more skilled players allows students to observe and write about the correspondence of movement with its purpose. Observing the harmony of movement with purpose in professional games helps students realize how congruence contributes to the aesthetic quality of sports activities. It also can help them improve their own performance. Using viewing, discussing, and writing, this comparative study of increasingly skilled players assists students in recognizing the aesthetic component of congruent movement.

Asymmetric: When a design is not exactly the same on opposite sides when folded in half.

What Are the Characteristics of Movement Patterns and How Do They Function?

The information about movement patterns discussed here builds on the material in Themes 2 (shapes of nonmoving people and objects) and 3 (features of moving people and objects). Here movement patterns—symmetric, asymmetric, random, regular, irregular—involve people moving together in multiple pathways. This builds on the separate pathway dimension of movement and individuals moving in space.

Symmetric: When a design is folded in half, it is the same on both sides of the fold.

A symmetrical design is one that, if folded in half, is exactly the same on both sides of the fold (see Figures 19 and 20). The beginning positions of people in a doubles tennis game can create a symmetrical pattern. Once the players begin to play, their movement patterns become asymmetric and do not exactly match on both sides of the net (see Figures 20 and 21). People walk in the street in random patterns with irregular strides, whereas members of a marching band synchronize the length and height of their stride in a regular, unified pattern (see Figures 22 and 23). In movement, asymmetrical shapes and irregular movements tend to be more interesting than symmetrical and regular ones.

Play strategies in team sports utilize these different kinds of movement patterns, formations, and designs. After teachers focus students' attention on how these line-ups and strategies function in games, they can point out the aesthetic component of these moving patterns. Dance performances depend on patterns of movement. Folk dance performers often maintain symmetrical patterns, whereas modern dancers rarely do. Folk danc-

---

Example 12

High School Example: Grade 12

Concept/Principle: Games and folk dances from different areas in the United States and other countries illustrate the aesthetic movement preferences of those regions.

Students choose games from three countries for in-depth study, relating the cultural, geographic, ethnic, social, religious, and economic context of these games to the movement choices in them. Writing a report about their findings gives students the opportunity to clarify their understanding of these subtle differences and similarities. Students teach one of these games to their classmates, relating the game to its cultural context.

---

ers often balance the stage with equal lines of dancers moving toward and away from each other. Modern dance choreographers deliberately place dancers on stage in uneven groupings, and dancers move in unpredictable patterns (see Figures 24 and 25).

Movement patterns function strategically in the activities and, when they produce success, experts describe them as congruent (fits exactly) with their goal. When they are beautiful or elegant in design and motion, they also serve an aesthetic function. For instance, someone may awkwardly hit a tennis ball that lands in a far corner. Although the shot earned the player a point and was congruent with the goal of the game, judges would not consider the movement beautiful. Or, the same individual may successfully serve the ball using perfect form with complete ease and grace, and judges would consider that serve both congruent with its goal and beautiful.

Figure 19

Examples of symmetry. (Courtesy of Hollingsworth, p. 74.)

Reprinted by permission, from Hollingsworth, Patricia and Stephen (1989). *Smart art: Learning to classify and critique art.* (Zephyr Press, Tucson, AZ).

Figure 20

Human figures in symmetric and asymmetric positions.

Courtesy of Anita Klebanoff.

Figure 21

Asymmetric design made by a tree and its shadow.

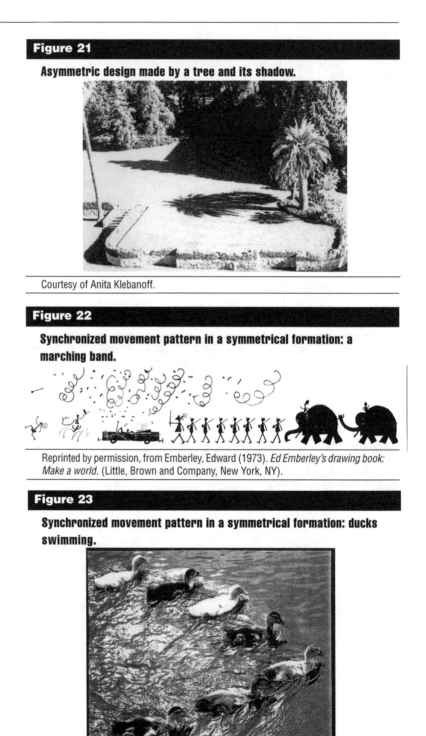

Courtesy of Anita Klebanoff.

Figure 22

Synchronized movement pattern in a symmetrical formation: a marching band.

Reprinted by permission, from Emberley, Edward (1973). *Ed Emberley's drawing book: Make a world.* (Little, Brown and Company, New York, NY).

Figure 23

Synchronized movement pattern in a symmetrical formation: ducks swimming.

Used with permission. Photograph by Kwan Lam Wong.

The obvious, regular, and required patterns in physical activities depend on the kind of game, event, or performance—they depend on the form the activity takes. People use the word form in many ways. Here it means "the shape of something, its outward or visible appearance," and "a fixed or usual method of doing something." For instance, runners in relay races run in predictable pathways—the usual form—and, therefore, four teams of runners create describable movement patterns. Experienced observers of soccer and ice hockey can follow the ir-

Figure 24

Movement patterns: pathways of people moving together making regular patterns.

Courtesy of Anita Klebanoff.

Figure 25

Movement patterns: pathways of people moving together making irregular patterns.

Courtesy of Anita Klebanoff.

regular and unpredictable movement patterns of the players in these sports. Highly skilled team players synchronize their actions to achieve the goals of the game. When they play elegantly together, their movement patterns create aesthetic and congruent action. And when they also win in this manner, their aesthetically congruent actions achieve the dual goals of aesthetically excellent and successful play.

The expressive power of movement influences its impact on observers and participants. People feel the impact of this characteristic of movement when viewing movement patterns made by individuals—such as a graceful jump shot in basketball and especially in large groups of people in, for instance, marching band formations, the parade at the beginning of the Olympics, or a bicycle race. Experts in aesthetics usually associate expressivity with events and products in the arts (dramas, bal-

Example 13

Elementary School Example: Grade 4

Concept/Principle: Preferences for movement qualities influence how the aesthetic experience is judged.

Students can list their most and least favorite movement activities and then discuss with the class the kinds of movement qualities these activities utilize. For instance, the flow in bicycling and skateboarding contrasts with the intense bursts of energy used in basketball and soccer. Drawing and writing require precise use of energy, while sweeping and washing the car require a larger and stronger output. Once students understand the pattern of their preferences, they can begin to understand why they appreciate some activities more than others, because the energy output is similar to their favorite activities.

Example 14

Middle School Example: Grade 8

Concept/Principle: People understand the expressive qualities of movement activities through their kinesthetic sense.

To help students understand how they kinesthetically respond to the expressive qualities of movement, have them watch a movie without the sound turned on and discuss what emotions the actors are conveying. Then, have them watch people walk in the street or on the playground to study what that particular walk might convey. Their observations can center on energy and space use and not necessarily on the particular emotion the person may feel. Let the students discuss their observations to discover agreement and disagreement. Then, have them relate their preferences to the aesthetic dimensions of what they do or do not prefer.

Example 15

High School Example: Grade 12

Concept/Principle: Aesthetic criteria can describe progress toward achieving physical competency.

Making videotapes of games early in the semester and then later can provide tools by which students can study their progress. Although aesthetic qualities occur more frequently at a higher skill level, once students learn and practice an activity, they can begin to watch for, describe, and take pride in aesthetically significant moments during their practice sessions. Watching professional athletes or dancers to spot their occasional awkward and careless movements also can help students pinpoint the relationship between a well-executed skill and its aesthetic quality. Such active and engaged spectator skills can enhance the students' sensitivity to their own progress and that of their peers.

---

lets, paintings, and novels, for example). The aesthetic features of expressivity also apply in a general way to physical education activities. They include balance—a combination of elements or features such as fast and slow, as in different parts of a baseball game; contrast—combining distinguishable opposites such as wide and narrow, which can increase interest (for example, when groups of marathon runners change their initial positions after they start) or the feelings of tension and relaxation (for example, before and after a basketball player successfully shoots a foul shot); accent—the main point or points of interest, such as at the end of a game; and dynamism—a sense of liveliness or active involvement, such as when team members overcome their fatigue.

In Theme 2, the aesthetic characteristics of movement contribute to its expressive features: flow—variations of energy; tempo—fast, medium, or slow; weight of the body—heavy or light; dynamics of energy expenditure—smooth or rough (including all the variations in between); and style—where unique individuals establish their own recognizable structure and form. Individuals learn to analyze these aesthetic features of movement by studying the time, space, energy, pattern, congruence, expressivity, and style and then connect them when they see and appreciate the entirety of a movement event.

Concepts/Principles

Kindergarten: *Variations of the same movement in space create a simple movement pattern.* Individual children walking in straight, curved, and zig-zag pathways and then repeating the sequence, can make a visible pathway—especially if the children trace their patterns by drawing them on the ground or floor. Two or three children doing this together create a simple movement pattern.

Second Grade: *Commonly used forms of games utilize symmetric to asymmetric formations and movement patterns.* Circle games, relay races, and simple folk dances utilize symmetrical individual pathways and group patterns seen on the ground or floor. Changing the group formations of these activities can introduce students to the function of these symmetrical formations (balance) and give them experience in recognizing and following symmetric and asymmetric patterns.

Fourth Grade: *Combinations of locomotor movements in space and time create movement patterns.* Jumping, skipping, and leaping make different level changes and, thus, make different patterns in space if observers watch the heads of the groups of moving students. Students can cover more distance when doing these movements and change the patterns of the pathways on the ground. They can carry out these locomotor movements at different speeds and also can change the spatial patterns.

Sixth Grade: *The combination of the basic elements of movement (shape, motion, time, space, energy, and flow) creates regular or irregular movement patterns.* If students watch or play tag, baseball, or soccer, they will see or experience variations of running that require changes of the shape of the body before moving and in motion; the length of time running; the speed and energy used; and the amount of time spent in continuous, smooth, and flowing running. Taken together, these variations of running make different and primarily irregular movement patterns.

Eighth Grade: *Aesthetically carried out movement becomes congruent with its goal when people achieve the goal directly, elegantly, and efficiently.* When learning movement skills, students experience increased mastery with practice, age, and coaching. They can sense the changes in their skill level as they progress. At this point in their development they can feel, observe, and describe when their skill levels increase from just successful, to efficiently successful, and then to exquisitely performed. They can begin to aim for aesthetic congruence in their actions.

Tenth Grade: *Observing others achieve aesthetic congruence of movement with its goal sharpens observation skills and facilitates self-observation.* Watching and identifying aesthetic congruence of actions made by professional teams during a time when students are practicing the same activity helps them appreciate aesthetically performed movements and movement patterns. They can understand how these beautiful actions contribute to the success of the game and the pleasure gained by the observers. Watching these models can motivate students to attend to the aesthetic quality of their own activities.

Twelfth Grade: *Games and folk dances from different areas of the United States and other countries illustrate the movement patterns and aesthetic preferences of those regions.* By the end of high school, students will have studied and participated in a variety of games and folk dances from the U.S. and other countries. These games and dances use space, time, energy, and flow differently, although they also have commonalities. These activities reflect many factors, such as the climate and topography of the location, and the occupation and class of the people who participate in them. For instance, games and dances use different amounts of space depending on whether people play them indoors or outdoors, on open plains, deserts, or mountain paths; require different amounts of energy in cold, warm, humid, or rainy weather; last longer or shorter amounts of time when people have a lot of or a little free time. These factors combine in the aesthetic dimensions these activities reveal.

What Factors Help Determine Criteria for Judging the Aesthetic Quality of Movement in One's Own and Other Cultures?

The criteria for making choices and judging quality depend on a person's goals, experiences, knowledge, preferences and those of the culture to which that person belongs. Only after students have learned to identify and apply the aesthetic components of movement, presented in the first four themes, can they adequately articulate criteria for judging them. High school students with sufficient background can begin this ongoing process.

The particular features of a person, action, or object that people consider beautiful stimulate aesthetic responses. Something specific evokes these responses. Special qualities of a separate action, for instance, add up to make that one lay-up shot much better than the others. Even though the specific shot is beautiful, it has properties present in other special shots that others players have made and will make again.

Most people intuitively resonate to their own personal internal aesthetic criteria while participating in or watching physical activities. They may not realize that their responses integrate their personal, cultural, and learned experience. These multifaceted experiences influence learning even while students and teachers focus attention and effort on other dimensions of the activities, such as learning and improving skills. Personal, cultural, and learned aesthetic standards interact with, change, and—at times—contradict each other.

People use the word "taste" when they discuss their personal aesthetic standards. Others who disagree may dismiss the judgments as unsophisticated, or in poor taste. Personal aesthetic standards probably stem from the earliest positive experiences students had with the persons, actions, or objects (e.g., the first, best, lay-up shot a person ever made or saw). The physical and emotional context of these early experiences—friendly or hostile—such as at home, in a public playground, or at a school game, also may effect students' early tastes.

When teachers understand that initial learning can determine subsequent standards of taste, they can help students to articulate their existing aesthetic standard and enable students to develop and improve their tastes along with their abilities. These criteria should align with healthy and biomechanically accurate information. Cultural, economic, social, and educational factors influence internal aesthetic standards. Because many factors contribute to personal taste, teachers can respect the tastes of students while encouraging them to remain receptive to new information as they grow and mature.

Cultural, generational, and regional differences in aesthetic criteria and responses can confuse students. These differences, however, can widen and deepen students' understanding of varied aesthetic criteria. For instance, students dress in particular ways and cultivate particular looks that mirror their age, interests, and peers; these choices reflect the time and place in which they live. The students who conform to these fads have adapted their aesthetic tastes to value this particular look. When asked, students may identify and articulate the criteria they use when they choose to dress in a particular way. To do so they will need to focus on the personal aesthetic decisions they made and clarify their choices to others who do not understand or appreciate their taste.

External aesthetic standards evolve from these same personal, cultural, and learned sources. Experts more often write and talk about external standards than internal ones, although one influences the other. When, for instance, a sports commentator raves about a superb shot in golf, the commentator will often state why he or she thinks the play is superb and describe the special qualities of how the golfer accomplished it. Television and radio broadcasts of special events provide a public forum where experts disseminate these external, recognized, and agreed upon standards. Broadcasters frequently played as star players in the sport on which they report. They combine their internalized standards from training and playing with expertise gained from observing and reporting on the game. Sports broadcasters knowingly allow their personal preferences to enter into their judgment when reporting on games; they often debate their viewpoints on the air. Many sports fans listen and privately debate these public standards in the light of their personal ones.

Major disagreements among experts can challenge the established aesthetic criteria. Eventually, some new consensus emerges. Thus, aesthetic standards change as time passes. Members of the public then compare their personal aesthetic criteria with updated ones. For instance, students see new aesthetic criteria of beauty emerge in many areas of daily life, such as fashion, car design, and, of course, the arts.

Concepts/Principles

Kindergarten: The practice of movement skills helps develop an understanding of excellent movement. When students' skills improve, their sense of improvement automatically helps them develop standards of quality. Often their improved skills feel easier and more direct, and look nicer than when they began. These internal aesthetic criteria result from each individual's aesthetic impulse.

Second Grade: Watching others in an activity develops an understanding of excellent movement. In everyday play settings, younger children watch older children playing the same games. Sometimes they play together in mixed age groups. Since children often learn by imitation, they model their skills on older, more skillful players. In this way they can gain an understanding that as they grow older and gain height and strength, they can improve their skills.

Fourth Grade: Preferences for movement qualities influence how the aesthetic experience is judged. Soon after they are born, children begin to show their individuality in energy use, movement range and frequency, and the kinds of stimuli they prefer. These movement and energy factors contribute to their personalities and to their preferences in what they enjoy doing and watching. Varied experiences during and after school can educate their aesthetic perception and broaden students' preferences.

Sixth Grade: Aesthetic guidelines for movement activity make meeting the goals of that activity easier. When students understand how to improve their physical skills using the knowledge of the space, time, energy, and the flow factors of movement, they have precise tools to help them. By now, students can grasp that the goals of physical activity include pleasure, concentration, focused energy, beautiful movement sequences, and, at times, winning. The aesthetic dimensions of movement they are learning contribute to many educational goals.

Eighth Grade: People understand the expressive qualities of movement activities through their kinesthetic sense. Since life's activities require movement, students intuitively and nonverbally understand them by using their eyes and muscles, which combine in the kinesthetic sense. Translating their intuitive grasp of the expressive qualities of these activities requires paying attention to and verbalizing the impact of the factors students learned in the other themes and concepts. The expressive qualities of sport and game activities remain general, whereas in the movement arts, aesthetically expressive movement communicates specifically and directly. The general or specific expressive qualities of any movement event affect each person's aesthetic perception and experience of it.

Tenth Grade: Individual aesthetic criteria for excellence develop from personal, academic, and professional sources. When people participate in physical activities, they continuously judge the results by a variety of criteria, some of which involve intuitive aesthetic criteria. Understanding the aesthetic dimensions of movement can clarify and develop people's intuitive criteria. This knowledge will help them understand, appreciate, and assess professional judgments made by sports commentators and judges.

Twelfth Grade: Aesthetic criteria can describe progress toward achieving physical competency. After their study of the aesthetic dimensions of movement, students gain an understanding of the terms to describe their own increased capabilities in the activities they undertake. These aesthetic criteria explain how they succeed in carrying out the necessary mechanical skills and interactive actions and provide further guidelines for improvement.

Placing Concepts of Aesthetic Experience in the Curriculum

Before teachers can integrate aesthetic concepts of movement into their physical education programs, they must decide where to place them. The placement of concepts throughout the chapter provides developmentally appropriate material for different grade levels in each theme. The sequence can help teachers decide when to introduce these concepts into their physical education activities. If students have not had the opportunity to learn the concepts identified in earlier grades, teachers need to include activities that give students this underlying knowledge. The basic concepts of the aesthetic component of movement concentrate first on teaching students to see and think with an aesthetic attitude and then to learn about the parts: shape, movement through space and time with varying energies, and patterns. Then, students focus on integrating the parts into a whole. Finally, they gain the ability to determine criteria for evaluating them.

Student learning involves the dual focus of recognizing the features of aesthetic experience in others as well as in themselves. Understanding aesthetic experience comes from learning first to recognize and then focus on it. In the last analysis, words may not fully express aesthetic experience, but when students excitedly shout, "Beautiful!" "Awesome!" or, "Wow!" they see and feel it.

Integrating Concepts of Aesthetic Experience into Instruction

Teachers can integrate the aesthetic component of physical activity into almost all content components and activities—physical and analytical—in the study of physical education. Often teachers, in their initial instruction, concentrate their efforts on training students in skills and game strategies. They tend not to introduce the aesthetic component until the training progresses to the advanced level. This need not be the case. When teaching physical education, teachers assume responsibility for pointing out the aesthetic component of the various activities. And, responsive students pay attention to the qualities that trigger their aesthetic responses. When someone calls out, "Nice shot!"

or "Beautiful play!" these comments show appreciation of the quality of the action itself, whether or not it is successful. These comments focus not only on what the student did, but also on how the student achieved the action.

Four major processes in physical activity provide occasions for developing aesthetic sensitivity. They include learning and training (practicing), participating and playing, watching, and reconciling different opinions about the aesthetic qualities of the event. Perhaps the best time to focus on the aesthetic qualities inherent in movement occurs when teachers begin to teach new physical skills to their students. During this learning and training phase, students can repeatedly and thoughtfully focus on the movement skills and sequences in a slower and more considered manner than when they actually play the games or engage in the activity. Students can learn and practice movement guidelines based not only on the success of their actions but also on the inherent qualities of them. Students then can apply these qualities while they participate in the activity. During these times, action occurs quickly with limited time to focus on each segment of the action. Movement habits built on aesthetic physical principles can contribute to students' satisfaction during their play and can enable them to watch their peers and professionals engaged in similar activities with enriched criteria for assessing what they see. When students and teachers assess what they did and saw, knowing the aesthetic dimensions of movement can deepen discussion and help reconcile different opinions. These processes develop both internal and subjective and external and objective standards. They foster discussion among participants about the validity of their aesthetic standards.

Theme 1 focuses on learning how to respond to aesthetic experience. Human beings respond intuitively with all their senses to this dimension of life. Participation in an event, whether at the elite or entry level, stimulates personal aesthetic responses whether or not players meet all their goals. Beginners can easily distinguish their ineffective from their effective plays or movements by using both physical skill goals and aesthetic criteria. They sense that a beautiful play feels easy and natural. They concentrate and unify their muscles, eyes, ears—even skin and nose—in this process Although differing sensory modes of recreating the personal aesthetic experience appear difficult to articulate, teachers can guide students to use all of their senses to become self-reflective and, thus, able to appreciate their unique physical achievements while engaged in learning skills and playing games. Players experience and, thus, learn what the results feel like on two levels: the success or not of their physical skills and the elegant beauty of the movement itself. This unity of senses helps players learn the "how" of performing at their highest, most beautiful level.

When teaching about the shapes of nonmoving people and objects (Theme 2), teachers can ask students to imitate these shapes with their bodies. Then, students can practice this special kind of seeing and become familiar with the words used to describe aesthetic features of people and objects in place or in motion. Movement exploration activities allow inexperienced students to participate at their own developmental level. Directed exploration works well for young and shy children; visual and observation skills improve as children mature.

Teachers can introduce the concepts of how space, time, energy, and flow influence the aesthetic experience of movement (Theme 3) one at a time; then, they can ask students to identify these features during their skill training or games. Teachers also can use these dimensions when instructing and correcting their students' actions. To clarify how effort contributes to movement performance, teachers can invite their students to experiment with various efforts when learning new skills or overcoming problems in executing complex movement sequences. Teachers can encourage students to find flowing moments in their daily activities as well as in physical activities. Their increased awareness of the ongoingness of movement can enhance understanding of how much of their movement contains flow (i.e., coasting on a bicycle, sliding down a slide, and gliding on a scooter).

Once they have practiced describing the features of movement in individuals, students can look for movement patterns in groups (Theme 4). Parades, dance performances, synchronized sports such as swimming and ice dancing give students an opportunity to study and describe obvious patterns. Then, students can look for less obvious and quickly changing patterns in groups of moving people, animals, and games.

After students have learned how to describe the aesthetic component of movement, they can understand the criteria for assessing the quality of aesthetic action (Theme 5). Students benefit from seeing and appreciating their own movement, with its individual style. Videotape reviews of performance can facilitate this self-observation. They can learn to discern when they achieve beautiful movement in design and motion, and when it is congruent with its goal. Students should identify the congruent movements based on criteria established from understanding how function, skill, and form fit together.

Students can study the aesthetic features of activities in daily life as participants and observers. For example, they can watch how people walk in the street, gesture to one another, and sit or stand together in groups. In big cities with recent immigrant populations, students can observe daily activities to understand cultural differences and similarities among people. Media presentations offer numerous opportunities to appreciate these qualities: television commercials with sports performances, super-slow-motion filming of athletic events, documentaries of sports heroes, and even video game graphics. Using the tools and concepts of the aesthetic component of movement, students can gain an understanding of people with movement limitations due to disability, injury, or age. With focused attention, students can appreciate the special aesthetic features found in restricted movement.

Students often associate self-expression and communication with the artistic and theatrical activities of dance and mime, rather than with recreational activities and competitive games and sports. Dance and mime activities center their skill training on aesthetic goals and standards. Physical education activities can include these art disciplines, but without dance and theater specialists to teach them, they generally do not appear in the curriculum. Although self-expression and communication play a small part in games and sports activities, how a person participates in these activities may be understood as self-expression. The nature of this self-expression differs from the basic role personal and cultural expression plays in dance and mime activities. Teacher preparation in the future must include the aesthetic component of movement. Such training can help teachers to understand how this focus enhances the enjoyment of all movement activities.

The instructional suggestions that follow include some dance and mime activities with aesthetic goals embedded in them; teachers and students primarily evaluate these activities by aesthetic criteria. Most of the suggestions, however, focus on games, social and folk dance, and recreation activities included in the training of most physical educators who may be unfamiliar with teaching and evaluating them using aesthetic characteristics and criteria.

Assessing Student Learning

When students can use aesthetic concepts to understand their own performance or the performance of others, the instructor has been effective in teaching about aesthetic features of physical education activities. Some assessment techniques follow. The 1995 NASPE publication, *Moving into the Future: National Standards for Physical Education*, contains detailed assessment information.

Journal Writing

Regular written self-assessment exercises become useful tools to help revitalize student performance and help them understand the features of the aesthetic component of physical education. The format of these exercises follows the guidelines used in authentic assessment methods discussed in many books and state assessment manuals.

> *Examples:* What did I learn about... (e.g., space or time or authenticity)? What risks did I take when... (e.g., working on improving the regular rhythmic quality of my dribbling)? What would I change the next time I... (e.g., have an opportunity to practice my dribbling)?"

The examples include the most useful questions to trace the development of understanding of concepts and skills (what was learned), experimentation with new ways of doing things (risks), and goal setting for improvement (revision).

Observations

The videotaping of activity sessions offers another way for students and teachers to refine their observation skills and observe growth. When watching the videotapes, students can watch specific executed skills or plays. They can focus their attention on a selected aesthetic dimension. They can record their responses on a tape recorder and transcribe their ideas into writing and illustrations. In time, such a record enables students and teachers to trace the development of their comprehension and execution of central concepts.

> *Examples:* Watch and describe in writing the rhythm of your running in those plays, the shape of your body at the end of your swing, and how your energy diminishes at the end of your action.

Student Projects

Visual projects such as a photo-collage poster, video production, or computer digital imaging serve as public assessment tools. They allow students to demonstrate their understanding of the aesthetic component. These can illustrate what students consider outstanding examples of athletes and dancers, as well as everyday people engaged in motion. They can arrange the examples by theme. Students should articulate the criteria by which they chose their photos or images and explain them to their classmates. A display of these posters can help others grasp the aesthetic dimensions of physical activity.

Concluding Comments

Integrating aesthetic awareness into the teaching of physical education can enhance the quality of students' lives. Aesthetic awareness remains one of the primary characteristics of a civilized way of life. It allows human beings to bring order out of chaos. When students become aesthetically sensitive to their movement activities, this sensitivity can transfer to other areas of their lives. Because human beings' sense of self begins in their physical selves, when students work toward achievable aesthetic standards in their physical activities, they focus on enhancing their body image—the basis of their self-image. The reward does not come from winning, earning points, or breaking records, but from students becoming the best and/or most beautiful that they can become. This internally motivated, self-powered goal provides unifying and satisfying experience. It can help students to empathize with and appreciate the great diversity of movement in their lives and the lives of others.

References

Arnold, N. (1976) *The interrelated arts in leisure: Perceiving and creating.* St. Louis: Mosby.

Brooks, M. (1986). *Drawing with children: A creative teaching and learning method that works for adults too.* Los Angeles: Jeremy Tarcher.

Dissanayake, E. (1995). *Homo aestheticus: Where art comes from and why.* Seattle, WA: University of Washington.

Downer, M. (1947). *Discovering design.* New York: Lothrop, Lee and Shepard.

Emberley, E. (1972). *Ed Emberley's little drawing book of birds.* Boston: Little Brown and Company.

Emberely, E. (1973). *Ed Emberely's drawing book: Make a world.* Boston: Little Brown and Company.

Gardner, H. (1991). *The unschooled mind: How children think and how schools should teach.* New York: Basic Books.

Hollingsworth, P., & Hollingsworth, S. (1989). *Smart art: Learning to classify and critique art.* Tuscon: Zephyr.

National Association for Sport and Physical Education. (1995). *Moving into the future: National physical education standards. A guide to content and assessment.* Reston, VA: Author.

Perkins, D. (1994). *The intelligent eye: Learning to think by looking at art.* Santa Monica, CA: The Getty Center for Education in the Arts.

Watts, E. (1977). *Towards dance and art: The relationships between two arts forms.* London: Lepus Books.

Unidentified drawings and photographs by Anita Klebanoff.

Resources

Dinhofer, S. M. (1990). *The Art of Baseball.* New York: Harmony Books.

Glasser, W. (1976). *Positive addiction.* New York: Harper & Row.

Kash, M. M., & Borich, G. D. (1978). *Teacher behavior and pupil self-concept.* Reading, MA: Addison-Wesley.

Lancy, D. F., & Tindall, B. A. (Eds.) (1977). *The study of play: Problems and prospects.* West Point, NY: Leisure Press.

Lieberman, J. N. (1977). *Playfulness: Its relationship to imagination and creativity.* New York: Academic Press.

Salter, M. A. (1978). *Play: Anthropological perspectives.* West Point, NY: Leisure Press.

Wingfield, M. A. (1988). *Sport and the artist, Volume I: Ball games.* Woodbridge, Suffolk, England: Antique Collectors' Club.

Chapter **9**

Putting It All Together

Bonnie S. Mohnsen

T hroughout this book, the authors—having reviewed multiple national resources—have defined the important con-
cepts/principles students must know in order to meet the
National Physical Education Standards and to live high-quality
lives in the 21st century. Each chapter presented one subdiscipline
in isolation, including learning experiences and assessment ideas.
This is a constructive approach in helping us to understand, teach,
and assess each area of physical education. However, in the actual
instructional environment, concepts/principles from each subdiscipline are best addressed in a more holistic manner. Integrating
several concepts/principles in one lesson or assessment is more time-
efficient and realistic in terms of how the information will ultimately be used.

This chapter focuses on how to integrate the concepts/prin-
ciples from the different subdisciplines into physical education
learning experiences and assessment opportunities. Ideas for
integrating these concepts/principles with other subject areas
also are provided, since this is even more realistic and time-
efficient. Sample learning experiences from a variety of instructional units serve to illustrate the implementation process
necessary to teach and assess students' cognitive understand-

Figure 1

Five Steps for Addressing Concepts

1. Select concepts
2. Sequence concepts
3. Select assessment tools
4. Select instructional units
5. Select instructional strategies

ing while simultaneously helping them to improve their motor skills and fitness levels.

Selecting, Sequencing, and Assessing

Looking at the variety of concepts/principles identified in Chapters 2 through 8 (see Appendix A) may cause anxiety in many physical educators who typically teach an activity-based curriculum. Even those who are using a conceptual-based (discipline-centered) curriculum may be concerned at the number of concepts/principles that are identified. Therefore, this section is designed to help physical educators select and sequence concepts/principles based on their unique situation.

The first question that physical educators need to address is whether to include all of the concepts/principles identified by the authors, or to select only a few. The concepts/principles identified in each chapter are based on the authors' perspectives—along with input from reviewers and other experts—of what students need to know in order to meet the standards identified by the National Association for Sport and Physical Education (NASPE, 1995). However, it is the responsibility of each school district to identify its own local standards, concepts/principles, and related curriculum. In districts where this has not yet occurred, resources such as *Designing the Physical Education Curriculum* (Melograno, 1996) and *Teaching Middle School Physical Education* (Mohnsen, 2003) will assist the reader in developing standards and curriculum. When local standards differ from the National Standards, the selection of concepts/principles also may differ. Even if the standards match the National Standards, local variables may limit the number of concepts/principles that are addressed during each school year. For example, teachers who meet once a week with students are far more limited in what they can address than are teachers who meet with their students daily. Teachers should choose the concepts/principles that are most important for their students.

Once the concepts/principles are selected, the second step is to sequence them from kindergarten through twelfth grade. The concepts/principles presented in Chapters 2 through 8 are sequenced by: K, 1-2, 3-4, 5-6, 7-8, 9-10, and 11-12 in order to align with the National Physical Education Standards. However, it is recommended that districts and schools sequence their concepts/principles as follows: K, 1, 2, 3, 4, 5, 6, 7, 8, 9, 10, 11, and 12. This will provide for more focus and less repetition, and if you have decided to go with the concepts/principles identified in this book, you can narrow the number of concepts per grade level to approximately 25.

For those who have selected their own concepts/principles, or who have chosen to adapt the concepts/principles identified in Chapters 2 through 8, there are four guidelines to consider when sequencing the concepts/principles. The first guideline is to list your concepts/principles from the most simple to the most complex. For example, consider Theme 5 from motor learning:

Kindergarten: Some skills are used in many different activities (e.g., throwing).

Second Grade: Striking with implements has many similarities to striking with your hand.

Fourth Grade: Throwing a large ball has some characteristics that are similar to throwing a small ball and some that are different.

Sixth Grade: The more closely related one skill is to another, the more likely the transfer of learning (e.g., throwing a variety of objects).

Eighth Grade: Transfer from practice to the game is subject to the same identical element issues of transfer.

Tenth Grade: Knowing how one skill is the same and different from another skill (or game) will facilitate transfer from one skill to another.

Twelfth Grade: Although there is no such thing as general motor ability, there are a set of perceptual motor abilities related to performance of different motor skills that may impose limits on individual performance and may explain why some students seem to be good at many skills.

Notice that, at each subsequent grade level, the information becomes more detailed and advanced.

The second guideline is to look at the concepts/principles from other themes in the subdiscipline, and from other subdisciplines, for natural connections. For example, at the kindergarten level, looking at the subdiscipline of aesthetics, you will notice the connection between the concepts from Themes 2 and 3:

Theme 2: Naming the shapes of nonmoving objects in the environment introduces this basic aesthetic feature.

Theme 3: Naming movements of people or things in the environment helps describe their aesthetic dimensions.

Or, consider the connection between exercise physiology and motor development concepts at the twelfth grade:

Exercise Physiology: People need to adjust their fitness activities as they mature and age.

Motor Development: Accumulating at least 30 minutes of activity most days of the week is important to maintain adequate fitness throughout one's adult years.

In each example, there is overlap between themes or subdisciplines. This overlap can facilitate student learning and reduce the amount of information presented at any specific grade level.

The movement forms (Standard 1) addressed at each grade also provide opportunities for connections and give us guideline three. For example, at the upper elementary level (third and fourth grade), students are demonstrating the mature form for selected manipulatives (e.g., throw, catch, kick) and "adapting skills to the demands of a dynamic, unpredictable environment" (NASPE, 1995). Notice how the concepts selected for third and fourth grade contribute to learning these motor skills:

Motor Learning: If you can identify the cues for a skill you are more likely to perform it correctly.

Motor Learning: Good performance of open skills requires a performer to adapt performance to an environment (e.g., modifying a forward roll to meet the size of a mat or performance with a partner).

Motor Learning: Throwing a large ball has some characteristics that are similar to throwing a small ball and some that are different

Motor Development: Fundamental skills are the building blocks of more complex actions such as sport-specific skills

Motor Development: More advanced form usually leads to more successful results.

Biomechanics: For every action there is an equal and opposite reaction.

Biomechanics: Large muscles generate more force than smaller muscles.

Biomechanics: Increasing the size, number, or speed of moving body segments tends to increase the force generated. Movement speed and the number of moving body segments should be adjusted in accordance with the force requirements of the activity.

Sociology: Using courtesy and complimenting in all games and activities makes the activities successful for everyone

Sociology: Positive self-talk increases self-confidence and one's ability to perform physical activities.

Sociology: Working in small groups with peers enables students to practice giving appropriate feedback, verbal persuasion, and encouragement.

Each of these concepts/principles provides the learner with information critical for mastering and applying manipulative skills.

The fourth guideline focuses on looking at concepts/principles from other subject areas and making natural connections. In general, biomechanics aligns well with physical science—specifically, physics, exercise physiology with biology and health, aesthetics with the arts, social psychology with the social sciences, and historical perspectives with history/social science. However, when looking to align concepts/principles with other subject areas, it is important to make sure that the alignment is specific to the grade level. For example, historical perspectives align well with the subject area of history/social science; but how much richer that alignment will be when it is specific to the area of history being studied in the history/social science class. In many states, ancient civilizations are studied in sixth grade history/social science. So, the concepts/principles for historical perspectives at the sixth grade level do more than link historical ideas, they specifically align with the concepts/principles addressed in the history/social science class. For example:

Sixth Grade Historical Perspectives

- The first ancient Olympics had only one event (stade), but each year new events were added (i.e., pentathlon, wrestling, chariot races, boxing).
- The ancient Olympics were considered both a sport and a religious festival.
- Each of the ancient civilizations (Chinese, Indian, Near Eastern, Greek, and Roman) had different reasons for participating in exercise.
- The purpose of games, dance, and sport in the ancient world was to maintain the culture, train for combat, perform religious ceremonies, and respond to a need for physical activity.
- In ancient Athens, music and gymnastics were the two focuses of the curriculum.

Another example involves biomechanics and physical science. Some educators may believe that addressing any biomechanics concept or principle in physical education is a good thing. But again, how much richer and deeper the learning when the concepts/principles are presented in a methodical manner from kindergarten through twelfth grade, and when they are aligned with the concepts/principles taught in science. It is suggested in Chapter 4, that Newton's Third Law (for every action there is an equal and opposite reaction) be addressed at the fourth grade level. This suggestion works well, except when a particular district or school focuses on Newton's Laws in the sixth grade. In that case, it might be prudent to address this concept/principle at the sixth grade level.

As we recognize relationships between concepts/principles from within a subdiscipline, between subdisciplines, and with other subject areas, it becomes apparent that we also can assess several concepts/principles simultaneously. For example, at the sixth grade level there are five concepts/principles related to historical perspectives that address the ancient Olympics. So, a report or project can be assigned that measures student learning related to the five concepts/principles. In addition, the history teacher and the physical educator can assign a joint project that gets at five of the historical perspective concepts/principles along with critical information from the subject area of history/social science. In addition, at the sixth grade level, stages of learning and progression are highlighted in the subdisciplines of motor development and motor learning:

Motor Development: People pass through developmental sequences at different speeds.

Motor Learning: In the first stage of learning a motor skill you should seek to get a clear idea of how to do the skill and should be able to describe what you should be doing.

Motor Learning: In the second stage of learning a motor skill you should work toward consistent performance in more complex environments.

One project or report can be assigned to get at all three of these concepts/principles. Finally, it is always possible to give one written test with questions from each of the subdisciplines.

Selecting Instructional Units

Once the concepts/principles are identified and sequenced, it may be helpful to assign them to one or more instructional units. A concept or principle may be taught in one instructional unit, taught again in another instructional unit, and reviewed in a third instructional unit. Or, the concept/principle may be addressed in its entirety during one instructional unit or broken down into parts that are addressed in different lessons or instructional units. What is important is that the teacher devise a strategy for teaching the concepts/principles. And, the strategy and its implementation should be documented, along with the assessment of student learning.

Figure 2

A Three-Part Model for Including Concepts in Instruction

Integrated: One or more selected concepts taught within a lesson.

Segregated: One or more complete lessons on a concept, which may or may not be related to the current unit of study.

Separated: Concept(s) taught as a unit of instruction.

Organizational Model

The actual learning experiences can be organized in a variety of ways. In the *Basic Stuff in Action* series (Bressan, 1987; Kneer & Heitmann, 1987; Lambert & Trimble, 1987) the authors created a three-part organizational model (see Figure 2) to describe the methods for including concepts/principles in physical education instruction. Teachers can select one of these models or use a combination of all three.

The **integrated model** uses an activity-based curriculum (e.g., volleyball unit, softball unit, badminton unit) and integrates each concept/principle throughout the different lessons. Some concepts/principles are addressed in one unit, while others are addressed in several different units. For example, while teaching the overhand throw in softball, the teacher emphasizes the biomechanical concepts/principles related to projectiles (biomechanics). The teacher reviews the projectile information again in the volleyball and badminton units. In order to address more than one concept/principle, the teacher also relates the overhand softball throw to the overhand serve in volleyball and the overhand clear in badminton, emphasizing transfer of learning (motor learning). It is the inclusion of these concepts/principles that enrich the learning activities and improve students' understanding of movement.

The **segregated model** brings in a one or two-day lesson on a concept or principle while the students are involved in a particular activity, such as gymnastics or dance. This is often seen with concepts/principles related to exercise physiology. Once a week, the teacher focuses on exercise physiology and facilitates student learning of a particular concept or principle. The concept/principle may or may not be related to the unit of study. For example, the teacher might emphasize cardiorespiratory concepts/principles during a dance unit, since dance is an aerobic activity, and flexibility concepts/principles during a gymnastics unit, since gymnastics requires flexibility. On the other hand, the teacher may have sequenced the concepts/principles for exercise physiology and may address them one after the other, regardless of the current unit of study.

The **separated model** identifies the concepts/principles as the actual unit of study. The emphasis shifts from activity to the knowledge; however, this does not mean that physical activity does not occur. Rather, the activities are selected based on the concept(s)/principle(s) taught. For example, a unit may focus on projectile concepts/principles and a variety of object handling activities (e.g., throwing a football, kicking a soccer ball, putting a shot) may be included in order to facilitate student learning of these concepts/principles. Other units may include cooperation (subdisciplines of sociology and psychology), learning a new closed skill (subdiscipline of motor learning), the

---

Figure 3

Interdisciplinary Models

Sequenced:	Topics are rearranged and sequenced to coincide with each other.
Shared:	Two subject areas with overlapping concepts are team-taught.
Webbed:	A theme of interest is webbed in curriculum content and subject areas.
Threaded:	Major concepts are threaded throughout various subjects or units.
Integrated:	Several subject areas with overlapping concepts are team-taught.
Immersed:	The learner chooses an area of interest and incorporates curricular areas within it.

Adapted from Fogarty, R. (1991). *The mindful school: How to integrate the curricula.* Palatine, IL: IRI/Skylight.

---

history of the Olympics (subdiscipline of historical perspectives), activities for the elderly (motor development), the beauty of sport (aesthetics), and health-related fitness (exercise physiology).

Interdisciplinary Model

Physical educators do need to keep in mind that they must first be true to their own subject area. They must ensure that they are facilitating student learning as it relates to the physical education grade level standards and concepts/principles. In many cases, integration with other subject areas can facilitate this process. And, as discussed previously, it can deepen the learning experience and provide for more lifelike learning experiences. There are several educational models available for integrating information with other subject areas. Fogarty's (1991) framework for interdisciplinary instruction (see Figure 3 for a review) was described in Chapter 1 and used in many of the examples presented in this chapter.

Regardless of which organizational pattern or interdisciplinary model is used, students should be able to demonstrate their understanding of the concepts/principles. If the separated model works best for a particular learning environment, that model should be used. If the segregated or the integrated model works best, that should be used. If an interdisciplinary model works best, that should be used. If a program is already based on an activity model, the concepts/principles can be addressed as described, using the integrated model.

Learning Experiences

While it is true that some learning occurs as a result of everyday experience, a comprehensive physical education program comes from teachers who provide learning experiences that ensure the concepts/principles are learned. Discussing the concepts/principles with the students and modeling their application is a good beginning. However, it is only through active learning that students make personal meaning out of the information. Active, hands-on learning experiences include problem solving, creating, and exploring. The strategy of starting with an initial question, placing students in a variety of contexts in which to experiment with different answers, and allowing them to draw their own conclusions engages students in active learning. It is through these types of carefully designed learning experiences that physical educators will ensure that students are able to understand the concepts/principles and demonstrate that understanding.

In Chapters 2 through 8, the authors provide ideas for teaching concepts/principles in the subdisciplines. The purpose here is to illustrate how a number of different concepts/principles are addressed simultaneously in a logical manner related to the current curriculum and not simply added on indiscriminately. Concrete learning experiences (one instructional unit from a yearly plan) for primary, elementary, upper elementary, middle school, and high school levels that address concepts/principles from two or more subdisciplines (and standards) along with practice and/or participation in motor skills or fitness activities are shown. These examples illustrate a variety of organizational and interdisciplinary models to provide the teacher with different options for addressing the physical education concepts/principles. Remember, these are instructional units, and they fit into the larger structure of a yearly plan.

Physical educators need to adjust these instructional units to coincide with their preferred teaching style and the specific learning needs of their students. Readers are referred to a number of books, including *Teaching Physical Education for Learning* (Rink, 1998), *Teaching Physical Education* (Mosston & Ashworth, 1994), and *Developing Teaching Skills in Physical Education* (Siedentop, 1991) for more information on instructional strategies, styles, and behaviors. Although readers may teach at only one grade level, they are encouraged to read all of the examples, since the key to including concepts in learning experiences is understanding the process involved, and not simply following a few isolated examples.

Example 1
After reviewing the concepts/principles and standards for kindergarten, the teacher chooses a skill theme approach for developing a yearly plan. The instructional units for this approach typically include: introduction, space awareness, effort, relationships, traveling, chasing/fleeing/dodging, jumping and

landing, rolling, balancing, transferring weight, kicking and punting, throwing and catching, volleying and dribbling, striking with objects, fitness concepts, and closure. Each of these units lasts from one to three weeks in a five-day-a-week program. For more information on the skill theme approach for teaching elementary physical education, readers are referred to *Children Moving: A Reflective Approach to Teaching Physical Education* (Graham, Holt/Hale, & Parker, 1993).

Once the instructional units are identified, the teacher using the integrated model decides which standards and concepts/principles to address during each instructional unit. This may sound like a contradiction, but it is not. At this stage of the process, there is a continual shifting back and forth between selecting the instructional units and determining where the standards and concepts/principles are addressed. Specifically, the distinct aspects of standards and concepts/principles are assigned to one or more instructional units.

Example 1

Traveling Unit

Day	Motor Skill Focus	Conceptual Focus
1.	Traveling in space	
2.	Traveling in different directions	
3.	Traveling and freezing at different levels	1
4.	Traveling at different speeds	
5.	Traveling and changing force qualities	
6.	Traveling along pathways	
7.	Animal movements	1, 2, 4
8.	Animal movements	1, 2, 4
9.	Animal movements	1, 2, 4
10.	Traveling activities	1, 2, 3
11.	Traveling activities	1, 2, 3
12.	Traveling activities	1, 2, 3

Conceptual Focus

1. Lowering the body's center of gravity (bending the knees), widening the base of support (stance), and leaning away from any force increases the ability to maintain balance (stability).
2. Learning how the body moves helps people feel good about themselves.
3. Games that are played at school today may have looked different long ago.
4. Naming movements of people or things in the environment helps describe their aesthetic dimensions.

The traveling instructional unit consists of 12 one-day lessons (see Example 1) that address the locomotor movements of running, hopping, galloping, sliding, and jumping, along with the qualities of movement. Looking at the standards and concepts/principles for kindergarten, the teacher decides to focus on skills and concepts/principles from Standards 1, 2, 5, 6, and 7 during this unit:

- Standard 1: Skill development in the locomotor movements (running, hopping, jumping, galloping, and sliding).
- Standard 2 (Biomechanics): Lowering the body's center of gravity (bending the knees), widening the base of support (stance), and leaning away from any force increases the ability to maintain balance (stability).
- Standard 5 (Social/Psychological): Learning how the body moves helps people feel good about themselves.
- Standard 6 (Historical Perspectives): Games that are played at school today may have looked different long ago.
- Standard 7 (Aesthetics): Naming movements of people or things in the environment helps describe their aesthetic dimensions.

Looking at the instructional units for kindergarten, the reader may be thinking, "Shouldn't the biomechanical concept/principle of lowering the body's center of gravity to increase stability be aligned with the balance unit?" The answer is definitely yes, but that doesn't prevent the teacher from also addressing the concept/principle during this unit.

The next step in the process is to look for interdisciplinary links. This unit is ideal for integrating with language arts. Students read a story, e.g., *Pretend You're a Cat* (Marzollo, 1990), or any story that involves animals moving (different locomotor movements). The reading and vocabulary lessons take place during language arts. Then, during physical education lessons seven through nine, the students mimic the animal movements. Pretending to be different animals provides students with the opportunity to practice different movements using different qualities of movement (e.g., bears walk heavily, rabbits hop, horses gallop fast).

This unit also lends itself to integration with visual and performing arts, since the animal movements can be performed to music (e.g., animal walks, or any music that contains a variety of rhythms). Science also can be integrated, since students can study stability principles during science and apply them during the traveling unit in physical education. History/social science is integrated into lessons 10 through 12 as students discuss with their parents how games they play at school were played differently by their parents and grandparents. Notice that the integration was not forced in any of these examples. Rather, it grew naturally from the instructional unit designed for physical education.

There are three major learning experiences (days one through six, seven through nine, and 10 through 12) in this unit. In lessons one through six, the students are improving their ability to demonstrate the basic locomotor skills (run, hop, jump, gallop, slide, walk, skip, leap) while applying the components of movement (space and time). In kindergarten, students are taught the basic locomotor skills, and prior to this learning experience, they are taught some of the qualities of movement. Since this is a review of the locomotor skills involving the application of components of movement, the teacher prompts the students with questions such as:

- Can you show me your body walking at a high level in general space?
- Can you show me your body sliding at a medium level?
- Can you show me your body running fast?
- Can you show me your body jumping slowly?
- Can you show me your body hopping forward?

In addition, the teacher addresses the biomechanical concept on day three while asking students to demonstrate the locomotor movement skills at the three levels (high, medium, and low). After the students run at each of the three levels, the teacher asks them to identify the level at which they felt the most stable. The teacher repeats this question after each movement. At the conclusion of the lesson, students discuss whether one level is more stable than the others.

In lessons seven through nine, a variety of environmental stimuli (music, stories, pictures) are used to assist students with their animal imitations. The teacher shows the students pictures of various animals from stories they have read and asks them to imitate that animal. Students select one locomotor movement skill and one component of movement to depict the animal (e.g., cows walk slowly, cats leap forward). The learning experiences provide students with an opportunity to continue to improve their locomotor movement skills and thereby increase their enjoyment of movement. Simultaneously, they discover stability concepts as they move at different levels.

During the next learning experience, the teacher asks the students to pretend to be the animal in the picture, but this time they must move at a low level, then at a medium level, and finally at a high level. For the next learning experience, the teacher turns on music and has the students listen to the rhythm. Each time the rhythm changes, the teacher asks the students which type of animal might move to that rhythm and why. The teacher plays the music again, but this time the students move to the music, changing animals as the music changes rhythm. The teacher debriefs these learning experiences by asking students several closure questions:

1. What do animals that are not likely to fall down when running have in common? Guide the discussion toward being low to the ground. (Biomechanics concept.)
2. How did you feel pretending to be animals? Why? (Social/psychology concept.)
3. Which locomotor movement did you use when pretending to be a bear, a kangaroo, and a rabbit? (Aesthetics concept.)
4. Which quality of movement did you use when you were pretending to be a cat, a lion, and a deer? (Aesthetic concept.)

In lessons 10 through 12, the students participate in activities that help them practice locomotor movements. These activities include hopscotch and obstacle courses. As each new activity is taught, students are asked to go home and ask their parents and other older relatives if they played the game when they were in elementary school, and if so, how was it played.

This provides students with an understanding of how games have changed over time. Again, the teacher uses debriefing questions to reinforce the concepts addressed earlier in the unit. These might include:

1. When balance was important in the game, was it better to be at a high level, medium level, or low level? Why? (Biomechanics concept.)
2. How did you feel about participating in the activities? Why? (Social/psychology concept.)
3. How are the games we play today the same or different from the games played by parents and other older relatives? (Historical perspectives concept.)

Example 2
After reviewing the concepts/principles and standards for third and fourth grade, the teacher decides on an eclectic approach for developing a yearly plan. The instructional units for this approach typically include: introduction, fitness, jump rope, throwing, striking with hands, striking with feet, striking with implements, tumbling, new games, rhythm, folk dance, and closure. Each of these units lasts from one to three weeks in a five-day-a-week program. Once the instructional units are identified, the teacher using the integrated model decides which standards and concepts/principles to address during each instructional unit.

The folk dance instructional unit consists of 15 one-day lessons (see Example 2) that address combining the locomotor movements of walking, running, hopping, galloping, sliding, skipping, jumping, and leaping in formal dance movements. Looking at the standards and concepts/principles for third/fourth grade, the teacher decides to focus on the skills and concepts/principles for Standards 1, 5, 6, and 7 during this unit:

- **Standard 1 (Motor Skill):** Performing formal dances to music.
- **Standard 5 (Sociology):** Positive self-talk increases self-confidence and one's ability to perform physical activities.

■ **Standard 6 (Historical Perspectives):** Many of today's physical activities, dances, and sports had their beginnings in ritual and religious activities.

■ **Standard 7 (Aesthetics):** Combinations of locomotor movements in space and time create movement patterns.

The next step in the process is to look for interdisciplinary links. This unit is ideal for integration with other subject areas around the theme of pioneer days, since this is the period that the students are studying in history/social science. Language arts, mathematics, science, and visual/performing arts also can be integrated into the theme of pioneer days. Physical education can address the dances, visual/performing arts can address the art and music, science can address the technologies, mathematics can use word problems, and language arts can do reading/writing activities associated with this time period.

Example 2

Folk Dance Unit

Day		Conceptual Focus
1.	Locomotor movements to sound of music	1
2.	Virginia Reel	4, 3, 2
3.	Oh Johnny	4, 3, 2
4.	Red River	4, 3, 2
5.	Review Virginia Reel, Oh Johnny, and Red River	2, 1
6.	Nobody's Business	4, 3, 2
7.	Alabama Gal	4, 3, 2
8.	Review Nobody's Business and Alabama Gal	1, 2
9.	Yankee Doodle	4, 3, 2
10.	Chorus Jig	4, 3, 2
11.	Review Yankee Doodle and Chorus Jig	4, 2, 1
12.	Create a dance	4, 2
13.	Create a dance	4, 2
14.	Create a dance	4, 2
15.	Perform dance	4, 2

Conceptual Focus:
1. Aerobic exercise provides people with many personal benefits, both physical and mental.
2. Respecting others shows a willingness to consider their thoughts and feelings during participation in games, activities, and sports.
3. Many of today's physical activities, dances, and sports had their beginnings in ritual and religious activities.
4. Combinations of locomotor movements in space and time create movement patterns.

There are three major learning experiences (day one, days two through 11, and days 12 through 15) in this unit. In lesson one, the teacher reviews, and the students practice, all eight of the locomotor movements (walk, run, hop, skip jump, gallop, leap, and slide). The students then practice the movements to music: jumping, hopping, leaping, running, and walking are performed to an even rhythm, while galloping, skipping, and sliding are practiced to an uneven rhythm. At the conclusion of the lesson, students discuss whether performing the locomotor movements is an aerobic activity.

In lessons two through 11, the students learn and review dances from the pioneer days. Each dance builds on the previous one, moving from simple to more complex movement combinations. During the introduction to each dance, the teacher demonstrates how locomotor movements are combined to create the dance (combinations of locomotor movements in space and time create movement patterns), and describes the history of the dance (many of the dances had their beginnings in ritual and religious activities). For many of the students, performing formal dances is new. Because they have a tendency to react negatively to their own performances, the teacher should emphasize that positive self-talk increases self-confidence and one's ability to perform physical activities. On day two, the teacher uses a T-chart to help students understand self-talk. Then, throughout the unit, the teacher questions the students about their use of positive self-talk and provides reinforcement for its use.

In lessons 12 through 15, students create their own dances. The emphasis here is on the aesthetic concept, "combinations of locomotor movements in space and time create movement patterns." Closure questions during the unit include:

- Which locomotor movements are you using in the dance?
- What popular dances today are similar to this dance?
- How did you use self-talk during this unit?
- How did self-talk assist you with your dance performance?

A final project for this unit centers on the historical perspectives concept. Students research the history of one of the dances taught during the unit. In their written summaries, the students explain the connection between the history of the specific dance and the concept, "many of the dances had their beginnings in ritual and religious activities."

Example 3
Fifth/sixth grade teachers often continue with the skill theme approach in developing a yearly plan, but they may add a few activity-based units. The following instructional units might comprise the fifth/sixth grade curriculum: introduction, fitness concepts, cooperative activities, throwing and catching, striking with hands, striking with feet, rhythm, stunts and tumbling, striking with implements, multicultural-cultural games, dance, and closure. Each of these units lasts approximately three weeks in a five-day-a-week program.

Example 3

Cooperation Unit

Day	Game Description	Conceptual Focus
1.	Introduction to Cooperation	1, 2, 3, 4
2.	Everyone Up (Partners) In groups of two, partners sit facing each other with knees bent, bottoms of toes touching with heels on the ground, and hands joined. The objective is to pull one another up.	1, 2, 3, 4
3.	Stand Up Sit on the ground, back to back with a partner. With knees bent and elbows linked the objective is to stand up at the same time.	1, 2, 3, 4
4.	Knee Touch In groups of two, partners stand facing each other. The objective is to touch your partner's knees while preventing your partner from touching your knee.	1, 2, 3, 4
5.	Minefield In groups of two, one partner is blindfolded. The partner not blindfolded must verbally direct the other person around polyspots (randomly distributed around the area) to safety.	1, 2, 3, 4
6.	Booop In groups of four, members form a circle and join hands. One person tosses a balloon into the air. The objective is to keep the balloon in the air while group members maintain joined hands.	1, 2, 3, 4
7.	Circle the Circle In groups of four, members form a circle and join hands with a hula-hoop around a pair of joined hands. The objective is to pass the hula-hoop around the circle without letting go of joined hands	1, 2, 3, 4
8.	Warp Speed A group of eight forms a circle with one person holding a fleece ball. The group establishes a tossing pattern, so that everyone in the group tosses and catches once. The group practices the pattern in order to complete the pattern as quickly as possible.	1, 2, 3, 4

9. Blind Polygon   1, 2, 3, 4
    In groups of four, members (blindfolded) form a circle while holding onto a rope. The objective is for the group to form different shapes (e.g., square, triangle, polygon) as directed by the teacher or leader.

10. Across the Great Divide   1, 2, 3, 4
    In groups of four, members stand side by side with elbows locked and sides of feet touching. The objective is for the group to move from point A to point B (approximately 15 feet) keeping their elbows locked and sides of feet touching.

11. TP Shuffle   1, 2, 3, 4
    Two groups of four stand on a horizontal telephone pole or a raised curb facing the center. The objective is for the two groups to change ends of the pole without touching the ground.

12. Knots   1, 2, 3, 4
    In groups of six, members form a circle while standing. Each member extends his or her right hand grasping someone's hand (except the person standing next to you) and extends his or her left hand grasping someone's hand (except the person standing next to him/her and the person whose hand he or she is already holding). The objective is to get untangled without letting go of joined hands.

13. Traffic Jam   1, 2, 3, 4
    The teacher lays out nine polyspots in a line. Two groups of four stand on the polyspots facing each other with the middle spot empty. The objective is for the people on the right side of the middle polyspot to end up on the left side of the middle polyspot, and vice versa, only stepping on polyspots. A person can move onto an empty polyspot in front of him or her or a person can move around a person facing him or her onto an empty polyspot on the other side of the person.

14. Sherpa's Walk   1, 2, 3, 4
    In groups of eight, seven members (blindfolded) form a line. The leader (not blindfolded) guides the group through an obstacle without speaking or touching the group.

15. Unit Closure   1, 2, 3, 4

Conceptual Focus

1. Opportunities to practice inclusion of all kinds of individuals help your groups/teams to function more effectively.
2. Listening without judgment, paraphrasing thoughts and feelings, and clarifying for mutual understanding enhances people's ability to understand and appreciate others.
3. When students have abundant opportunities to alternate leadership roles, give feedback, practice social skills, and contribute to the success of the group, they learn to work successfully with people in any activity.
4. Achievement is directly related to effort and motivation put forth.

Once the instructional units are identified, the physical educator decides which standards and concepts/principles to address during each instructional unit. For example, the cooperative activities instructional unit consists of 15 one-day lessons that specially address the social skill of cooperation as applied in movement activities (see Example 3). Looking at the standards and concepts/principles for fifth/sixth grade, the teacher decides to use the segregated model and focus exclusively on Standard 5:

- **Standard 5 (Social Psychology):** Opportunities to practice inclusion of all kinds of differences and similarities in individuals helps groups/teams to function more effectively.
- **Standard 5 (Social Psychology):** Paraphrasing is the ability to restate something that another person said to you, to check for understanding and to demonstrate that you cared enough to listen well.
- **Standard 5 (Social Psychology):** When students have abundant opportunities to alternate leadership roles, give feedback, practice social skills, and contribute to the success of the group, they learn to work successfully with people in any activity.
- **Standard 5 (Social Psychology):** Achievement is directly related to the effort and motivation put forth.

The next step in the process is to look for interdisciplinary links. This unit lends itself to the web interdisciplinary model involving physical education, health education, and language arts. It uses the theme of cooperation. In physical education, students participate in cooperative activities. After physical education, students go to their health class, where they debrief the activity in order to improve their cooperation, communication, and listening skills. Then, in their language arts class, students write an essay describing the social skills they learned during the physical education activities. Notice again that in each of these examples the integration was not forced. It grew naturally from the physical education unit.

In this instructional unit, students experience a wide variety of cooperative activities. Notice that only one activity is suggested per day. In reality, a class may address from one to four activities per lesson, depending on the length of time needed to accomplish each one. However, as discussed previously, it is not enough to introduce the cooperative activities and expect the students to understand the cognitive concepts associated with the sociology subdiscipline. Specific learning experiences must occur that provide students with opportunities to learn, understand, and practice the social skills.

The sociology concepts are addressed starting on day one and continuing through the end of the unit. During each subsequent lesson, the concepts are addressed at a deeper level. Notice that the activities on days two through five involve partners. Thus, the social skills of cooperation and listening only involve one other person. The activities can be set up so that students initially participate with friends as their partners, then with acquaintances, and finally with students who are different from themselves. This process is then repeated during days 6 through 14 as the groups become larger and the difficulty of the activity increases.

A T-chart is a very effective strategy for introducing the concepts of cooperation, inclusion, effective listening, and brainstorming for problem solving, motivation, achievement, and providing feedback. For example, on day one, the teacher sets up a T-chart with the word "cooperation" at the top. The students are asked to identify what cooperation looks like and sounds like. The cooperative activities throughout the unit then provide an opportunity for the students to practice cooperation. During each lesson, selected students may be asked to chart the number of times they observe an individual or team cooperating. The information provides feedback to the individual or group, and helps members reflect on their social performance.

Equally important is the end of each lesson, when the teacher debriefs the activities. Sample questions include:

- What did you try?
- How did it work?
- What would you do differently next time?
- Did your partner or group listen to you? How do you know they were listening?

- How did it feel when someone gave you feedback?
- Describe how you demonstrated cooperation today.
- How did it feel to work with someone who is different from you?
- How did you go about including someone different from you in the activity?
- How were you able to utilize the strengths/weaknesses brought to the group by each individual?
- How were you able to demonstrate leadership in the activity?
- How did you contribute to the group?
- Was your group motivated? How do you know your group was or was not motivated?
- Was your group successful? Why do you think your group was or was not successful?

These same questions may be used after each lesson; however, the responses of the students should become increasingly sophisticated. Remember, without the debriefing, the games stand alone as simple physical activities. With the debriefing, the games provide a context for discussing and reflecting on the understanding and use of social skills. The debriefing also ensures that the students learn the concepts/principles related to this unit.

Example 4
Seventh/eighth grade teachers often use activity-based instructional units. The following instructional units might comprise the eighth grade curriculum: introduction, square dance, project adventure, volleyball, softball, basketball, team handball, soccer, football, and closure. Each of these units may last three to four weeks.

Once the instructional units are identified, physical educators must decide which standards and concepts/principles will be addressed during each instructional unit. For example, the basketball unit consists of 20 one-day lessons that address the motor skills of stopping (two-step stop, jump stop), passing (chest, overhead, and bounce), catching, pivoting, dribbling, one-handed set shot, lay-up, and rebounding. Looking at the standards/concepts for seventh/eighth grade, the teacher decides to focus on some of the concepts/principles related to Standards 2, 5, and 6 in addition to the motor skills:

- **Standard 1 (Motor Skill):** Application of locomotor, nonlocomotor, and manipulative skills to basketball.
- **Standard 2 (Motor Development):** Practice with increasingly complex interactions among teammates and opponents can help individuals become better players.
- **Standard 2 (Motor Development):** People pass through developmental sequences at different speeds.
- **Standard 2 (Motor Learning):** In the first stage of learning a motor skill you should seek to get a clear idea of how to do the skill and should be able to describe what you should be doing.
- **Standard 2 (Motor Learning):** In the second stage of learning a motor skill you should work toward consistent performance in more complex environments.
- **Standard 5 (Social/Psychology):** Consistent use of short-term goals and self-evaluation when learning a new skill or activity makes it easier for people to recognize and appreciate the things that they are doing well.
- **Standard 6 (Historical Perspectives):** Team sports emerged after the Civil War.

Many additional seventh/eighth grade concepts/principles could be addressed in this unit. However, the selection was based not only on its alignment with basketball, but also on its alignment with other concepts/principles. You will see that all of these concepts/principles address improving one's performance. This alignment to one central idea makes it easier to address during the lessons.

The next step in the process is to look for interdisciplinary links. This unit (see Example 4) lends itself to integration with history/social science. Many eighth graders study United States history during the 1800s in their history/social science classes. Therefore, students can learn about the history of that era during history/social science and then participate in basketball, which was invented during the same period, during physical education. Students can consider why basketball was invented during the 1890s, what social factors influenced its development, and how the game has changed during the last 100 years. The answers to these questions can be generalized to a number of team sports and lead to the concept/principle, "team sports emerged after the Civil War." Notice that the lessons on days

17 through 19 focus specifically on the history of basketball. On these days, students work in small groups and present one historical version of the game of basketball. The project is assigned early in the unit to provide students with sufficient time to gather information and determine how they will present their games. The project uses a cooperative learning structure known as coop coop. Each group of five students investigates the game of basketball at various points throughout its history. Each stu-

Example 4

Basketball Unit

Day	Motor Skill Focus	Conceptual Focus
1.	Passing (chest, overhead, bounce)	2, 3, 4, 5
2.	Stopping (two step, jump stop)	2, 3, 4, 5
3.	Dribbling	2, 3, 4, 5
4.	Combinations (pass, catch, stop, pivot, dribble)	2, 3, 4, 5
5.	Combinations (pass, catch, stop, pivot, dribble)	2, 3, 4, 5
6.	One handed set shot	2, 3, 4, 5
7.	One handed set shot	2, 3, 4, 5
8.	One-on-one strategies	1, 2, 3, 4, 5
9.	Two-on-two strategies	1, 2, 3, 4, 5
10.	Lay-up shot	2, 3, 4, 5
11.	Lay-up and rebounding	2, 3, 4, 5
12.	Two-on-two strategies using lay-up	1
13.	Two-on-two strategies using lay-up	1
14.	Three-on-three strategies	1
15.	Three-on-three strategies	1
16.	Three-on-three strategies	1
17.	Two basketball games–early history	1, 6
18.	Two basketball games–middle history	1, 6
19.	Two basketball games–later history	1, 6
20.	Project	1, 6

Conceptual Focus

1. Practice with increasingly complex interactions among teammates and opponents can help individuals become better players.
2. People pass through developmental sequences at different speeds.
3. In the first stage of learning a motor skill you should seek to get a clear idea of how to do the skill and should be able to describe what you should be doing
4. In the second stage of learning a motor skill you should work toward consistent performance in more complex environments.
5. Consistent use of short-term goals and self-evaluation when learning a new skill or activity makes it easier for people to recognize and appreciate the things that they are doing well.
6. Team sports emerged after the Civil War.

dent in the group has a specific responsibility for the project that is different from that of the other group members. In addition to learning the rules and strategies of the time period they are researching, each group must determine the influence of societal events on the game rules.

Notice that this integration with history/social science only works because basketball is an appropriate activity for seventh/ eighth graders. It would not, for example, be appropriate for second graders. As the students trace the development of basketball throughout its 100-year history and speculate about how the game may change during the next 10 years, language arts or visual/performing arts can be integrated into the unit. For example, students might choose an essay, a video, or a model format for their project.

During the instructional unit, students have the opportunity to review and practice the basic skills related to basketball in a variety of games. As the teacher introduces the motor skills related to basketball, the students will observe a wide variety of skill levels among their peers. This provides the teacher with an opportunity to discuss and illustrate the motor development, motor learning, and social psychology concepts/principles:

- People pass through developmental sequences at different speeds.
- In the first stage of learning a motor skill, you should seek to get a clear idea of how to do the skill and should be able to describe what you should be doing.
- In the second stage of learning a motor skill, you should work toward consistent performance in more complex environments.
- Practice with increasingly complex interactions among teammates and opponents can help individuals become better players.
- Consistent use of short-term goals and self-evaluation when learning a new skill or activity makes it easier for people to recognize and appreciate the things that they are doing well.

At the beginning of the unit, students write short-term goals related to the accomplishment of basketball skills. Throughout the unit, the concepts provide students with information on how best to practice, given their current level of skill. At the end of each lesson, the teacher asks the students to use a rubric to assess their performance, paying close attention to the improvement that occurs with practice. The opportunity to apply the concepts/principles reinforces the students' understanding and shows the students the real life value of the concepts/principles.

This instructional unit also takes students from two-on-two basketball, to three-on-three basketball, to basketball in the 1890s, to basketball in the new millennium. Throughout the unit, the teacher addresses the motor development concept, "Practice with increasingly complex interactions among teammates and opponents can help individuals become better players," by first setting up isolated skill practice, then combined skill practice, one-on-one situations, two-on-two situations, three-on-three situations, and then finally game situations. Debriefing questions at the conclusion of several lessons will determine student understanding of this concept. These questions might include:

1. Are you getting better at playing basketball?
2. Why do you think you are getting better at basketball?
3. What would happen now if you stopped trying more complex drills and activities?

Example 5
In many states, high school physical educators are required by law to provide a one-year, one-semester, or one-quarter course on health-related fitness. Often, a physical education textbook containing information on health-related fitness—e.g., *Fitness for Life* (Corbin & Lindsey, 1997), *Personal Fitness: Looking Good, Feeling Good* (Williams, et al., 2000), or *Moving for Life* (Spindt, et al., 1991)—is central to the course of study. In other states, high school physical educators provide a one quarter course on health-related fitness, but they also address one or more of the following areas: team sports, individual/dual sports, self-defense, tumbling and gymnastics, dance, and/or aquatics. Students may be required to participate in one unit related to each of these content areas in some states, and they may choose the courses they will take in others.

Example 5

Health-Related Fitness Unit

Day	Fitness Focus	Conceptual Focus
1.	Introduction to physical fitness	
2.	Introduction to physical fitness, day 2	
3.	Introduction to physical fitness, day 3	
4.	Introduction to physical fitness, day 4	
5.	Introduction to physical fitness, day 5	
6.	Components of fitness	
7.	Components of fitness, day 2	
8.	Components of fitness, day 3	
9.	Components of fitness, day 4	
10.	Components of fitness, day 5	
11.	Guidelines	
12.	Guidelines, day 2	
13.	Principles	
14.	Principles, day 2	
15.	Evaluation of activities	
16.	Evaluation of activities, day 2	
17.	Goal setting	
18.	Goal setting, day 2	
19.	Flexibility	6, 7, 8
20.	Flexibility, day 2	6, 7, 8
21.	Flexibility, day 3	6, 7, 8
22.	Flexibility, day 4	6, 7, 8
23.	Cardiorespiratory endurance	2
24.	Cardiorespiratory endurance	2
25.	Cardiorespiratory endurance	2
26.	Cardiorespiratory endurance	2
27.	Body composition and nutrition	9
28.	Body composition and nutrition	9
29.	Body composition and nutrition	9
30.	Body composition and nutrition	9
31.	Body composition and nutrition	9
32.	Muscular fitness	1, 4, 8
33.	Muscular fitness, day 2	1, 4, 8
34.	Muscular fitness, day 3	1, 4, 8
35.	Muscular fitness, day 4	1, 4, 8
36.	Program design	3, 5
37.	Program design, day 2	3, 5
38.	Program design, day 3	3, 5
39.	Program design, day 4	3, 5
40.	Program design, day 5	3, 5

Conceptual Focus

1. Changing the moment arm of the involved muscles or the resistance forces can alter the difficulty of an exercise.
2. Females who participate in vigorous, regular physical activity can lessen the effects of age-related diseases.

3. Maintaining a regular physical fitness program and its benefits requires preparation, dedication, and updated information.
4. The FITT principles of strength training include frequency of training (F), intensity/amount of weight (I), time/sets of repetitions (T), and type of exercise/using body weight, free weights, or weight machines (T).
5. Physical, emotional, and social growth influence the individual needs and results of a regular physical fitness program.
6. Muscles, joints, and range of motion of the arms and legs are similar.
7. The different designs of synovial joints facilitate the range of movement found in the body.
8. Specific dangerous exercises that should be avoided include neck circles, hurdler's stretch, deep knee bends, back arching, and double leg lifts.
9. Body composition and nutritional needs interact and change as students grow, engage in different physical activities, increase their fitness levels, and commit to ongoing after-school obligations.

The sample unit provided consists of 40 one-day lessons (see Example 5) that address the health-related fitness components (cardiorespiratory endurance, flexibility, body composition, muscular strength, and muscular endurance). Looking at the standards and concepts for tenth grade, the teacher decides to focus on Standards 2 and 3 in addition to Standard 4, which is the focal point of the instructional unit:

- **Standard 2 (Biomechanics):** Changing the moment arm of the involved muscles or the resistance forces can alter the difficulty of an exercise.
- **Standard 2 (Motor Development):** Females who participate in vigorous, regular physical activity can lessen the effects of age-related diseases.
- **Standard 3 (Exercise Physiology):** Maintaining a regular physical fitness program and its benefits requires preparation, dedication, and updated information.
- **Standard 4 (Exercise Physiology):** Bouncing, swinging, over-stretching, strengthening fast, locking, over-bending, arching, and clicking the joints are harmful aspects of some exercises.
- **Standard 4 (Exercise Physiology):** Physical, emotional, and social growth influence individual needs and the results of a regular physical fitness program.
- **Standard 4 (Exercise Physiology):** Muscles, joints, and range of motion of the arms and legs are similar.
- **Standard 4 (Exercise Physiology):** Specific dangerous exercises that people should avoid include neck circles,

hurdler's stretch, deep knee bends, back arching, and double leg lifts.

- **Standard 4 (Exercise Physiology):** Body composition and nutritional needs interact and change as students grow, engage in different physical activities, increase their fitness levels, and commit to ongoing after-school obligations.
- **Standard 4 (Exercise Physiology):** Design strength-training programs for individuals based on body composition, current strength, and the specific requirements of the activity.

The next step in the process is to look for interdisciplinary links. This unit lends itself to the web interdisciplinary model involving physical education, health education, science, and math using the theme of wellness. In physical education, students learn about health-related fitness; in health education, students study personal health; in science, students study the muscular/skeletal system; and in math, students graph their fitness improvement throughout the unit. Again, this interdisciplinary model works well because it includes content that should be addressed in tenth grade physical education, health education, science, and math.

As noted earlier, state law often requires fitness instructional units. The intent is to ensure that students understand the various concepts/principles associated with health-related fitness. In some situations this will be a review of information presented previously; in other situations this will be new information. The sample unit is divided into eight sections:

1. Introduction
2. Components, Guidelines, and Principles
3. Evaluation and Goal Setting
4. Flexibility
5. Cardiorespiratory Endurance
6. Body Composition and Nutrition
7. Muscular Fitness
8. Program Design

During sections one through three, concepts/principles from previous grade levels are reviewed. Starting in section four, specific ninth/tenth grade concepts/principles are addressed. For example, during the flexibility segment, three of the concepts/principles are taught:

- Muscles, joints, and range of motion of the arms and legs are similar.
- Bouncing, swinging, over-stretching, strengthening fast, locking, over-bending, arching, and clicking the joints are harmful aspects of some exercises.
- Specific dangerous exercises that should be avoided include neck circles, hurdler's stretch, and back arching.

Notice that only some of the dangerous exercises are covered during the flexibility section. The rest are covered during the muscular fitness section.

During the cardiorespiratory endurance segment, the concept/principle, "females who participate in vigorous regular exercise can lessen the effects of age-related diseases such as osteoporosis," is addressed. One of the learning activities in this section has students working in groups to research the benefits of good cardiorespiratory endurance for various groups of people. One group of students is assigned females over the age of 50. The students use the Internet, books, and interviews to answer the research question. Students then share their findings with the rest of the class.

During the body composition and nutrition segment, the concept/principle, "body composition and nutritional needs interact and change as students grow, engage in different physical activities, increase their fitness levels, and commit to ongoing after-school obligations," is addressed. An instructional activity for this section includes having students calculate their caloric input and output on a daily basis and observe the effects of additional physical activity on their caloric output.

The learning experience for muscular fitness relates directly to strength-training programs for individuals based on body composition, current strength, and the specific requirements of the activity. Initially the FITT principles of strength training— which include frequency of training (F), intensity/amount of weight– (I), time/sets of repetitions (T), and type of exercise/using body weight, free weights, or weight machines (T)—are reviewed. For this activity, the teacher uses a cooperative learning structure known as a jigsaw. In a jigsaw experience, students work in groups of four (home groups), and select one aspect of information to study in detail. Detailed information includes frequency, intensity, time, and type of variables related to muscular strength development. The students read about their topic and then meet with students from other home groups who have the same topic (expert groups). If groups are larger than six people, then the teacher forms double expert groups (e.g., two groups meet together to study frequency). Each expert group discusses the information and prepares a presentation. The intensity group is given information related to "changing the moment arm of the involved muscles or the resistance forces can alter the difficulty of an exercise." The type group is given information related to "specific dangerous exercises that should be avoided include: deep knee bends and double leg lifts." Students then return to their home groups to share their presentations on the variables related to muscular strength development. This activity is followed by lessons revolving around the adaptation of muscular strength programs based on individual body composition, strength, and needs.

Finally, in the last section of the unit, students bring all of their learning together to create a personal health-related fitness plan. The concept/principle, "physical, emotional, and social growth influence individual needs and results of a regular physical fitness program," is addressed as students analyze their own personal strengths and weaknesses along with their short and long-term goals before creating their fitness plan. The concept/principle, "maintaining a regular physical fitness program and its benefits requires preparation, dedication, and updated information," is addressed as students not only design but also implement their fitness plan.

In order to ensure understanding of the process for addressing the concepts in a variety of lessons, the reader should now return to each lesson, look at the list of concepts for that grade level, and determine if and how any additional concepts can be addressed during each instructional unit. This will provide good practice before beginning to adjust current lesson plans.

Concluding Comments

The concepts/principles outlined in Chapters 2 through 8 provide the knowledge base or content to ensure that students have sufficient information to demonstrate the National Physical Education Standards and live high quality lives in the 21st century. This chapter provides several examples of learning experiences and assessment examples that bring together concepts from the different subdisciplines and shows how they can be integrated with other subject areas. These examples serve as models that teachers can use to create their own learning experiences. It is important to remember two points when doing so: incorporate one or more concepts/principles into each learning experience when feasible, and identify the link between the learning experience, assessment, and the related concepts/principles and the National Standards.

References

Bressan, E. S. (1987). *The basic stuff in action for grades K-3.* Reston, VA: American Alliance for Health, Physical Education, Recreation and Dance.

Corbin, C. B., & Lindsey, R. (1997). *Fitness for life.* (4th ed.). Champaign, IL: Human Kinetics.

Fogarty, R. (1991). *The mindful school: How to integrate the curricula.* Palatine, IL: IRI/Skylight.

Graham, G., Holt/Hale, S., & Parker, M. (1993). *Children moving: A reflective approach to teaching physical education.* Mountain View, CA: Mayfield.

Kneer, M. E., & Heitmann, H. M. (1987). *The basic stuff in action for grades 9-12.* Reston, VA: American Alliance for Health, Physical Education, Recreation and Dance.

Lambert, L. T., & Trimble, R. T. (1987). *The basic stuff in action for grades 4-8.* Reston, VA: American Alliance for Health, Physical Education, Recreation and Dance.

Marzollo, J. (1990). *Pretend you're a cat.* New York: Dial Books for Young Readers.

Melograno, V. J. (1996). *Designing the physical education curriculum,* (3rd ed.). Champaign, IL: Human Kinetics.

Mohnsen, B. S. (2003). *Teaching middle school physical education* (2nd ed.). Champaign, IL: Human Kinetics.

Mosston, M., & Ashworth, S. (1994). *Teaching physical education.* New York: Macmillan.

National Association for Sport and Physical Education. (1995). *Moving into the future: National physical education standards. A guide to content and assessment.* Reston, VA: Author.

Placek, J. H., & O'Sullivan, M. (1997). The many faces of integrated physical education. *Journal of Health, Physical Education, Recreation & Dance, 68*(1), 20-24.

Rink, J. E. (1997). Teacher education programs: The role of context in learning how to teach. *Journal of Physical Education, Recreation & Dance, 68*(1), 17-19, 24.

Rink, J. E. (1998). *Teaching physical education for learning* (3rd ed.). Boston: McGraw Hill.

Siedentop, D. (1991). *Developing teaching skills in physical education.* Mountain View, CA: Mayfield.

Spindt, G. B., Monti, W. H., & Hennessy, B. (1991). *Moving for life.* Dubuque, IA: Kendall/Hunt.

Williams, C. S., Harageones, E. G., Johnson, D. J., & Smith, C. D. (2000). *Personal fitness: Looking good, feeling good.* Dubuque, IA: Kendall/Hunt.

Resource

Animal walks. Long Branch, NJ: Kimbo Educational.

Appendix A

Grade Level	Subdiscipline	Concept/Principle
K	Aesthetics	Naming the shapes of objects clarifies how they differ or compare to others.
K	Aesthetics	Naming movements of people or things in the environment helps describe their aesthetic dimensions.
K	Aesthetics	Variations of the same movement in space create a simple movement pattern.
K	Aesthetics	The practice of movement skills helps develop an understanding of excellent movement.
K	Aesthetics	People gain aesthetic awareness by seeing, hearing, touching, smelling, and tasting.
K	Biomechanics	More force must be applied to move heavy objects than light objects.
K	Biomechanics	Muscles move the body.
K	Biomechanics	Lowering the body's center of gravity (bending the knees), widening the base of support (stance) , and leaning away from any force increases the ability to maintain balance (stability).
K	Biomechanics	The faster a ball is thrown or kicked, the farther it tends to go.
K	Biomechanics	It is easier to float in water while holding a big breath.
K	Biomechanics	When lifting or carrying something, it is important to hold it close to your body.
K	Exercise Physiology	Moderate physical activity contributes to a healthy body.
K	Exercise Physiology	Moderate physical exercising makes the heart beat faster and the lungs work harder.
K	Exercise Physiology	Every activity in life requires movement.
K	Exercise Physiology	Exercising muscles makes them stronger.
K	Exercise Physiology	Food provides the body with energy for daily life and vigorous physical activity.
K	Historical Perspectives	The Olympic Games began a long time ago.

K	Historical Perspectives	Throughout history, people have exercised.
K	Historical Perspectives	Games that are played at school today may have looked different long ago.
K	Historical Perspectives	Physical education is good for people, and that is why it is taught in school.
K	Motor Development	Getting better at motor skills requires lots of practice.
K	Motor Development	People may differ physically, even though they are the same age.
K	Motor Development	People may differ cognitively even though they are the same age.
K	Motor Development	Regular participation in physical activities is good for people of all ages
K	Motor Learning	Practice and experience makes you better at motor skills.
K	Motor Learning	You are good at a motor skill when you perform the skills with the correct cues.
K	Motor Learning	When you first begin to learn a motor skill you will not be good at it.
K	Motor Learning	Self-assessment of how good you are at learning a motor skill should be considered in terms of your improvement.
K	Motor Learning	The more practice the more learning.
K	Motor Learning	Some skills are used in many different activities (e.g., throwing).
K	Sociology	Learning how the body moves helps people feel positively about themselves.
K	Sociology	Practice and positive self-talk makes people feel pleased.
K	Sociology	Students learn best by doing and watching a model of the movement form.
K	Sociology	Including everyone in activity makes learning fun for everyone.
K	Sociology	Using caring words and actions makes everyone feel good.
K	Sociology	All of your actions are choices.
K	Sociology	It is OK to make mistakes.
2	Aesthetics	The size of an object influences people's aesthetic response to it.
2	Aesthetics	Terms such as level, direction, range of personal space, and pathway, identify how one moves in space.

2	Aesthetics	Commonly used forms of games utilize symmetric to asymmetric formations and movement patterns.
2	Aesthetics	Watching others in an activity develops an understanding of execellent movement.
2	Aesthetics	Special beautiful moments give sudden aesthetic pleasure.
2	Biomechanics	Force can cause both motion and change in shape of the body acted upon.
2	Biomechanics	Muscles move the body by producing force.
2	Biomechanics	Muscles act by pulling on the bones to which they are attached.
2	Biomechanics	Faster movement produces greater force.
2	Biomechanics	The greater the angle at which a ball is thrown or kicked, the higher the projectile travels.
2	Biomechanics	It is harder to push heavier objects than lighter objects across a table or floor surface.
2	Biomechanics	When lifting something, it is important to bend your knees.
2	Biomechanics	Giving with the force gradually reduces its speed.
2	Exercise Physiology	Cardio-respiratory endurance; muscular strength, endurance, and flexibility; and body composition are the major components of health-related fitness.
2	Exercise Physiology	Vigorous activities that make the heart beat faster also make the heart stronger.
2	Exercise Physiology	A coordinated system of bones, joints, and muscles moves the body
2	Exercise Physiology	Exercising muscles in many activities (such as jumping rope, playing tag, shooting baskets) makes them stronger in different ways.
2	Exercise Physiology	Muscles need safe stretching to be ready to exercise.
2	Exercise Physiology	Breads, crackers, and muffins made of whole grain supply better sources of energy than those made with only refined white flour and lots of sugar.

2	Historical Perspectives	Summer Olympics are now held during the summer every four years.
2	Historical Perspectives	Winter Olympics are now held during the winter every four years.
2	Historical Perspectives	Throughout history, there have been many reasons why people exercise.
2	Historical Perspectives	There are many reasons why games change.
2	Historical Perspectives	The local climate influences the kinds of physical activity in which people participate.
2	Historical Perspectives	Physical education looked different long ago.
2	Historical Perspectives	There is a difference between someone who pursues a single sport (athlete) and someone who wants to stay healthy by becoming physically educated.
2	Motor Development	Change in motor skills occurs gradually over many years
2	Motor Development	Bigger, stronger people tend to perform physical skills better.
2	Motor Development	People may understand instructions for performing motor skills differently.
2	Motor Development	Learning many different motor skills gives people more choices for movement as they grow older.
2	Motor Learning	Knowing how to perform a skill will help you learn that skill.
2	Motor Learning	Two or more skills (serial) are combined correctly when they flow smoothly from one skill to another without any breaks (e.g., running into a jump).
2	Motor Learning	Continuous skills (same skill performed over and over again) need to be modified when more than one is performed in a row.
2	Motor Learning	You can do a motor skill more consistently when you get good at it.
2	Motor Learning	Feedback provides information on your performance and can enhance the quality of practice.
2	Motor Learning	External feedback that informs the learner on how to improve performance is usually the best kind of feedback.
2	Motor Learning	Striking with implements has many similarities to striking with your hand.

2	Sociology	Moving with personal control gives people a sense of self, purpose, and control.
2	Sociology	Exploring a variety of movement skills and concepts enables people to develop motor skills and identify movements and activities they do and do not enjoy.
2	Sociology	Encourage students to use imagery to think and recreate why a movement or social interaction was successful.
2	Sociology	Boys and girls can learn to be partners and respect each other.
2	Sociology	Listening means that you can say what you heard and ask questions to make sure you understand.
2	Sociology	Problem solving is a process that involves thinking about more than one possible way to do something and choose the one that you think will work the best.
4	Aesthetics	The rhythm of a movement along with meter and tempo effects its outcome; rhythm organizes movement.
4	Aesthetics	Combinations of locomotor movements in space and time create movement patterns.
4	Aesthetics	Preferences for movement qualities influence how the aesthetic experience is judged
4	Aesthetics	Varying distances between objects create differing aesthetic relationships among them.
4	Aesthetics	Paying attention to aesthetic experience requires appreciative concentration and personal commitment.
4	Biomechanics	For every action there is an equal and opposite reaction.
4	Biomechanics	Large muscles generate more force than smaller muscles.
4	Biomechanics	Increasing the size, number, or speed of moving body segments tends to increase the force generated. Movement speed and the number of moving body segments should be adjusted in accordance with the force requirements of the activity.

4	Biomechanics	The speed and angle of an object when it is released, or a person takeoff, determine the flight path.
4	Biomechanics	Increases in weight or the roughness of the surfaces in contact increase the friction between a moving body and the surface underneath it.
4	Biomechanics	When lifting something, it is important to bend your knees and not let your back slump.
4	Biomechanics	Raising the body's center of gravity, narrowing the base of support, and leaning in the direction of movement allows for a quicker start.
4	Exercise Physiology	Aerobic exercise provides people with many personal benefits—both physical and mental.
4	Exercise Physiology	People inherit their ligament, tendon, and bone structure.
4	Exercise Physiology	Regular monitoring of progress in gaining muscular strength, endurance, and flexibility, demonstrates the benefits of engaging in and adding variety to a fitness program.
4	Exercise Physiology	Body composition refers to lean and fat components of the human body; both affect and are affected by vigorous physical activity.
4	Exercise Physiology	Carbohydrates, proteins, and fats should be eaten every day.
4	Exercise Physiology	Aerobic activity should be performed for at least 15 to 20 minutes three times per week.
4	Historical Perspectives	New venues (e.g., gymnasiums, pools) are built by the country hosting the Olympics.
4	Historical Perspectives	Various cultures have had an impact on sports and leisure-time recreational activities throughout the local area.
4	Historical Perspectives	Many of today's physical activities, dances, and sports had their beginnings in ritual and religious activities.
4	Historical Perspectives	Many states have laws governing physical education instruction in both elementary and high school.
4	Historical Perspectives	There are many traditions associated with the Olympics Games.

4	Historical Perspectives	Throughout history, there have been many reasons why people exercise, including religious, military, and health.
4	Historical Perspectives	Throughout history, people have performed exercises that are potentially harmful.
4	Motor Development	Fundamental skills are the building blocks of more complex actions such as sport–specific skills
4	Motor Development	Equipment should be selected based on an individual's physical development.
4	Motor Development	Cognitive abilities influence complex skill performance.
4	Motor Development	Older adults have a difficult time performing two tasks simultaneously.
4	Motor Development	More advanced form usually leads to more successful results.
4	Motor Development	There are virtually no differences between boys and girls in body proportions throughout childhood.
4	Motor Learning	You get better at many motor skills as you get bigger and stronger.
4	Motor Learning	If you can identify the cues for a skill you are more likely to perform it correctly.
4	Motor Learning	Good performance of open skills requires a performer to adapt performance to an environment (e.g., modifying a forward roll to meet the size of a mat or performance with a partner).
4	Motor Learning	You can begin to concentrate on other parts of performance after you get some consistency in the skill itself (e.g., dribble by yourself before you have a defender).
4	Motor Learning	Where you look during performance has a lot to do with skillfulness. Visual focus during a skill is an important aspect of skill.
4	Motor Learning	Throwing a large ball has some characteristics that are similar to throwing a small ball and some that are different.
4	Sociology	Safe and appropriate physical activity helps people feel secure.
4	Sociology	Working in small groups with peers enables students to practice giving appropriate feedback, verbal persuasion, and encouragement.

4	Sociology	Respecting others shows a willingness to consider their thoughts and feelings during participation in games, activities, and sports.
4	Sociology	Using courtesy and complimenting in all games and activities makes the activities successful for everyone.
4	Sociology	Collaboration happens when you are working together with someone or a team for different results, such as sharing equipment or space to make up separate games.
4	Sociology	Positive self-talk increases self-confidence and one's ability to perform physical activities.
6	Aesthetics	People's bodies combine different shapes and kinds of shapes.
6	Aesthetics	Movement qualities, or many ways of using energy, whether regular or irregular contribute to the aesthetic dimension of physical activity.
6	Aesthetics	The combination of the basic elements of movement (shape, motion, time, space, energy, and flow) create regular or irregular movement patterns.
6	Aesthetics	Aesthetic guidelines for movement activity make meeting the goals of that activity easier.
6	Aesthetics	Shared receptive and generous feelings contribute to seeing and experiencing beautiful action.
6	Biomechanics	Spin occurs when a force is applied anywhere on the object except through the center of gravity.
6	Biomechanics	Muscles are arranged in functional pairs that can move our body segments in opposite directions.
6	Biomechanics	When we tense both muscles in a functional pair equally, no body motion occurs.
6	Biomechanics	The larger the range of motion the greater the potential for angular velocity and force production.
6	Biomechanics	Longer or heavier bats and clubs tend to produce more force than shorter or lighter ones.

6	Biomechanics	The greater the height from which something is projected the longer it tends to remain in the air.
6	Biomechanics	Increases in contact force or the roughness of the surfaces in contact produce more friction between the two objects in contact.
6	Biomechanics	Gravity causes objects dropped from the same height to fall at the same speed (neglecting air resistance).
6	Biomechanics	Perform lifts and exercises in a slow and controlled fashion.
6	Biomechanics	The longer the contact and the greater the area of absorption of a force, the less chance of injury.
6	Exercise Physiology	Personal preferences, skills, and talents influence students' choices, successes, and pleasure when engaging in vigorous physical activity.
6	Exercise Physiology	The principles of cardio-respiratory fitness program include frequency, intensity, time, and type (FITT).
6	Exercise Physiology	Most of the largest and strongest muscles of the body—the gluteal, hamstring group, and calf muscles—are located in the back lower half of the skeleton to help hold it up.
6	Exercise Physiology	For vigorous physical activity, proper stretching exercises serve to warm up and cool down muscles and maintain their contracting function.
6	Exercise Physiology	Performing isotonic, isometric, or isokinetic exercises every other day improves muscular strength.
6	Exercise Physiology	Regular monitoring of changes in body composition demonstrates the benefits of engaging in a fitness program.
6	Exercise Physiology	Inherited, familial, and cultural factors influence the size and shape of peoples' bodies.
6	Exercise Physiology	Because muscles only contract, they are typically found in functional pairs.
6	Exercise Physiology	The principles of muscle strength, endurance, and flexibility (adequate stretch) include overload, individual differences, progression, regularity, and specificity.

6	Historical Perspectives	The first Ancient Olylmpics had only one event (stade), but in subsequent years new events were added (i.e., pentathlon, wrestling, chariot races, boxing).
6	Historical Perspectives	The ancient Olympics were considered both a sport and a religious festival.
6	Historical Perspectives	Each of Ancient Civilizations (China, India, Near East, Greeks, and Romans) had a different reasons for participating in exercise.
6	Historical Perspectives	The purpose of games, dance, and sport in the ancient world was to maintain the culture, train for combat, perform religious ceremonies, and to respond to a need for physical activity.
6	Historical Perspectives	During Medieval times, jesters, squires, and knights participated in different activities; the knights and squires were preparing for combat while the jesters were entertainers.
6	Historical Perspectives	In Ancient Athens, music and gymnastics were the two curricular foci.
6	Historical Perspectives	During the Dark and Middle Ages, fitness was a requirement for survival.
6	Historical Perspectives	During the Renaissance, there was a renewed interest in studying the human body and related health issues.
6	Historical Perspectives	During the dark and middle ages, physical education was virtually nonexistent.
6	Motor Development	Experience in a variety of movement settings improves motor performance.
6	Motor Development	Some children begin puberty earlier than others, resulting in dramatic physical differences between same-aged individuals.
6	Motor Development	During the adolescent growth spurt, more time may be necessary to adjust motor patterns to rapidly changing body dimensions and physical attributes.
6	Motor Development	Pre-adolescents may need concrete instruction regarding how to perform specific skills or playing strategies.
6	Motor Development	Regular participation in physical activity can help delay or minimize effects of age-related diseases.
6	Motor Learning	Different skills require different physical abilities that can be developed through training programs.

6	Motor Learning	Game tactics are a decision of what to do in a competitive situation. Some tactics are correct but executed poorly.
6	Motor Learning	The selection of a game tactic is dependent on what your teammates and opponents do in a game.
6	Motor Learning	Movement sequences, routines, and combinations of skills should have as their goal the smooth flow from one movement to another. Preparation for a subsequent movement occurs in the previous movement.
6	Motor Learning	In the last stage of learning a motor skill the skill becomes automatic.
6	Motor Learning	Good practice will help you move more quickly from one stage to another.
6	Motor Learning	Practice that promotes processing of how to do the skill is better practice.
6	Motor Learning	Skills should be practiced in conditions that are game-like and performance-like as much a possible.
6	Motor Learning	The more closely related one skill is to another the more likely the transfer of learning (e.g., throwing a variety of objects).
6	Sociology	Working productively in cooperative and competitive settings establishes purpose.
6	Sociology	Setting and achieving goals based on personal strengths and weaknesses creates a sense of personal responsibility for one's own learning.
6	Sociology	Achievement is directly related to the effort and motivation put forth.
6	Sociology	Opportunities to practice inclusion of all kinds of differences and similarities in individuals helps your groups/teams to function more effectively.
6	Sociology	Paraphrasing is the ability to restate something that another person said to you, to check for understanding, and to demonstrate that you cared enough to listen well.
6	Sociology	When students have abundant opportunities to alternate leadership roles, give feedback, practice social skills, and contribute to the success of the group, they learn to successfully work with people in any activity.

6	Sociology	Practicing the skills of conflict resolution helps to resolve problems that occur naturally in games, sport, and physical activities.
8	Aesthetics	The size of nonmoving people and distances among them influence aesthetic responses to them.
8	Aesthetics	Space, time, and energy come together in flow ("ongoingness") activities
8	Aesthetics	Aesthetically carried out movement becomes congruent with its goal when people achieve the goal directly, elegantly, and efficiently.
8	Aesthetics	People understand the expressive qualities of movement activities through their kinesthetic sense.
8	Aesthetics	Recognizing and appreciating how all parts of a special physical moment fit together as a whole develops aesthetic perception.
8	Biomechanics	When more than one force acts on a body, the effect on the body is the result of the sum of the sizes and directions of the forces.
8	Biomechanics	Muscles with larger cross-sectional areas can produce more force than smaller muscles.
8	Biomechanics	The longer the distance between a bat, club, or racket's center of rotation and contact point with a ball (radius of rotation) the greater the amount of force that tends to be delivered to the ball. The radius of rotation for a bat or club striking a ball should be adjusted in accordance with the force requirements of the activity.
8	Biomechanics	Extension of the joints of moving body segments increases the radius of rotation for throwing or striking motions.
8	Biomechanics	If air resistance is absent, trajectory (flight path) of a projectile is determined by the initial speed, angle, and height of projection.
8	Biomechanics	The optimum projection angle for maximum projection distance is 45 degrees when projection and landing heights are the same, but less than 45 degrees when projection height is greater than landing height.

8	Biomechanics	Streamlined shapes and smooth surfaces reduce air and water resistance on a moving body.
8	Biomechanics	A ball with top spin rebounds on a lower trajectory and a ball with back spin rebounds on a higher trajectory than the same ball without spin.
8	Biomechanics	Always face the object you are lifting so you do not have to twist or bend to the side.
8	Biomechanics	Both the size of the force and the distance of the force from the center of rotation contribute to torque.
8	Exercise Physiology	Regular vigorous physical activity and proper nutrition contributes to physical and mental health.
8	Exercise Physiology	The FITT guidelines for a cardiorespiratory fitness program include exercising a minimum of 20 to 30 minutes three days per week to a maximum of 50 to 60 minutes every other day, within one's target heart rate range.
8	Exercise Physiology	Flexion, extension, abduction, adduction, and rotation of muscles at their joints provide the body's range of motion.
8	Exercise Physiology	Different synovial joints (nonaxial, uniaxial, pivot, biaxial, and triaxial) have different functions.
8	Exercise Physiology	Hold stretches for major muscle groups for 30 to 60 seconds.
8	Exercise Physiology	The FITT principles of strength training include frequency of training (F), intensity—amount of weight (I), time—sets of repetitions (T), and type of exercise—using body weight, free weights, or weight machines (T).
8	Exercise Physiology	Family, school, community, and commercial information about proper nutrition influence an individual's commitment to his or her physical fitness program.
8	Exercise Physiology	Proper nutrition contributes to physical and mental health while excess sugar, starch, fat, alcohol, and food supplements impede performance of physical activities and can cause permanent harm.

8	Historical Perspectives	The modern Olympics (revived by Pierre de Coubertin and held in Athens, Greece) had its roots in furthering the cause of world peace, highlighting athletes from different parts of the world, and in preparing individuals to become highly-trained athletes.
8	Historical Perspectives	The late 1800s marked a time when researchers studied strength training and fitness testing.
8	Historical Perspectives	As leisure time increased, so did the interest in playing and watching sports.
8	Historical Perspectives	The Industrial Revolution was a catalyst for the development of playground and recreational facilities.
8	Historical Perspectives	Many American sports and games have their roots in other countries; this accounts for many of the similarities between sports in different cultures.
8	Historical Perspectives	Team sports emerged after the Civil War.
8	Historical Perspectives	During the nineteenth century, three major programs (English sports and games, German gymnastics, and Swedish calisthenics) influenced American physical education.
8	Historical Perspectives	Public schools begin to include physical education programs in the 1850s.
8	Historical Perspectives	Medicine was very influential on early physical education.
8	Historical Perspectives	Colleges and universities began training physical educators in the late 1800s.
8	Motor Development	People pass through developmental sequences at different speeds.
8	Motor Development	Physical abilities contribute to one's potential in motor ability and level of participation.
8	Motor Development	Practice with increasingly complex interactions among teammates and opponents can help individuals become better players.
8	Motor Development	A variety of activities is necessary to maintain a high level of function throughout life.
8	Motor Learning	Motor skills that are learned well enough for long-term memory are kept for a long period of time.

8	Motor Learning	Good performance of closed skills should result in practice and performance that is done in the same way each time. Some closed skills are done in different environments and require adaptation.
8	Motor Learning	In the first stage of learning a motor skill you should seek to get a clear idea of how to do the skill and should be able to describe what you should be doing.
8	Motor Learning	In the second stage of learning a motor skill you should work toward consistent performance in more complex environments.
8	Motor Learning	Most skills should be practiced as a whole so that you maintain the rhythm of the skill. If you practice parts they should not be practiced for too long a period of time before they are put back in the whole.
8	Motor Learning	There is a speed-accuracy trade off in many striking/throwing skills.
8	Motor Learning	Transfer from practice to the game is subject to the same identical element issues as transfer from skill to skill.
8	Sociology	Consistent use of short-term goals and self-evaluation when learning a new skill or activity makes it easier for people to recognize and appreciate the things that they are doing well.
8	Sociology	Relaxation techniques help relieve stress, improve attention and focus, and assist with impulse and anger control.
8	Sociology	Practicing the use of empathy during physical activity with others will be especially helpful in developing effective communication skills.
8	Sociology	Providing specific feedback will enable you to develop communication skills, increase content knowledge, and improve oral speaking skills.
8	Sociology	Identifying behaviors that are supportive and inclusive of others in physical activity builds people's sense of self.
8	Sociology	Understanding of the brain (brain stem, limbic system, and neo-cortex) can help people understand why they react as they do during interactions with others.

8	Sociology	Moral and ethical interactions with others in physical activity include holding one's self accountable to rules and predetermined standards of behavior that affect the ability of all students to be successful.
10	Aesthetics	Identifying and describing the aesthetic features of nonmoving objects and people facilitates understanding their complexity.
10	Aesthetics	Shape, motion, time, space, energy, and flow interact differently across various movement activities.
10	Aesthetics	Observing others achieve aesthetic congruence of movement with its goal sharpens observation skills and facilitates self-observation.
10	Aesthetics	Individual aesthetic criteria for excellence develop from personal, academic, and professional sources.
10	Aesthetics	Focusing on the unity of all the factors in a beautiful physical event develops aesthetic sensitivity.
10	Biomechanics	A body's motion is determined by the net forces and torques acting upon it.
10	Biomechanics	Muscle forces and resistance forces combine to produce joint torque.
10	Biomechanics	Changing the moment arms of the involved muscles or the resistance forces can alter the difficulty of an exercise.
10	Biomechanics	Positioning moving body segments close to the major joint center of rotation facilitates faster movement.
10	Biomechanics	Forces applied to a stationary object must overcome the mass of the object, so heavier people tend to be better at activities involving stability and shorter people tend to be better at activities involving body rotation.
10	Biomechanics	Projection speed is usually the most important factor in projecting for maximum horizontal distance.
10	Biomechanics	The shape of a projectile's trajectory is symmetrical in the absence of air resistance.
10	Biomechanics	Increasing relative projection height or projection angle tends to increase flight time.

10	Biomechanics	Whether a body sinks or floats depends on whether the weight of the volume of water displaced by the body is greater or less than body weight.
10	Biomechanics	Lift is a force produced by a foil shape or spin that alters the path of a body moving through air or water.
10	Biomechanics	Always use a spotter when exercising with heavy free weights.
10	Exercise Physiology	Physical, emotional, and social growth influence individual needs and results of a regular physical fitness program.
10	Exercise Physiology	Muscles, joints, and range of motion of the arms and legs are similar.
10	Exercise Physiology	Bouncing, swinging, over-stretching, strengthening fast, locking, over-bending, arching, and clicking the joints are harmful aspects of some exercises.
10	Exercise Physiology	Specific dangerous exercises that people should avoid include: neck circles, hurdler's stretch, deep knee bends, back arching, and double leg lifts.
10	Exercise Physiology	Body composition and nutritional needs interact and change as students grow, engage in different physical activities, increase their fitness levels, and commit to ongoing after-school obligations.
10	Exercise Physiology	Maintaining and benefiting from a regular physical fitness program requires preparation, dedication, and updated information.
10	Historical Perspectives	The country hosting the Olympics receives many benefits.
10	Historical Perspectives	Fitness tests are currently conducted in most schools and are changed regularly based on research findings.
10	Historical Perspectives	The results of early fitness tests such as the Kraus-Weber indicated a need to focus on the fitness of American youth.
10	Historical Perspectives	There is currently an emphasis on health-related fitness and moderate physical activity directed towards health enhancement.
10	Historical Perspectives	Understanding the purpose and history of sport helps people to make informed decisions regarding education and recreation.

10	Historical Perspectives	Laws such as Title IX and Section 504 of the Rehabilitation Act have had an impact on who can participate in sports and physical education.
10	Historical Perspectives	Sports rules are influenced by societal events; as is most noticeable in women's sports.
10	Historical Perspectives	Physical education has emphasized different aspects (e.g., calisthenics, marching, recreation activities, fitness, movement, lifetime sports, social activities) of physical education at different times in the last 100 years.
10	Historical Perspectives	During war times, fitness is emphasized in physical education programs.
10	Historical Perspectives	The poor fitness levels of the WWI and WWII draftees heightened the public's awareness of the need for exercise programs.
10	Historical Perspectives	Women pioneers in athletics have paved the way for today's female athletes.
10	Historical Perspectives	The meaning of amateur status in the Olympics has changed over the years.
10	Motor Development	There is a specific sequence of changes that people pass through to become better movers.
10	Motor Development	Physical activity patterns typically change throughout the life span.
10	Motor Development	As adolescents mature, they become capable of more advanced cognitive and motor skills.
10	Motor Development	Females who participate in vigorous, regular physical activity can lessen the effects of age-related diseases.
10	Motor Learning	Short-term improvement in motor skills can be achieved without learning if the practice isn't long enough.
10	Motor Learning	Open skills are performed in unpredictable and unstable environments and should be practiced in variable conditions.
10	Motor Learning	In the third stage of learning a motor skill, your responses should be automatic. Difficult motor skills never reach 100 percent reliability
10	Motor Learning	Distributed practice is better than massed practice.

10	Motor Learning	You can increase your performance by improving your physical and motor abilities that play a major role in the skill to be learned.
10	Motor Learning	Knowing how one skill is the same and different from another skill will facilitate transfer from one skill to another.
10	Sociology	Clarity and consistency in creating and following game rules gives people a sense of security as well as purpose and competence.
10	Sociology	Pursuing multicultural and new activities and sports both alone and with others allows people occasions to use self encouragement and positive self-talk while discovering more about their own abilities.
10	Sociology	An increasing willingness to learn about others can include exploration of and participation in cultural and ethnic dances, games, and activities.
10	Sociology	Integrity is the ability to adhere to a strict moral code with others and it fosters cooperative efforts.
10	Sociology	Keeping the importance of winning and losing in perspective during physical activities and sports helps maintain positive feelings about self and others.
10	Sociology	Participating and succeeding in challenging and culturally diverse physical activities develops positive attitudes, openness, and a sense of accomplishment.
10	Sociology	Imitation of positive interactions with others, asking for feedback, and formulating goals enhances self-confidence and self-actualization.
10	Sociology	Empathy enhances effective communication skills.
10	Sociology	Frequent self-reflection about interaction skills creates deeper understanding and development of those skills.
12	Aesthetics	The skillful execution of movement and representation of that movement experience in a variety of ways (words, pictures, poetry, video, or sculpture) can depict understanding of aesthetic features.

12	Aesthetics	Artists and photographers utilize the components of movement: shape, motion, time, space, energy, and flow in their different renditions of movement activities.
12	Aesthetics	Games and folk dances from different areas in the United States and other countries illustrate the movement patterns and aesthetic preferences of those regions.
12	Aesthetics	Aesthetic criteria can describe progress toward achieving physical competency.
12	Aesthetics	Understanding aesthetic experience in physical activities enhances pleasure for participants and observers.
12	Biomechanics	A force's magnitude and moment arm contribute equally to the torque generated by the force at the body's center of rotation.
12	Biomechanics	Equilibrium is a state of balanced forces and torque (a body in equilibrium can be stationary or moving at a constant speed in a given direction).
12	Biomechanics	Forcefully stretching a muscle immediately before a concentric contraction increases the force of that contraction.
12	Biomechanics	Movement speed, range of motion, joint extension, and the number of moving body segments should be adjusted in accordance with the force requirements of the activity.
12	Biomechanics	Body anthropometry can make skillful performance of some motor skills easier or harder. Equipment should be selected to match the anthropometric characteristics of the user.
12	Biomechanics	When projection and landing heights are equal, a projectile's landing speed is the same as its projection speed.
12	Biomechanics	There are trade-offs among optimum projection speed, angle, and height when projecting for maximum horizontal distance when the human body is either applying force to a projectile or serving as the projectile.
12	Biomechanics	Fluid forces increase with the density and viscosity of the fluid.

12	Biomechanics	Buoyancy increases with the volume of the submerged body.
12	Biomechanics	Perform exercises in a slow and controlled fashion unless training for muscular power development.
12	Biomechanics	To minimize spinal load when lifting, avoid bending or twisting, keep the trunk erect, and hold the load close to the body.
12	Biomechanics	Friction is reduced by the presence of a layer of fluid between two surfaces in contact.
12	Exercise Physiology	Family, school, and community attitudes toward vigorous physical activity influence an individual's commitment to that fitness program.
12	Exercise Physiology	Regular aerobic activity releases endorphins that allow people to enjoy and sustain commitment to their fitness programs.
12	Exercise Physiology	People need to adjust their fitness activity as they mature and age.
12	Exercise Physiology	Neurons enable the brain to send and receive signals to and from the muscles and organs.
12	Exercise Physiology	Design strength-training programs for individuals based on body composition, current strength, and the specific requirements of the activity.
12	Exercise Physiology	Setting goals and recording progress in a stretching and strengthening program enable students to overcome barriers to continued participation.
12	Exercise Physiology	Nutritional and exercise needs change and people must adapt them to various stages of life.
12	Exercise Physiology	Health experts can treat the potentially life-threatening eating disorders, such as anorexia nervosa and bulimia.
12	Historical Perspectives	There have been many political events (i.e.,. war in 1916, 1940, 1944; boycotts in 1956, 1976, 1980, 1984; terrorism in 1972; racial conflicts in 1936, 1968) that have affected the Olympics.
12	Historical Perspectives	The host country also may choose one demonstration sport for inclusion in the Olympics.

12	Historical Perspectives	Research has improved the way people exercise and the equipment they use.
12	Historical Perspectives	Every game and sport we play has a history.
12	Historical Perspectives	The popularity of most sports in different countries can be linked to the geographic conditions or the influence of immigrants or settlers to the area.
12	Historical Perspectives	Understanding the purpose and history of sport around the world helps people to better understand different cultures and appreciate the contributions of different groups of people.
12	Historical Perspectives	In 1977, Public Law 94-142 stated that all children from ages 3 to 21 with a handicapping condition had the right to receive specialized physical education instruction.
12	Historical Perspectives	There are programs and careers that are related to the physical activities and the sports in the United States and around the world
12	Historical Perspectives	After a war is fought and won, there is a tendency for a society to exercise less.
12	Motor Development	Individuals who have had more practice and experience will have better skills than individuals with less practice and experience. The first individual to master step one of a skill may not be the first to master step three.
12	Motor Development	Training (recommended after pubertal growth spurt) can help emphasize physical attributes.
12	Motor Development	Increased activity levels reduce the slowing of reaction time in the elderly.
12	Motor Development	Accumulating at least 30 minutes of activity most days of the week can improve self-esteem, decrease stress, anxiety, and depression, and improve health
12	Motor Learning	As you move into adulthood, you will want to learn different motor skills.
12	Motor Learning	Learning is assessed after a break between practice and testing (retention).
12	Motor Learning	Good practice plans spend the majority of practice working to get better at combining and adapting skills.

12	Motor Learning	Mental practice can increase performance particularly at higher skill levels.
12	Motor Learning	Although there is no such thing as a general motor ability, there is a set of perceptual motor abilities related to performance of different motor skills that may impose limits on individual performance.
12	Sociology	Community service and cross-age projects develop sense of purpose and belonging as well as competence for physical activity.
12	Sociology	Developing numerous strategies for preparing to succeed in movement challenges (visualization, positive self-talk, or relaxation exercises) can help people become successful in any activity.
12	Sociology	Levels of self-efficacy may predict whether or not individuals function independently to pursue physical activity outside of high school.
12	Sociology	Community service projects involving physical activity provide opportunities to learn about the needs of others in a real life, meaningful way while also providing the opportunity to practice social skills.
12	Sociology	Constructive communication (active listening, empathy, paraphrasing, questioning, and clarifying) builds shared understanding and an appreciation of diverse points of view.
12	Sociology	Decisions about pursuing regular physical activity will be determined by a person's combined knowledge, experience and attitude about a wide variety of physical activities.
12	Sociology	Ethical decision making involves the attainment of a number of learned social skills, including empathy, respect for other persons/property, honesty, integrity, and self discipline.
12	Sociology	Distributed leadership allows the development of a sense of responsibility for self and others and the chance to be perceived as a meaningful member of the group.

Index

A

AAHPERD. *See* American Alliance for Health,
Physical Education, Recreation, and Dance
abdominal muscles, 177–79
accent
definition, 327
acceptance
definition, 254
accuracy
vs. speed, 49–50, 53
achievement motivation
stages of, 260
activities of daily living (ADLs), 95
activity-based curriculum, 354, 360, 371, 375
adenosine Triphosphate (ATP), 185, 187
aerobic
definition, 144
aerobic activity, 149–50
concepts, principles for grade levels, 154–55
fitness testing, 151
heart rate, 151–52
aerobic exercise
benefits, 147–48
over exercise, 151–52
aesthetic experience, 309–10
concepts, principles, 317–18
for grade 2, 388–89
for grade 4, 391
for grade 6, 394
for grade 8, 398
for grade 10, 402
for grade 12, 405–6
for kindergarten, 387
criteria, 344–45
dispositional atmosphere, 316
guidelines for teachers, students, 315–16
importance of, 311
instant access, 315
instruction example
early elementary, 313
high school, 314
middle school, 313
integrating into curriculum, 346–50
learning to respond to, 313–16
movement, 325–29
concepts, principles for grade levels, 330–31
energy and shape, 333
instruction examples, 338, 339
movement patterns
concepts, principles for grade levels, 340–41
high school instruction example, 334
multiconnectedness, 316
and National Standards, 311–12
personal engagement, 316
responding to, 347–48
sensory anchoring, 315
and skiing, 314
standards, 342–44
guidelines for teachers, students, 346–50
themes, 312–13
wide-spectrum cognition, 316
aesthetics
assessing student learning, 350–51
and environment, 318, 321–22
concepts, principles for grade levels, 324–25
instruction examples, 322, 323
shapes, 319, 320
themes, 347–49
affective domain, 293
affiliation/belongingness, 254
definition, 250
aging
and falls, 95–96
and motor performance, 93–98
aisthetikos
definition, 309
alignment
definition, 19
amateurism
and Olympics, 210
amenorrhea, 76
American Alliance for Health, Physical Education,
Recreation, and Dance (AAHPERD), 219
amino acids, 188
anaerobic, 150
anatomy, 157–58
elementary school instruction example, 158
Andry, Nicholas, 215–16
anorexia nervosa, 192
anthropometrics
definition, 235
anthropometry, 125

and force, 122–23
appreciation
    definition, 254
archery, 224
arching, 176
arm swings, 177
arousal level, 50–51
asanas, 213
ascesis, 213
assessing student learning
    in aesthetics, 350–51
    in biomechanics, 138–40
    in exercise physiology, 198–200
    in historical perspectives, 239–40
    in motor development, 100–2
    in motor learning, 60–63
assessment
    definition, 11
assessment tools, 23–25. *See also under
    names of tools*
associative stage (Stage 2), 42
assymetric
    definition, 334
    example, 335, 336
ATP. *See* adenosine triphosphate
attention. *See* arousal level
authentic assessment
    definition, 23
automatic stage (Stage 3), 42–43
autonomous competence stage, 260

B
back, lower
    and exercise, 135–36
back bends, 178
balance, 50, 94
ballistic stretching, 175, 219
baseball, 118–19
Basedow, John Bernhard, 233
Basic Stuff in Action, 360
Basic Stuff Project, 4
basketball, 228
    instructional unit, 375–79, 377
Basmajian, John, 215
Beecher, Catherine, 234
bicycling, 150
biomechanics. *See also* force; projectiles
    assessing student learning, 138–40
    concepts, principles
        for grade 2, 389
        for grade 4, 391–92
        for grade 6, 394–95
        for grade 8, 398–99
        for grade 10, 402–3
        for grade 12, 406–7

for kindergarten, 387
    definition, 107–8
    external forces, 128–32
    importance of, 108
    integrating into curriculum, 138
    and National Standards, 108–9
    safety concerns, 134–36
    themes, 109
blocked practice, 47, 48
body composition, 80–82, 191–93
    concepts, principles for grade levels,
        82–83
    and metabolism, 185–91
    middle school instruction example, 186
body fat, 189, 191
body mass
    and force, 122
body proportion
    changes in, 73
    and motor development, 73–74
bone loss. *See* osteoporosis
boule, 226
bouncing, 175
boxing, 224
Brooks, William Penny, 208
buoyancy, 129, 134
Bush, George W., 9

C
calf muscles, 158, 164, 173, 180
calories, 190, 191
    definition, 189
cancer, 82, 143
carbohydrates, 188
cardio
    definition, 144
cardiorespiratory development, 79–80
cardiorespiratory program
    factors, 145–47
    instruction example,
        elementary school, 145
        high school, 145
cardiorespiratory training, 150–52
cardiovascular disease, 7–8
Carlos, John, 209
carrying
    biomechanics and safety, 134–35
celebration, 277
Center for Disease Control and Prevention
    (CDC)
    reports, 12–13
center of gravity
    definition, 111
center of rotation
    definition, 113

challenge
    definition, 257
checking for understanding, 23
    in exercise physiology, 198
    in historical perspectives, 239
    for motor learning, 60–61
checklists
    to assess social psychology, 300
Cheyne, George, 215
cholesterol, 189
circuit training, 152
circular reaction, 86
clarifying
    definition, 278
closed skills, 37–38, 41
cognitive development
    concepts, principles for grade levels,
        92–93
    concrete state, 88–89
    information processing, 90
    information retrieval speed, 90–91
    and language skill, 87
    and motor development, 84–85
    Piaget stages of, 85
    preoperational stage, 87–88
    sensorimotor stage, 85–87
cognitive stage (Stage 1), 42
collaboration, 288
competence, 254
    definition, 250
competition, 282
    and moral development, 285
concentric, 167
    definition, 116
*Concepts of Physical Education: What Every
    Student Needs to Know*, 15
concrete state, 88–89
conflict resolution, 285–87, 289
    middle school instruction example,
        283–84
constructive communication, 277, 280
Content standards. *See* National Standards
continuous skills, 34, 39, 40
contrast
    definition, 314
cool-down, 148
Cooper, Kenneth, 147, 149
Cooper Institute, 199
cooperation unit, 371–72
cooperative groups
    definition, 282
cooperative learning, 294, 295, 296–97
coordination, 121–22
criteria
    definition, 25

crunches, 178, 179
Csikszentmihalyi, Mihaly, 193
Cureton, Thomas K., 218

D
Da Feltre, Vittorino, 232
da Vinci, Leonardo, 214
debriefing questions, 367
de Coubertin, Pierre, 208–9
developmental perspective, 66
developmental sequence, 68
Dewey, John, 222
diabetes, 144, 147
discrete skills, 34, 38
discus, 125, 132
disordered eating, 76
dispositional atmosphere, 316
Dissanayake, Ellen, 313
distributed leadership, 294
distributed practice, 47, 54
diversity, 273–75
    concepts, principles for grade levels,
        276–77
    definition, 254
    high school instruction example, 274
drag
    definition, 131
dynamism
    definition, 331

E
eating habits, 188, 190–91. *See also*
    nutrition
eccentric, 167
    definition, 116
education
    future trends, 10–12
effort, 328, 329
Eisenhower, Dwight, 218
empathy, 279
encouragement, 262–63
Enlightenment, 216
environment, aesthetic features
    concepts, principles for grade levels,
        324–25
    instruction example
        elementary school, 322, 323
        high school, 322, 323
    shapes, 319, 320, 321
environment, aesthetic features environ-
    ment, 318, 321–22
equilibrium, 112–13
ergogenics, 193
ethical skills, 281

ethics, 281, 289. *See also* moral development
exercise. *See also* physical activity
  in 17th, 18th centuries, 215–16
  in 19th, 20th, 21st centuries, 216
  aerobic activity, 149–50
  aerobic testing, 151
  in ancient times, 211
  appropriate clothing, 181
  benefits, 147–48
  biomechanics and safety, 135–36
  cardiorespiratory training, 150–52
  for children, 153
  concepts, principles for grade levels, 137, 154–57
  cool-down, 149
  harmful exercises, 177–80
  and heart rate, 151–52
  history of, 211
  and mental health, 147, 155
  in Middle Ages, 214
  over exercising, 153–54
  during Renaissance, 214–15
  surfaces for, 181
  time, 153
  type, 153
  warm-up, 148
exercise physiology
  assessing student learning, 198–200
  concepts, principles, 163–66
    for grade 2, 389
    for grade 4, 392
    for grade 6, 395
    for grade 8, 399
    for grade 10, 403
    for grade 12, 407
    for kindergarten, 387
  definition, 143
  importance of, 143–44
  integrating into curriculum, 197–98
  and National Standards, 144
  themes, 144

F

falls, 95–96
fats, 188–90
feedback, 50, 51–52, 263
  concepts, principles for grade levels, 52–53, 271
feedback, specific, 279
  definition, 278
Feiring, Jesse, 235–36
Female Athlete Triad, 76, 83
Fit, Healthy, and Ready to Learn: A School Health Policy Guide, 13

fitness testing, 218–19
Fitnessgram, 199
FITT. See frequency, intensity, time, and type
flexibility, 169
  definition, 79
flexor reflex, 171
floatation, 129
flow, 193–94, 329, 330, 332
  middle school instruction example, 332, 333
fluid forces, 134
foil shape, 131
folk dance, 334–35, 341
  instructional unit, 369
food pyramid, 187
foot racing, 225
football, 132
  knee injuries, 179
force
  and anthropometry, 122–23
  applied to projectiles, 125–27
  body coordination, 121–22
  body's generation of, 114–17
  concepts, principles for grade levels, 113–14, 123–25
  definition, 107
  description, 109
  effects of, 110
  instruction example
    elementary school, 110
    high school, 115
    middle school, 110
  and motor skill requirements, 118–19, 121–23
  muscle length, 117
  net force, 111–12
  radius of rotation, 119, 121
form
  definition, 310
frequency, 150
frequency, intensity, time, and type (FITT), 150, 155–56, 168, 184
friction, 109, 130, 134
Fuchs, Leonard, 215
functional reach, 94
  testing, 95
fundamental movement skills
  definition, 69

G

game tactics, 40–41
Gardner's theory, 20
glucose, 186
gluteal muscles, 158, 164

goal setting, 260–61
  concepts principles for grade levels,
    264–65
good performance, 36–39
  concepts, principles for grade levels,
    40–41
Goos, Karl, 222
gravity, 128–29
  center of, 111
  definition, 110
group projects. *See also* student projects
  for biomechanics, 140
  for social psychology, 299–300
growth. See skeletal development
growth plates, 75
*Guidelines for School and Community
  Programs to Promote Lifelong Physical
  Activity Among Young People*, 12–13
Gulick, Luther, 222
Guts-Muths, Johann Christoph Friedrick,
  232

H
Hall, G. Stanley, 222
hamstrings, 158
handball, 150
head circles, 177
Healthier Us, 9
*Healthy People 2010: Physical Activity and
  Fitness Objectives*, 9
heart disease, 7
heart rate, 151–52
Hegel, George, 216
Herannic Games, 208
heterogeneous grouping, 294
historical perspectives
  in 17th, 18th centuries, 226–27,
    232–33
  in 19th, 20th, 21st centuries, 227–29,
    233–37
  ancient times, 224–25, 231–32
  assessing student learning, 239–40
  basketball, 228
  concepts, principles, 220–21, 229–31,
    237–38
    for grade 2, 390
    for grade 4, 392–93
    for grade 6, 396
    for grade 8, 400
    for grade 10, 403–4
    for grade 12, 407–8
    for kindergarten, 387–88
  definition, 205
  importance of, 206
  integrating into curriculum, 238–39

in Middle Ages, 225–26, 232
middle school instruction example,
  222, 223
and National Standards, 206
North America, 226–27
physical activity, sport, 221–24
physical education, 231–37
during Renaissance, 232
secondary school instruction example,
  207, 211
and sixth-grade curriculum, 358
themes, 206–11
Hitchcock, Edward, 235
Hitler, Adolph, 209
Hoffman, Friederich, 215
hormone replacement therapy (HRT), 77
human genome, 7
hurdler's stretch, 180
hypertrophy
  definition, 77
hypothetical deductive reasoning, 89–90

I
"I" statements, 286
ice hockey, 229
imagery, 270
  concepts, principles for grade levels,
    270–71
immersed model, 22
immersion (project) approach, 59–60
individual differences, 150
inertia
  definition, 113
injuries
  football, 132
  prevention, 172–76
instant access, 315
integrated model, 22, 360
integrated stage, 260
integrity, 269, 279
*Intelligent Eye, The: Learning To Think by
  Looking at Art*, 315
intensity, 148
interdisciplinary instruction, 20
  immersed model, 22
  integrated model, 22
  sequenced model, 21
  shared model, 21
  themes, 20
  threaded model, 22
  webbed model, 21–22
interdisciplinary model, 361, 362
interpersonal skills, 6
interval training, 152

interviews
  for motor development, 101–2
isokinetic, 168
isometric, 168
  definition, 116
isotonic, 167

J

javelin throwing, 125
joints, 153, 158–61
  locking, 176
  over bending, 176
  synovial joints, 160, 165
jousting, 226
  definition, 225
juggling, 225

K

Kennedy, John F., 219
kinesthetic awareness, 50
knee
  injury prevention, 172–74
knee bends, 179–80
knowledge of performance (KP), 51
knowledge of results (KR), 51
Krau-Weber Test, 218
kyphosis
  definition, 77

L

lacrosse, 69, 227
lateral flexion, 135
leadership, 288, 290
  distributed, 294
learning opportunities. *See also* motor
  learning
  definition, 17
leg lifts, 179
leisure trends, 10
life expectancy, 7, 93
  gender and longevity, 94
lift, 131–32
  definition, 132
lifting
  biomechanics and safety, 134–35
  concepts, principles for grade levels,
    137
  injury prevention, 172
ligaments, 158
line of action
  definition, 112
line of pull, 167
listening, active, 277, 279, 282
  definition, 278
long-term memory, 90

M

Magnus effect, 131–32
  definition, 132
Marx, Karl, 216
Maslow, Abraham, 266
massed practice, 47, 54
McCloy, C. H., 236
melee, 222, 225
memory, 90
mental health
  high school instruction example, 93
  and physical activity, 97, 156
mental practice, 54
Mercurialis, Hieronymus, 215
metabolism, 185–91
meter
  definition, 327
mode, 150
moment arm, 118
  definition, 112
moment of inertia
  definition, 123
Moore, Arabella, 221
moral development
  competition, 285
  and sports, 282–85
morbidity
  definition, 96
Morgan, William, 228
mortality
  definition, 96
motivation, 257, 259
  achievement, stages of, 260
  concepts, principles for grade levels,
    272
motor development, 65–66
  assessing student learning, 100–2
  and body composition, 80–82
  and body proportion, 73–74
  and cardiorespiratory development,
    79–80
  catching, 68–69
  concepts, principles, 70-72
    for grade 2, 390
    for grade 4, 393
    for grade 6, 396
    for grade 8, 400
    for grade 10, 404
    for grade 12, 408
    for kindergarten, 388
  definition, 65
  developmental sequence, 68
  fundamental skills, 69
  importance of, 67

instruction example
  elementary school, 69
  middle school, 72, 84
and muscular development, strength, flexibility, 77–79
and National Standards, 67
performance improvement, 68–69
and physical development, 72
process of, 66
running, 68
and skeletal development, 74–77
themes, 67–69
motor learning
  assessing student learning, 60–63
  balance, 50
  concepts, principles,34–36, 44–45, 355
    for grade 2, 390
    for grade 4, 393
    for grade 6, 396–97
    for grade 8, 400–1
    for grade 10, 404–5
    for grade 12, 408–9
    for kindergarten, 388
  definition, 31
  feedback, 50, 51–52
  and feedback, 47
  good performance, 36–39
  importance, 32
  improving in, 33–35
  instruction example
    elementary school, 47, 56
    secondary school, 43, 46
  integrating into curriculum, 56–57, 57–63
  measuring, 34
  NASPE documents, 17
  National Standards, 32, 32–33
  perceptual motor abilities, 54, 56
  and practice, 46–52
  skill-to-skill transfer, 54, 55
  stages of proficiency, 42–43
  themes, 33
  threading, 58
  webbing, 58, 59
motor performance
  and aging, 93–98
  and stages of cognitive development, 84–90
motor skills
  concepts, principles for grade levels, 34–36
  continuous skills, 34
  discrete skills, 34

requirements, and force, 118–19, 121–23
stages of proficiency, 42–43
movement
  aesthetic components of, 325–29
  concepts, principles for grade levels, 330–31
  effort, 328, 329
  energy and shape, 333
  instruction example
    elementary school, 338
    high school, 339
    middle school, 338
  speed
    and force, 119
movement patterns, 334–39
  concepts, principles for grade levels, 340–41
  high school instruction example, 334
  pathways, 337
  synchronized, 336
Moving into the Future: National Physical Education Standards, 15
multiconnectedness, 316
multiple intelligences, 305
muscle mass, 78
muscle tension, 114–16
muscles, 161–62
  concepts, principles for grade levels, 163–66
  contraction, 163
  functional pairs, 118
  major, 162
muscular strength, 166–67
  concepts, principles for grade levels, 117–18
muscular strength training, 167–68
  concepts, principles for grade levels, 181–85
  guidelines, 168–69
  harmful exercises, 176–80
  high school instruction example, 166
  injury prevention, 172–76
  isokinetic, 168
  isometric, 168
  sets, 178
muscular stretching, 166, 169–72
  concepts, principles for grade levels, 183, 184, 185
  don'ts, 175–76
  harmful exercises, 176–80
  injury prevention, 172–76
  PNF, 171
  training principles, 169

N

Naismith, James, 228
National Association for Sport and
Physical
Education (NASPE)
  assessment publications, 16–17
  curriculum publication, 15
  instructional publication, 16
  learning opportunities documents, 17
  Outcomes Committee, 1
  physical education standards, 2, 4
  Standards and Assessment Committee,
  2
National Standards
  and aesthetic experience, 311–12
  and biomechanics, 108–9
  and exercise physiology, 144
  and historical perspectives, 206
  and local standards, 354
  and motor development, 67
  and motor learning, 32–33
  and social psychology, 248
  Standard 5
  grade-level expectations, 3–4
nationalism
  definition, 233
Native Americans, 224, 227
NBPTS Physical Education Standards, 16
net force, 111–12
neurons, 162–63
notebook assessment
  for motor learning, 61
nutrition. *See also* eating habits
  concepts, principles for grade levels,
  194–97
  food pyramid, 187
  and health, 193–94
  instruction example
  middle school, 186
  elementary school, 185

O

Oberteuffer, Delbert, 236
obesity, 8, 81–82, 189
observation
  to assess aesthetic learning, 350–51
  for exercise physiology, 199
observations, 24
Olympic Festival, 207, 208
Olympics, 207
  concepts, principles for grade levels,
  212
  economic advantages of hosting, 211
  grooming for, 210
  political pressures on, 209

traditions, 209–10
  Wenlock Olympics, 208
  women in, 209
ongoingness, 329
open skills, 38, 39, 40, 41
ossification
  definition, 74
osteoporosis
  definition, 76
outcome orientation, 263
outcome-oriented sports, 284
Outward Bound, 6
over bending, 176
overload, 150, 167
  definition, 151
  muscle, 145, 167, 168, 169, 179, 183
Owens, Jesse, 209
oxygen carrying capacity, 80

P

paidotribe
  definition, 232
pair share
  to assess social psychology, 298
palestra
  definition, 232
pancratium
  definition, 232
pankration
  definition, 208
paraphrasing, 277, 279, 287
  definition, 278
pathways, 333, 337–38
  definition, 326
  example, 337
PECAT. *See* Physical Education Curriculum
Analysis Tool
peer assessment
  for motor learning, 61
peer observation
  in biomechanics, 139
pentathlon
  definition, 208
performance, "good", 36–39
  concepts, principles for grade levels,
  40–41
Perkins, David, 315
personal engagement, 316
physical activity. *See also* exercise
  and aesthetic sensitivity, 347
  among children, 8
  attitudes toward, 12
  concepts, principles for grade levels,
  82–83, 98–99

ethical skills, 281
Healthy People 2010 fitness objectives, 9
high school instruction example, 93
importance of, 81
to improve self-concept, 257–64
and mental health, 97, 156
performed by adolescents and young
adults, 81
and self-actualization, 267
and self-concept, self-esteem, 252–54
social skills, 277–79, 281
sports, recreation programs, 229
Surgeon General's 1996 report, 12
*Physical Activity and Health: A Report of
the Surgeon General*, 7, 144, 220
physical development
and motor development, 72
physical education
assessment publications, 16–17
basketball unit, 375–79, 377
concepts, principles for grade levels,
237–38
connection to academic curriculum,
358–59
connections among concepts, 356–57
content standards, 2, 4
cooperation unit, 371–72
curriculum documents, 14, 15–16
and diversity, 273–75
folk dance unit, 369
health-related fitness unit, 379, 380–81
history of, 231–37
instructional publications, 16
integrated model, 360
interdisciplinary instruction, 20
interdisciplinary model, 361, 362
learning experiences, 361–62
selecting, 353–59
planning instructional units
grades 5–6, 371–75
grades 7–8, 375–79
grades 3–4, 368–71
high school, 379–84
kindergarten, 363–68
programs, teacher- vs. student
centered, 291
and Public Law 94–142, 236
segregated model, 361
separated model, 361
student-centered, definition, 292
Title IX, 236
traveling unit, 364
Physical Education Curriculum Analysis
Tool
(PECAT), 15–16

physical education trends, 12–18
physical inactivity among children, 8
physically educated, 2
assessment, 60, 62–63
and National Standards, 248
twelfth-grade exit goal, 57
Piaget, Jean, 85, 222–23
Plato, 216, 231
PNF. *See* proprioceptive neuromuscular
facilitation
portfolios
to assess social psychology, 300–2
definition, 25
positive interdependence, 294–95
postural alignment, 173
slump position, 174
power
definition, 144
practice
amount of, 49
concepts, principles for grade levels,
52–54
speed vs. accuracy, 49–50
transfer of, 48
types, 47
whole vs. part, 49
preoperational stage, 87–88
Presidential physical fitness programs,
218–19
processing, 297
progression, 151
Project Zero, 315
projectiles, 109
angle and height, 125–26
concepts, principles for grade levels,
127–28
human performance, 126–27
speed, 125
trajectories, 126
*Promoting Better Health for Young People
Through Physical Activity and Sports: A
Report to the President*, 13
prone arch, 178
proprioceptive neuromuscular facilitation
(PNF), 171
proteins, 188
psychology
definition, 246
puberty, 74, 83, 101, 192
Public Law 94–142, 236
public service announcements, 13
purpose, 254
definition, 250

R

radius of rotation, 124
  definition, 121
  and force, 119, 121
  middle school instruction example,
    120, 121
random practice, 48
range of motion, 124, 161
  and force, 119
  middle school instruction example, 120
reaction force
  definition, 113
reaction times, 91
regularity, 152
relaxation techniques, 270
  concepts, principles for grade levels,
    272
  middle school instruction example,
    268–69
research reports, 24
  for motor development, 101
resistance, 167
resistance forces, 129–31
  concepts, principles for grade levels,
    132–33
  and joint movement, 116–17
  middle school instruction example, 130
resistance torque
  and joint movement, 116
resistance training
  free weights, 136
respiratory
  definition, 144
reversibility, 88
rhythm, 327, 328
  definition, 327
role playing, simulations, 24
Rousseau, Jean Jacques, 216
rubrics, 25
  definition, 24
  for social psychology, 298, 299

S

Sargent, Dudley Allen, 235
*School Health Index for Physical Activity
  and Healthy Eating: A Self-Assessment
  and Planning Guide*, 14–15
schools
  future trends, 10–12
secondary memory, 90
Secretary of Labor's Commission on
  Achieving
Necessary Skills (SCANS), 5
security, 252
  definition, 251

segregated model, 361
self-actualization, 267
  concepts, principles for grade levels,
    272
self-assessment, 263–64
  in biomechanics, 139–40
  for motor learning, 61
self-concept, 250. See also self-esteem
  concepts, principles for grade levels,
    254–57
  definition, 246
  elementary school instruction example,
    253
  and physical activity, 252–54
self-determination, 254
  definition, 250
self-efficacy, 267, 269–70
  concepts, principles for grade levels,
    272–73
self-encouragement, 263
self-esteem, 250. *See also* self-concept
  concepts, principles for grade levels,
    254–57
  definition, 246
  and physical activity, 252–54
selfhood, 252, 254
  definition, 251
self-reflection, 287, 289
self-talk, 261–63
  concepts principles for grade levels,
    264–66
  definition, 262
  elementary school instruction example,
    258
sensorimotor stage, 85–87
sensory anchoring, 315
separated model, 361
sequenced model, 21
sequencing, 59
serial skills, 38–39, 40
seriation, 88–89
sets, 178
shared model, 21
short-term memory, 90
side bends, 177
sit-ups, 178
skeletal system, 158, 159
  and motor development, 74–77
skin fold test, 191
Smith, Tommie, 209
social comparison stage, 260
social psychology. *See also* sociology
  assessing student learning, 297–302
  definition, 246
  importance of, 247–48

integrating into curriculum, 290–92
  modeling, 292–93
  teaching strategies, 293
  and National Standards, 248
  themes, 240–51
social skills, 277–79, 281
  concepts, principles for grade levels,
    279–81, 288–90
  conflict resolution, 285–87, 289
  definition, 249
  elementary school instruction example,
    278
  steps to teaching, 295
sociology. *See also* social psychology
  concepts, principles
    for grade 2, 391
    for grade 4, 393–94
    for grade 6, 397–98
    for grade 8, 401–2
    for grade 10, 405
    for grade 12, 409
    for kindergarten, 388
  definition, 245
softball, 69, 360
sound pattern
  definition, 327
Spartans, 214
Spaulding, A.G., 228
Special Olympics, 209
specificity, 152
speed
  vs. accuracy, 49–50, 53
Spencer, Herbert, 222
spinal laoding friction, 134–35
sport psychology, 246–47
sport sociology, 245–47
sports
  ethical skills, 281
  social skills, 277–79, 281
  task- vs. outcome-oriented, 284
squat thrusts, 179
stade, 358
  definition, 207
standards
  definition, 10
standards-based
  definition, 15
standards-based assessment
  definition, 11
starch, 185, 187–88, 195, 196
  refined, 188
stereotyping, 273
strength, 78
  definition, 67

strength training program. *See also*
  muscular training
  for children, adolescents, 78–79
stress reduction, 245, 268. *See also* mental
  health
stretching, 169. *See also* muscular stretching
student-centered physical education
  definition, 292
student journals, logs, 24
  for aesthetic learning, 350
  for exercise physiology, 199
  for motor learning, 61–62
  for social psychology, 298–99
student learning
  and aesthetics, 347
student projects, 24. *See also* group
  projects
  for aesthetic learning, 350–51
  for exercise physiology, 199
  for historical perspectives, 240
  for motor development, 101
  for motor learning, 62
style
  definition, 309
Surgeon General's Report on Physical
  Activity. *See*
  Physical Activity and Health
swimming, 150, 224
swinging, 176
symetric
  definition, 334
  example, 335
synovial joints, 160, 165

T

T-chart, 295, 374
  definition, 296
task-oriented goals
  definition, 260
task-oriented sports, 284
taste, 311, 314, 342–43
teaching strategies
  cooperative learning, 294
  distributed leadership, 294
  group autonomy, 295–96
  heterogeneous grouping, 294
  positive interdependence, 294–95
  social skills acquisition, 295
teamwork, 6
technology
  in education, 4–5, 11, 22
telecomputing, 10
tennis, 226, 227

tempo
definition, 327
tendons, 158
tennis, 150
tension
definition, 116
thirty-second wonders, 25
for biomechanics, 139
for motor development, 100–1
for motor learning, 61
Thorpe, Jim, 210
threaded model, 22
threading, 36, 37, 58
time, 153
time management, 10
timed up and go (TUG), 94
Tissot, Joseph-Clement, 216
Title IX, 236
toe touch, 180
tolerance, 277
torque
definition, 112
and joint movement, 116
schematic, 112
Total Fitness in 30 Minutes a Week, 153
training
history of, 211
traveling instructional unit, 364
trunk lift, 178
TUG. *See* timed up and go

V

variable practice, 47, 48
virtue, 254
definition, 251
volleyball, 228, 229, 360

W

waist twists, 177
walking, 150
warm-up, 148
Watts, Elizabeth, 311
webbed model, 21–22
webbing, 38, 58, 59
Webster, Noah, 233
weight-bearing activities, 77
Wenlock Olympics, 208
wide-spectrum cognition, 316
Williams, Melvin H., 193
Windship, George Barker, 217
work force
performance expectations, 5–6
wrestling, 196
written tests, 25, 102
for biomechanics, 139
for exercise physiology, 198–99
for historical perspectives, 239–40
for motor development, 102
for motor learning, 62

Y

yoga, 213
Young Men's Christian Association
(YMCA), 228, 229

Z

Zappa family, 208

Resources

Published by the National Association for Sport and Physical Education for quality physical education programs:

Moving Into the Future: National Standards for Physical Education, A Guide to Content and Assessment (1995), Stock No. 304-10083

Beyond Activities: Elementary Volume (2003), Stock No. 304-10265

Beyond Activities: Secondary Volume (2003), Stock No. 304-10268

National Physical Education Standards in Action (2003), Stock No. 304-10267

Active Start: A Statement of Physical Activity Guidelines for Children Birth to Five Years (2002), Stock No. 304-10254

Physical Activity for Children: A Statement of Guidelines (1998), Stock No. 304-10175

National Standards for Beginning Physical Education Teachers (1995), Stock No. 304-10085

Appropriate Practice Documents
Appropriate Practice in Movement Programs for Young Children, (2000), Stock No. 304-10232

Appropriate Practices for Elementary School Physical Education (2000), Stock No. 304-10230

Appropriate Practices for Middle School Physical Education (2001), Stock No. 304-10248

Appropriate Practices for High School Physical Education (1998), Stock No. 304-10129

Opportunity to Learn Documents
Opportunity to Learn Standards for Elementary Physical Education (2000), Stock No. 304-10242

Physical Education Program Improvement and Self-Study Guides (1998) for Middle School, Stock No. 304-10173, for High School, Stock No. 304-10174

Assessment Series

Assessment in Outdoor Adventure Physical Education (2003), Stock No. 304-10218

Assessing Student Outcomes in Sport Education (2003), Stock No. 304-10219

Video Tools for Teaching Motor Skill Assessment (2002), Stock No. 304-10217

Assessing Heart Rate in Physical Education (2002), Stock No. 304-10214

Authentic Assessment of Physical Activity for High School Students (2002), Stock No. 304-10216

Portfolio Assessment for K-12 Physical Education (2000), Stock No. 304-10213

Elementary Heart Health: Lessons and Assessment (2001), Stock No. 304-10215

Standards-Based Assessment of Student Learning: A Comprehensive Approach (1999), Stock No. 304-10206

Assessment in Games Teaching (1999), Stock No. 304-10212

Assessing Motor Skills in Elementary Physical Education (1999), Stock No. 304-10207

Assessing and Improving Fitness in Elementary Physical Education (1999), Stock No. 304-10208

Creating Rubrics for Physical Education (1999), Stock No. 304-10209

Assessing Student Responsibility and Teamwork (1999), Stock No. 304-10210

Preservice Professional Portfolio System (1999), Stock No. 304-10211

Order online at www.aahperd.org/naspe
or call 1-800-321-0789
Shipping and handling additional.

National Association for Sport and Physical Education
an association of the
American Alliance for Health, Physical Education,
Recreation, and Dance
1900 Association Drive
Reston, VA 20191
naspe@aahperd.org
703-476-3410